MUSIC AND THE WESLEYS

Music and the Wesleys

Edited by
NICHOLAS TEMPERLEY
AND STEPHEN BANFIELD

UNIVERSITY OF ILLINOIS PRESS
URBANA, CHICAGO, AND SPRINGFIELD

Publication of this book was supported by a grant
from the Henry and Edna Binkele Classical Music Fund.

Excerpts from "The Music of Poetry" from *On Poetry and Poets* by
T. S. Eliot. Copyright © 1957 by T. S. Eliot. Copyright © renewed 1985
by Valerie Eliot. Reprinted by permission of Farrar, Straus and Giroux,
LLC. Copyright © the Estate of T. S. Eliot and reprinted by permission
of Faber and Faber Ltd.

Library of Congress Cataloguing-in-Publication Data
Music and the Wesleys / edited by Nicholas Temperley
and Stephen Banfield.
p. cm.
"This book originated in a conference, Music, Cultural History
and the Wesleys, hosted by CHOMBEC (Centre for the History of
Music in Britain, the Empire and the Commonwealth) and held at
the University of Bristol in July 2007" —Preface.
Includes bibliographical references and index.
ISBN 978-0-252-03581-4 (cloth : alk. paper)
ISBN 978-0-252-07767-8 (pbk. : alk. paper)
1. Wesley family. 2. Church music—Methodist Church. 3. Church
music—England. 4. Church music—United States. 5. Hymns,
English—England—History and criticism. 6. Hymns, English—
United States—History and criticism. I. Temperley, Nicholas.
II. Banfield, Stephen, 1951–
ML410.W51M87   2010
781.71'700922—dc22   2010024823

CONTENTS

Editors' Preface   *vii*

Family Tree   *ix*

Abbreviations   *xi*

Introduction   *xiii*
  Nicholas Temperley

PART 1: MUSIC AND METHODISM

1. John Wesley, Music, and the People Called Methodists   *3*
   Nicholas Temperley

2. Charles Wesley and the Music of Poetry   *26*
   J. R. Watson

3. *Psalms and Hymns* and *Hymns and Sacred Poems*:
   Two Strands of Wesleyan Hymn Collections   *41*
   Robin A. Leaver

4. John Frederick Lampe's *Hymns on the Great Festivals
   and Other Occasions*   *52*
   Martin V. Clarke

5. Methodist Anthems: The Set Piece in English
   Psalmody (1750–1850)   *63*
   Sally Drage

6. The Music of Methodism in Nineteenth-Century America   *77*
   Anne Bagnall Yardley

7. Eucharistic Piety in American Methodist
   Hymnody (1786–1889)   *88*
   Geoffrey C. Moore

8. The Musical Settings of Charles Wesley's Hymns
   (1742 to 2008)   *103*
   Carlton R. Young

PART 2: THE WESLEY MUSICIANS

9. Style, Will, and the Environment:
   Three Composers at Odds with History   *121*
      Stephen Banfield

10. Charles Wesley's Family and the Musical Life of Bristol   *141*
      Jonathan Barry

11. Pictorial Precocity: John Russell's Portraits
    of Charles and Samuel Wesley   *154*
      Peter S. Forsaith

12. Harmony and Discord in the Wesley Family Concerts   *164*
      Alyson McLamore

13. Father and Sons: Charles, Samuel, and Charles the Younger   *175*
      Philip Olleson

14. Samuel Wesley as an Antiquarian Composer   *183*
      Peter Holman

15. The Anthem Texts and Word Setting of Sebastian Wesley   *200*
      Peter Horton

16. The Legacy of Sebastian Wesley   *216*
      Stephen Banfield and Nicholas Temperley

    Appendix 1: Catalogue of Compositions
    by Charles Wesley the Younger   *231*
      John Nightingale

    Appendix 2: Denominational American
    Methodist Hymnals Cited   *242*

    Bibliography   *245*

    Contributors   *263*

    Index   *267*

EDITORS' PREFACE

This book originated in a conference, *Music, Cultural History and the Wesleys,* hosted by CHOMBEC (Centre for the History of Music in Britain, the Empire and the Commonwealth) and held at the University of Bristol in July 2007 to mark the tercentenary of Charles Wesley's birth. As the title of the book implies, the emphasis has shifted in the direction of greater concentration on music. Partly for this reason, we have not used all the papers delivered at the conference but have commissioned five additional essays that were not represented there. We also include a catalogue of the compositions of Charles Wesley the younger, the least-studied of the three composers in the family. By a happy coincidence, publication of the book is taking place in the bicentennial year of the youngest of them, Samuel Sebastian.

Since many Wesleys are discussed in the course of the book, we have provided a family tree to help identify them. Charles the elder and younger are so designated whenever necessary. Of the several Samuels in the family, we have fully identified John Wesley's father and brother whenever they are mentioned and called Charles's son "Samuel" without further definition. Samuel Sebastian's name was sometimes shortened to Sebastian in his lifetime (Gauntlett: 118): the same has often been done in these pages. Charles's wife and daughter were both named Sarah: we have followed family custom by referring to the daughter as Sally.

Original punctuation, spelling, and layout have been used wherever possible in quotations and music examples from historical sources. Acknowledgments for the reproduction of illustrations and music examples are given in their captions.

Research and production have been assisted by small grants from the University of Bristol. We are especially grateful to Carlton Young for help with many bibliographical questions.

FAMILY TREE

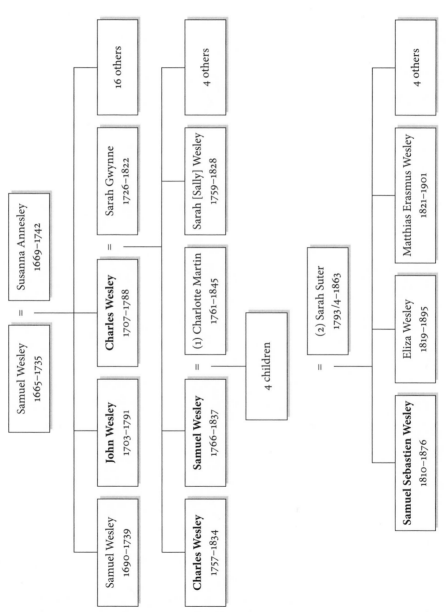

Samuel Wesley 1665–1735 = Susanna Annesley 1669–1742

- Samuel Wesley 1690–1739
- John Wesley 1703–1791
- Charles Wesley 1707–1788 = Sarah Gwynne 1726–1822
- 16 others

Charles Wesley 1707–1788 = Sarah Gwynne 1726–1822

- Charles Wesley 1757–1834
- Samuel Wesley 1766–1837
- Sarah [Sally] Wesley 1759–1828
- 4 others

Samuel Wesley 1766–1837 = (1) Charlotte Martin 1761–1845 — 4 children

Samuel Wesley 1766–1837 = (2) Sarah Suter 1793/4–1863

- Samuel Sebastien Wesley 1810–1876
- Eliza Wesley 1819–1895
- Matthias Erasmus Wesley 1821–1901
- 4 others

ABBREVIATIONS

For full citations of published works, including *HTI* codes where applicable, see the Bibliography.

AMEC   The African Methodist Episcopal Church (see Appendix 2)
BPC   *The Book of Common Prayer*
BWV   Bach-Werke-Verzeichnis (Bach catalogue)
CPM   *The Catalogue of Printed Music in the British Library to 1980*
DSM   double short meter
HLS   J. and C. Wesley, *Hymns on the Lord's Supper*
HTI   Temperley, *The Hymn Tune Index*
JN   John Nightingale, "Catalogue of Compositions by Charles Wesley the Younger," Appendix 1 in this volume
KO   Kassler and Olleson, *Samuel Wesley: A Source Book*
LM   long meter
MEC   The Methodist Episcopal Church (see Appendix 2)
MECS   The Methodist Episcopal Church, South (see Appendix 2)
MPC   The Methodist Protestant Church (see Appendix 2)
ODNB   *The Oxford Dictionary of National Biography*
OED   *The Oxford English Dictionary*
UMC   The United Methodist Church (see Appendix 2)

INTRODUCTION

Nicholas Temperley

"What a family!" exclaimed the late John Betjeman. He was discussing the hymn "O thou who camest from above," where the text is Charles Wesley's and the customary tune, HEREFORD, is by his grandson (Betjeman: 54). It is difficult, indeed, to think of many families that have supplied at least two pre-eminent figures in each of two different areas of cultural activity. Such was the case with the Wesleys. John and Charles revived religious passion in an age when the English churches were declining toward a state of apathy. Charles's sons Charles and Samuel, and Samuel's son Samuel Sebastian, kept the flame of English music alive in a period of foreign domination and relatively modest creative achievement.

There is no question that music was a dominant force in the lives of all five men. Its role differed greatly between the generations, but the sum of the Wesleys' influence on musical history, especially in Britain and the English-speaking world, is incalculable. This book gives some idea of its scope over the last three hundred years.

Neither John nor Charles the elder was particularly musical, though Charles played the flute in his youth. As children they became acquainted with music mainly as a handmaid of religion. Their mother, Susanna, who personally undertook the education of all her children, made a point of singing metrical psalms with them both before and after lessons, morning and evening (Lynch). Their father, Samuel, introduced a religious society in his parish at Epworth, Lincolnshire, which promoted a rehearsed choir in the parish church; the Wesley children would have heard the singing every Sunday (Temperley 1979b, 1:43).

From these experiences John and Charles learned of music's immense power to enhance feelings specified by sung words. They carried it from Epworth, through their schooling at Charterhouse and Westminster, respectively, to the "Holy Club" at Oxford, and then on to the societies of the Methodist movement. The importance they attributed to music is demonstrated not only in their writings, but in the pains they took to supervise and direct every aspect of the singing in their societies. Hymns were fully as significant for their mission as preaching.

The role of hymns as Methodism changed from a movement to an independent denomination is discussed in Chapter 3 by Robin Leaver, who also investigates their relationship with German Pietism. The theology of Charles Wesley's sacramental hymns, as modified in American Methodism, is Geoffrey Moore's subject in Chapter 7. As J. R. Watson tells us in Chapter 2, Charles's hymns can also be seen as poems for silent reading, with their own internal music. But they have inspired an extraordinary range of musical settings. In the 1740s, Lampe wrote the first custom-made tunes for Wesleyan hymns, examined in Chapter 4 by Martin Clarke. Sally Drage in Chapter 5 explores some musical developments in northern England that exceeded John Wesley's tolerance for choirs, soloists, and textual repetition. Nineteenth-century American musical practices are the subject of Anne Yardley's Chapter 6, while Carlton Young in Chapter 8 offers a historical survey, bringing the story up to modern times. Indeed, hymns written, translated, or introduced by the Wesleys are sung worldwide today, and in many languages.

Charles had to take serious account of music in another way when he was blessed (or burdened) with two sons who were among the most remarkable prodigies of their time. Their musical talent must have been inherited chiefly from their mother, Sarah.

This was an age when Rousseauian ideas placed a high premium on the natural genius that child prodigies were thought to embody. A long succession of them was displayed in public and courted by the world of fashion: four, from the city of Bristol alone, are listed on page 141. The most famous of all, Mozart, was nearly two years older than young Charles. Something of this philosophy can be sensed in the pictorial representations of the two boys, explored by Peter Forsaith in Chapter 11. An essential point was that natural talent should be allowed to express itself in free and untrammeled form. But these ideas, tending toward Deism, did not fit comfortably with the Puritanism that was a strong element in the Wesleys' inheritance, nor with the educational legacy of Susanna, who had stated that "In order to form the minds of children, the first thing to be done is to conquer their will" (Lynch: 200), nor with Wesleyan views on the centrality of adult conversion and rebirth in Christ. Charles's own doubts on the matter are vividly expressed in his second hymn on "The True Use of Musick," quoted on page 29.

As Chapter 12 makes clear, it is highly probable that Sarah was the primary influence on the boys' musical development. Her family, the Gwynnes, could claim several accomplished amateur musicians, including Sarah herself, who sang and played harpsichord and guitar. She also possessed inherited wealth, and her friends were drawn from the gentry and aristocracy. Charles, who was already more at ease than John in such company, moved more rapidly in the direction of high society after his marriage in 1748 (Lloyd 1998: 23). In those circles it was entirely acceptable to cultivate secular music as a delightful art, and it seems clear that Sarah's influence would have been in that direction.

Confronted with a dilemma, Charles decided that his sons' gift came from God and must be nurtured, though properly disciplined. His consideration and careful supervision of their musical training are clearly documented by Jonathan Barry in Chapter 10 and Philip Olleson in Chapter 13; but he allowed them to take their studies far beyond the limits of church music (to the dismay of his brother and several other Methodist leaders), notably in the series of concerts detailed by Alyson McLamore in Chapter 12.

The elder son, Charles, though famous as a child prodigy, made little impact as a mature composer. As Stephen Banfield points out in Chapter 9, his gifts have not yet been understood; and John Nightingale's catalogue (Appendix 1) includes a large number of compositions quite unknown to musicologists, let alone performers. On the other hand, his younger brother Samuel is now regarded as the premier English composer of his generation, distinguishing himself particularly in organ voluntaries, other instrumental music, and settings of Roman Catholic liturgical texts. But Peter Holman believes that his originality and his importance in musical history have still not been properly recognized, as he argues in Chapter 14.

Samuel's son Sebastian was generally esteemed in the Victorian era as the leading English organist and composer for the Church, though Peter Horton has shown that he distinguished himself in several other branches of composition (Horton 2004). He succeeded, by the expressive power and intensity of his anthems and services, in bringing new life to the ancient tradition of cathedral music, starting a revival that lasted for more than a century. In Chapter 15 Horton now discusses Sebastian's boldly individual approach to the selection and setting of anthem texts. His free cutting and mixing of biblical words to bring their meaning home to the worshipper, and even to modify that meaning, offers a parallel to John and Charles Wesley's paraphrases of biblical words in their hymn texts. His personal reputation and influence have outlasted the general rejection of Victorian arts that was dominant in the twentieth century. Chapter 16 brings this other side of the Wesley story up to the present time.

A common factor of the "famous five" was their relationship with the Church of England. John and his brother Charles, like their father, were ordained priests, immovably devoted to the Church's symbolic authority if not to its current practice. Charles's sons were baptized on January 7, 1758, and March 15, 1766, respectively (*BRro*, St. James parish registers), and raised as strict church members in the strongly evangelical culture of Bristol, explored in Chapter 10. Charles the younger became a prominent organist in London, where his final post was at St. Marylebone parish church. Samuel left the Church for a brief spell as a Roman Catholic convert but was still involved from time to time in the music of Anglican worship, for which he composed some thirty-five anthems and an ambitious and successful service setting. In the life and music of his son Sebastian the Anglican element came to the fore again. He was organist and choirmaster at a series of cathedrals and, for a period in middle life, at Leeds parish church.

Outspoken criticism of the established clergy and their behavior was something that any Wesley felt free to indulge in, even though none of them were notably successful in moving the Church authorities to change their ways. That illustrates another quality the Wesleys shared in varying degrees: a rugged independence of mind and spirit, sometimes going over the line to arrogance, and often accompanied by an insensitivity to the feelings of others. They were brilliantly creative thinkers, and having made up their minds, they had little patience with those who disagreed. They would use their reason and force of character to challenge any authority, however widely respected, but when in authority themselves they were often ruthless in their treatment of those under their charge. The result could be disastrous, but in the best cases it produced a new synthesis of permanent value. (Charles Wesley the younger was an exception to most of this paragraph. It is no coincidence that his milder temperament and willing submission to parental authority resulted in a comparatively reclusive career with little public acclaim, though his natural gifts were second to none: see Lloyd 1998 and Chapter 9.)

"I can only declare this truth, that my aversion to constraint is invincible," wrote Samuel to his mother in 1791 about his contempt for the conventional view of marriage (Olleson 2001: xxxii). It could well have been the motto of the whole family (again excepting his brother). Both John and Charles the elder, from the beginning of their ministry, adopted a relentlessly combative stance that doubtless played a vital part in establishing the Methodist movement but also alienated many Anglicans, Dissenters, and fellow evangelicals, causing untold strife and discord (Lloyd 2007b: 58–63). John "was insistent that he and his brother knew what was best for the Methodist movement and that preachers and people alike were under his personal charge" (62). For instance, in a letter to Edward Perronet in 1750 he wrote: "I have not one preacher with me, and not six in England, whose wills are broken enough to serve me as sons in the gospel" (J. Wesley 1975–, 26: 431).

This autocratic mindset naturally governed the brothers' approach to music. In his selection and editing of tunes John showed admirable taste and judgment, but he refused to be swayed by professional musicians ("masters of music"). As he wrote, "I was determined whoever compiled this [book], should follow *my* direction. . . . At length I have prevailed" (J. Wesley 1761: iii). And as I will show in Chapter 1, both he and Charles, once they were personally convinced of the value of a tune, assumed that all their followers would accept it too. John actually raised objections when he found them straying from the tunes he had authorized.

The same overweening self-confidence shows in the later generations. For instance Samuel, once he was persuaded of the supremacy of J. S. Bach, had only scorn or pity for those who could not see the truth. Indeed, there is much in the tone of his letters on the subject to suggest that he regarded his promotion of Bach's music in a religious light: not a simple effort to persuade others of its merits, but a "zealous Promotion of advancing the cause of Truth & Perfection," which he compared to the work of Martin Luther (Olleson 2001: 71), and perhaps by extension (though he did not say so) to that of his father and uncle.

Sebastian's frequent quarrels with his ecclesiastical superiors and with contemporary musicians were often about questions of authority. He would brook no rivals in musical matters, or in his control of the choirs he supervised (Horton 2004:

122, 311–12). In a more quixotic vein he stubbornly upheld the merits of meantone temperament in the face of the prevailing trend toward the equally divided octave (Thistlethwaite: 372), though it would have made some of his own works, such as the anthem *The wilderness* or the Service in E Major, sound intolerably out of tune.

This leads us to yet another family tendency: to favor the past over the present. All five Wesleys were musical conservatives, preferring older traditions to current fashions. John condemned some of the fundamental characteristics of modern music, such as counterpoint and even harmony (C. Young 1995a: 84–88), though he did not succeed in banishing them entirely from his societies. Charles the elder, according to his son Samuel, was "fond of the Old Masters Palestrina, Corelli, Geminiani, Handel, and among the English chamber composers Croft, Blow, Boyce, Greene" (*Lbl* Add. 27593). He wrote tributes to Handel as an immortal (Baker 1962: 311) and lines expressing scorn for modern composers like Felice Giardini and Johann Christian Bach, who, he said, "Have cut Old Music's throat, / And mangled ev'ry Note." He wrote a longer poem in 1783 savagely attacking the piano, which was just then beginning to overtake the harpsichord in popularity. As he sarcastically put it, "Loud as a spanking Warming-pan its tone, / Delicious as the thrilling Bagpipe's Drone" (Baker 1962: 363).

His sons maintained his partiality for older styles. Charles made Handel his master for life, generally though not uniformly resisting the fashionable *galanterie,* and many of his compositions reflect this preference. Samuel, throughout his career, continued to uphold the "ancient" style, with its diatonic dissonances, energetic basses, and counterpoint (see Chapter 14), and to adopt it whenever he considered it appropriate. Indeed, it was his passion for plainsong and the learned style of renaissance church music that induced him to convert to Rome, as Olleson points out in Chapter 13. Like his elder brother, he adopted the organ as his principal instrument and used it to pursue his bent for a fundamentally linear, contrapuntal style. Both brothers, to their lasting honor, would rather suffer hardship than yield to the dictates of fashion. Even in his piano music Samuel resisted the temptations of flashy virtuosity offered by the rapidly developing instrument, as well as its capacity for romantic mystery: he did not rely on the sustaining pedal, unlike his younger contemporaries John Field, John Baptist Cramer, and others. Instead, he invented bold new combinations and harmonic progressions in the spirit of late baroque and even older music (Temperley 1985: xiv–xvi).

Sebastian also hewed his own path, maintaining elements of the ancient style for yet one more generation. Though he was not impervious to the attractions of sentimental chromaticism after the manner of Louis Spohr, he did not surrender to it, as some of the lesser Victorians did. He maintained contrapuntal and structural discipline and a fundamentally diatonic harmonic palette. Sebastian in his cathedral posts kept to an extremely conservative repertory of choir music, populated by some of the same late-baroque English composers preferred by his grandfather (Horton 2004: 269, 287, 311–12). His attitude to Continental musicians of his own time was even less enthusiastic than that of his contemporary William Sterndale Bennett (Temperley 2006: 22). Like Bennett, he ignored his avant-garde contemporaries Berlioz, Chopin, Liszt, and Wagner.

So, in stark opposition to the prevailing xenophilia of English musical life (Temperley 1999: 3–19), the three composer Wesleys found most of what they needed at home, or in the distant past. They never left the shores of Britain. They rarely tried to associate with the distinguished foreign musicians who visited London or toured the country. They were not much impressed by, or even interested in, the dazzling virtuosos who gained the lion's share of applause (not to mention money) in every season. Each was entirely his own man. They must have had a potent inner reserve of confidence to draw on. Perhaps it can be traced to that unshakable faith in God's love that radiates from the hymns of their father and grandfather Charles.

Music and Methodism

CHAPTER 1

John Wesley, Music, and the
People Called Methodists

Nicholas Temperley

All human societies use music in the course of religious worship. It has been adopted everywhere to unify cultures, to confront other cultures, and to communicate with the supernatural (Nettl). When associated with words conveying both a rational and an emotional message, the prime function of music is not usually to specify either ideas or feelings, but to enhance and intensify the ideas and (especially) the feelings that those words articulate. John and Charles Wesley had been brought up to think of music as a vehicle of Christian texts, and they clearly recognized its enormous power over the heart and soul. They set out, thoughtfully and deliberately, to harness that power for their religious goals.

It is generally recognized that one of the Wesleys' great accomplishments was to broaden and enrich the scope of religious poetry by adding hymns to the standard Anglican corpus of metrical psalms and other Bible-based lyrics (though they were not, of course, the first to do so). By this means they could raise the artistic level of the sung words; they could link them more directly to the subject of a sermon; they could interpret Christianity in their own way and in tune with the times; they could put the expression of personal religious feeling into the mouths of their followers.

But these goals, in varying degrees, all depended on music for their full fruition. In 1787 an Anglican parson, Dr. William Vincent, concluded that "for one who has been drawn from the Established Church by preaching, ten have been induced by music" (15). Not hymns: music. The question I hope to answer in this chapter is how music played so decisive a role in the overall function and effect of Methodist hymnody.

Methodist Singing

Today one thinks of hymn singing as something one does in church. Although the Wesley brothers (as well as George Whitefield, who has equal claims to be a founder of Methodism) were clergymen in the Church of England, they normally

ILLUS. 1.1. John Wesley (Kingswood School, Bath). Oil portrait thought to be by
John Russell. Kingswood School archive collection. Reproduced by permission.

had no control over the singing in church and had to be content to supplement
it with their own kind of singing in other places. The only time John Wesley was
actually in charge of an Anglican parish was in Savannah, Georgia, from 1735
to 1737. He used his authority there to introduce a number of hymns, including
translations of pietistic German songs he had learned from the Moravians. But
he changed their verse meters to those already known from metrical psalms
(common meter, short meter, and the like), presumably so that they could be
sung to the familiar psalm tunes in the old way, with Wesley probably reading
out each line before it was sung.

When the Wesleys experienced their respective "conversions" in 1738, their new spiritual standing did not include any desire to leave the Church. Since the music in church was inadequate from their point of view, they encouraged the singing of hymns at family prayers and private gatherings, and at their own public meetings and preaching services in whatever buildings could be appropriated for their use, such as barns, warehouses, assembly rooms, upper rooms of inns, and the like. Gradually they acquired or rented rooms set aside for their meetings in a few large towns, beginning with the New Room in Bristol and the Foundry in London. In these respects they were following the older Dissenting bodies, which had been shut out of the churches in 1662 and for a while even banished from the towns, and were accustomed to conducting their meetings in small prosaic rooms or in the open air.

Methodists, like Anglicans and most Dissenters, would sing before and after a sermon, and they took up and renewed the still-surviving Anglican custom of the communion hymn (Temperley 1979a). The Wesleys also borrowed some practices from the recently revived Moravians, whose customs deeply impressed them during their voyage to Georgia and afterward in London. On the Moravian model they adopted special services, such as watch nights and love feasts, which often included singing.

The difference between singing in a parish church and at a Methodist meeting could not have been more striking. A church was usually an imposing Gothic building designed in Roman Catholic times, when the laity had played no part in the singing. It had its social hierarchy, separating parson, squire, and gentry from the common people—and this was emphasized by its Georgian furnishings, still to be seen in full glory at Whitby in Yorkshire and in some remote villages (see Chatfield). In most churches the clergy and gentry thought it beneath their dignity to sing, while their servants and tenants no doubt felt too inhibited to sing heartily in their presence. Women were even more diffident than men about raising their voices. Before the advent of voluntary choirs, the only leadership was provided by an unmusical, uneducated parish clerk, who droned out each line before leading the singing of it at an extremely slow pace. This practice, generally known as "lining out," had originated in the 1640s as a reading out of the line by a minister or clerk for the benefit of those who could not read or had no books, but over time it had turned into a ritualized monotone (see Temperley 1979b, 1:82). The vicar generally left the church during the singing to change from a surplice to a Geneva gown or vice versa. In some churches a voluntary choir was formed, but it more often than not had the effect of silencing the congregation altogether (Temperley 1979b, 1:85–97).

Methodist singing, by contrast, took place in an ordinary room, and (ideally at least) it was free, informal, lively, well led, and open to all. It was communal singing such as people might have experienced in a tavern, a mill, or a hayfield. Indeed, outdoor hymn singing became a badge of the Methodists. Charles Wesley or George Whitefield, leading their followers from village to village, would sing as they walked or rode in carts, or would sit on the "leads" (the roofs of extensions to cottages) to sing a rousing song of praise (C. Young 1995a: 118–52). People would gather to listen or take part, without having made any formal decision to "go to church." We will see how this free and secular character was displayed in certain characteristics of Methodist singing.

It had been a cardinal principle of the Reformation that in public worship all the people were to sing, as they were ordered to do in several much-quoted biblical texts. But the tradition had eroded in two ways. First, women were asking for trouble if they sang out strongly, let alone attempted to lead the singing. St. Paul had said that they must be silent in church, and the Puritans had had to argue ingeniously from other biblical texts to show that he did not mean to silence them during singing (see, for instance, Cotton). But they generally sang quietly, if at all. That is why in harmonized settings of hymn tunes designed for Anglican use, the tune was allotted to the tenors until late in the eighteenth century. John Wesley, following Isaac Watts, was determined that all should sing, but he ordered men not to sing the women's parts. We will return to this later to see exactly what he meant by it.

The other danger to universal singing was to admit a special group of leading voices, in other words a choir. The high-church religious societies, which were an important factor in the Wesley brothers' background, had tried to improve the singing of metrical psalms by having the young people of a parish learn them under the direction of a singing teacher (Temperley 1979b, 1:141–51). The Presbyterians and Independents did the same thing at the London Weighhouse in Eastcheap, starting in 1708 (*Practical Discourse;* Benson: 89–90). The idea was for these rehearsed singers to be scattered among the people, and so encourage a generally more disciplined and inspiring congregational praise. This was the origin of both the choir of charity children in many town churches and the voluntary adult choirs in rural ones. But the singers, once they had got under way, wanted to sing together from their own pew or gallery, and then aspired to more difficult music. It was soon found that congregations, instead of feeling encouraged to join, tended to fall silent and listen to the music (Temperley 1979b, 1:151–62).

John Wesley (Illus. 1.1) was critical of choirs that performed on the people's behalf. "Exhort every one in the congregation to sing, not one in ten only," he wrote in 1766 (*Minutes,* 1:532). At Neath on August 9, 1768, he recorded: "I began reading prayers at six, but was greatly disgusted at the manner of singing: (1) twelve or fourteen persons kept it to themselves, and quite shut out the congregation" (J. Wesley 1872, 3:339). But he certainly wanted the people to learn the many new tunes and hymns he introduced, and his tune books were of course published for this purpose. In the preface to the first definitive one, *Select Hymns with Tunes Annext: Designed Chiefly for the Use of the People Called Methodists* (J. Wesley 1761), his famous "directions" for singing began: "I. Learn *these* tunes before you

TABLE 1.1. Hymn tune collections published or sanctioned by John Wesley

---

[Wesley, John.] *A Collection of Tunes, Set to Music, as They Are Commonly Sung at the Foundery.* London, 1742. (#CTSF)

[Lampe, John Frederick.] *Hymns on the Great Festivals, and Other Occasions.* London, 1746. (#HGFOO)

[Butts, Thomas.] *Harmonia-Sacra, or A Choice Collection of Psalm and Hymn Tunes.* London, [c.1754]. Later eds. 1767, 1768, 1785. (ButtTHS a–d)

[Wesley, John.] *Select Hymns with Tunes Annext.* Tune supplement, untitled. [London], 1761. [✱TS Wes a] — Tune supplement: "Sacred Melody." London, 1765. Later eds. 1770, 1773. (✱TS Wes b–d)

[Wesley, John.] *Sacred Harmony, or a Choice Collection of Psalms and Hymns.* [For use with *A Collection of Hymns for the Use of the People Called Methodists*, 1780.] [London?, 1781.] Later ed. [c. 1790]. (#SHCCPH a, b)

Note: Codes in parentheses refer to the *Hymn Tune Index*, where fuller information is provided.

learn any others; afterwards learn as many as you please." (See C. Young 1995a: 72–73 for the full directions.) The tunes were probably taught in classes and other meetings of the societies. In preaching services and public worship, generally he insisted that all who could sing should do so. His attitude to anthems and set pieces varied, as we will see in Chapter 5.

Most early Methodist singing was entirely unaccompanied, whether from principle or from necessity. Hymns sung at impromptu meetings in barns or inns, let alone on the roadway, were unlikely to be supported by keyboard instruments. Even in permanent meeting houses, organs were rare, and John Wesley explicitly disapproved of them. Only three are known to have existed in his lifetime (Lightwood 1927: 40). Conference continued to discourage organs until the late 1820s, when the matter came to a head in the well-known dispute over an instrument presented to Brunswick Chapel, Leeds (Curwen: 29).

Wesley's own tune books of 1742, 1761, and 1765 have no accompaniments. (Table 1.1 lists the principal Wesleyan tune books of the eighteenth century.) Lampe's hymns had instrumental figured basses. Butts changed these to accommodate voices in his 1754 collection but retained the figures indicating chordal accompaniment. In later editions these were erased, no doubt under pressure from Wesley, but most other Methodist collections did include figured basses. Presumably they were meant for use in family devotions, or for teaching and rehearsing in class meetings music later to be used in worship.

Vocal harmony was another matter. Charles warmly accepted it: in his "Musician's Hymn" (in C. Wesley 1747, repr. C. Young 1995a: 178–80), he calls God "the God of harmony" and Jesus "the soul of harmony." Even if this is only metaphorical in intent, he seems to dedicate all the resources of music to the praise of God:

> If well I know the Tuneful Art
> To captivate an Human Heart
> The Glory, LORD, be Thine:

A Servant of thy blessed Will
I here devote my utmost Skill,
To sound the Praise Divine.

But John seems to have been, at best, uninterested in harmony and unconvinced of its value in religious music. As I have said, his tune books before 1781 are for melody only. In his 1779 treatise "Thoughts on the Power of Music" (J. Wesley 1781a), he concluded that "modern music has no connexion with common sense, any more than with the passions" and that "it is harmony (so-called) that destroys the power of music." (This bizarre notion was partly based on a misleading passage in Charles Avison's *Essay on Musical Expression,* which seemed to suggest that harmony dated only from the sixteenth century.)

Wesley tempered his views, realizing that harmony was a permanent feature of modern music, and that among his followers many choirs had formed to lead the singing. Two years after condemning harmony in the treatise, he published *Sacred Harmony,* "in two or three parts for the Voice, harpsichord or organ." Most of the harmony in it comes, in fact, from Butts's *Harmonia-Sacra.*

The typical arrangement of harmonized tunes in Methodist collections was in three staves, as in Illustration 1.2. The tune, in the G clef, was on the middle staff;

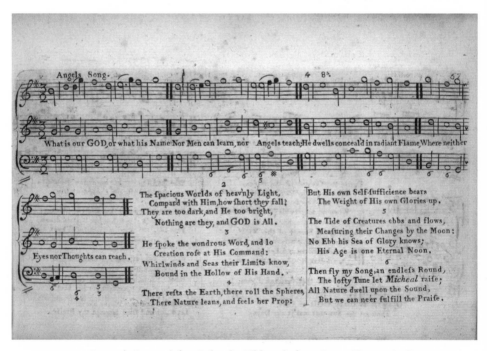

ILLUS. 1.2. ANGEL'S SONG (after Orlando Gibbons), from Butts, *Harmonia-Sacra* [1754]. Image © The British Library Board (shelfmark B.771).

the upper staff carried a subordinate part in the G clef; and the lower staff carried the vocal bass, with or without figures. This arrangement of the score seems to have been invented by Independents, later known as Congregationalists. It had the advantage for keyboard players of placing the tune right over the bass, but Butts was the first to combine it with figures. It became the signature format for Methodists and Dissenters well into the nineteenth century. The congregation, male and female, sings the tune in two octaves. The upper part is available for altos, singing an octave below the written notes.

John Wesley summed up his ideas about singing one more time, in the document called the Large Minutes, promulgated at the Methodist Conference of 1780. These included "9. Let the women constantly sing their parts alone. Let no man sing with them, unless he understands the notes, and sings the bass, as it is pricked down in the book." What does this mean? In *Sacred Harmony*, all but 7 of the 119 tunes are scored for two vocal parts, one the tune, the other the bass. If "parts" were interpreted as vocal parts in this sense (melodic lines in a harmonic texture), the injunction would have no plausible meaning. By "parts" Wesley meant portions or phrases of the melody. A custom had developed by which women sang certain phrases alone—phrases of the tune, without the men who sang the rest of the tune with them. A Swedish visitor to the Foundry chapel in 1769, Johan Henrik Liden, wrote a highly complimentary account of the singing in his journal, and continued: "It added not a little to the harmonious charm of the song that some lines were sung only by the women and afterwards the whole congregation joined in the chorus" (Bretherton: 3, repr. C. Young 1995a: 64).

Wesley, as a rule, did not specify which lines were for women only, but some later editors did (see Ex. 1.5, for instance). The practice was sometimes shown by dynamic marks in the score: *p,* or "soft," meaning women alone; *f,* or "loud," meaning everybody. In harmonized settings, the dynamics are generally given only for the tune-carrying part, so the "women only" direction applies to the congregation, not the choir members who were singing the subordinate parts. Typically, a repeated line was sung first by women alone, then by all; sometimes another section was sung by men alone. In several eighteenth-century collections this meaning of *p* and *f* is explicitly stated in the preface (see Smith 1779: 2–3, passage repr. Temperley and Drage: 325; Addington, quoted Temperley 1979b, 1:213). In some hymns, directions such as "Women alone" and "All together" are printed over the congregational part (see Temperley and Drage: 73, 74, 222–25). But it may also have been the normal practice in tunes like HOTHAM (Ex. 1.3), and in HELMSLEY, best known today as "Lo, he comes with clouds descending" in Ralph Vaughan Williams's majestic reharmonization. Another tune from the period, from a Catholic source but popularized by Dissenters, is ADESTE FIDELES, and there is still a living tradition of letting the women and children sing "O come let us adore him" twice, quietly, on their own before everybody comes in for the final phrase.

Methodist Hymn Tunes

So much for the change in character and meaning that the Wesleys brought about in hymn singing. Now we will consider the tunes they used. The most definitive book appeared in 1761 as *Select Hymns with Tunes Annext*. In later editions the tune supplement was separately titled *Sacred Melody*. In its often-quoted preface, Wesley said that he had been planning the book for more than twenty years. He praised the collection published some seven years earlier by Butts, then added, "But this, tho' it is excellent of its kind, is not the thing which I want. I want the people called Methodists to sing true, the tunes which are in *common use* among us." In fact all but 8 of the 102 tunes in Wesley's selection were taken straight from Butts's book, with only minor revisions. The chief difference was one of omission. Sixty-eight of Butts's tunes were passed over, presumably because Wesley did not like them or because they had not caught on in his societies.

In the gradual buildup of this core repertory, the starting point had been a group of English psalm tunes, which were familiar to everyone, being widely used by Dissenters as well as Anglicans. Most came from seventeenth- and early-eighteenth-century England, and they include fine tunes by Thomas Tallis, Orlando Gibbons, Thomas Campion, William Croft, and Jeremiah Clarke, as well as anonymous ones like EASTER HYMN. The Wesleys would have known them from early childhood. A group of fifteen or more of them is found in every collection sanctioned by John Wesley. Illustration 1.2 is a good example. It is a remote descendant of Gibbons's SONG 34, changed in the process of oral transmission but widely popular in this form in the early eighteenth century.

To these were added German melodies learned from the Moravians. As Robin Leaver has pointed out, some of these were old Lutheran chorales, some came from Freylinghausen's *Geistreiches Gesangbuch* (1704), while others were composed by the newly reorganized Moravians themselves (Leaver 1996: 32–33). It was from Germany, and from the Moravians specifically, that a number of new verse meters entered English hymnody, though many of them were already familiar in English secular song. The most significant were trochaic, where lines begin with a stressed syllable and hence call for a musical phrase with no upbeat (as in, for instance, Ex. 1.3). The newer Moravian tunes are distinctive in themselves but were not much imitated, perhaps because the Wesleys very soon fell out with the Moravian Brethren: they and their supporters left the Moravian congregation at Fetter Lane in July 1740 (Lloyd 2007: 48–49). But John Wesley, once he had come to know and love a tune, tended to remain loyal to it. He included fourteen tunes of Moravian origin in his Foundry collection of 1742. Of these, eleven survived into the later collections and became part of the permanent Methodist repertory.

The largest group of tunes were a kind of distillation of the English art-music style of the day, whether derived from the theater, the public concert, or domestic song. Some of these were actual adaptations of secular music: we will return to these later. Others had been printed for the first time in Butts's collection, or in Whitefield's *Divine Musical Miscellany* for the Calvinistic Methodists (both books appeared in about 1754, and it is hard to tell which was printed first). They are largely anonymous. Example 1.1 is an appealing one, which John Wesley attached to his own revision of a hymn by Joseph Addison. It was a winner, appearing in all major Methodist hymnals and many Dissenting and Anglican books during the next sixty years.

The text is in common meter, but the melody is greatly extended by melismas (groups of two or more notes sung to one syllable) and text repetitions. Some features of its musical style had seldom been found in traditional psalm tunes: modulation (to D major in bars 5–7), sequence (the phrase sung to "Why, my cold heart" is repeated at a higher pitch), structural repetition (the cadence in 5–7 repeated in the home key in 16–18). These tend to remind one of Handel, but they are actually just a part of the common musical language of the time. Indeed, it is quite possible that this tune originated as a secular song, like many others used by Butts.

Another source of tunes for the Wesleys had a more decided link with art music: John Frederick Lampe's *Hymns on the Great Festivals and Other Occasions,* which appeared in 1746. It will be discussed in depth by Martin Clarke in Chapter 4. In this series of twenty-four tunes, Lampe transferred the style of his theatrical songs directly, making no attempt to adapt it to English church traditions. I do not see any specific influence here either of Handel or of Moravian tunes, as Robin Leaver does (1996: 34). Lampe's tunes were an undoubted success with the Wesleys. Charles listed them as the preferred tunes in several of his hymn collections (C. Young 1996: 12). All twenty-four were reprinted by Butts in *Harmonia-Sacra,* and fifteen of them in each of Wesley's subsequent collections.

EX. 1.1. MORNING SONG, as printed by John Wesley in 1761.

The Wesleys' continued endorsement of Lampe's tunes is a little puzzling. It is easy to imagine why they gave them a favorable reception at first. Here was a leading, accomplished professional musician, converted to the cause at a time when influential support was crucially needed. Charles's eighty-line "Musician's Hymn," already cited, is thought by some to be a celebration of Lampe's conversion (see C. Young 1995a: 178). And now Lampe quickly produced a well-planned collection of twenty-four well-written tunes custom-made for Wesleyan hymns. (For further discussion see Chapter 4.)

But John in his famous preface of 1761 wrote: "Sing *All*. See that you join with the congregation as frequently as you can," and "Sing *lustily* and with a good courage," and "strive to unite your voices together, so as to make one clear melodious sound." It is difficult to reconcile these precepts with the fussy, clearly soloistic texture of many of Lampe's tunes. They are sprinkled with trills, slides, and other ornaments; nineteen of them use the fashionable Lombardic rhythm; two of them include upward leaps of a tenth. Examples 4.1 and 4.2 show all these features. Martin Clarke will argue that Wesley saw Lampe's tunes as a way of attracting members of the theatrical community and its patrons to his cause.

As for ornaments, many hymnal compilers, including Wesley himself, gave instructions in prefaces about their interpretation. But they seem to have been intended for solo singing. When Samuel Porter gave instructions for how to "grace a note," he cautioned that this was "not very proper in a whole congregation" (1700), and Robert Barber asserted that "The Trill is only an ornament for one Part, or two to be sung alone, of a few Voices together" (1727). One writer in Wesley's own *Arminian Magazine* had this to say in 1791, the year of Wesley's death: "Gracing or ornamenting tunes may do very well for a single voice (if done with judgement) but it is by no means proper in a congregation. On this account it has been, and will be found best to use plain tunes in all places of public worship, without any embellishments, but such as may be easily and naturally sung together" (J—S—, organist: 103). This does imply that "gracing" had been attempted, even if unsuccessfully, in some congregations, but it is difficult to reconcile the practice with Wesley's exhortations. Quite possibly, as Leaver suggests in Chapter 3, Wesley had two standards, one for private singing within his societies, the other for public worship.

"The Invitation" is Lampe's most durable tune and the only one that spread far outside Methodist circles. It is one of the simpler ones, in four regular phrases, but still decked with various types of ornament. Example 1.2 shows how it was gradually simplified over the decades. Interestingly, Wesley left out most of the trills when he printed the tune in 1761 but restored them in *Sacred Harmony* (1781). In the Wollaston version (from an Anglican book of 1813), almost all the original ornaments and melismas have gone, but two new ones have appeared (in bars 0 and 13), of the kind that often emerge in the process of oral transmission. Such "slides" were also found in the "old way of singing" of earlier times (see

EX. 1.2. Four printings of John Frederick Lampe's hymn 18, "The Invitation," originally set to Charles Wesley's hymn "Sinners, obey the gospel word."

Temperley and Drage, No. 5). It may be doubted whether the word *ornament* is appropriate for this involuntary process.

The Parody Hymn Tune

A historically important feature of Methodist music was the parody hymn tune, that is, a tune taken from another source (often secular) and given new words. The practice had been common enough at the time of the Reformation, but it had been suppressed in England for generations. As early as 1619, George Wither had condemned the use of "those roguish tunes, which have formerly served for profane jigs," and in 1630 the Court of High Commission censured one William Slatyer for adding to his psalm book a "scandalous table" proposing secular ballad tunes for many of the psalms (see Temperley 1979b, 1:66–67). Now the Methodists revived the practice. John Wesley himself was responsible for the very first known instance from this period, when he introduced a march from Handel's *Riccardo primo* into the "Foundery Collection" of 1742. Charles Wesley explicitly advocated the practice, as is made very clear in his hymn "Listed into the cause of sin," discussed in Chapter 2.

It is useful to distinguish between three differently motivated types of religious parody. One results simply from the search for a good but *unfamiliar* tune, without reference to its secular context. This was surely Wesley's reason for taking the Handel march. The opera it came from was obscure; the march was little known and was not one of the many excerpts from Handel operas that had been reprinted; Wesley did not acknowledge the source or even hint at it when he named the tune JERICHO. But he liked it and found it suited the words.

The second and most common type of religious parody was an open borrowing of a *familiar* secular tune, with full knowledge of its pagan, blasphemous, lascivious, or merely non-religious text, but on the principle that the music itself was innocent, as Charles Wesley declared. The best way to get new hymns sung was to attach them to tunes already known, and it was hoped that people would come to prefer the new religious words to the old secular ones. John Day in his 1562 title page had urged "the laying apart of all ungodly songes and balades" (*Whole Booke*); now Charles Wesley wanted to "plunder the carnal lover." The first to carry this out on any large scale was Thomas Butts, who must have gained the Wesleys' approval for doing so. I have found eleven cases in Butts's 1754 collection, and more are almost certainly waiting to be identified.

The third type is the *pointed* parody, where the original secular words are an integral part of the plan. A likely model for this game was *The Beggar's Opera* (1728), where no less than sixty-nine well-known popular airs were given new texts by John Gay. Yvonne Noble has pointed out many cases where the original text of a song, presumably well known to the audience, gave additional meaning to the new text and to the stage action that went with it. For example, when Macheath sings, "My heart was so free," he is making a pretty compliment to Polly:

CAPTAIN PLUME:	CAPTAIN MACHEATH:
I still will adore,	My heart was so free,
Love more and more,	It rov'd like the Bee,
But by *Jove* if you chance to prove Cruel,	Till *Polly* my passion requited;
I'll get me a Miss,	I sipt each flower,
That freely will Kiss,	I chang'd ev'ry hour,
Tho' after I drink Water-gruel.	But here ev'ry flower is united.
—George Farquhar	—John Gay

He is saying that whatever his previous conduct, he will now be faithful to Polly forever, and Polly takes him at his word. Yet the scene that this tune called up to contemporary audiences, from Farquhar's *The Recruiting Officer* (1706), shows a very different morality (in the left-hand column above), which turns out to be Macheath's actual code of behavior.

Charles Wesley adapted this technique to sacred music when he wrote the hymn "Love divine, all loves excelling" to be sung to Henry Purcell's tune for John Dryden's "Fairest isle, all isles excelling":

Fairest Isle, all isles excelling,
   Seat of pleasure and of love,
Venus here will choose her dwelling,
   And forsake her Cyprian grove.
Cupid from his fav'rite nation
   Care and envy will remove,
Jealousy, that poisons passion,
   And despair, that dies for love.
             —John Dryden

Love divine, all Loves excelling,
   Joy of Heav'n, to Earth come down,
Fix in us thy humble Dwelling,
   All thy faithful Mercies crown.
Jesu, thou art all Compassion,
Pure unbounded Love thou art;
Visit us with thy Salvation,
Enter ev'ry trembling Heart.
            —Charles Wesley

In *King Arthur* (1691), Dryden was writing in honor of Cupid, Venus, and sexual freedom. Wesley substituted the love of the Christian God, while at the same time appropriating one of the most beautiful songs in the English canon; as a hymn tune it was given the name WESTMINSTER. The singers or hearers were thus invited to compare the relative merits of the two kinds of love. A similar case, which John Wesley added to *Sacred Melody* in 1765, is "Thou Shepherd of Israel, and mine," a parody of "My fond Shepherds of late were so blest" from Richard Rolt's *Eliza* (1754), set to its tune. The unalloyed pleasures of the pastoral life, Wesley seems to tell us, can be legitimately enjoyed only if the Lord is our shepherd.

Another subclass of pointed parody is the heroic. Charles Wesley's "Christ the Lord is risen today" was matched by Butts to "See, the conquering hero comes" from Handel's *Judas Maccabaeus,* composed in 1746. Handel and Thomas Morell had chosen to celebrate the military victory of the biblical hero Judas and his triumphant return as a metaphor for the recent defeat of the Jacobite rebellion by the Duke of Cumberland. But by setting Charles Wesley's Easter hymn to Handel's instantly famous tune (borrowed in turn from Gottfried Muffat), Butts asserts that the victory of Christ over the forces of darkness and his return to the living trumps the glory of any human hero. This telling stroke was immediately taken up by the Calvinistic Methodists, and from them ultimately by John Wesley, who accepted the text–tune match in his *Sacred Harmony* of 1781. Again, "He comes, he comes, the judge severe," from Wesley's *Hymns of Intercession* (1758), was written for the tune of "He comes, he comes, the hero comes" from Henry Carey's masque *Britannia* (1734). Other Methodist collections made similar adaptations of "God Save the King" and "Rule, Britannia."

There is no doubt that John approved of these parodies. Although seven of them were among the many tunes he did not take over from Butts, he retained at least five, added two more in 1761, and added yet another in 1781. The parody principle then continued far into the nineteenth century, the prime Victorian example with a Wesleyan text being "Hark, the herald angels sing," its tune adapted from a song honoring Gutenberg in Mendelssohn's *Festgesang* (1840).

John Wesley's Musical Taste

Art music was clearly the idiom preferred by the Wesleys. Charles had considerable reservations about it when used in a secular context, as we will see in Chapters 10 and 12, but was always ready to exploit its powers for religious purposes, as already shown. John, who made the final selection of tunes for "the people called Methodists" in his *Sacred Harmony,* shows a consistent taste and sensitivity, and an understanding of current ideas of musical quality. And that quality was inevitably defined by the taste of the nobility and gentry. If John was somewhat disapproving of Charles's eventual encouragement of his sons' music, it was not the musical style itself that he disliked, but the idea of showing off children's performances to worldly people.

Secular art music was more complex than street ballads or traditional psalm tunes. It had more graces, melismas, repetitions, melodic leaps, rhythmic and harmonic variety. We might expect, therefore, that Methodist hymn tunes of the period would be more complex than those of other groups, and such indeed proves to be the case. Table 1.2 shows the results of an analysis comparing new Methodist tunes, first printed between 1750 and 1779 (and thus excluding Lampe's), with three other categories in the same period. First, Methodist collections tended to have more new tunes than others (line 3). By almost every measure, their tunes were more complex than those of the other groups: they were longer (lines 5, 6), used more and longer melismas (lines 9, 10) and more melodic leaps (line 11), and had a larger total range (line 12), though the differences are not huge. In one respect—textual repetition—they were far ahead of urban Anglican and Dissenting tunes (lines 7, 8) but neck-and-neck with rural Anglican: more tunes had some verbal repetition, but the number of notes involved was slightly less. (This is somewhat ironic, in view of Wesley's dislike of "vain repetitions," discussed later in this chapter; but it is consistent with the development of Methodist "repeating" tunes, where women sang a line that was then repeated by the whole congregation.)

All these characteristics probably reflect the influence of secular art music, though there is no corpus available for comparative analysis. The more general "urban" influence, shared by the urban Anglican and Methodist categories, may account for the lower proportion of tunes in minor mode (line 4), which was rapidly losing popularity in that milieu during the second half of the eighteenth century, and the greater number of exact repetitions of musical lines (line 13). Line 14 is a count of musical sequences, or lines repeated at a higher or lower pitch, a relatively modern and sophisticated element in eighteenth-century art music: here Methodist tunes are far ahead of the other categories, though the proportion is still small.

At all events, John Wesley was firmly convinced that he could rely on his own judgment in the selection of music. What he recognized as good must be good for everyone. Today we tend to consider that musical excellence is not absolute

TABLE 1.2. Analysis of hymn tunes newly printed in England between 1750 and 1779

	Urban Anglican	Rural Anglican	Dissent	Methodist
1. Number of printed sources in sample	35	58	24	22
2. Number of new tunes in sample	313	573	226	341
3. New tunes per printed source	8.9	9.8	9.4	15.5
4. Tunes in minor mode	20%	29%	28%	24%
5. Notes per tune	61.8	52.4	49.3	72.4
6. Lines of music per tune	6.4	5.2	5.1	7.0
7. Tunes using verbal repetition	19%	46%	22%	54%
8. Proportion of notes using repeated text	9%	18%	7%	16%
9. Tunes with melismas	94%	97%	93%	98%
10. Proportion of notes that are the second or subsequent notes of a melisma	22%	24%	24%	28%
11. Average interval size (in scale steps)	1.31	1.24	1.30	1.35
12. Average tune range (in scale steps)	9.07	8.01	8.32	9.79
13. Exact repetition lines of music	4.4%	2.1%	2.7%	4.7%
14. Sequential repetition lines of music	0.7%	0.3%	0.7%	2.0%

Note: Data from the *Hymn Tune Index* (2006 revision). Sources were used only if they could be confidently assigned to one of the four categories heading the columns. "Methodist" sources include those for non-Wesleyan Methodists. Unfortunately, it was not possible to compare rhythmic or harmonic complexity, or melodic chromaticism, from this corpus, since these elements are not recorded in the *HTI* database. Analysis by David Temperley

but culturally determined. We can hardly blame Wesley for not recognizing this truth, since it only began to dawn on musicologists in the late nineteenth century. His stance was paternalistic, as one would expect in his time. But it was in conflict with another principle that was equally strong in his mind, summed up in those two words "Sing *all*." He truly wished to bring all classes of society to Methodism. He did not see that if he wanted to appeal to the poor, the unlettered, the laborers and the mill workers, sophisticated songs with graces like those of Handel, Lampe, or Arne were not going to do the trick. It is true that crowds of people unfamiliar with art music may have been quite capable of ornamenting a melody, as they do today in "You'll Never Walk Alone" at soccer matches or, for that matter, in "Amazing grace." But the Lampe style of ornaments patently belonged to the world of fashion.

At the same time, there were aspects of art music that Wesley opposed. As already mentioned, he had a rooted dislike of what he called "vain repetitions," music that repeated the same words over and over again. In the 1768 Conference minutes he made a well-known statement to this effect, specially singling out the addition of hallelujahs. (On the other hand, he had included the Easter Hymn, "Jesus Christ is risen today," which has a hallelujah after each line.) He went on: "The repeating of the same words so often (but especially while another repeats different words, the horrid abuse which runs through the modern church-music), as it shocks all common sense, so it necessarily brings in dead formality, and has no more of religion in it than a Lancashire hornpipe."

On the whole, the disavowal of counterpoint was in line with the *galant* taste of the times, reacting against the late-baroque style. But Wesley's position was more extreme and was based on theological principle. His pungent condemnation has been many times quoted and was repeated a number of times in slightly different forms (C. Young 1995a: 96–97). It seems to rule out most anthems, unless they were entirely homophonic; but see Chapter 5. It also excludes fuging tunes (those in which voices enter some phrases successively in counterpoint, normally resulting in text overlap between the voices). These did, indeed, mostly stay out of Methodist tune books for several decades after Wesley's edict. Like the early Puritans, he was, above all, concerned that every word of a hymn, psalm, or anthem should be heard and understood. He did sometimes acknowledge the sublime effect of anthems and oratorio choruses, and indeed an anthem at St. Paul's cathedral had played a part in his personal conversion experience in 1738. This was the Anglican side of his multilateral persona. He could appreciate in a cathedral things that he wanted no part of in Methodist meetings, where they might confuse his flock.

After the Wesleys

When John Wesley's authority was no longer supreme, as in America after Independence and in Britain after his death, Wesleyan Methodism tended to split into two or more movements, largely along class lines. The middle-class urban Wesleyan societies in Britain, and on the Eastern Seaboard of the United States, became in each case a fully-fledged Methodist Church. Their music continued to move in the direction of art music (see Chapters 6 and 8). They gradually introduced organs, choirs, and elaborate musical settings such as anthems, set pieces, solos and duets, and eventually even Anglican chants.

Let us see what happened to one of Charles Wesley's most admired hymns, "Jesu, lover of my soul." The tune that was first printed with it, Martin Madan's HOTHAM (Ex. 1.3), was an instant hit and was adopted in over 90 percent of the 232 musical printings of the hymn in the next sixty years. It first appeared in Madan's "Lock Hospital Collection" but was quickly picked up by John Wesley in the 1765 edition of *Sacred Melody*. It was just the sort of tune he most admired. Madan had printed it in three parts, but Wesley reduced it to melody alone, removed a trill, and cut out the repeat, with pauses, of the last four measures. Even in its monophonic form, its implied harmony is obvious and is even outlined in parts of the melody (as in bars 9–11 and 17). Very probably, bars 15 and 16 would have been sung by women alone.

HOTHAM lasted a hundred years but was replaced in *Hymns Ancient and Modern* by John Bacchus Dykes's equally accomplished tune HOLLINGSIDE (its first half shown in Ex. 1.4), which was soon adopted in most English Methodist hymnals. It is in the same key, with very similar phrases in the first part, but the elegant fripperies are all gone and are replaced by rich and solid four-part har-

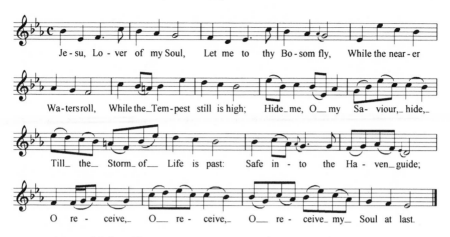

EX. 1.3. Martin Madan, HOTHAM.

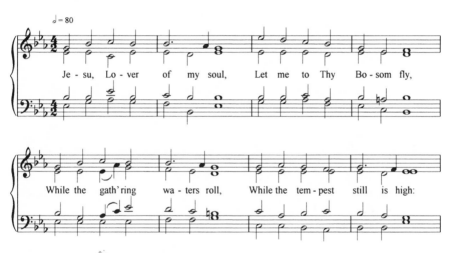

EX. 1.4. J. B. Dykes, HOLLINGSIDE, first half.

mony. John Wesley, I think, would have admired its tunefulness and directness, but he would not have liked the fact that it depends for so much of its effect on harmony. For instance, in bars 2 and 6 the melody is almost identical to that of bar 2 in HOTHAM. But Dykes's two harmonizations of this three-note phrase, unlike Madan's, could not be surmised from the melody alone, and differ between themselves. (More recently the hymn has often been matched to John Parry's minor-mode tune ABERYSTWYTH. In North America its tune history has been quite different, as discussed in Chapter 6.)

Other branches of Methodism moved in the opposite direction, one that the Wesleys would not have endorsed. Revival meetings were held in frontier regions, attracting large numbers of people with no books, little education, and

often little experience of worship. These meetings were severely criticized by the
central Methodist Conferences in both Britain and America. The camp meeting
and its musical tradition was established in America in about 1800 and was soon
dominated by Methodists (Hulan). They alone had a built-in itinerant ministry
that could cope with the expanding frontier. To encourage those who could not
read, the texts depended at first on lining out by the preachers; and as there was
little possibility of musical instruction or accompaniment, the tunes had to be
either well known, as with "folk hymns," or very easily learned, as with "spiritual
songs" (see Eskew and McElrath: 160–68; Hatchett: 9–13).

This type of "spiritual song," or simply *spiritual*, traded on easy accessibility of
both text and music. The text was consciously popular in diction, avoiding theological niceties, complexity of thought, and the type of self-questioning severity
that the Wesleys often stressed, and appealed directly to feeling. Its simplistic
message of hope in the future life as consolation for present misery would become
quite general to Methodism in the nineteenth century. Many have a powerful
aura of fighting against evil, which Hulan attributes in part to the influence of
Bunyan's *Pilgrim's Progress* (117–41):

> 'Tis glorious hope upon my head,
> And on my breast, my shield;
> With this bright sword I mean to fight,
> Until I win the field. (Tiebout: 50–51, cited Hulan: 121)

Some spirituals made use of call-and-response structures, and also of refrains,
which were often transferred from one hymn to another. Here is one printed by
Stith Mead, a Methodist preacher in Virginia, under the title "Shout Old Satan's
Kingdom Down" in his *General Selection* in 1807:

> This day my soul has caught on fire, Hallelujah!
> I feel that Heaven is coming nigher, O glory Hallelujah!
>
> *Chorus:*
> Shout, shout, we're gaining ground, Hallelujah!
> We'll shout old Satan's kingdom down, Hallelujah!

Revival meetings soon came to Britain, most famously at Mow Cop in 1807,
led by the American revivalist Lorenzo Dow. This event, usually regarded as the
beginning of a new kind of popular revivalism in Britain, led to the formal organization in 1810 of the Primitive Methodists, who had been expelled from the main
Conference in 1808 because it could not approve their meetings. They were soon
nicknamed Ranters, probably because of the loud and harsh voice production
they had to cultivate in order to be heard out of doors. Their singing resembled
that of the American revivalists, being constrained by the same need to involve
large numbers of people. They too used simple-minded hymns with shouted
refrains and set new words to well-known popular tunes. There was no reason

to write the tunes down; so, as in America, there are few contemporary musical sources. (For an account of early Primitive Methodist music see Stokes.)

But there is suggestive evidence that this type of song also had earlier English roots. William Edward Miller, who compiled *David's Harp*, an English Wesleyan collection published about 1803, said in his preface that Wesley's *Sacred Harmony* had tried to preserve "a distinction . . . between *sacred* and *prophane* music," but that since then "a light, indecorous style of music has been introduced," notably some "effusions of folly and ignorance . . . lately brought over from America." This echoes a complaint that we sometimes hear in our own time, but it may be that the Americans were not solely responsible for populist innovations, any more than they are today.

The English roots can be traced back to the lifetime of the Wesleys, who, however hard they tried, could not control every aspect of the movement they had founded. The Conference minutes, which were largely dictated by John Wesley, repeated from time to time his injunction to use "our" tunes, suggesting that there were others creeping in that he considered undesirable.

The most popular hymnbook of early American Methodism was in fact a revised edition of an English collection, *A Pocket Hymn Book Designed as a Constant Companion for the Pious,* compiled by Robert Spence and published in York in 1781. Most of the hymns in it were selected from the Wesleys' books, but other texts were added, often substituting emotional appeal for theological substance. They lacked Charles Wesley's discourse on difficult subjects. Instead, they presented religion as a simple matter of following God's word and fighting off Satan, which quickly caught on in some Methodist societies. John Wesley dismissed most of them as "grievous doggerel." We know exactly which ones he meant, because he quickly brought out his own revision of Spence's book (J. Wesley 1785), with thirty-seven of its hymns expunged (see C. Young 1993: 97–108 for a comparative analysis of the contents of these books).

A few of these rejected hymns have repeated refrains and call-and-answer structures of the type that would later become characteristic of American spirituals. Example 1.5 shows "Salvation, O the joyful sound," an Isaac Watts hymn, which appears in Spence with the addition of an anonymous doxology refrain ("Glory, honour, praise and power"). It was one of those rejected by Wesley. The refrain has its own tune, which was apparently first used in the Countess of Huntingdon's Connexion, a branch of Calvinistic Methodism, with Watts's hymn "Come happy souls, approach your God."

The first eight bars are the sort of tune Wesley would have liked—ornate, balanced, shapely. It was first printed in *The Gospel Magazine* in April 1774 with the Watts hymn but without the refrain. The text and tune of the refrain, by contrast, are a popular rouser with repeated hallelujahs of the kind that Wesley deeply distrusted. The combination is to modern ears more cheerful than we might think "proper for Good-Friday," as the heading states. Paul Gailiunas has told

EX. 1.5. SALVATION.

me that the tune was popular in English Primitive Methodist circles throughout
the nineteenth century. It made its first American appearance in Amos Pilsbury's
United States' Sacred Harmony (1799).

This brings us to the "folk hymn," more properly defined as a hymn set to an
existing secular folk tune. It formed the backbone of the American Sacred Harp
tradition, which is still flourishing today. It is, of course, a kind of parody hymn
of the second category as defined earlier in this chapter (the "familiar tune" type),
but using a very different kind of model than the ones favored by the Wesleys.
Some folk hymns are first found in print in Pilsbury's book and in Jeremiah Ingalls's *Christian Harmony* (1805). They have been much discussed by American
scholars (see, for instance, G. P. Jackson; Eskew and McElrath). David Klocko
conducted extensive research on secular concordances of tunes in the Ingalls
volume (1978, 1981). Example 1.6 is one of these.

Staff 1 shows the tune as Ingalls printed it, underlaid with the first verse of a
long anonymous hymn. This is the second of two hymns printed by Ingalls for use
with this tune, and it seems to have given the tune its name, SHOUTING HYMN.
Staff 2 shows a slightly earlier Masonic hymn by Robert Burns, which Klocko
considers to be Ingalls's likely source. Nobody seems to have noticed that the same
melody became the basis for one of Ralph Vaughan Williams's finest hymn tunes
a century later, the one he used again in his *Five Variants of "Dives and Lazarus"*
(1939). It is shown in staff 3. There may also be a relationship to the still-popular
ballad tune "The Wraggle Taggle Gypsies, O."

This is an example of the more modal (or pentatonic) kind of tune that was
most likely to be familiar to rural communities in both England and America,
and hence was more useful for country revival meetings than the urban type of

EX. 1.6. (1) SHOUTING HYMN compared with (2) "The Farewell" and (3) KINGSFOLD.

melody favored by the Wesleys. It uses a "gapped" scale with final on E, missing out F♯ in the version used by Burns (staff 2), and also employs the flat seventh (D). Ingalls also omitted F♯ but "modernized" the tune by sharpening all but one of the D's, even when this produced a melodic diminished fourth (staff 1, bars 1–2, 6, and 16). Vaughan Williams, of course, had quite different motives: he was appealing to a sophisticated nostalgia rather than looking for tunes that were already familiar to his audience. He clearly relished the sense of antiquity imparted by flat sevenths. He used D♮ consistently but had no special objection to F♯. The emotional tone of his version is worlds away from that of Ingalls, but each is well matched to its text.

The most popular folk hymn of all is surely "Amazing grace," written by the evangelical poet John Newton and gaining an enormous following in the United States after it was matched to the tune NEW BRITAIN (first printed in 1829 with another text) in William Walker's *Southern Harmony* (1835). (Its popularity in Britain is a relatively recent development.) It is essentially pentatonic, and in the general idiom of Anglo-Celtic folk song, but no secular original has been unearthed so far. Whether real or imitation "folk," it demonstrates the level of cultural penetration that a hymn can achieve when it finds a tune that appeals intimately to its audience. No tune approved by Wesley can come close to matching this record.

These relationships with folk song gave the common people full access to religious expression and can be seen as the triumphant realization of John Wesley's first principle of hymn singing: "Sing *All*." Yet he resisted, with all his authority, the popularization of texts and tunes that was a necessary precondition for their acceptance by all classes of Anglo-Saxon society. Still more radical changes of style would be demanded by the eventual worldwide mission of Methodism and other branches of evangelical Christianity: the development of Negro spirituals, the embracing by missionaries of musical norms from all parts of the world, and in more recent times the adaptation of commercial popular music. It is difficult to imagine what Wesley would have made of these developments.

Conclusion

What, then, was John Wesley's purpose and ideal for Methodist music? He had a mixed inheritance of high-church, Puritan, and Pietist elements, and each of them played a part in his views. For the high churchman singing was an offering to God, and as such must be of the best quality that could be attained. For the Puritan it was an obedient carrying out of God's command that all men and women should praise their maker with understanding. And for the Pietist it was an expression of love coming truly from the heart. From these three vantage points sprang the Wesleyan ideal: tunes must be of good quality, regardless of their origin; must be uttered and understood by all; and must be sung with energy and devotional feeling.

But Wesley evidently had additional, unstated goals that may be called political in nature. He found, as Luther and Watts had before him, that putting emotional words into the very mouths of the people was the most effective way possible of promulgating new religious principles. Finally, music was probably the greatest factor in increasing the numbers and hence the power of the movement, as William Vincent ruefully acknowledged. The paradox is that the full extent of that power could be realized only when it was set free from the constraint of the Wesleys' relatively narrow musical tastes.

I am grateful to Sally Drage, Harry Eskew, Julian Onderdonk, David Temperley, and Carlton Young for their help and advice on various matters covered in this chapter.

CHAPTER 2

Charles Wesley and the Music of Poetry

J. R. Watson

Introduction

Music and poetry are closely allied: "Blest pair of Sirens, pledges of Heav'ns joy, / Sphear-born harmonious Sisters, Voice, and Vers," as Milton, Charles Wesley's beloved forbear, put it. Wesley himself was acutely aware of the closeness of music to poetry: in the hymn "For the Anniversary Day of One's Conversion," published in *Hymns and Sacred Poems* (J. and C. Wesley 1740), he wrote in verse 7 (now traditionally verse 1), "O for a thousand tongues to sing." "Sing" here may be simply a metaphor for poetic utterance, but it may also refer to the musical element of hymns and to the praise of God in sacred song. Wesley did not write "O for a thousand tongues to preach," but "to *sing.*"

Moreover, the word "sing" suggests a discourse that is not merely the singing of hymns to a tune. Whether sung or read, the hymns of Charles Wesley "sing" in the mind's ear in ways that are instantly recognizable: the lines in their verses *move* in the mind, sound and sense coming together in a precision and harmony that makes them seem exactly right for what they want to say. This is partly, of course, a matter of the presentation and re-presentation of scripture, but the hymns are then involved in human response and interpretation. They also articulate feeling, the fluctuating moods of the mind and heart. They do so in such a way that these things are subsumed into the art of the hymn, its formal structures; they make up, in all their variety and force, the convincing whole that we recognize as the hymnody of Charles Wesley and no one else.

This chapter argues that he was always conscious of music and its relationship to the words in the line; the rhythms, cadences, and movements of the verse; the rising and falling of verbal sound; the sense of the "music" of a whole hymn. His poetic art, honed to a fine point by years of writing classical verse at school, was wonderfully sensitive to meters, word sounds, and the ways in which sound and sense go together. Specific examples of his utterances on the subject have been collected by Carlton R. Young in *Music of the Heart* and need not be repeated here; but Young's description of Wesley as a "lyrical theologian," taken (and expanded)

ILLUS. 2.1. Charles Wesley the elder (Museum of Methodism, John Wesley's Chapel, City Road, London). Oil portrait by John Russell. Reproduced by permission of the Trustees of Wesley's Chapel, London.

from S T Kimbrough, is of great importance and underpins much of what has been said up to this point (C. Young 1995a: 28ff.).

He loved music and was very proud of his two sons, whom he encouraged and promoted; and because of his love of music, he was concerned that it should be used properly. He knew that music was a great and precious art, and he was acutely conscious that (like other great human gifts and attainments) it could be used or misused. The most obvious statement of its importance is in two hymns titled "The True Use of Musick" (C. Wesley 1749a, 2: hymns 189, 190). One of them, "Jesus, Thou Soul of all our Joys," is still in Methodist hymnbooks (it is no. 761 in *Hymns and Psalms,* 1983). The other, "Listed into the Cause of Sin," has long been forgotten, but it is worth revisiting for what it says about music. It is clear that Wesley saw music as good but believed that it had been misused:

> Listed into the Cause of Sin,
> Why should a Good be Evil?
> Musick, alas! too long has been
> Prest to obey the Devil:
> Drunken, or lewd, or light the Lay
> Flow'd to the Soul's Undoing,
> Widen'd, and strew'd with Flowers the Way
> Down to Eternal Ruin.

This uncompromising stuff is followed by a commendable instruction to use music for its right purposes:

> Who on the Part of God will rise,
> *Innocent Sound* recover,
> Fly on the Prey, and take the Prize,
> Plunder the Carnal Lover,
> Strip him of every moving Strain,
> Every melting Measure,
> Musick in Virtue's Cause retain,
> Rescue the Holy Pleasure?

This is a clear statement of the practice that Charles Wesley followed in his writing, which frequently took a secular text, especially one of profane love, and altered it to make it refer to divine love: it is a snatching back of the phrases of lovers from them, and giving them to Christ, as it is in "Love divine, all loves excelling" (see page 15). At this point, however, "Listed into the Cause of Sin" turns to celebrate the "music" of the name of Jesus, the music of the heart. Now the name of Jesus is itself a sacred music:

> Harmony all its Strains may bring,
> JESUS's Name is sweeter.

Because of this, "Jesus the soul of music is," and this is what will make us rejoice:

> Melody in our Hearts we make,
> Melody with our Voices.

Finally the music of the name of Jesus is what will "carry us up to heaven":

> Only believe, and still sing on,
> Heaven is Ours for ever.

Wesley had celebrated the music of the name before, in "Glory to God, and Praise, and Love" (J. and C. Wesley 1740: 120, later excerpted as "O for a thousand tongues to sing"):

> JESUS the Name that charms our Fears,
>   That bids our Sorrows cease;
> 'Tis Musick in the Sinner's Ears,
>   'Tis Life, and Health, and Peace!

"Music to my ears" is a cliché, here daringly adopted to become both the original proverbial saying *and something else*—a "music" that is agreeable and necessary comfort, but also music, song in the mind and in the heart.

The other hymn on "The True Use of Musick" follows the same pattern, but more gracefully:

> JESUS, Thou Soul of all our Joys,
> For whom we now lift up our Voice,
>   And all our Strength exert,
> Vouchsafe the Grace we humbly claim,
> Compose into a Thankful Frame,
>   And tune thy People's Heart.

The verbs "compose" and "tune" point the way forward to the hymn's central idea, that in "the true use of music" the praise of Jesus should be the sole aim, and that our lives, our hearts, should be directed to this end. It is not a matter of singing, but of living. We are to be "on our guard" against the temptation to neglect Christ, a temptation that can be encouraged by music itself, if improperly used:

> Still let us on our Guard be found,
> And watch against the Power of Sound,
>   With sacred Jealousy;
> Lest haply Sense should damp our Zeal,
> And Musick's Charms bewitch and steal
>   Our Heart away from Thee.

The true aim of music is that we should sing together, "sweetly join with one accord." But that means living a life in accordance with God's will, a life that is "in tune with Heav'n" (Milton again), so that we should feel in all our faculties the power of "thine harmonizing name." If we do so, we shall find ourselves, both in life and in death, "singing" the "music" of salvation:

> With calmly reverential Joy
> We then shall all our Lives employ
>   In setting forth thy Love,
> And raise in Death our Triumph higher,
> And sing with all the Heavenly Choir
>   That endless Song Above.

For Wesley the word "music" was constantly associated in his mind with "the Name of Jesus," the name that is above every name: in that name the pilgrim on this earth rejoices as he journeys towards heaven: indeed, the music on earth is a foretaste of heaven, what Wesley in his "conversion hymn" calls an "Antepast of Heaven." He would have known Herbert's celebration, "Church-musick," which begins by addressing sacred music as "sweetest of sweets" and ends,

> But if I travel in your companie,
>   You know the way to heavens doore.

These hymns indicate the ways in which music becomes for Charles Wesley a divine gift. It is also an element of the spiritual life, the singing of the soul on its pilgrimage from earth to heaven. In "Father of everlasting Grace," a hymn for Whit Sunday (J. and C. Wesley 1746d: hymn 1), Wesley prays for the coming of the Holy Spirit, so that the congregation may "bless, and praise Thee evermore / And serve Thee like thy Hosts above," until the time when they will, at death, sing in heaven as they have sung on earth, only better:

> Till added to that Heavenly Quire,
> We raise our Songs of Triumph higher,
>   And praise Thee in a bolder Strain,
> Outsoar the firstborn Seraph's Flight,
> And sing with all our Friends in Light,
>   Thy everlasting Love to Man.

To Wesley, our life is itself a music, and we "sing" that life. The result is a body of hymnody that expresses his devotion *as* music, but also *in* music; because his art is always conscious of its ability not merely to expound scripture, but to versify it lyrically. It was his great gift to be able to transform the exposition into singable poetry. As Kimbrough has written, "Charles Wesley's imaginative poetic art sets Holy Scripture and theology in a symphonic language of many keys" (1992: 136).

Kimbrough is drawing attention to the immense variety of Wesley's work, the way in which his use of scripture has many different ways of presenting and modifying it, as different as G major is from A minor. We cannot, obviously, identify hymns with specific keys, although we might be able to construct a rough sense that some hymns are in a major key and others in a minor. But Kimbrough is writing figuratively, and we should not seek to press his sentence too far. It is a powerful and effective metaphor to conclude his fine essay, and what follows is an attempt to disentangle that metaphor in a discussion of some Wesley hymns.

The Poet's Music

The poet Anne Stevenson has remarked that every poet has his or her own music. It is helpful to explore Wesley's verse in the light of this observation, and in the light of T. S. Eliot's essay "The Music of Poetry." One of Charles Wesley's finest hymns is titled "To the Trinity" (C. Wesley 1747: hymn 34). (As it happens, the

tune to which it is generally sung today, now called R IDGE (KO 117), from the
village in Hertfordshire where he lived, is by Samuel Wesley. Tune and words
here make an extraordinary combination.)

> Father, in whom we live,
>   In whom we are, and move,
> The Glory, Power, and Praise receive
>   Of thy Creating Love:
> Let all the Angel-Throng
>   Give Thanks to G OD on high;
> While Earth repeats the Joyful Song,
>   And ecchoes to the Sky.
>
> Incarnate Deity,
>   Let all the Ransom'd Race
> Render in Thanks their Lives to Thee,
>   For thy Redeeming Grace;
> The Grace to Sinners shew'd,
>   Ye Heavenly Quires, proclaim,
> And cry Salvation to our God,
>   Salvation to the Lamb!
>
> Spirit of Holiness,
>   Let all thy Saints adore
> Thy sacred Energy, and bless
>   Thine Heart-renewing Power[.]
> Not Angel-tongues can tell
>   Thy Love's extatic Height,
> The Glorious Joy unspeakable,
>   The Beatific Sight!
>
> Eternal Tri-une L ORD,
>   Let all the Hosts above,
> Let all the Sons of Men record,
>   And dwell upon thy Love;
> When Heaven and Earth are fled
>   Before thy glorious Face,
> Sing all the Saints thy Love has made,
>   Thine Everlasting Praise!
>   (*Hymns and Psalms,* 4)

The first thing to be said about this hymn is that it has a robust and clear structure. It is in four movements, like a modern symphony (Kimbrough's "symphonic
language"), although those movements are theological rather than musical. There
are verses to Father, Son, and Holy Spirit, with a concluding verse to the triune
God. In this respect it imitates Watts's "We give immortal praise," a hymn with
an identical structure but a different "music" (because it is by a different author).

Both hymns are very grand; and here I want to suggest a variant of Kimbrough's musical analogy of the symphonic language. I would put forward the idea that this is in a major key, with the last line as the verbal equivalent of the final cadence, after intermediate verses ending in related keys:

> Sing all the Saints thy Love has made,
>   Thine Everlasting Praise!

One identifying characteristic of this hymn is that it is to be sung in the grand manner. This is Charles Wesley *maestoso;* elsewhere he is found in many differ-ent moods: *allegro* and *allegretto, largo* and *lento, andante* and *adagio.* We will encounter some of these in the course of this chapter: I record them now by way of putting down a marker to indicate the extraordinary range and variety of the many thousand hymns he wrote—certainly six thousand plus, and perhaps nine thousand if you count the one-verse hymns in *Short Hymns on Select Passages of the Holy Scriptures* of 1762.

In the introduction to his classic *Representative Verse of Charles Wesley* (1962), Frank Baker wrote of Charles Wesley's "word-music," later adding:

> Although he could make no great musical claims as vocalist, instrumentalist, or composer, his musical sons acknowledged that his ear was impeccable. . . . His inventiveness and his mastery in lyrical form were without parallel in the verse of that century, and perhaps only paralleled by Shelley in the century that followed.

A little later Baker wrote:

> Any musician knows that if he remains in the same key for too long monotony sets in. This he avoids by modulations, passages in a different, though related key, passages short or long, obvious or subtly concealed beneath the melody, varying both with the occasion and with the technical command and musical sensitivity of the composer. The same kind of thing is true in verse. (Baker 1962: xxiii, xxxiv–xxxviii)

Baker spends much time, very profitably, on Wesley's use of different meters, his understanding of rhetorical patterns such as *anaphora* (repetition of a word or phrase at the beginning of successive lines) and *antanaclasis* (repetition with a difference), and his modulations on expected forms. Thus he points out that the opening line of "Soldiers of Christ, arise" is a variation on what he calls "the other-wise docile iambics of the double short meter" by using "an opening choriambus, or a foot consisting of a trochee followed by an iambus" (xlviii). The choriambus, with its distinctive rhythm, gives life and energy to the line. It occurs in many of the succeeding verses, though not always to the same extent (the variety is part of the attraction): whereas "Stand then in his great might" (verse 2), "Leave no unguarded place" (verse 3), and "Pray, without ceasing pray" (Part 2 verse 4) begin with choriambuses of varying assertiveness, "To keep your armour bright" (Part 2, verse 3) returns to the normal iambic pattern. It is interesting that *Hymns Ancient and Modern*, from 1861 to the present day, uses William Henry Monk's tune St. Ethelwald, which removes any suggestion of the choriambic rhythm by presenting the line as five quarter-notes followed by a dotted half-note, with the first syllable on an upbeat. The two eighth-notes into which the fifth quarter is divided give some life to the line, but the pattern is basically that of Baker's "docile" DSM. Edward Woodall Naylor's From Strength to Strength, written for this hymn, does the opposite: the dotted eighth-note in the first bar picks up Wesley's choriambic rhythm and even exaggerates it. "Soldiers" becomes a startlingly uneven trochee, where in Monk's tune it feels like two equal syllables.

Poetry, Music, and Meaning

The music and the meaning of a lyric are inseparable, as critics have always known and as the first paragraph of Eliot's essay reminds us. A verse from the hymn "Come let us anew / Our journey pursue" (C. Wesley 1749b: hymn 5) offers an example:

> Our life is a dream,
> Our time as a stream
> Glides swiftly away,
> And the fugitive moment refuses to stay,
> The Arrow is flown,
> The moment is gone,
> The millennial year
> Rushes on to our view, and Eternity's here!

This pattern of three successive lines of five syllables, followed by one of twelve syllables, is an unusual combination. Because the ear has grown used to the five syllables in each phrase (though "the millennial year" already has six), the twelve-syllable line comes as a sudden rush of sound: the temptation is to try to fit it into the same space, like thirty-second-notes. Another way of seeing the lines would be not as five-syllable lines but as two-beat ones, "The *arrow* is *flown*, / The *moment* is *gone*," with the long lines as having six syllables to each of the long beats, like two sets of triplets to each beat. Whatever the metrical or musical analysis, however, the effect is one of remarkable acceleration. But that effect is one of meaning as well as sound: "The millennial year / Rushes on to our view, and Eternity's here." The line begins with "rushes on," continues with "our view" as it comes into sight, and ends "here." The process is one of something coming toward the reader at great speed, and it is therefore threatening. But it also conforms to what we know of time and space: the arrow flies through the air, the moments pass one after the other. And then, suddenly, "Eternity's here."

The "millennial year," strictly speaking, means the thousandth year. But it was customary to use it to mean the time when Christ would come in person to rule on earth, following an interpretation of the references in Revelation 20: 1–5. It packs into itself the meaning of the Second Coming, with all that is implied for the world and the people who live in it: the prospect of judgment and the end of all things as we know them. The opening of the verse, "Our life is a dream," takes us back to Isaac Watts and the "busy tribes of flesh and blood / With all their hopes and fears" who disappear "as a dream / Dies at the opening day," and before Watts to Shakespeare: "We are such stuff / As dreams are made on" (*The Tempest* 4.1.156–57). Watts's "Time, like an ever-rolling stream / Bears all its sons away" is imported for the next lines, as part of the rich accumulation of meaning that is summed up at the end in the word "millennial."

The placing of that word, and its sound, are clearly part of the poetic effect, just as with "fugitive." We might say that "millennial" sounds rather beautiful here, a mellifluous set of syllables; whereas "fugitive" sounds much less attractive to the ear. But that would be foolish. "A poem is not made only out of beautiful words," as Eliot put it. "The music of a word . . . arises from its relation first to the words immediately preceding or following it, and indefinitely to the rest of its context" (32). There have been studies of Charles Wesley's vocabulary, notably by Frank Baker, Henry Bett, Oliver Beckerlegge, and Donald Davie. Most of these have drawn attention to the astonishing range and versatility of his word usage, from an Anglo-Saxon simplicity to the complex uses of words of Latin and Greek derivation: "amaranthine" or "panoply" (Greek), "latent" (Latin). Davie suggests that he threaded Latinisms on to the staple Anglo-Saxon of his diction (Baker 1962: xviii), so that they "criss-cross and light up each the other's meaning" (Davie: 78). The Latin words, says Davie, are "refurbished," so that "the blunted meaning or the buried metaphor comes sharp and [live] again, by a sort of Latinate pun" (Baker 1962: xvii, adapted by Davie: 77). We might find this in "fugitive" and "millennial" in the verse already quoted. But the vocabulary is a matter of the words in their context, as Eliot pointed out: the simplest words can be used to remarkable effect. They are the "notes" of the piece, and they come to life in their relationship to one another. They can be dense and complex, like the harmonies of Schumann, or exquisitely simple, like a sequence of single notes. Davie's essay chooses as an example of a classical moment the line "This man receiveth sinners still." He does not say what that particular line does that is specifically classical, but I would agree with him that it is: it comes from the simplicity of "this man," referring to the incarnate God in Jesus Christ, so that a whole christological theory is condensed into two words; and also from the word "still," which incorporates within its simplicity the whole sense of the never-ending love of God, a love that persists "still," meaning not only "forever" but also "in spite of."

Simplicity, in music and in poetry, depends for its effect upon the surrounding complexity. As with "millennial," the force of "still" lies in the compression of meaning into a small space; but it is also dependent on the other words in the line. Eliot was writing before the days of structuralist criticism (although not before Saussurian linguistics), and he did not use concepts of sign systems that have become commonplace, such as those of *langue* (the language system) and *parole* (the individual speech taken from that language). But in the passage quoted in the previous paragraph, he was engaging with the same concepts. In the line that Davie quotes, "This man receiveth sinners still," we discover the meaning because it uses signs that have crucial relationships with the signs before and after them. The choice of words is vital, and the relationship of the words to one another even more so, like the notes of a chord, or the intervals between single notes in a melody.

Words, Lines, and Verses

Sometimes a word will be expressive in itself, transforming the line in which it appears. Thus we have the line from "Jesus the good shepherd is" (a variant on the twenty-third Psalm) describing the generosity of the Lord as "All the pleni-tude of God," in which the word "plenitude" expresses in its three syllables, set against the monosyllables of the line, a certain amplitude and abundance. The same thing could be said of the second line of "Author of faith, eternal Word" (J. and C. Wesley 1740: 6), where the line is "Whose Spirit breathes the active Flame." We might expect the word "breathes" in connection with the Holy Spirit, from the Hebrew *ruach,* meaning "breath," or "spirit," or "wind"; but the crucial word is "active." Where we might expect the word "living," which a lesser writer might have used, we have an adjective that implies action, movement, the active mode rather than the passive mode, the "acting upon" someone rather than just "being," which the word "living" might have conveyed.

That verse is worthy of some study:

> Author of Faith, Eternal Word,
>> Whose Spirit breathes the active Flame,
> Faith, like its Finisher and Lord,
>> To day, as yesterday the same;

It begins with another feature of Charles Wesley's word-music, and that is the unexpected and spectacular. At one level the first line is simple. It addresses the eternal Word, Jesus Christ the incarnate God, who is (in the words of Hebrews 12:2) "the author and finisher of our faith." Linguistically, however, it presents us with two words, "author" and "word," which are here conflated. If we say that Jesus is an author, is he also a word? The two words look at each other from either end of the line. It is perfectly possible to make sense of them in various ways, but the effort of doing so is an enlivening one. It requires us to make a certain imaginative leap, as it does when we think of an author and his or her words as being one, or the words as part of the author, or the words as inscribing the author (it is, for example, perfectly possible for us to argue, as a post-structuralist critic might do, that the words inscribe the author rather than the author the words—that all that we know of Charles Wesley is what we can gather from the hymns and sermons and journals and letters). Here the questions about the relationship between the author and the word are solved by christological doctrine: it is all quite simple if we remember the first chapter of St. John's gospel and the idea of the *logos*. But to get to that point requires a step that suggests another musical analogy: we have to "play" the piece according to the composer's intentions for it to make sense. And here the piece is (deliberately) quite difficult, so that "playing" it becomes a test of technique.

Words here, as Eliot noted, are in relation to the words preceding and following them, and "indefinitely to the rest of [the poem's] context." The words "active," "author," and "Word" are part of the whole stanza, the whole music of the verse itself. That music moves from the unexpected to the expected: a musician might say that it modulates from an interrupted cadence to a perfect cadence on a major chord. The verbal excitement of the first two lines is completed and explained by the appositional phrase of the second two lines, and that clause at first makes explicit the half quotation of "Author" in line 1. We now recognize the "author and finisher" idea, and the word "Lord," occurring for the first time, explains "eternal Word." The tangle of line 1 is now disentangled in a lovely clarity, a simplicity that is continued in the quotation from the next chapter of Hebrews, "Jesus Christ the same, yesterday, and today, and for ever."

"At one stage," Eliot writes, a stanza "is a right and natural formalization of speech into pattern," but then it tends to become a hindrance rather than a help, because "it quickly loses contact with the changing colloquial speech." This can happen in hymn writing, and it is one reason why the hymn as a literary form had, until recently, a bad name. But we may wonder if the age of Watts and Wesley was one in which writers were exploring what Eliot called "the idiom of the moment of its perfection." (He goes on to write of the sonnet, but his point is equally valid for the hymn stanza.) I would argue that whatever stanza form Wesley chooses (and there are many), each, in its different way, has a "music" that comes from the sound and sense held in that specific line- and rhyme pattern. Consider the third verse of his hymn "Come Holy Ghost, all-quickning Fire" (J. and C. Wesley 1739: 184). The preceding verse ended with the line "Eager I ask, and pant for more," which is picked up as the next verse gets under way:

> Eager for Thee I ask and pant,
>   So strong the Principle Divine
> Carries me out with sweet Constraint,
>   Till all my hallow'd Soul be Thine:
> Plung'd in the Godhead's deepest Sea,
> And lost in thy Immensity.

The repetition of the first line, echoing the last line of the verse before, holds up the ongoing movement of the verse for a moment. It is followed by "so strong," two syllables that are followed by an implied comma (added by later editors), so that the caesura is early in the line, and the music again stops: it pauses twice, once at the end of line 1 and now here. Then the movement of the verse sweeps forward, as the lines explore the image of being carried out, like a swimmer on the tide. The carrying out is a sweet constraint, a phrase taken from Shakespeare—"love's own sweet constraint" (*All's Well That Ends Well*, 4.2.16)—and used beautifully here to describe a joyful sense of being helplessly in the power of a benevolent force. The sea metaphor is implied throughout these lines and is made explicit in the last two lines, "Plung'd in the Godhead's deepest Sea, / And lost in thy Immensity." Word after word here seems exactly right and in its place: "plung'd," "lost," "Immensity." And the stanza form carries the expression with an exquisite lyrical movement, starting, pausing, and then running free: as Eliot put it, Wesley has made the pattern comply with what he has to say. The "music" of the verse is in its beautifully judged tempi.

The Musical Structure of the Whole

We pass, therefore, from the word to the line, and from the line to the verse, and from the verse to the whole hymn. The following is one of the best known of Charles Wesley's hymns, often (indeed, usually) sung to Sebastian Wesley's tune Hereford:

> O thou who camest from above
> The pure, celestial fire t' impart,
> Kindle a flame of sacred love
> On the mean altar of my heart;
>
> There let it for thy glory burn
> With inextinguishable blaze,
> And trembling to its Source return,
> In humble prayer, and fervent praise.
>
> *Jesus*, confirm my heart's desire
> To work, and speak, and think for thee;
> Still let me guard the holy fire,
> And still stir up thy gift in me,
>
> Ready for all thy perfect will,
> My acts of faith and love repeat,
> 'Till death thy endless mercies seal,
> And make my sacrifice complete.
>
> (*Hymns and Psalms*, 745)

It comes from *Short Hymns on Select Passages of the Holy Scriptures* (C. Wesley 1762: hymn 183), where it is found, improbably, at Leviticus 6:13, where there are elaborate instructions to Aaron and his sons about the management of sacrifices: "The fire must ever be burning upon the altar; it shall never go out." This need not detain us, except as an excuse for yet another musical analogy, for this is a theme and variation: Wesley's New Testament hermeneutics provide an original composition starting from a given theme. The verse from Leviticus, which begins with fire, suggests to Wesley the fire that descended on the apostles at the first Pentecost, as described in Acts 2. It is the transformation of an unrewarding text into a prayer for the indwelling power of the Holy Spirit in the human heart.

But what seems more important than this transformation is the perfection of form. In four verses of four lines (originally two eight-line stanzas), Wesley produces a beautifully paced statement of prayer and dedication. The lines depend on one another to form verses that are separate, yet interlinked, with variations in the structure that please the ear and prevent repetition or boredom. Certain lines are of course unusual: "inextinguishable" may be the longest word in English hymnody, and certainly its six syllables are an astonishing tour de force in the line, for they occupy six of the eight available spaces.

Almost as bold is the unexpected trochaic opening of the last verse. It interrupts the lyrical movement that is established at the outset by the running on of the adjectival clause after "O thou" and the postponement of the main verb to the beginning of line 3. "Kindle," we might say, comes at precisely the right moment in the verse and leads through its predicate to the "heart" that ends the verse. The movement is from the Holy Spirit, in all its wonder, to the individual heart of the speaker or singer. This is carried on and underlined by the "There" of verse 2, after which the implications of the flame of sacred love are explored: the hope that it will never be put out and that it will return itself to God, who gave it: it is a recapitulation of George Herbert's image for prayer—"God's breath in man returning to its birth"—here in the double process of prayer and praise, humble prayer and fervent praise.

The two verses outline a threefold process: kindling, burning, and returning. And what is noticeable is the way in which the verse elaborates on those three verbs: how the speed of the lines, the pauses at the end of the line, the rhymes, all unite to present a vital process. The stanza form has not yet become just a mold in which to pour things, but it is a way of giving form to an aspiration. Despite the simple *abab* rhyming scheme, the formal effect is complex, artificial (using the word "artificial" in its good sense of having artifice), and yet also natural, in that it is, for a Christian believer, an expression of a common human desire.

The last verse is a profound statement of a Christian life. The first line combines "ready" with God's perfect will, and the word suggests a disciplined preparedness, like an athlete beginning a race or a soldier about to go into battle. What that readiness involves is the acts of faith and love. The word "repeat" is important: it suggests a pattern of living, day after day, month after month, year after year, devoted to acts of Christian duty. This is no sudden or temporary change: the Holy Spirit's descent leads to a continuous process, keeping the fire going to the end. And the final act, which crowns all the other mercies, is death. Death fittingly concludes the fire in the heart, the sacred love, the inextinguishable blaze, the working, speaking, and thinking for Christ. These are the daily stuff of the Christian life, lived at full stretch, lived at the uttermost stretch of human ability: and if that life is lived properly, then death comes to complete what is a fully lived human existence, so that the word "complete" comes as the final statement of an ideal. It is "complete" in the sense of being entire, but also in the sense of being finished, properly finished; and just as the meaning is concluded with "complete," so the poem too is "complete" at its end. The line and the poem are brought to an end with a proper resolution, one that allows a formal satisfaction as well as a finished understanding. The piece finishes as one feels it ought to: whatever the various movements, variations, and modulations on the way, the end draws them together, the word "complete" acting as a final chord.

Conclusion

Eliot's lecture concluded with a disclaimer, but also with a robust claim for the idea of the music of poetry: "I think that a poet may gain much from the study of music." From his own experience he noted "that a poem, or a passage of a poem, may tend to realize itself first as a particular rhythm before it reaches its expression in words, and that this rhythm may bring to birth the idea and the image." This seems to me to describe Charles Wesley's hymn writing very accurately. If you think of "Jesu, lover of my soul" (J. and C. Wesley 1740: 67), it is possible to see the music of that hymn as directing the expression of intimacy and dependence that characterizes that text:

> Other Refuge have I none,
>> Hangs my helpless Soul on Thee,
> Leave, ah! leave me not alone,
>> Still support, and comfort me.

"Hangs," surprising the reader at the beginning of the line, provides a sound that suggests an emotional dependence, using a physical word for "depending" or "hanging down"; and "Leave, ah! leave" interrupts the rhythm with a further emotional exclamation of the need for Christ. The reiterated note of "me," sufficient to provide a continuity but different enough to let the meaning modulate— "leave me not . . . support and comfort," gives the music of the verse a stability and a gentle change.

Perhaps this is Charles Wesley *andante con moto*. At another extreme there is the *maestoso* of "Let earth and heaven agree" (C. Wesley 1742: hymn 11), which is written in an entirely different medium. The first four lines have three heavy beats each, a verbal equivalent of a percussion section:

> Let Earth and Heaven agree,
>   Angels and Men be join'd
> To celebrate with me
>   The Saviour of Mankind;
> T' adore the All-atoning Lamb,
> And bless the Sound of Jesu's Name.

The final two lines change the rhythm to a four-beat line, brilliantly announced by "T' adore," where the second syllable of "adore" is a splendid piece of bravado, a trombone *fortissimo* of a word. And the hymn ends with the verse, "O for a trumpet voice / On all the world to call."

Charles Wesley liked trumpets. His hymn later named "The Year of Jubilee" (C. Wesley 1749b: hymn 3) begins and ends with them:

> Blow ye the trumpet, blow
>   The gladly solemn sound:
> The gospel trumpet hear,
>   The news of heavenly grace,

I have tried to avoid making facile comparisons in this chapter, but we might like to think of these last two hymns as played by the brass section, and of "Jesu, lover of my soul" as written for a verbal equivalent of woodwind and strings. The moods are different: the one all triumphant and celebratory, the other all introspection and prayer.

We are back where we began, with the "music" of Wesley's hymns, in this particular case a music that is written in two contrasting modes. Examples such as this could be multiplied and discussed almost ad infinitum, for every hymn has its own music. But that music is more than sounds, more than the placing of words in a line, more than the structure of verses to make a hymn. It is the music of the soul's journey. In Wesley's case it was a journey that began in enthusiasm and evangelical energy, and continued in controversy and debate, his spirit overflowing in its espousal of one cause after another: first the revival of religion in Britain, and then the struggle to preserve the Methodist energy within the Church of England and not apart from it (see Lloyd 2007b).

His hymns present us with an ever-restless energy, controlled and shaped into the "music" of his life; and that life was represented by the fluctuating, evanescent, ever-varying sound and sense of his hymns. Sometimes he celebrates, sometimes he is full of wonder, sometimes he is questioning and hesitant, and sometimes he is full of a blessed assurance; but always he preserves, in the face of an indifferent or hostile world, his own kind of evangelical idealism. His ideal was to "sing" on earth, to lead a life that would be "complete," and thus sing his way to heaven; till he was added to that heavenly choir, where he would sing for ever, praising God in a nobler strain among the saints in light (see *Hymns and Psalms*, 300).

CHAPTER 3

Psalms and Hymns and Hymns and Sacred Poems

TWO STRANDS OF WESLEYAN HYMN COLLECTIONS

Robin A. Leaver

It is a familiar truism to state that Methodism was born in song. But it was not only born in song, it also matured, grew, and continues in song, vigorous hymn singing being the hallmark of denominational Methodism. What is not so read- ily recognized is that denominational Methodism was a late development of the movement begun by the Wesley brothers in Oxford in the 1730s. Their Method- ism was not an attempt to create a new church body but to revitalize the old one, the Church of England. The singing of hymns, in lively tempi, in contrast to the slow, ponderous singing characteristic of much Anglican psalmody of the time, became an essential part of the spiritual method of the Wesleys. In the course of time the two brothers, John and Charles, published an impressive sequence of hymnals over a period of forty years or so. These collections of hymns they edited are usually considered in a chronological sequence, culminating in *A Collection of Hymns for the People Called Methodists* (London, 1780; with many later reprints and editions). But such a classification disguises the fact that there appear to have been at least two fairly distinct strands in these publications: one reflecting the concerns of the weekly meetings of the Methodist societies, the other reflecting the structure and content of the Anglican *Book of Common Prayer*. This chapter attempts to clarify and explore these two strands of hymnody as Methodism evolved from being a movement within a denomination to becoming denomi- nationally independent.

Methodism in Oxford and Georgia

The Holy Club came into existence after John Wesley's Oxford studies, ordination, and curacy with his father in Epworth, when he returned to Oxford in 1729. It was founded by his brother Charles and was in many respects an intensification of the activities of the societies their father had organized in Epworth: fasting until 3:00 P.M. on Wednesdays and Fridays, weekly attendance at the Lord's Supper, daily study and discussion of the New Testament in Greek, visiting prisoners and the sick, and other charitable works. The singing of hymns, individually and corporately, was a fundamental part of the spiritual exercises of the members of the Holy Club. For example, both Benjamin Ingham (1712–1772) and John Wesley frequently note in their manuscript diaries of the 1730s that their individual early-morning devotions began with a hymn. Ingham also records singing with others. (Ingham 1985: especially 85, 198, 288.)

The recently founded colony of Georgia had been a haven to thousands of German-speaking Lutheran refugees between 1732 and 1735 (Threinen). In the hope of gaining converts to the renewed Unitas Fratrum, or Moravians, around twenty-five German missionaries sailed for Georgia with Wesley on the ship *Simmonds* toward the end of 1735, arriving in February 1736. The Moravian movement, under the leadership of Count Nikolaus Ludwig von Zinzendorf (1700–1760), was in many respects an offshoot of Halle Pietism (see Nagler). Hymnody, much of it authored by the count himself, was fundamental for the public, private, and personal worship of Moravians, and Wesley was enamored by the singing of the Moravian missionaries in their daily services on board ship and encouraged to learn German and translate some of their hymns into English.

Both Lutherans and Moravians made extensive use of a wide variety of hymns. This practice was in sharp contrast to the practice of Anglicans, who sang almost exclusively metrical psalms in their public worship and relatively few hymns in private, such as those by Thomas Ken, George Herbert, and perhaps one or two others, as well as the small selection of hymns found in the Sternhold and Hopkins psalter, or the newer scriptural paraphrases appended to the *New Version* of Tate and Brady. Few Anglicans at this time would knowingly sing the hymns of Isaac Watts, but Wesley was one of them!

It is possible that John Wesley formed the idea of creating an English collection of hymns while he was on board, being inspired by the singing of the Moravians. It seems likely that some, perhaps most, of his translations of German hymns were done while on the long sea passage to Georgia (Nuelsen; Hatfield: 171–99). Within weeks of arriving in the colony, in a letter to Count Zinzendorf dated March 15, 1736 (Hatfield: 175), Wesley cited the penultimate stanza of Freylinghausen's "Wer ist wohl, wie du," which may indicate that he had already prepared the translation ("Jesu, source of calm repose") that would be included in his 1737 collection. This suggests that almost as soon as he arrived in Savannah he was at work compiling what is generally considered to be the first Anglican hymnbook in contrast to metrical psalms: *A Collection of Psalms and Hymns* (J. Wesley 1737). It includes five translations of German hymns. Wesley also had some personal knowledge of Lutheran hymnody in Georgia, as shown by his journal entry for October 18, 1736.

Of the seventy-eight texts in the 1737 *Collection,* nine were written by his father; five were by his eldest brother, also named Samuel; and seven significantly were taken from an anonymous collection that had appeared in 1700, *Devotions in the Antient Way of Offices,* promoted by the high church, nonjuring bishop of Thetford, George Hickes (1642–1715). This was an Anglican version of the English daily offices that John Austin (1613–1669), under the pseudonym William Birchley, created for English Roman Catholics in exile in France. It was revised by Susanna Hopton (1627–1709), who eliminated all expressions of specific Catholic doctrine, increased the biblical content, and utilized the language of the *Book of Common Prayer* for such things as the Lord's Prayer, creed, and canticles. It includes forty office hymn texts, mostly written in the familiar psalm-tune meters, which implies that they were intended to be sung rather than corporately recited. This is confirmed by the second and third editions of *Devotions,* each of which included a supplement of ten tunes. It seems likely that the volume was used by both Samuel Wesley in Epworth and John Wesley in Oxford. Six of the remaining texts in Wesley's Savannah hymnal were written by George Herbert and three by Joseph Addison, but most of the psalms and hymns—almost half of the total—were the work of Isaac Watts, the implication being that most of the psalms and hymns sung by members of the Holy Club in Oxford in previous years had been those of Watts.

Instead of an unstructured anthology of hymns, Wesley created three distinct sections, each with its own heading and each containing metrical psalms in biblical order followed by hymns by various authors. The second section, for Wednesdays and Fridays, seems to have been compiled mainly for society meetings that gathered on these traditional fast days, while the third, to be sung on Saturdays, gives the impression of having been intended primarily for personal use in preparation for the worship of the following day, Sunday. But it is the first and largest section, for Sundays, that is the most intriguing, because it strongly suggests that Wesley did intend that its ten psalms and thirty hymns should be sung in the public worship of prayer-book services. If so, it was a radical innovation.

Ten years before Wesley produced his Charleston hymnal, a small anthology had appeared, published by Joseph Downing: *A Collection of Psalms and Divine Hymns, Suited to the Great Festivals of the Church, for Morning and Evening, and Other Occasions.* It was intended to complement the devotional publications of the Society for Promoting Christian Knowledge. It contained a number of hymns for the seasons of the church year, but the anonymous compiler made it clear that they were intended for private use: "I Have no Thought of proposing the Use of any Part of this *Collection* in the Publick Service. For which Reason I did not think myself oblig'd to take those *Hymns* which are collected out of the Psalms, from any of the *Versions* allow'd by *Authority* to be Sung in Churches (*Collection:* 3)."

Wesley's ministry in Georgia was not without controversy, partly owing to the fractious nature of many of the colonists, but also because of his high-handed conduct as a pastor, which has been described by an otherwise sympathetic biographer as arrogant, foolish, offensive, and intolerant (Tyerman, 1:159). A significant group of colonists thought he was too strict and overbearing in enforcing discipline, especially with regard to admission to communion, which he did by appealing to the directions found in the *Book of Common Prayer*. His antagonists took action by following his example: since he had used the regulations and formularies of the Church of England against them, they would charge him by appealing to similar sources. A list of twelve grievances was drawn up, and he was called upon to answer them at the Savannah court on August 22, 1737. The third item charged Wesley with deviating "from the principles and regulations of the Established Church in many particulars inconsistent with the happiness and prosperity of the colony . . . By introducing into the church, and service at the altar, compositions of the psalms and hymns not inspected or authorized by any proper judicature" (Tyerman, 1:159).

The complaint confirms that Wesley's *Collection* must have been published during the first half of 1737 and that Wesley was censured for using congregational songs in public worship other than those thought to be authorized in the Church of England, meaning the psalms of either Sternhold and Hopkins or Tate and Brady. But the complaint is explicit that the newly printed psalms and hymns had been introduced into the church, especially into the service at the altar, that is, the sacrament of the Lord's Supper. Following the example of Lutherans and Moravians, who sang more than metrical versions of the psalms in their public worship, Wesley had sought to introduce into the Anglican services in Savannah a broader range of congregational song than had been customary hitherto. It is not surprising that such unauthorized hymn singing was added to the list of grievances that the Savannah colonists brought against John Wesley.

Wesley was never thereafter able to establish a good pastoral relationship with the colonists, and within a few months, more than a little disillusioned, he left for England, as did his brother Charles.

The Awakening and the Early Wesley Hymn Collections

On their return from Georgia in 1738, the two Wesley brothers experienced the spiritual awakening that changed their lives and their ministries. John embarked on a vigorous program of itinerant preaching and teaching, and Charles overflowed with an expanding stream of remarkable poetry. In nearly every year thereafter, newly edited collections of hymns were published, usually jointly by the two brothers, in London and Bristol, together with reprints and editions in other cities and countries. Although not the first collection of hymns published by the Wesleys after their return from Georgia, *Hymns and Sacred Poems* (London, 1739), with 138 items, charted new directions. Two further imprints followed in the same year, and another was issued in Philadelphia in 1740. Strahan (and Hutton) issued an abbreviated selection in 1742, reprinted in Dublin and Belfast in 1749 and 1750 respectively. In 1740 another collection was issued in London with the same title but different content (87 items), and in 1742 yet another, published at

Bristol, with 155 items (for full details, see Baker 1991). The use of the same title created some confusion, implying that they were different editions of the same work, whereas together they formed a three-part collection comprising a total of some 370 hymns and sacred poems, though most were hymns. That the three collections should be regarded together as a three-part anthology is confirmed by references found in Wesley's "Foundery" tune book, where the three books are cited as "Vol. 1," "Vol. 2" and "Vol. 3," respectively (J. Wesley 1742).

Over the following years, in addition to small collections for special events and occasions, the Wesleys produced hymn collections for the use of societies, notably *Hymns and Spiritual Songs: Intended for the Use of Real Christians of All Denominations* (1752: twenty-four editions by 1786), *Select Hymns, with Tunes Annext: Designed Chiefly for the Use of the People Called Methodists* (1761: ten editions by 1787), and supremely, *A Collection of Hymns for the Use of the People Called Methodists* (1780, with numerous later editions). Some colleagues of the Wesleys produced their own collections, such as Ingham's *Collection of Hymns for Societies* (1748). Ingham's preface anticipates Wesley's well-known "Directions for Singing," appended to the index of tunes in *Select Hymns* (1761):

> In Singing two Things ought to be regarded. The one is, to Sing in outward Harmony, keeping the Tune; and if we do not understand it, 'tis better to be Silent and hear others, or to Sing low and after Others; that we may not make a Discord, which is disagreeable and causes Confusion. And in general, it is not well to Sing so very high and loud. But the other and more Material thing to be regarded is, seriously to mind what we are about; to be present with our Thoughts; to meditate upon the Matter; and above all to Sing with Grace in the Heart to the Lord. This makes Singing sweet and heavenly; and without this our Singing can neither be edifying to ourselves, nor to others. (Ingham 1748: [2])

By *harmony,* both Ingham and Wesley meant voices in unison, not singing in parts.

That there was a distinction drawn between Christians of all denominations and "people called Methodists" reflects the divisions that occurred around 1740. On the one hand, Wesley, who had had close relations with Moravians, especially those connected with the Fetter Lane Society in London, rejected their quietist tendencies and separated from them. On the other hand, he, an Arminian, found himself at variance with the Calvinism of George Whitefield (1714–1770) and others. Further, by the beginning of 1739 most pulpits of the Established Church were barred to him as bishops and clergy reacted against what they saw as the dangers of enthusiasm, antinomianism, and fanaticism. Wesley's hymn collections were therefore offered to all who thought of themselves either as real Christians or Methodists, whatever their confessional or theological position might be (Arminian, Calvinist, or Moravian, within or without the Anglican Church), wherever people met together in societies for spiritual edification. Wesley, of course, thought that his Arminian Methodism within Anglicanism was the authentic Christian position, but others were free to use his collections of hymns if they so chose.

Whitefield and the Hymn Collections
of Calvinist Methodists

Just before Wesley and Whitefield went their separate ways, Whitefield compiled a modest hymnal: *Divine Melody: or, a Help to Devotion, Being, a Choice Collection of Hymns, Psalms, and Spiritual Songs for the Use of the Pious Sincere Christian* (London, 1739). There is no apparent structure for the order of the hymns, but a closer inspection reveals that metrical psalms are given together in groups in which, apart from a small deviation in one group, the psalms always appear in their biblical sequence, in exactly the same way John Wesley included such psalms in his 1737 Charleston collection. There is no hint that these items might be sung in public worship: on the contrary, the title speaks in the singular ("for the use of the pious sincere Christian"), as does the preface. However, many of the items have a clear affinity with the *Book of Common Prayer*. For example, the paraphrase of the Proper Preface in the communion service headed, "A Hymn, Composed by the Reverend Mr. Charles Wesley" (Meet and right it is to sing, / Glory to our God and King) makes its first appearances in this collection (see Baker 1962: 113–14).

Presumably, Whitefield had learned from John Wesley's experience in Georgia that congregational song, other than metrical psalmody, would be strenuously opposed if he attempted to introduce it in parish churches; hence the emphasis on personal devotion in the title of his 1739 collection. Like Wesley, he was opposed by mainstream Anglicanism, and most churches were off-limits for his preaching. So he too created his own meeting place. About a year after Wesley had opened his Foundry meeting house in Moorfields, Whitefield's followers built, in the same area of London, a wooden structure that came into use in 1741. Again like Wesley, Whitefield considered himself a loyal Anglican and was committed to the services of the *Book of Common Prayer*. At some time in the years following 1741, congregational hymnody was no doubt introduced into the public worship of the Moorfields chapel. This was certainly the case from 1753, when a brick-built tabernacle replaced the earlier wooden building. Whitefield and his congregation came under the patronage of Selina, Countess of Huntingdon (1707–1791). Unlike a parish church, they were not directly under episcopal authority and therefore had greater freedom in the conduct of worship. To coincide with the opening of the new building, Whitefield created a new hymnal for his congregation: *A Collection of Hymns for Social Worship: More Particularly Design'd for the Use of the Tabernacle Congregation* (1753). An accompanying tune book was issued the following year: *The Divine Musical Miscellany*.

The collection was immensely popular and was widely circulated, reaching its thirty-second edition by 1788, with numerous other reprints and editions well into the nineteenth century (R. Roberts: 11–15, 54). Whitefield made it clear that the hymns in this new collection were for corporate worship: "[These hymns] . . . are intended purely for social worship . . . They are short, because I think three or four stanzas, with a Doxology, are sufficient to be sung at one Time[.] I am no great Friend to long Sermons, long Prayers, or long Hymns: they generally weary instead of edifying, and therefore I think should be avoided by those who preside in any public worshipping Assembly."

The hymnal is in two parts, the first, "Hymns for Public Worship," comprising 132 hymns to be sung in regular public worship; the second, "Hymns for Society and Persons meeting in Christian-Fellowship," comprising 38 hymns to be sung in society meetings. In the preface Whitefield draws attention to the innovation of congregational antiphony, a feature that would mark later Evangelical hymnody: "I think myself justifiable in publishing some Hymns by way of Dialogue for Use of the Society, because something like it is provided in our Cathedral Churches, but much more so because the Celestial Choir is represented in the Book of Revelation, as answering one another in their heavenly Anthems."

The originator of the dialogue hymn was John Cennick (1718–1755): the exchange was often between men and women (Cennick 1743). It was indicated by the alternate use of roman and italic type, usually in paired lines within the stanzas. Cennick explicitly designated his dialogue hymns for the use of societies rather than for congregational hymnody, and Whitefield followed this model by placing all eight dialogue hymns in the second part of his book. (For an example, see Temperley and Drage, No. 81.) This perhaps suggests that the congregational hymnody of public worship was somewhat more formal than the singing in the fellowship meetings of the societies.

Later collections of hymns for independent Calvinist Methodist chapels (Maxfield, Dyer), or for charity chapels (Madan 1760), as well as those of the Countess of Huntingdon, which were outside direct episcopal oversight, were strongly influenced by Whitefield's *Hymns for Social Worship*. In these chapels and meeting houses, congregational hymns were regularly sung in public worship, as well as in society meetings and for personal devotion.

Psalms and Hymns for Public Worship?

Calvinist Methodism had separated from Arminian Methodism, and also in many cases from the Church of England, so there is the question: did the early Wesleyans also sing hymns in the Prayer Book services used for public worship in their chapels, as these other congregations certainly did? The early evidence is somewhat ambivalent. There is no doubt that what John Wesley had begun in

Savannah was continued in England. In the first few years after his spiritual awakening, in parallel with his compilation of various editions of *Hymns and Sacred Poems*, John Wesley issued a succession of three editions of *A Collection of Psalms and Hymns*, which were in effect revisions of his 1737 Charleston collection. But unlike the three volumes of *Hymns and Sacred Poems*, which together formed a three-part anthology, these three editions were successive attempts to establish a definitive collection. By a process of addition, subtraction, and substitution, John Wesley (according to the title pages) apparently worked alone on the editions of 1738 and 1741, being joined by his brother Charles in creating the 1743 edition. (See J. Wesley 1738, 1741; J. and C. Wesley 1743.)

For the first edition of 1738, Wesley closely followed the structure of his Charleston collection issued the previous year but offered a different selection of psalms and hymns, though with some overlap. They were arranged in the same three sections: for Sundays, for Wednesday or Friday, and for Saturday, with metrical psalms in biblical order appearing before the hymns in each section. There are significant changes in the 1741 edition: first, in contrast to the anonymously issued collections of 1737 and 1738, it was explicitly "published by John Wesley"; second, it is structured in just two sections that are simply headed "Part the First" and "Part the Second," with roughly the same number of items in each: seventeen metrical psalms and sixty-two hymns in the first part, and forty-five metrical psalms and thirty-six hymns in the second. The omission of any reference to Sunday, or any other day, was perhaps conditioned by the need to avoid any overt suggestion that these psalms and hymns might be sung in the public worship of the church and to deflect any rumors that might be emanating from Georgia. In the 1743 edition, the first part has seventy items, beginning with seventeen metrical psalms (a different selection from that of 1741); part two has sixty-eight items, beginning with forty-nine metrical psalms.

Once the content of the 1743 edition was established, it was constantly in print throughout the rest of the century and also well into the next. There were sixteen more London editions (1744–1829), six published in Bristol (1744–73), two in Burlington, New Jersey (1771, 1773), and one in Philadelphia (1781). The content, remaining essentially stable in all these later reprints, tended to be more objective than that of the *Hymns and Sacred Poems,* or at least more corporate rather than personal, though personal hymns were not entirely absent. The first part included hymns under such headings as "Hymn for Sunday," "A Hymn for Easter Day," "A Morning Hymn," "An Evening Hymn," and no fewer than eight "for Charity Children." But it is the second part that seems particularly suited to regular corporate worship. There are forty-five metrical psalms, immediately followed by six hymns addressed to the Trinity, and a little later by five hymns that together form a paraphrase of the *Benedicite.* Another important difference between the two series is that the *Collection of Psalms and Hymns* included many items already published, some not authored by Wesleys, whereas *Hymns and Sacred Poems* were largely new or translated hymns offered to the public for the first time.

As observed earlier in this chapter, by the end of 1738 hardly any parish church was open to John Wesley. This was an important factor that led to his itinerant open-air ministry. There was therefore the need for permanent meeting places for him, his brother, and his followers. In May 1739 the foundations were laid for what was to become the New Room in Bristol, and in November of the same year Wesley took over the old Foundry in Moorfields, London, which he refurbished as a meeting house and chapel. In addition to the weekly society meetings, daily worship, morning and evening, was conducted in these chapels. The *Collection of Psalms and Hymns* was used for these daily worship services, which, given the Wesley brothers' love of and commitment to Anglican worship, must have been morning and evening prayer of the prayer book. (It might be suggested that John Wesley's *Collection of Forms of Prayer for Every Day in the Week,* first published in 1733 and reprinted at least twelve times by 1755, was used for daily worship in London and Bristol, but this anthology was specifically intended for personal rather than corporate use.)

In the early years, the Wesleys were often accused by bishops and other clergy of creating a parallel church. Their response was that while they did gather their adherents for regular worship, they always instructed the members of the Methodist societies to attend the sacrament in their parish churches on Sundays. (See Leaver 1992: 157–75.) But when Charles Wesley celebrated communion, hymns were sung in the prayer book order of the Lord's Supper. The Welsh evangelist Howell Harris, after attending a celebration conducted by Charles, wrote in his diary, under the date August 28, 1743: "In his singing the hymns between every company of communicants, I was much humbled" (cited Bowmer: 87). John Wesley may have been slow to resume his Savannah practice of hymns at communion; at least, he did not do so at every celebration. A letter from John Fletcher, dated December 13, 1756, encouraged Wesley to follow what he (Fletcher) regarded as a common practice by singing a verse or two of a hymn during communion: many, he said, had found benefit of that method. But the same letter makes it clear that while John Wesley might not have always included hymn singing at communion, it was only in parish churches that he had abandoned the celebration of the Lord's Supper, since Fletcher also records: "I received the sacrament in your chapels" (Bowmer: 88). Thus by the mid-1750s the full range of prayer-book services was commonly used in the Wesleyan chapels, at which appropriate items from the *Collection of Psalms and Hymns* were sung.

But there is evidence that other hymns were sung as well. Between 1744 and 1746 the Wesley brothers published a rapid sequence of hymnals (see Bibliography). Since the *Hymns on the Lord's Supper* were appropriately focused on the passion and death of Jesus, the sacramental hymns also doubled as hymns for Lent and

Holy Week. With this realization it becomes clear that during this three-year period the Wesleys created a series of supplementary hymn collections that covered
the major Prayer Book festivals and celebrations of the church year from Advent
to Trinity (J. and C. Wesley 1744, 1745, 1746a, 1746b, 1746c). The additional collections were usually produced in the same format as the editions of the *Collection of
Psalms and Hymns* so that they could be bound together. For example, I have in
my possession a copy of the eighth edition of *A Collection of Psalms and Hymns*
(1773) in a contemporary binding that includes the sixth edition of *Hymns on
the Lord's Supper* (1761) and the fifth edition of *Gloria Patri, &c., or Hymns to the
Trinity* (1771), all published by Pine of Bristol. That these additional collections
for the major festivals were conceived as a connected sequence is confirmed by
the tunes composed and published by John Frederick Lampe for a selection of
texts from these supplements, significantly appearing in 1746, the year that the
church-year sequence of hymn supplements was completed (Lampe). Similar
selections of hymns on the festivals of the church year, mostly made up of hymns
by Charles Wesley, can be found, for example, in such later collections as Maxfield (1766) and Ramsden (1775). Thus in the *Collection of Psalms and Hymns,*
together with the supplements for the major festivals and fasts of the church year,
John and Charles Wesley created a body of hymnody for Anglican-Methodist
use that approximated to major sections of hymns found in the comprehensive
congregational hymnals used by both Moravians and Lutherans.

When in 1784 John Wesley literally took it into his own hands to ordain Thomas
Coke for episcopal oversight of congregations in America, he in effect created
denominational Methodism. One of the first things he did was to prepare his
own version of the *Book of Common Prayer* for American congregations: *The
Sunday Service of the Methodists in North America: With Other Occasional Services* (London, 1784). Because he was convinced that hymnody had a vital place
in such worship, Wesley arranged for a collection of hymns to be bound up with
the *Sunday Service*. Given the later use and significance of *A Collection of Hymns
for the People Called Methodists,* published just a few years earlier in 1780, the
expectation is that this would have been the collection that Wesley had in mind
for his version of Prayer Book services. But that is not case. Instead he and his
brother created a slightly revised edition: *A Collection of Psalms and Hymns for
the Lord's Day* (London, 1784). Here the title is unequivocal: these items were
congregational songs that were intended to be sung in the Sunday Service. Of
course, the *Collection of Hymns for the People Called Methodists* continued to be
widely used for personal devotion and in society meetings. But, from the evidence
that I have reviewed here, as far as the Wesley brothers were concerned there were
two types of hymn collection required for Methodists: *Psalms and Hymns* (with
their occasional supplements) for corporate worship, and *Hymns for the People
Called Methodists* for personal and society use. This was not always understood
in the various branches of denominational Methodism that followed over the

next decades, well into the nineteenth century, since most of them used the *Collection of Hymns for the People Called Methodists,* with various supplements, as their congregational hymnal.

There were, however, some Methodists who did understand that the *Collection of Hymns for the People Called Methodists* had been compiled for society and personal use rather than public worship and that the Wesleys had published two major strands of hymnal collections. For example, early in the nineteenth century Thomas Roberts argued for the compilation of another collection of hymns for public worship that could be used alongside the 1780 collection. His essay was published in 1808 as *Hymnology: A Dissertation on Hymns; with Particular Reference to the Propriety of Having an Additional Volume of Hymns for General Worship, among the People Called Methodists.* The fifth section of the dissertation has a rather lengthy heading: "The Question, Is the Hymn-Book [i.e., the 1780 collection] fully adapted to all the purposes of general worship, more particularly in the present state of Methodism? Answer, No . . . The Hymn-Book is, however, truly excellent; but another is indispensably necessary for all the purposes of general worship" (T. Roberts: 26). He goes on to argue that the then current use of the 1780 collection was by accident rather than design. He continues:

> The Writer of most of the hymns (Mr. Charles Wesley), never designed, nor composed them, for the purposes of general worship. He always looked upon the means of grace among the Methodists, as customs of a religious society, and not the ordinances of a church. . . . The Publisher of the [1780] Hymn-Book (Mr. John Wesley), did not intend it to answer all the purposes of general worship. That book was not introduced by him, in London, Bristol, or any place, when the [Prayer Book] liturgy was read, and service performed by him in canonical hours. For that occasion, from almost the commencement of Methodism, a collection of Psalms and Hymns had been used . . . And therefore . . . after he had published the Hymn-Book, when he made the Abridgement of the liturgy . . . he printed with this service . . . a new edition of the Psalms and Hymns for the Lord's Day. To conform, then, to Mr. Wesley's opinion, not to say to enter into Mr. Wesley's design, that volume, and not the Hymn-Book, should be used, on the Lord's day mornings . . . These two books were used for the distinct services . . . till Mr. Wesley's death, and are so used to this day, in the New Chapel City Road [Wesley's chapel in London], and many other places. (T. Roberts: 28)

CHAPTER 4

John Frederick Lampe's
Hymns on the Great Festivals
and Other Occasions

Martin V. Clarke

John Frederick Lampe's *Hymns on the Great Festivals and Other Occasions* (1746) is the first collection of hymn tunes by a single composer associated with the Methodist movement. In it, Lampe sets twenty-four texts, twenty-three by Charles Wesley, the movement's pre-eminent hymn writer, and one by Charles's older brother Samuel. This chapter examines the texts and music of Lampe's collection in relation to Methodist theological and doctrinal principles and practices in order to explain the enduring popularity of many of the hymns in subsequent Methodist publications, specifically those under the editorial guidance of John Wesley.

Methodism and the Liturgical Year

Nineteen of the texts set by Lampe focus on specific liturgical feasts and had been published previously in a variety of collections; Frank Baker notes that "From December 1745 to October 1746 Charles had published no fewer than five distinct pamphlets offering hymns dedicated to worship at different seasons of the church year" (Baker 1996: 21). In the light of his loyalty to the Church of England, it is not surprising that he should address the liturgical seasons in his poetical writings; as a key feature of Anglican spirituality they presented an obvious opportunity to express characteristically Methodist theological interpretations of events that were steeped in both scripture and the traditions of the church. The hymn by Samuel Wesley also fits into this framework. Titled "A Hymn to the Trinity," it was published in his 1736 collection *Poems on Several Occasions*. The five hymns not associated with the liturgical calendar are nonetheless designed for liturgical use; two are on the subject of the Church Triumphant, while the remaining three are funeral hymns.

John and Charles Wesley's shaping of early Methodist worshipping practices clearly reflected their Anglican background and training, as discussed by Robin Leaver in Chapter 3. Furthermore, John's regulations for the Methodist societies were designed to ensure that Methodists participated fully in the liturgical life of the Church of England, as prescribed by the *Book of Common Prayer* (Chapman: 10–15).

As Methodism grew, its adherence to the Church of England became more difficult to maintain; fewer of the new members had any close affiliation to its worshipping life, and more saw Methodism as their sole form of religious participation. To address this trend, John Wesley produced abridged versions of the *Book of Common Prayer,* firstly for use in America, and latterly for the societies in Britain under the title of the *Sunday Service.* The content of these volumes reveals a Puritan influence with regard to the liturgical calendar, which was reduced significantly from the *Book of Common Prayer* version. There are no commemorations of saints, the seasonal pattern of Sunday worship is significantly simplified, and the number of christological feasts that could occur outside of Sunday worship is reduced, leaving the whole calendar rather diminished (Table 4.1, from J. Wesley 1784: 325).

Hymnody played a crucial role in virtually all areas of Methodist life; the Wesleys' realization of its powerful effect is seen in the many collections of hymns they published for use among the Methodists. While some of these were designed for specific liturgical seasons or applications, the larger collections for general use among the societies were structured according to a distinctively Methodist pattern. This emphasized the requisite elements of a personal faith and sought to provide guidance and inspiration for the various stages of the Christian life. Hymns associated with the liturgical calendar played a far less prominent role. The contents list of the seminal *Collection of Hymns for the Use of the People Called Methodists* (1780), regarded by John Wesley as "containing all the important truths of our religion" and analyzed in the final column of Table 4.2, arranges the hymns "under proper heads, according to the experience of real Christians" (Hildebrandt, Beckerlegge, and Baker: 74). Such collections were evidently designed as hymnbooks for use within a religious movement rather than mere resources for a liturgically self-sufficient church. They mark a significant shift in emphasis from the earlier, smaller Methodist collections that were more liturgically focused.

In the context of Methodism's development as a religious movement, the selection of texts set by Lampe is rather different from the type of collection that later achieved widespread use within Methodism. Nonetheless, it is an important representation of Methodism's early history and the desire of its leaders to remain

TABLE 4.1. Liturgical Calendar in the *Sunday Service* (1784/6)

Four Sundays of Advent	5 Sundays after Easter
Christmas Day	Ascension Day
5 Sundays after Christmas	Sunday after Ascension Day
Sunday before Easter	Whit Sunday [Pentecost]
Good Friday	Trinity Sunday
Easter	26 Sundays after Trinity

TABLE 4.2. Contents list of *A Collection of Hymns for the Use of the People Called Methodists* (1780), with numerical data added in the final column

Title				No.of Hymns
Part I. Containing Introductory Hymns				
Section I.	Exhorting Sinners to return to God			11
II.	Describing,	1.	The Pleasantness of Religion	10
		2.	The Goodness of God	19
		3.	Death	13
		4.	Judgment	13
		5.	Heaven	13
		6.	Hell	1
III.	Praying for a Blessing			10
Part II. Convincing				
Section I.	Describing Formal Religion			4
II.	Inward Religion			4
Part III.				
Section I.	Praying for Repentance			9
II.	For Mourners convinced of Sin			60
III.	For Persons convinced of Backsliding			14
IV.	For Backsliders recovered			7
Part IV. For Believers				
Section I.	For Believers Rejoicing			76
II.	Fighting			26
III.	Praying			14
IV.	Watching			16
V.	Working			8
VI.	Suffering			11
VII.	Seeking for full redemption			78
VIII.	Saved			23
IX.	Interceding for the World			37
Part V.				
Section I.	For the Society Meeting			10
II.	Giving Thanks			13
III.	Praying			32
IV.	Parting			7

firmly within the Church of England and to adhere to the format of its liturgical life. These hymns, written with specific liturgical contexts in mind, embody a strongly Methodist theological interpretation of the significance of the religious events and doctrines that inspired them. For example, hymn 5, "Lamb of God, whose bleeding Love," is a meditation on Christ's sacrificial death, intended for use on Good Friday and in preparation for receiving the sacrament of holy communion. Nonetheless, it is steeped in the Wesleys' belief in the universal offer of salvation and the human capacity for growth in holiness towards the attainment of Christian perfection. The first stanza is a plea for mercy, emphasizing the connection between active faith and salvation:

Lamb of God, whose bleeding Love,
　　We now recall to Mind,
Send the Answer from above,
　　And let us Mercy find,
Think on us, who think on thee;
And every Struggling Soul release;
O remember Calvary,
　　And bid us go in Peace.

The fourth stanza is rich in Wesleyan theological language, emphasizing the brothers' belief in the universality of the offer of salvation and the prospect of Christian holiness:

Never will we hence depart,
　　Till thou our wants relieve,
Write forgiveness on our heart,
　　And all thine image give:
Still our souls shall cry to thee,
Till all renew'd in holiness;
O remember Calvary,
　　And bid us go in peace!

Similarly, the first stanza of the Ascension Day hymn 12, "Hail, Jesus, hail, our great High-Priest," emphasizes that all believers can be saved through faith in Christ's resurrection and ascension:

The Conquest Thou hast more than gain'd,
The Heavenly Happiness obtain'd,
　　For all that trust Thy dying love.

The imagery of the third stanza illustrates the Wesleys' strong sacramental theology, which is wedded to the events of the crucifixion and the benefits it brings for believers:

Shed on the altar of Thy cross,
Thy blood to God presented was
　　Through the Eternal Spirit's power;
Thou didst, a spotless Victim, bleed,
That we from sin and suffering freed,
　　Might live to God, and sin no more.

The final, sixth stanza culminates with an eschatological vision of all the sanctified believers, the whole hymn having traced the connections between Christ's crucifixion, resurrection, and ascension and the believers' path of faith and salvation:

To us, who long to see Thee here,
Thou shalt a second time appear,
　　And bear us to Thy glorious throne.

These hymns can be readily understood as belonging to a revival movement, reflecting the Wesleys' zeal to reinvigorate the Church of England and to communicate their theological beliefs in a concise and memorable fashion. They sought to build upon existing customs and to use them to reinforce what they saw as their vital message; Temperley notes that hymns included in common Anglican psalm books such as the Old and New versions were generally associated with specific events in the liturgical calendar or with liturgical acts such as communion, a practice that seemingly informed Lampe's collection. In terms of eighteenth-century practice, he states that "The tradition of the communion hymn during the people's communion remained alive on Sacrament Sundays" (Temperley 1979b, 1:123).

The importance of the selection of texts in *Hymns on the Great Festivals and Other Occasions* lies in their wedding of ecclesiological and theological principles to create a distinctively Methodist response to the liturgical life of the Church. The potential that the Wesleys saw in congregational hymnody and its limited but accepted place in Anglican liturgy explain the seemingly atypical selection of texts, which are actually in keeping with Methodism's original revivalist ethos.

Lampe's Musical Settings

In the same way that the selection of texts is indicative of a particular aspect of Methodist religious belief and thought, Lampe's musical settings are likewise representative of one trait in musical style and practice associated with early Methodism. They form part of a broader and more diverse musical repertory that provided the movement's primary means for the memorable communication of its beliefs and values to those within and beyond its membership and across a wide social, cultural, and educational spectrum.

Lampe was a prolific composer in several genres and was acclaimed above all as a composer for the theater. Although Handel was the dominant composer in England at this time, Lampe's music has more in common with the idiom of Thomas Arne, who became his brother-in-law in 1738. Peter Holman notes that Lampe's only references to Handel's music are ironic in character: "Apart from those occasions when he parodied the Handelian style for comic effect, [he] tended to follow his brother-in-law in introducing elements of British popular song into his airs, including the Scotch snaps that proliferate in *Pyramus and Thisbe*" (2001). Dennis Martin comments on Lampe's elaborate melodic writing, arguing that its construction shows an acute awareness of the voice:

> Lampe's coloratura passages are well written for the voice, employing good vowels and idiomatic melodic figures . . . Lampe's coloratura technique seems to be related to the melodic embellishment practices in his thoroughbass book, where a simple melody is "varied" by the addition of passing and neighboring tones, passage work, and arpeggiation of triads. (94–95)

Another important element of Lampe's style highlighted by Martin concerns his responsiveness to texts:

> Lampe generally treats the text quite carefully and thoughtfully. Great concern for text setting was characteristic of [Georg Kaspar] Schürmann and [Reinhard] Keiser, whose ideas probably influenced the young Lampe. This is in sharp contrast to the practices of many opera seria composers, who often, it seems, considered their texts mere vehicles for the music, a suspicion affirmed by the not infrequent contrafacta and substitute-text arias in their works. One never finds such devices in Lampe, whose respect for the text also reflects his sense of drama, nurtured through his years with Handel. (96)

He also notes Lampe's rich harmonic vocabulary and the striking use of chromaticism that pervades much of his music, commenting that "the general chromaticism of Lampe's style and his harmonic adventurousness . . . contrast greatly with the practices of his English contemporaries" (99).

Martin is writing about Lampe's secular music, but such characteristics are also evident in his hymn settings. Carlton Young describes them as "in the prevailing popular strophic song-style form, intended to be performed by female soprano and tenor soloists of demonstrated competence and accompanied by harpsichord or chamber organ and cello" (1996: 15). The melodies are frequently adorned with ornaments, including trills and several types of appoggiatura, and are generally within the middle range of a soprano voice. A pair of examples will serve to illustrate different elements of Lampe's idiom.

In Example 4.1, Lampe's assimilation of elements of fashionable secular music can be observed in the frequent use of the "Lombardic" rhythmic figure (referred to by Holman as the "Scotch snap" in the earlier quotation), where one syllable is extended over two notes, of which the second is longer than the first (bars 1, 2, 3, etc.), and the highly embellished melodic writing, which exhibits the techniques outlined above, especially passing notes, often in conjunction with the Lombardic figures. This tune is also a good example of his broad and rich harmonic vocabulary; in keeping with many of the other tunes, first-inversion chords dominate, creating a smooth, often stepwise bass line, perhaps attributable to Lampe's skill as both a harpsichordist and bassoonist. It contains a long series of modulations, visiting several closely related keys: beginning in the tonic, Lampe modulates to the dominant (bars 13–14), then to the subdominant (bars 17–18) and its relative minor (bars 21–22), before a somewhat abrupt change of direction back to the tonic at bar 23. As with many of the settings, the final line of text is repeated, allowing a weak penultimate cadence based on first inversions to be followed by a strong, root-position perfect cadence. The tension created by the harmonic framework of the piece, together with the affective leaps of the melody, illustrates Lampe's skill in matching the sentiment of text and music, another characteristic shared with his secular vocal music. The modulation to E minor reflects the plea in the words "and every struggling soul release," while the return to the tonic in

EX. 4.1. Lampe, hymn 5, "On the Crucifixion."

the final phrases matches the reassurance suggested by the refrain of the text, "O remember Calvary / And bid us go in Peace."

Lampe's tune to hymn 8 (Ex. 4.2) shows the demands Lampe occasionally placed on the singer, by way of large melodic leaps of an octave, either between phrases (bars 2, 12) or within a phrase (bar 11), and even a tenth (bar 14). Again, there is much ornamentation, with decoration at the end of all but one of the main phrases. The harmonic structure in this setting is much simpler than in the previous example, which again reflects Lampe's efforts to match the sentiment of the text: Charles Wesley's text is a joyous and forthright celebration of the resurrection, characterized by the repeated imperative "rejoice." The consistent use of strong tonic and dominant harmonic progressions together with rhythmic, melodic, and harmonic sequences results in a purposeful setting in which the sense of the text is readily conveyed. Lampe's setting has been almost entirely

EX. 4.2. Lampe, hymn 8, "On the Resurrection."

superseded by Handel's GOPSAL (see p. 104), which was not discovered until 1826 (Handel 1988). The latter is more declamatory and readily suited to congregational singing, but there are harmonic and melodic similarities between the two.

These examples show Lampe's bold musical language, characterized by considerable momentum toward the cadence points, a firm harmonic grasp, melodically interesting bass lines, detailed figuring, and chains of modulations. The influence of musical theater is clear in the dramatic melodic leaps, heavy ornamentation, and close correlation between textual sentiment and melodic and harmonic features. Thus we see Lampe's assimilation of fashionable musical styles, transferred from the secular to the sacred. Robin Leaver takes the argument further: "these melodies were not simply designed to be fashionable: they were also intended to be popular. In many respects they are a continuation of the English broadside ballad tune tradition, refined and made widely acceptable through the ballad operas including Lampe's own of the immediately preceding decade" (1996: 34). Both tunes highlight Lampe's soloistic writing, reflecting the qualities of a proficient and experienced musician in using the voice to create a dramatic, affective quality that would have assisted their widespread appeal, thus furthering the reach of the message contained within the texts.

However, this musical style highlights a paradox between the appeal of the settings and their suitability in a congregational context. Although all Lampe's tunes were included in later general collections produced by John Wesley and Thomas Butts, many of them demand a higher level of musical skill and sophistication than most congregations would have mustered. Significantly, a number of the ornaments are omitted in these later versions, which indicates that some of the tunes had gained currency as congregational settings in slightly simplified forms (see Ex. 1.2 and its discussion). Even so, Wesley's approval of them undermines his staunch advocacy of melodic simplicity and full congregational participation in his writings on music. His "Directions for Singing" (in J. Wesley 1765) instructed his followers to participate in corporate hymn singing, while his "Thoughts on the Power of Music," written in 1779, advocated simple, unadorned melodic writing and was highly critical of modern harmonic and contrapuntal trends (J. Wesley 1781a). There seems therefore to be no convincing explanation for his adoption of Lampe's tunes for use across the whole of the Connexion when they were so far removed from the cultural experience and musical skill of many Methodist congregations.

Nonetheless, many of these tunes did enjoy a wide circulation within Methodism and therefore need to be assessed in terms of the movement's theological position and evangelical method. Considered as complete entities of text and music and in relation to one particular aspect of Methodism's evangelical outreach, the significance of *Hymns on the Great Festivals* as part of Methodism's cultural engagement may be more clearly understood.

Lampe's Contribution to Methodist Cultural Engagement

The Wesleys' evangelistic zeal manifested itself in a desire to communicate the message of the gospel to all, particularly those in areas where the presence or influence of the Established Church was limited. Although Methodism's growth in the expanding industrial towns, especially in the north, during the second half of the century is commonly cited (Rack 2002: 438), one of its earliest areas of influence was among the theatrical community in London, through which initial contact with Lampe was established. Indeed, in the 1740s the Wesleys leased a chapel on West Street (near Covent Garden) in order to pursue their ministry to these new converts of the West End. During the early part of that decade, Lampe conducted at Covent Garden Theatre and turned his compositional attentions to writing solo songs. In 1745 he was introduced to the Wesley brothers through Priscilla Rich, a Methodist convert, Covent Garden player, and wife of the proprietor. John Wesley's journal entry for November 29, 1745, notes that he "spent an hour with Mr. Lampe, who had been a Deist for many years, till it pleased God, by *An Earnest Appeal* [J. Wesley 1743] to bring him to a better mind" (Heitzenrater and Ward: 106). For Wesley, the gospel message was as relevant for London's theater professionals as for the industrial workers of the north and west. The centrality of hymnody to this work found a tailor-made outlet in Lampe's compositions: music that set Wesleyan texts in a style familiar to a particular group within Methodism.

The value and significance of these tunes for early Methodism lies not in the minutiae of their compositional style or their overall suitability for congregational singing, but in the opportunity they afforded for conveying Methodism's evangelical zeal to a distinct social group. John Wesley's subsequent use of several of the tunes in his general collections indicates that Lampe's collection was not regarded as a congregational volume in its own right, but that its stylistic qualities were of use to Methodism and some of the tunes were sufficiently adaptable to gain more widespread adoption.

Brian Wren offers a model for interpreting the significance of Lampe's settings in the context of Methodist theology and doctrine. He argues that "Congregational song is by nature corporate, corporeal, and inclusive; at its best, it is creedal, ecclesial, inspirational, and evangelical. Each characteristic is theologically important" (84). These settings can be seen to fulfill the corporate and inclusive aspects of congregational song; as stylistically familiar compositions wedded to theologically rich texts, they were intended to communicate with Methodism's musically literate members and embody the Wesleyan emphasis on unity within the Christian community through the universal relevance of the theological message they sought to preach, while avoiding the imposition of complete musical uniformity across the movement. Wren argues (84–85) that the corporate nature of congregational song makes the theological statement "We are the body of Christ" and represents the unity of the Church: "Though we do not submerge our identity in the crowd, singing together brings us together, demonstrating how we belong to one another in Christ."

In terms of the desirable characteristics outlined by Wren, Lampe's settings can be interpreted as creedal and evangelical, in accordance with Methodism's theological position and evangelical aims. As a creedal statement, according to Wren, "congregational song helps us express a believing response in a self-committing way" (90). Wesley's advocacy of Lampe's settings can be interpreted as offering a way for those to whom the music was stylistically familiar, such as the "wealthy theatre patrons" who attended the West Street chapel (C. Young 2007: 441), to respond to the theological message of the texts and affirm their own belief. As evangelistic tools, they demonstrate the Methodist practice of cultural engagement with different areas of society, emphasizing in particular the universal applicability of the message of salvation and the desire to impress upon people that from any personal, cultural, or social situation they were able to make a religious commitment. Although this was a common facet of Methodist hymnody, these specific examples represent a more focused expression of evangelical intent, directed at a particular section of society. Through using culturally familiar music, the intention was clearly to impress upon those singing and hearing the hymns that the theological message contained therein was both relevant and accessible to them. Even if the extent of their popularity or stylistic familiarity across eighteenth-century Methodism cannot be accurately assessed, the makeup of the congregation at West Street, along with Lampe's personal association with Methodism and the presence of converts such as Priscilla Rich, suggests that these tunes did achieve a wider popularity than simply appealing to the Wesley brothers' own musical tastes.

Thus it is the combination of text and music that is the most significant aspect of *Hymns on the Great Festivals* in terms of their place within early Methodism's worship and evangelical activity. Words and music together embody Methodism's distinctive theological ethos, emphasizing each of the elements of the "Wesleyan Quadrilateral" of scripture, tradition, reason, and experience (Outler, in J. Wesley 1964). This model describes Wesley's four areas of emphasis in religious formation and highlights his Anglican background, from which the first three elements are drawn, and the influence of the Moravians and his own conversion in terms of "experience." In hymnody the combination manifested itself in Methodism's emphasis on congregational song grounded in and inspired by biblical texts while embodying a distinctive theological interpretation that encouraged personal religious commitment. The liturgical nature of the hymn texts in Lampe's publication was inspired by scripture and grounded in the traditions of the Church of England, while the Wesleyan theological interpretation and emphasis on the universal offer of salvation was guided by reason and intellectual reflection. The particular cultural form of engagement that Lampe's music allowed was intended to enhance the religious experience of those people it appealed to by relating to their own musical and cultural environment. *Hymns on the Great Festivals* should be understood as a distinctively, though perhaps not typically, Methodist collection of hymns, in terms of both words and music and their combination.

CHAPTER 5

Methodist Anthems

THE SET PIECE IN ENGLISH
PSALMODY (1750–1850)

Sally Drage

A sacred set piece is essentially an anthem with a metrical text instead of prose. Although there are a few examples in Church of England psalmody, most are nonconformist in origin and are settings of evangelical hymns. Unlike a strophic tune, which may be used for different hymns with the same meter, a set piece is through-composed and the relationship of the words with the music is fixed, which enables composers to express the meaning of the text more directly. There is no exact definition: some set pieces are plain settings of a single verse, which could be performed by a solo voice with keyboard accompaniment, whereas others may include changes of time, key, and tempo, with solos, duets, or trios alternating with choruses. Other terms used for set pieces in the period include *hymn, ode, anthem, hymn-anthem,* and *select piece.*

This chapter traces the development of the set piece from early examples in John Wesley's collections of hymn tunes to the fully orchestrated miniature Handelian oratorios by northern composers such as James Leach of Rochdale and John Fawcett of Kendal. In particular, it considers whether such pieces were compatible with the Methodist ideal of united congregational singing. Two types of set piece are of particular importance in Methodist psalmody: the three-voice *galant* pieces by art composers favored by John Wesley, and the later, more homespun compositions of provincial musicians, which would probably not have met with his approval. The latter were often performed by a special choir and instrumental band on particular occasions such as Christmas and Easter, or the opening of a new chapel, and for fund-raising events including charity sermons and, from the 1790s, at Sunday school anniversaries.

Wesley and the Set Piece

John Wesley's views on singing have been explored in Chapter 1. Throughout his life he kept firm control of every aspect of Methodism, including its hymnody, and determined to regulate congregational singing by publishing three tune books

(J. Wesley 1742, 1761, 1781b). The music includes traditional English psalm tunes; plain Moravian Lutheran-style chorales; parody tunes based on popular secular airs, which would have already been known to many members of a congregation; and elaborate ornamented tunes in the fashionable operatic style of the period by John Frederick Lampe. Wesley expressed himself strongly against counterpoint with overlapping texts, excessive text repetitions, and long alleluias, and insisted that all who could do so should join in the singing. These firmly held views would seem to exclude set pieces. In the preface to *Select Hymns* he says that it contains "all the Tunes which are in *common Use*" among Methodists (1761: 74). And yet in the second edition of that book, generally called by its new title *Sacred Melody*, Wesley himself introduced a set piece named CHESHUNT.

CHESHUNT is an elaborate setting of Charles Wesley's words "The voice of my beloved sounds" (see Ex. 5.1), hymn 148 in *Select Hymns*. It had already appeared in Thomas Butts's *Harmonia-Sacra* (c. 1754). It is a sacred parody and has been identified by Maurice Frost as an adaptation of a popular song by Henry Holcombe titled *A Thought on a Spring Morning* (Frost: 71). It is best described as a set piece, as it is through-composed, with a change of time from 2/4 to 3/8, ending with a repeat of the first sixteen bars of words and music. In accordance with Wesley's preferences, the textual repetition does not obscure the meaning of the words, and only the melody is printed; so although it is quite florid, it was presumably intended to be sung unaccompanied. A second verse is printed in the words-only section of *Select Hymns*, but it may not always have been sung, as the words are not readily fitted to the music.

The Methodist Conference, however, was concerned that only plain tunes should be sung. In 1768 it echoed Wesley's letter to Thomas Rankin and warned against "vain Repetition" of words, and "those complex Tunes, which it is scarce

EX. 5.1. CHESHUNT, set piece melody, opening (J. Wesley 1765).

possible to sing with Devotion" (*Minutes,* 1768: 11–12), and in 1779 included a more comprehensive caution against "those complex tunes and anthems," stating bluntly, "Sing no anthems" (*Minutes,* 1779: 25). (By "anthems" they would have meant set pieces as well as prose anthems.) This comment may have been a reaction to Wesley's inclusion of CHESHUNT in *Sacred Melody.* When he published his third collection, *Sacred Harmony* (1781), he retained CHESHUNT, now in three vocal parts: two treble—largely in thirds and sixths, in the light, elegant style of the period—and bass. It is identical with Butts's setting, except for a few printing errors and the omission of the bass figures. In both Butts and Wesley the bass is textless, but as it is slurred to match the upper parts it was probably sung similarly to the one in Butts. Wesley added a second set piece, THE 100 PSALM by Martin Madan, more commonly known by its original title, DENMARK. He may have wished to widen the appeal of the book and hence increase its salability, as the title page states that it is for harpsichord and organ as well as voice, even though there is no figuring. However, if singers performed these pieces during Methodist services, this could explain why in 1787 the Conference reiterated that no anthems should be "introduced into our Chapels or Preaching-Houses for the time to come, because they cannot be properly called *joint* worship." In 1796 this resolution was modified to allow anthems "on extraordinary occasions and with the consent of the Assistant."

The Lock Hospital, like the Foundling and Magdalen hospitals and the Asylum for Female Orphans, relied on charitable donations for its funding. All four London institutions supported chapels, whose worshippers were attracted by the music. This was sung by inmates, except at the Lock Hospital. Here the patients were usually too ill to perform, as they suffered from venereal diseases. But music of a high standard was still needed to attract affluent patrons and compete successfully for their money against the choirs of the other institutions, so a solution was found whereby the visiting congregation at the Lock Hospital rehearsed regularly, performing in a style described in the Select Committee minutes of the hospital as a "peculiar mode of singing." Temperley (1993) has identified this as the way in which two vocal parts were both sung by men and women in octaves, even though the lower part occasionally went below the organ accompaniment and inverted the harmony.

A collection of music for the hospital was published cumulatively by its chaplain, Martin Madan. It contains music with two equally melodic upper parts and figured bass and was composed especially for the Lock congregation in the florid operatic manner of the period, and it would have appealed to fashionable benefactors. This *galant* style was imitated by later nonconformist composers, and pieces from the volume soon appeared in other psalmody collections. Madan's DENMARK (Ex. 5.2) became by far the most popular set piece in America (Crawford 1984: xxxiii) and was also very well known in England. The text is an adaptation by John Wesley of Isaac Watts's version of Psalm 100, "Sing to the Lord with joy-

EX. 5.2. DENMARK, set piece in three parts, opening (Madan 1769).

ful voice" (J. Wesley 1737: 5–6). In *Select Hymns* (1761), Wesley had designated an ordinary hymn tune, KETTLEBY, for this text.

Carlton Young has suggested that John Wesley included set pieces in his tune books "because of the popularity of the village singing groups and their influence on the singing practice of local Methodist societies" (C. Young 1995a: 71). Anglican societies of singers became increasingly common in the eighteenth century, and as their skill grew they began to sing anthems, often composed for them either by local musicians or by professional organists. Wesley would have been aware of these choirs and their near monopoly of parish church music, but he surely would not have wished to replicate this segregation of singers from the congregation, and he was probably more influenced by the distinctive singing at the Lock Hospital in London. His inclusion of set pieces in his tune books may indicate that he expected them to be sung congregationally. Alternatively, he may never have intended either these or the more elaborate hymn tunes to be sung in public and provided them only for domestic worship or for use at class meetings.

One wonders whether early Methodist congregations employed the Lock Hospital method of doubling both upper parts by men and women when they sang DENMARK and CHESHUNT, or whether performances were left to a select group of singers. Some Methodist chapels had choirs. For example, John Wesley provided for the singers at the New Room in Dublin a set of rules, which were copied into the Society Roll; but these singers were only supposed to lead the congregation and not to sing by themselves (Curnock, 5: illustration, 221). In 1787 the Methodist Conference considered it necessary to repeat yet again that no anthems should be sung, because they were not properly joint worship, but Wesley seems to have been unconcerned: a few years later, in about 1790, he produced a second edition of *Sacred Harmony* with a further three set pieces, all in the usual three-voice texture. Two are from sources he had used already. SPRING, to an anonymous, rather secular text, "Hail, hail reviv'd reviving spring," is from Butts, and YARMOUTH, a setting of Isaac Watts's "He dies, the friend of sinners dies," is from Madan. The third, *The Dying Christian,* is by a provincial composer, Edward Harwood (1756–1787).

"Vital Spark"

Harwood was a handloom weaver from Darwen, near Blackburn, who moved to Liverpool to become a professional singer and composer. At least five of his secular songs were published, as well as two books of church music. The texts of his sacred music suggest that he was a Dissenter, for they are nearly all to be found in *A New Collection of Psalms Proper for Christian Worship* of 1764, compiled by two Liverpool Unitarian clergymen, John Brekell and William Enfield. Harwood's first book, *A Set of Hymns and Psalm Tunes: In Three and Four Parts, Adapted to the Use of Churches and Chapels* of 1781, includes *The Dying Christian to His Soul,* a setting of Alexander Pope's "Vital spark of heav'nly flame, / Quit, O quit this mortal frame." (For a modern edition see Temperley and Drage, No. 86.) "Vital spark" became part of popular culture and the most famous funeral piece of the eighteenth and nineteenth centuries, and even the early twentieth, in both England and America. It was republished in numerous editions and arrangements throughout the period, including a setting for a reed band, complete with percussion, by J. Tidswell (c. 1877). The most far-flung performance may have been at the state funeral of a Polynesian prince in 1855 (*Evangelical Magazine, and Missionary Chronicle:* 728), and perhaps the most bizarre occurred in 1871 when it was played by a militia band at a concert in Hay-on-Wye during an exhibition of roller skating (Kilvert: 111). It was also imitated by other authors, and Samuel Pattison's "The Dying Saint's Soliloquy" (1790?: 208–9) was set by James Leach, whose compositions will be discussed later in this chapter. The anonymous parody, *Soliloquy of a Winter Bather*—"Timid mass of flesh and blood, / Plunge, ah! plunge, into the flood" (*Monthly Magazine,* 1822: 517)—is not known to have attracted a composer.

Perhaps the secularity of "Vital spark" was part of its appeal. The words are not overtly Christian. Pope, at the suggestion of Joseph Addison, created a text suitable to be set to music by combining a translation of the dying thoughts of the Roman emperor Hadrian, as recorded by Ovid, with a paraphrase of a fifteenth-century poem, "*A Thought on Death,*" by Thomas Flatman, together with a verse from I Corinthians 15.

As with the pieces already discussed, Harwood's music is in three vocal parts and its musical style is secular. It is similar to a glee, with short sections expressing the emotion of the text by changes of both key and time signature, and with contrasting dynamics, though notably without any fuging passages, thereby avoiding Wesley's disapproval. Temperley has described it as comparable to a "cantata with an amorous text," with "sentimental appoggiaturas" (1979b, 1:214). Wesley's edition has some alterations: the upper two parts are switched; tempo changes are omitted; crescendos are replaced with plain *fortes*, but trills are added; and a few notes are wrong or missing, with lower-octave bass notes added at some cadences. Wesley did not have to remove the bass figures, since there were none in the original, perhaps because Harwood intended it to be sung unaccompanied. It seems to have been well known before Wesley's version was published, for he thus described a performance at Bolton on July 27, 1787:

> Here are eight hundred poor children taught in our Sunday schools, by about eighty masters, who receive no pay but what they are to receive from their Great Master. About a hundred of them (part boys and part girls) are taught to sing; and they sang so true, that, all singing together, there seemed to be but one voice. . . . In the evening, many of the children still hovering round the House, I desired forty or fifty to come in and sing,
> Vital spark of heavenly flame.
> Although some of them were silent, not being able to sing for tears, yet the harmony was such as I believe could not be equalled in the king's chapel. (J. Wesley 1975–, 24:46.)

This may indicate another reason for the growing fame of "Vital spark." After their introduction in the later eighteenth century, Sunday schools, particularly in the north of England, educated an enormous number of children, and by 1851 three quarters of working-class children attended Sunday schools throughout the country (Laqueur: 44). If, as seems likely, "Vital spark" was taught to them, many thousands of young people would remember it into adulthood. The text continued to be included in numerous hymnbooks, particularly up to about 1830, although not in Methodist publications, despite Wesley's apparent approval of it. It would seem to be too complicated for full congregational participation (and the upper part starts on f"), but it may have been easier to sing when there was a large number of worshippers. In 1847, James Sherman, minister of Surrey Chapel in London, described how pieces such as "Vital spark," "by being frequently sung, are as familiar to the congregation as ordinary tunes . . . Nothing can be more imposing than the union of nearly three thousand voices rapturously, and harmoniously[,] singing the praises of their Saviour and God" (Novello: preface).

The children from Bolton and the congregation of the Lock Hospital were trained to sing set pieces, but if Methodist congregations could cope with the florid hymn tunes favored by Wesley, they would probably also have attempted to sing set pieces without rehearsals, even if there were not so many singers as at Surrey Chapel. Presumably, congregations were used to the ornamented style of fashionable eighteenth-century music, in the same way that the syncopation of pop music is familiar to modern worshippers. Some evidence of possible congregational singing of set pieces can be found in the word editions of hymn books, particularly those which include tune names. *A Pocket Hymn Book*, published by John Wesley in 1787 to counteract the pirated edition produced by a Methodist bookseller in York, has the tune name CHESHUNT affixed to "The voice of my beloved sounds," under the heading "For Believers saved" (J. Wesley 1787: 193).

Set Pieces in the North

As Lightwood noted, more tangible evidence that some congregations sang set pieces can be found in counties in the northern part of England (1928: 9). John Wilde, a Sheffield singing teacher, produced a series of pamphlets containing the words of "Hymns, Odes and Anthems" as sung in Methodist chapels in the Sheffield, Rotherham, Doncaster, and Nottingham circuits. The earliest surviving copy seems to be the fifth edition, dated 1797, although Eric Mackerness, in his book on the history of music in Sheffield, *Somewhere Further North*, noted a second edition of 1795, as "sung at Norfolk Street Methodist Chapel in Sheffield," which was apparently still extant in the middle of the twentieth century (Mackerness: 26).

The singing at this chapel was led by a choir, seated together in a singing pew, which in 1782 the chapel authorities agreed should have a carpet (perhaps to keep the noise down, rather than to provide comfort). Before an organ was erected in 1860, the singers were accompanied by a cello (Seed: 183, 196). Wilde particularly praised the congregational harmony at Norfolk Street, and whereas the choir may have used notated music, the congregation sang by ear in at least two parts, treble and bass, Wilde's selection of texts showing that their repertory included quite a few set pieces. Congregational part singing may have been made easier if Norfolk Street Chapel followed the Methodist Conference's instructions that men and women should sit separately (*Minutes*, 1770: 43), because the two vocal lines would have been more clearly heard, especially on repeats, when women sang the air alone. Despite its excellence, Wilde suggested further improvements to the singing and must have been familiar with John Wesley's directions for singers, as he quotes from them indirectly:

Let those Persons who are dispersed throughout the Chapel, and sing the Bass part, use the same Notes they hear from the singers; inattention to *this* produces discord. Secondly, keep time with the singers; that is to say, go not before, nor hang behind them; both of which cause disorder. Lastly, and above all things, let no MEN sing the repeats, which the WOMEN take; this destroys the beauty,

simplicity, and excellency for which Methodist singing has been so long celebrated (Wilde 1797).

In all, six different versions of Wilde's pamphlet have survived, ranging from
1797 to 1803. Wilde probably sold them himself: they would have been an inex-
pensive way for a congregation to acquire new texts, and if enough copies were
purchased they could sing without lining out. (It should be noted that there is
no evidence that through-composed pieces were ever lined out, even when sung
by a congregation.)

In some instances, Wilde heads texts with the name of the piece, the tune,
or the composer, but others are unidentified. The 1797 edition includes at least
two texts that can be positively classified as set pieces; the congregation presumably sang these together with the choir. *The Promised Land,* a setting of "Happy
beyond description he," is by James Leach (1761–1798), who called it CANAAN
(Leach 1794: 6–69). It is described by Wilde as a "celebrated Ode" and consists
of a trio, a duet, and a chorus. While the trio would have been relatively simple
for a congregation, the duet is quite florid, and a sixteenth-note bass run in the
chorus would have been particularly difficult to sing by ear. *The Fall of Babylon,*
a setting of Watts's dramatic hymn "In Gabriel's hand, a mighty stone," is by
John Beaumont (1762–1822), a Methodist minister who preached in the Sheffield
and Nottingham circuits and who seems to have had maverick tendencies. He
composed anthems; he must have approved of the organ in the chapel at New-
ark, because there is an engraving of him sitting at the console (John Beaumont
1793: frontispiece); and his grandson wrote that he took pleasure in a "blood
horse and a fine Psalm tune" (Joseph Beaumont: 6). Beaumont printed *The Fall
of Babylon* in 1795, then included it in his *New Harmonic Magazine* (1801: 68). In
his autobiography he explains his reasons for publication, which provide further
evidence of congregational singing of set pieces: "My chief design . . . was, to give
a few short pieces, proper to be sung before the sermon, easy to be learnt, and
in which the congregations might readily join" (1809: 398). *The Fall of Babylon* is
obviously not the work of a professional composer—the alto drops below the bass
in bars 53 and 54—but it illustrates the words well and is simple and rewarding
to sing. It is probably also the only set piece of this period in current use, as it
is still sung every Christmas by the carol singers of Foolow in Derbyshire, who
were originally all members of the local Wesleyan Methodist chapel.

John Wilde's six extant editions include fifty-three separate texts. Two were set
to music by Wilde, he arranged two more, and one was "composed and adapted"
by him, but in all instances his music cannot be traced. There are also two more
compositions by Leach, of which the first, JORDAN, to the words "Guide me, O
thou great Jehovah," is another set piece, consisting of a trio and a chorus, and is
from Leach's third psalmody collection (1798: 38–42).

At approximately the same date as Wilde's pamphlets, but sixty miles or so from
Sheffield in Hull, congregations were also singing set pieces. In *Stories of Methodist*

Music, James Lightwood, who wrote extensively on Methodist music but rarely gave any indication of where his sources might be found, noted another pamphlet, *Hymns Selected from Various Authors: To Be Sung at the Methodist Chapel, George Yard, Hull* (Hull, 1798). The original has yet to be traced, but Lightwood apparently transcribed the preface verbatim. The pamphlet was issued in order that "those detached pieces of music which are frequently sung in the Methodist Chapel in George Yard, before Sermons, may be more generally understood," and "those who have any taste for sacred Music, when they have the words in their Hands . . . may with ease attend to and obtain a perfect knowledge of the Tunes, so that in a very short time they will be generally sung throughout the Congregation at large" (Lightwood 1928: 16–17).

The author, who is identified only as T. H., probably knew of the Sheffield pamphlets, since Wilde makes very similar suggestions as to how the congregational singing might be improved. He could possibly have been Thomas Holy, one of the benefactors and founders of Norfolk Street Chapel. Lightwood lists twenty-seven texts and states that they are all "hymn-anthems," although one cannot be certain, for again few composers' names are given. Thirteen pieces are also found in the Sheffield pamphlets, including Beaumont's *The Fall of Babylon,* and William Miller's *The Methodist Parting* and KEDRON. One other set piece by Beaumont can also be identified, though he is not named as the composer. A short prose anthem, *The Barren Fig Tree,* is relatively easy for a congregation to sing, as it is in two parts throughout, despite some suspect word stresses in the opening bars. It was first published probably in 1795 and then appeared in Beaumont's collection (1801: 70). Manuscript copies of it were added to two printed books, Leach's *New Sett of Hymns and Psalm Tunes,* in the Royal School of Church Music copy, and Beaumont's *Four Anthems,* in the copy held at the Henry Watson Music Library, Manchester. The Hull pamphlet is perhaps closer to mainstream Methodism than those by Wilde, for it also contains three set pieces approved by Wesley: Butts's SPRING, Madan's DENMARK, and Harwood's "Vital spark." This would seem to provide further evidence that congregations joined in such pieces despite their complexity. However, some congregations may also have sung one setting that Wesley would have censured. Wilde's five main *Selections* and the Hull pamphlet all include "Rise, my soul and stretch thy wings," which Lightwood surmised may have been sung to DARTFORD (1928: 20), possibly the tune popular in Cornwall that was disliked by Wesley as it was too "full of repetitions and flourishes" to be sung "with devotion" (Telford 1931, 4:311; and see p. 000).

Special Services and Their Music

After John Wesley's death in 1791, the Methodist Conference continued to be concerned about the use of music in services and repeated the 1782 instructions that no anthems should be sung "unless on extraordinary occasions . . . because they cannot properly be called *joint* worship" (*An Extract,* 1796: 35). By 1800, matters seem to have deteriorated further, and capital letters were required when Question 15 asked, "Can anything be done to prevent, what appears to us a great evil, namely, BANDS OF MUSIC and THEATRICAL SINGERS being brought into our Chapels, when charity sermons are to be preached?" (*An Extract,* 1800: 26).

In theory, the answer was simple: "Let none in our Connexion preach Charity Sermons, where such persons and such music are introduced." In practice, chapels needed money, and as at the Lock Hospital, affluent worshippers were more likely to attend special sermons and contribute generously if the service was lightened with some musical interludes by fashionable composers.

Handel's music was universally popular. His oratorios were already important at provincial music festivals and meetings, and the north, the cradle of Anglican psalmody in the early eighteenth century, also maintained a strong oratorio tradition. There were at least thirty-one performances of Handel's oratorios, particularly *Messiah* or *Judas Maccabaeus,* in the area to the north of Manchester in a twelve-year period from 1765 to 1777 (G. Shaw: 141–239), and subscription lists to thirteen Handel oratorios show that the majority of music and singing societies that purchased copies were from east Lancashire and west Yorkshire (Burchell: 6–42). Lancashire singers became nationally famous, and some of them sang at the Handel Commemoration at Westminster Abbey in 1784. It was inevitable that excerpts from Handel's oratorios, if not complete works, would soon be a feature of charity and anniversary sermons.

In 1805 the Methodist Conference was so concerned about this culture that, after stating that only a cello was to be used to accompany worship, it made the following regulations:

> Let no *Pieces,* as they are called, in which *Recitatives,* by single men, *Solos,* by single women, *Fuguing,* (or different words sung by different voices at the same time,) are introduced, be *sung* in our chapels.
>
> Let the original, simple, grave, and devotional style be carefully preserved, which, instead of drawing attention to singing and the singers, is so admirably calculated to draw off the attention from both, and to raise the soul to God only.
>
> Let no musical *Festivals,* or, as they are sometimes termed, *Selections of Sacred Music,* be either encouraged, or permitted in any of our chapels: in which performances, the genuine dignity of spiritual worship is grossly abused under the pretence of getting money for charitable purposes, which we have sufficient proof, has been procured as amply, where nothing of the kind has been introduced, but the charity recommended to the people in the name of God.

However, "Selections of Sacred Music" were a money spinner, and many chapels seem to have taken little notice of these regulations and continued to hold special services where music was provided by an augmented choir and instrumentalists.

Donations were also needed by Sunday schools, many of which were opened in the industrialized towns of northern England to educate both child and adult factory workers. By 1784 there were apparently 1,800 pupils in Manchester and the same number in Salford and Leeds (Kelly: 75). In 1837 Stockport had just under 5,500 pupils and had educated more than 40,000 (Morgan: 12, 18). Although many Sunday schools were interdenominational, they were often managed by nonconformists, in particular Methodists, and again, the music performed at special services could arouse opposition. In 1824 Dr. Thomas Chalmers, the famous Church of Scotland preacher and reformer, was invited to deliver the annual Sunday school sermon at Stockport. Having traveled solidly for nearly three days, he was not amused by the advance notice of the event in the local newspaper, writing in his memoirs that "On reading the advertisement I was well-nigh overset by the style of it. They are going to have a grand musical concert along with the sermon . . . this is really making it a theatrical performance, and me one of the performers." There were "three rows of female singers, so many professional male singers, and a number of amateurs," accompanied by "one pair of bass drums, two trumpets, bassoon, organ, serpents, violins (without number), violincellos [*sic*], bass viols, flutes and hautboy." Chalmers agreed to preach only if his sermon and prayers were not mixed up with the music, and he stayed in the vestry during the performance, but whatever his misgivings there were 3,500 in the congregation and £401 was raised (Wild: 221–24).

James Leach and John Fawcett

The music at Stockport Sunday School was exceptional. Not all schools, nor indeed all nonconformist chapels, could coopt such a large number of singers or such a wide variety of instrumentalists, and some would have found Handel's music too difficult. But they still wanted to perform special music, and a solution was to be found in the work of James Leach, an enterprising Methodist who was the first psalmody composer to write extended set pieces with instrumental accompaniment for amateur performance, and specifically for Sunday schools. Since he came from Rochdale, north of Manchester, Leach would certainly have known Handel's music, and his own has Handelian characteristics, which would also have been familiar to performers. An early biographer stated that Leach played in the King's Band and sang in "one of the great musical festivals" at Westminster Abbey (Hirst: 136–37). No evidence has yet been found to support the former claim, but he may have been the Mr. Leach who was one of the countertenors in the chorus at the Westminster Abbey Handel Commemoration in 1784 (Burney: 22). If so, he would have sung with another Lancashire countertenor, namely Harwood, composer of "Vital spark." (They were both originally handloom weavers, and both died young: Leach was killed in a stagecoach accident, aged about thirty-six.)

Two set pieces with instrumental accompaniment are included in Leach's first book of sacred music, *A New Sett of Hymns and Psalm Tunes* (1789), and three in his *Second Sett* (c. 1794). The title pages of both books state that the music was "adapted for the Use of Churches, Chapels & Sunday Schools." After his death, a volume of his previously unpublished compositions was issued in periodical numbers to support his widow and children (1798–). This volume contains twenty-eight longer pieces: twenty-three set pieces, four anthems, and one hybrid piece with prose and metrical texts as well as three hymn tunes. Bass parts are figured, but all the hymns and psalms could equally be performed unaccompanied, and particularly in the first set, most follow John Wesley's constraints that there should be no "vain repetitions" or overlapping text. The melodies, like so many others sung by Methodists during the later eighteenth century, are light and tuneful in the popular theater style of the day.

Leach's two set pieces in his first book have separate instrumental parts. *The Tribunal,* to Charles Wesley's "He comes, he comes, the judge severe," consists of a chorus, a trio with a separate figured bass, and a chorus with three unidentified treble instrument parts and bass, again figured. *The Second Coming of Christ* is an extended setting of "Lo, he comes with clouds descending," Charles Wesley's adaptation of John Cennick's "Lo, he cometh, countless trumpets." Indeed, only the first line of text is used for the opening thirty-eight bars of a bass solo and chorus, accompanied by two clarinets and an unnamed instrumental bass that continues throughout the piece. Next come a short treble duet with violin, a chorus with three treble instruments (presumably clarinets and violin), a bass solo, a treble duet, a chorus with an extra cello part, and a final chorus with named clarinets and violin. It is essentially a miniature oratorio, thirty-two pages in length, and although the book's pagination is continuous, it may also have been sold separately, as it is headed "P^r. 1s."

Perhaps these two pieces were considered too elaborate for anniversary and charity services. The three set pieces in Leach's second book—REUMAH, CALVARY, and CANAAN—are simpler and contain no separate instrumental parts. CANAAN, as noted earlier in this chapter, was included in Wilde's pamphlets, and also in the one from Hull. The selection of set pieces and anthems in Leach's posthumous *Collection,* "Composed and adapted for a Full Choir," is more diverse, as might be expected, for it was made up after his death from his unpublished manuscripts and some engraved plates. Most of the set pieces have choruses alternating with solos, duets, or trios, and some of the longer ones again imitate oratorios. Nine can be sung unaccompanied but have bass figures; a further ten have a separate figured instrumental bass. One of these, GILEAD, has a duet section marked "violoncello," but in general bass instruments are not named.

Five longer pieces are scored more extensively. RESURRECTION, "Anthem from the 41 Psalm," and ASYLUM have parts for two oboes and two violins and a separate bass; *New Year's Day* has the same scoring, but the oboes may be replaced with horns for a bass solo; and *The Last Trial* is set for two violins, two oboes, and two horns. The latter also includes a double chorus, as does ASYLUM, which at forty-seven pages is the longest piece of all. In common with Anglican psalmody, there are no parts for violas or other tenor instruments, but "organ" is specified in a number of pieces, and if one were available, it is likely that it would have been played together with the other instruments. The bass would probably be supported by a cello or perhaps a bassoon: wind parts may have been played by members of local militia bands, recruited for the occasion. If instruments were used, they would have doubled the voices when there were no separate instrumental parts.

It is difficult to determine how many of Leach's set pieces were performed at special services. Despite his pioneering efforts, only two of his less complicated pieces, CRUCIFIXION, a setting of "When I survey the wondrous cross," and CANAAN, seem to have become well known, appearing in various manuscripts. His hymn tunes were more popular, and twenty-six of them were included in an American Methodist book compiled by James Evans (1808), with another twenty-one added to later editions.

Other composers followed Leach's example and began to add one or more set pieces to their collections of hymn tunes. In particular, another Methodist, John Fawcett (1789–1867), a shoemaker from Kendal, successfully imitated Leach's Handelian style and produced a succession of orchestral set pieces, some of which were written for amateur choral societies. Fawcett, like Leach, was self-taught, but he became more accomplished musically. He learned to play a variety of wind instruments by joining the Kendal militia band, and he sang in the chorus at local festivals. In 1814 he was employed by the Wesleyan Sunday School at Farnworth, just south of Bolton, to lead the singing and train the choir and instrumentalists. By the time he was forty-one he could proudly advertise that he was the author of fifteen books of sacred music (1830: title page), and his obituary noted that the final number of his compositions was in excess of two thousand (*Bolton Chronicle*, November 2, 1867).

Fawcett's early collections of psalm and hymn tunes are written in the traditional florid nonconformist style. According to the title page his first book, *A New Set of Sacred Music* (c. 1811), was designed to be interdenominational, in the hope of wider sales. It includes one short set piece, DISMISSION, with keyboard accompaniment, whereas his *Second Sett* (1813–14) contains six "select pieces" (as Fawcett describes them on his title page), one of which, *The Promis'd Land,* is eleven pages long, with parts for two horns, two violins or flutes, and a separate figured bass for organ. (The Sunday school band at Farnworth may have included horns, as five hymn tunes in the same collection are also written for two horns and organ.) *The Promis'd Land* is advertised separately on the title page of a later edition of his first *Set* ([1837]) and may be all or part of an oratorio, *The Promised Land,* which he apparently composed at about the same date (*Bolton Chronicle*, November 2, 1867). It seems that the term *oratorio* could also be used to describe a long set piece, at least in Lancashire. The unpublished "Salvation O the joyful sound," by James Nuttall, is sixteen pages long and is headed "an oratorio" in one manuscript (*PRlro* DDX. 1468. Acc. 4986 box 5: 97–112). There are two more "select pieces" in Fawcett's *Third Sett*. "Hark me thinks I hear a voice" is titled "Anthem," although the text is metrical. The opening and closing choruses are scored for two violins, two oboes, two trumpets, bassoon and cello, and organ, with a central trio accompanied just by organ. The second set piece, *Chorus* ("Blessed be the name of the Lord"), uses the same mixed wind and string instrumentation. There could be further pieces in Fawcett's fourth, fifth, and sixth sets, but these are missing, and there are none in his *Seventh Set of Hymn Tunes* (1830). However, there are three set pieces in his *Harp of Zion* (c. 1834): *A Funeral Piece,* DEDICATION, and CELEBRATION, all of which have a written-out organ part and instrumental parts for pairs of violins, flutes, clarinets, horns, and trumpets, which are printed in a separate section at the back of the book.

Fawcett's most extensive collection of orchestral set pieces is unfortunately incomplete. *The Voice of Harmony* (c. 1850?) contained ninety pieces and could be purchased in three volumes, or in six books, or in fifty-nine parts. However, apart from the first volume of thirty pieces, only another twenty-one are known, and ten of these have survived only in tonic sol-fa notation. According to the title page, the music was "suited for Sunday School and other Anniversaries, and for Missionary Meetings" and was "complete without the Orchestral Parts, but the addition of these renders this work more useful to those Societies which number instrumentalists among their members." The scoring is varied, but some pieces are for full classical orchestra, including violas and even timpani.

By the later nineteenth century, restrictions of working hours for children and improvements in education meant that Sunday schools could focus more on religious instruction and less on basic literacy. Anniversary services continued to be important, particularly in the north of England, and local composers wrote special pieces for Sunday school anniversary services, with band parts, until the mid-twentieth century. But the music became simpler, perhaps because there were fewer young adult pupils and because oratorios were increasingly performed by municipal choral societies. John Wesley would have approved.

CHAPTER 6

The Music of Methodism in Nineteenth-Century America

Anne Bagnall Yardley

Introduction

The history of nineteenth-century American Methodist music reflects and parallels the complex evolution of the various Methodist denominations during the period. The hymn texts compiled by John Wesley in his 1780 volume *A Collection of Hymns for the Use of the People Called Methodists* continued to form the backbone of Methodist hymn singing, even as the particularly American developments of camp meeting music, the "better music" movement, Sunday school hymnody, Negro spirituals, and gospel hymnody inculturated these texts into their various American contexts (Graham: 1–17). The publication of hymnals and tune books throughout the nineteenth century offers us abundant source material for the actual music sung, while descriptions of religious events and essays in contemporary journals (e.g., *The Christian Advocate*) illuminate such areas of controversy as the use of choirs and organs in seeming contradiction to John Wesley's own precepts on church music (Yardley 1999a: 39–64; C. Young 1995a). The resulting picture of a vibrant musical life among American Methodists demonstrates the ways in which the denominations themselves, especially the Methodist Episcopal Church (MEC), rose in social status during the period. (See Marti: 159–66, on increasing wealth in Methodism.)

Music plays a central role in catechesis within Methodism. John Wesley himself emphasized the importance of hymn texts in the formation of Christian disciples. Through the choice of musical settings for these formative texts, American Methodists expressed the Wesleyan message in appropriately American musical vehicles, dependent on the geographical region and cultural biases of specific groups. As each branch of Methodism formed, it created two documents: a discipline and a hymnbook. These documents expressed both the particularity of each group and the genetic code of the Methodists embodied in the writings and hymn translations of John and the hymn texts of Charles.

The Methodist connection in the United States experienced numerous schisms during the nineteenth century, including the breaking off from the Methodist Episcopal Church (founded 1784) of the Free African Society (1787); the African Methodist Episcopal Church (formally organized 1816); the African Methodist Episcopal Zion Church (formally organized 1821); the Methodist Protestant Church (1828); the Methodist Episcopal Church, South (1844); the Free Methodists (1860); and the Colored Methodist Episcopal Church (1870). Most of these divisions occurred over issues of clerical authority and race, not primarily because of differences in worship practices, although as the denominations developed, certain ritual distinctions, including differences in hymn repertory and performance practice, resulted as well. And certainly the schisms created a wealth of opportunity for musicians and clergy to create new volumes geared to each denomination's predilections. Each of these groups published hymnbooks containing text only (listed in Appendix 2) and, to varying degrees, tune books as well (Graham; Temperley 2001; Spencer; Yardley 1999b). These will be explored in more detail in Chapter 8.

In many ways, Methodist music reflects the great variety of American sacred music of the century. Geographical differences had a major effect on the musical tastes of churches. North-south and rural-urban distinctions created markets for different musical compositions (Crawford 1993: 7). Was the untutored early American style or the imported European "better music" more appropriate for worship? The camp meeting offered a stage upon which black musical traditions shared space with rural white musical styles, each affecting the other (Hulan). Many Methodists participated in the growth in midcentury of music for the Sunday school and the subsequent development by Ira Sankey and others of the gospel hymn.

Prefaces to published tune books often give some indication of the musical proclivities of the compilers. While these cannot be examined here in detail, one example points to the type of information often included. In the preface to the MECS 1860, L. C. Everett, the editor, talks about the need of the MEC-South to have its own tune book. In supplying this need, he artfully hit upon a method of also promoting his compositions and those of his brother Asa B. Everett. As he explains in the preface, "the one on the left hand page is an old standard tune with which every congregation is presumed to be somewhat acquainted; and that on the right, a *new* tune, in some instances known to a limited extent, and in others not known at all, being published for the first time in this work." With few exceptions, the texts on either page can be sung with either tune. Thus in this volume he is attempting both to represent the currently used tune repertory and to expand that repertory through the addition of new tunes. He has entered this task with the explicit idea of making good matches between texts and tunes. As he states in the preface: "It has been the constant and prayerful aim of the author to associate together hymns and tunes of kindred spirit, in every instance to secure an appropriate adaptation of song to sentiment, and to produce a work in every respect equal to the demands of the Church, and, as a whole, inferior to none of the kind ever before published in this country."

At the beginning of the nineteenth century, there was little expectation that tune and text would be married together, although there were certainly exceptions to this rule. By the end of the nineteenth century, largely as a result of Sunday school hymnody and gospel hymnody, hymnals included a one-to-one correspondence between text and tune. In many cases the stanzas were still formatted as poetry. Everett's volume, like others of the midcentury, shows a state of concern with the relationship but still an expectation that one could provide one or two tunes for six to eight texts.

Musical Settings of Charles Wesley's Texts

The musical settings of Charles Wesley's hymn texts provide one useful barometer for musical trends in the American Methodist Church during the nineteenth century. The presence of a substantial number of Wesley texts is one distinguishing characteristic of virtually all Methodist hymnals. While American Methodists often incorporated more popular hymnody into their volumes, as they did in the first authorized hymnal (MEC 1786), nevertheless all of the official Methodist hymnbooks contained a substantial body of Wesley texts. For example, MECS 1847 included 600 texts by the Wesleys out of a total of 1,047. While the percentage dropped drastically by MEC 1905 to just under 20 percent, a considerable number (125) of Charles Wesley's texts remained in that volume. These hymns thus carried the bedrock Wesleyan theology that formed Methodists as Methodists. In that sense they represent a conservative aspect of the hymnal. In the United States in the nineteenth century, editors of tune books regularly paired Wesley texts with tunes that marked the acceptable musical styles for their particular branch of Methodism.

Additionally, there were undoubtedly a number of musical renditions of Wesley texts that are outside of the published repertory. For example, lined-out versions of Wesley texts in the African American tradition existed in an oral, not written, tradition. Song leaders in individual congregations could choose from any tune in the appropriate meter when setting a hymn. Therefore, what we know about the tunes associated with Wesley texts is limited to the published written sources and some descriptive material. It is difficult for a scholar to do more than acknowledge both the existence and the importance of these oral traditions.

In order to explore the repertory of tunes connected with Wesley texts, I have traced the nineteenth-century musical lineage of about thirty hymns that subsequently appeared in both *The Methodist Hymnal* (MEC 1905) and *The United Methodist Hymnal* (UMC 1989) as well as in the majority of published tune collections of the nineteenth century. Working through these sources, it is possible to see which texts gravitated to a particular tune and were relatively stable, and which appeared with several different tunes in the collections.

Among the tunes associated with Wesley texts in American nineteenth-century sources, there are four main categories. First, English eighteenth-century tunes, many of which were part of the Methodist repertory in England and made their way to the United States in collections of the late eighteenth and early nineteenth centuries (e.g., ALMA, ARLINGTON, CARLISLE, DARWALL, EASTER HYMN (WORGAN), HANOVER (ST. MICHAEL'S), HOTHAM, ITALIAN HYMN, LITTLE MARLBOROUGH, PLEYEL'S HYMN, WARWICK, ST. MARTIN'S, TRURO,and WATCHMAN). Second, early American compositions, published before 1820 (e.g., CORONATION, ENNIUS, FILLMORE, KENTUCKY, and LENOX). Third, tunes by Lowell Mason (1792–1872) and his contemporaries, associated with what is known as the "better music" movement, including the incorporation of European tunes but moving by midcentury into the composition of tunes by such American composers as Isaac Woodbury and Thomas Hastings (e.g., AZMON, BEALOTH, BOYLSTON, DENNIS, HAMBURG, HEBRON, HENDON, LABAN, MARTYN, SELENA,and UXBRIDGE). Lastly, tunes that made their way to America from Victorian England, especially as represented by the Anglican publication *Hymns Ancient and Modern* (1861), an exceedingly influential book (e.g., DIADEMATA, FAITH, HOLLINGSIDE, ST. CATHERINE, and ST. FABIAN).

In many ways these tunes represent a fairly conservative musical approach to the setting of Wesley hymns. Of course there were other settings as well. For example, L. C. Everett's many pairings of his own tunes and those of his brothers gave a decidedly southern spin to the *Wesleyan Hymn and Tune Book* (MECS 1860). Within the MEC, the musical choices were clearly related to prevailing cosmopolitan tastes in the Northeast: Mason's "better music" in the middle third of the century and the hymns of the Oxford movement at the end of the century.

An examination of the range of tunes assigned to specific texts helps to establish an understanding of musical tastes. Of the texts studied, only a few demonstrate a close correspondence to the same tune throughout the period and across the branches of Methodism. For example, "Blow ye the trumpet, blow," in the unusual meter of 6.6.6.6.8.8., is first associated with the tune LENOX in the 1857 collection. (Both MEC 1822 and MEC 1833 associated it with PORTSMOUTH NEW.) Subsequently, the tune and text were matched in MECS 1860, MEC 1867, MEC 1878, AMEC 1898, MPC 1901, and MEC 1905, even retaining the connection all the way through to the 1989 hymnal. This is a robust American tune, composed by Lewis Edson (1748–1820). It was originally a fuging tune (Edson's background was Anglican) but is set homophonically in MECS 1874a and from 1878 onward in the MEC (Graham: 75). The two eight-syllable lines are a refrain and are further emphasized by a repeat of the text of the penultimate line, "the year of jubilee is come!," in both the fuging and homophonic versions. Examples 6.1a and -b show the way in which the lively fuging tune is condensed into the homophonic version.

a)

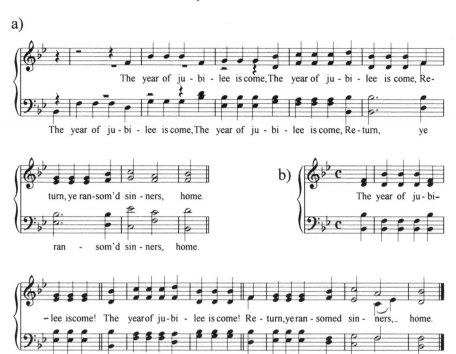

EX. 6.1. Lewis Edson, LENOX, ending: (a) fuging version (MEC 1867: 290); (b) homophonic version (MEC 1878: 122).

In other cases, the Methodist pairing in England did not survive the transplant to the United States. As Nicholas Temperley has shown in Chapter 1, the text "Jesu, lover of my soul" was regularly paired with Madan's HOTHAM until its association in the later nineteenth century with Dykes's HOLLINGSIDE. In the United States, however, HOTHAM appears only in MEC 1822 and 1833, where another British tune, Samuel Webbe's ALMA, is also offered as a choice. Beginning in MEC 1857, editors paired the American tune MARTYN with this text in every collection through 1905. MEC 1878 offers the tune REFUGE also. MEC 1905 supplies two additional settings for the text, both Victorian: HOLLINGSIDE (Dykes) and ST. FABIAN (Joseph Barnby). These offerings appear to let congregations continue to sing an old favorite at the same time that the editors give a nod to the latest fashions in hymn tunes and to their British connections. McCutchan credits Thomas Hastings with matching MARTYN with "Jesu, lover of my soul" (McCutchan: 359–61). MARTYN is a bland and repetitious tune (ABABCCAB) with a range of just a sixth. It does not seem to capture any of the restlessness of flying or tempests referenced in the text but rather to provide the safe haven that the singer seeks in Jesus (Ex. 6.2). This compact version shows the repetitiveness of the music very clearly and the move to a slightly higher register in the third

EX. 6.2. Simeon B. Marsh, MARTYN (MEC 1878: 242).

line in comparison with lines 1, 2, and 4. A look at the bass line makes the static nature of the harmony also evident.

In an interesting sidelight, AMEC 1898 pairs the text with MARTYN but also offers it in an extended setting for choir and soloists. The composer is John T. Layton, one of the editors of the volume. The soprano sings the first verse to a lyrical triple-time melody that modulates from G major to E flat major for the chorus rendition of the second verse. Other soloists sing verse 3, and the chorus re-enters with verse 4.

Both of the texts discussed so far have relatively stable musical histories. The great Wesley hymn "O for a thousand tongues to sing" appears with a wide diversity of musical settings in American sources. Since it is a common-meter text, there is no shortage of tunes that editors (or choir directors) can choose to pair with it. MEC 1822 and 1833 pair it with MELODY, by the English Methodist composer James Leach (see Chapter 5). MEC 1857 and MPC 1901 pair it with the tune NORTHFIELD. The MEC-South 1860 hymnal suggests only L. C. Everett's own tune CHAPPEL; MEC 1867 uses Oliver Holden's CORONATION. Three tune books pair it with AZMON, the tune with which American Methodists associate it now. This tune, a Lowell Mason arrangement of a German tune by Hans Georg Nägeli (1773–1836), is featured in MEC 1878, AMEC 1898, and MEC 1905. So this tune/text combination, which now epitomizes American Methodism, first appeared in 1878 (for Carlton Young's view, see p. 109).

One final hymn can conclude our excursion into specific hymn histories: "Lo, he comes with clouds descending." MEC 1822 includes two tunes, Wesley's own choice (*Select Hymns with Tunes Annext*, 1765) of HELMSLEY and Leach's JUDG-

MENT, renamed LAST DAY. The 1833 edition adds a third tune, MOUNT CALVARY by Uri K. Hill. By the 1837 publication *The Harmonist*, ZION from Thomas Hastings's *Spiritual Songs for Social Worship* (1831–32) appears with this text. One of the core tunes identified by Graham, ZION reflects the move from English tunes to American "better music" tunes. MEC 1857 and 1867 continue to pair the text with ZION; it is also one of the choices in MECS 1860. In MEC 1878 and 1905 it is paired with NOVELLO, a tune of uncertain origin arranged by the British editor Vincent Novello. AMEC 1898 uses ADVENT HYMN and MPC 1901 HAMDEN. By 1989, the United Methodist Church had returned to HELMSLEY, while the *Hymnal 1982* (Episcopal) includes both HELMSLEY and NOVELLO.

Just what can we learn from this foray into the tunes used for Wesleyan texts? First, we discover that the texts inherited from England became part of the American Methodist context through the use of tunes appropriate to that culture. Second, we see that the musical settings of Wesleyan texts, like the texts themselves, represented a fairly stable aspect of musical life. They were a continuation of hymn tunes for recognizable metric patterns, not the newer gospel tunes where tune and text were inextricably bound together. Third, we realize that the gradual expectation that certain tunes and texts belonged together eventually encouraged certain pairings that lasted through the twentieth century. Composers of the twenty-first century continue to find Wesley's texts worth setting in musical idioms of this era, as witnessed by the publication of new musical settings (see Chapter 8). The music continues to have the power to bring Wesley's texts to new generations of Christians as they journey toward perfection.

Methodist Musical Life

American Methodist music of the nineteenth century went well beyond the singing of Charles Wesley's texts and well beyond the official publications of the churches. Beginning in the early part of the century, Methodists took part in camp meetings, an area of particular musical fertility. There are very few tunes preserved from early camp meetings, but from the texts and from descriptions of the meetings we learn that the camp meeting was an important place of cultural exchange in primarily rural America. Americans of both European and African descent attended and had the opportunity to overhear each other's music. The music sung came from oral cultures of African origin, from the folk traditions of Scotland and England, and from American permutations of those traditions. The songs included refrains, the interpolation of "shouting words," and other repetitive characteristics that made them easy to sing. Like many of the important developments in church music of the nineteenth century, camp-meeting music was not confined to a specific denomination. Yet Methodists led the movement after its earliest years, and its practices affected the music of the denomination, especially in rural parts of the country.

In the Northeast, the "better music" movement influenced the taste of Methodists. Lowell Mason worked to improve the state of American music away from the untutored harmonies of such American composers as William Billings and Lewis Edson toward the prevailing understanding of harmony and counterpoint in European music. To further that aim, Mason adapted many European tunes to fit the prevalent hymn meters and composed many pieces himself. Within Methodist hymnody, *Sacred Harmony,* published in 1848, epitomized the move toward European music, including many examples of Anglican chant as well as hymn tunes from European and American composers. This volume clearly aimed to please the market in the northeastern part of the United States. In 1849 the MEC published a new tune book, *The Devotional Harmonist,* to accompany its new book of texts. It served as a corrective to the somewhat elitist nature of *Sacred Harmony.*

As Methodism grew and developed in this era, it moved from a church of circuit-riding pastors, assisted by lay class leaders, to an organized denomination with clergy resident in specific churches. As A. Gregory Schneider suggests, the focus of development shifted from the class meeting and making disciples of adults to the home and the nurture of children in the faith. Simultaneously, "a church focused increasingly on enterprise began to value the activity-centered patterns of voluntary associations more than the feeling-centered rituals of social religion" (Schneider: 197). One of these voluntary associations was the singing school or choral society. These groups, which often met weekly, created a tension between spirit-filled congregational music making and the more professionally led choir renditions of hymns and anthems. Although the stated intent of such organizations was to revitalize and aid congregational singing, onlookers often commented that they in fact discouraged singing, especially among those who did not read music (Yardley 1999a: 48–53).

In the post–Civil War period, many churches professionalized music even further by hiring a paid quartet to serve as a "quartet choir" (see C. Young 1993: 67–73 for coverage of urban Methodist music). These "choirs" included only the four paid soloists and no other members. Often they performed entire oratorios on Sunday afternoons or evenings. Parts of the Northeast also felt the impact of the Oxford movement on choral singing. Some churches began to vest their choir, even going so far as to imitate the Anglican phenomenon of a choir of men and boys. For example, an 1897 picture of such a choir from the Grace Methodist Episcopal Church in Worcester, Massachusetts, is reproduced in *Souvenir History of the New England Conference* (214).

The shift of emphasis to evangelizing children often meant that children's musical education centered in the Sunday school. The music-publishing industry produced a steady stream of songbooks aimed at the Sunday-school market from midcentury on. Mason himself was heavily involved, publishing music intended specifically for children and teaching music in the Boston public schools without payment to demonstrate the importance of including it in the curriculum. His pupil William B. Bradbury (1816–1868) created a real industry out of this market. Bradbury, composer of "Jesus loves me," published such volumes as *Fresh Laurels for the Sabbath School* (1867) and *Bright Jewels for the Sunday School* (1869). Although neither Mason nor Bradbury was a Methodist, their work profoundly affected the styles and goals of Methodist church music.

Sunday schools participated fully in the trend toward the conflation of sacred and secular on patriotic occasions. As Schneider comments, "using the Sunday school as their chief instrument, the evangelical churches turned July 4 into the cult day of the Protestant God, American flag, and middle-class domestic circle" (Schneider: 155). Such cults need music, and Sunday school hymnals happily supplied patriotic songs mingled with hymns. Musically these songs offered simple and rather static harmonic structures with considerable repetition. Both camp-meeting music and popular music of the time influenced the style of music composed for the Sunday school. As Edith Blumhofer describes it, the marriage of "light melodies and assuring words" gave hymns an important part in Sunday school pedagogy (182).

One of Bradbury's most significant moves was to create an association between his publishing company, later Biglow and Main, and the author Fanny J. Crosby (1820–1915), the most influential Methodist hymn writer after Charles Wesley. The beginning of her career overlapped the end of Bradbury's. Bradbury and Crosby collaborated on over twenty hymns, several of which appeared in *Fresh Laurels for the Sabbath School*. One of the patterns that Crosby followed was to take a tune and then write the words to go with it. For example, Phoebe Knapp composed a tune and played it for Fanny Crosby, who then said that it spoke to her of "Blessed Assurance." Thus a hymn was born (Blumhofer: 229). From Ex. 6.3, showing the first line of the hymn (Sankey: 151), the basic rhythmic pattern of three eighth-notes followed by two dotted quarters is evident. This pattern repeats throughout the song, and Crosby's words fit it aptly. The regular rhythm and the simple harmonic progressions are hallmarks of this style.

This close relationship between text and tune is a hallmark of not only the Sunday-school hymn, but also of the closely related gospel hymn, the genre with which Fanny Crosby and Howard Doane (1832–1915), who composed music to over 130 of Fanny's texts, are most closely connected. The gospel hymn arose to serve the needs of evangelists wooing a large audience more than those of Sunday-morning worship. Indeed, nineteenth-century Christians had a clear understanding of the differences among musical styles appropriate to specific kinds of religious situations: Sunday-morning worship, class meetings, Sunday school, home worship, and civic gatherings, for example.

The rise of gospel hymnody accompanied the popularity of such revivalists as Dwight Moody (1837–1899), who usually traveled with his musical partner Ira Sankey. In such situations, the music needs to have an immediate accessibility and

EX. 6.3. Phoebe Knapp, BLESSED ASSURANCE, opening (Sankey: 151).

appeal, it needs to prepare people emotionally to accept Jesus as their savior, and it needs to be memorable, so that people will leave the gathering with the words and tune still in their brain, inspired to find a local community of worship.

What kind of music can fulfill these expectations? The music of gospel hymns tends to be in a major key, to make use of repetition, to use the three primary chords of the key extensively, and to have a slow harmonic rhythm (the rate at which the chords change). Additionally, many gospel hymns have a refrain that further reinforces the textual message and embeds the music in the listener's brain. All of these features combine to create a genre that superbly fulfills its function as a vehicle for texts that call sinners to repentance and to the experience of joy that comes with the acceptance of Jesus. Gospel hymns share many musical traits with their earlier counterparts, camp-meeting hymns. Both rely on a style that is easily grasped by those in the congregation.

This repertory has often been criticized for its predictability, its banality, and the "Jesus and me" emphasis of its texts. Yet when understood in the context of purely evangelical events rather than as part of the ongoing worship life of a congregation, many of these features are perhaps essential to their purpose. It is clear that for music to be effective, it must have the right degree of predictability, which may be higher for a mass audience than for an elite one. The recent work of cognitive psychologist Daniel J. Levitin has described the ways in which our brains create "schemas" for understanding music expectations of the overall structure of a type of music and of the specific chords and melodies we might hear (Levitin: 240–46). For people who were being exposed to gospel hymnody for the first time, a close relationship to the popular music of the time allowed them to experience the hymns positively. For many musicians, the predictability makes the music unbearably banal.

Methodists were actively involved in the creation of this hymnody; indeed, Fanny Crosby is estimated to have contributed over nine thousand texts herself, but it was a cross-denominational American movement. Doane, for example, was a Baptist. Thus, as with several other trends (camp meetings, the "better music" movement, Sunday-school hymnody), the incorporation of gospel hymnody into American Methodist circles was part of the inculturation of the precepts of the Wesleys into the milieu of the United States.

Of equal importance in the latter part of the nineteenth and into the twentieth century was the importation of Victorian hymn tunes from England. The Anglican Church embraced hymn singing wholeheartedly during this period (Bradley), and many of its hymn tunes found their way to America. Some became the bedrock of urban congregations. For example, my research (unpublished) on hymn singing at the Highland Park Methodist Church in Dallas shows that the tunes of English composers John Bacchus Dykes, Frederick Maker, Henry Smart, John Hatton, Edward Hopkins, and Samuel Sebastian Wesley took their place alongside those of American composers Lowell Mason and Richard Willis as the most frequently sung in 1937 and 1947. This legacy from the nineteenth century still endures in many congregations today.

An essay of this length can only begin to hint at the rich trove of music associated with American Methodism in the nineteenth century. As Methodists came to populate all parts of the country and a great many walks of life, so too their music drew on the wide variety of musical styles that coexisted during the period. Music was, in many ways, an intensely local phenomenon reflecting the social status, geographic location, and ethnic nature of the worshipping community. The larger denominational bodies provided many resources and the texts of Charles Wesley continued to weave theological principles into this tapestry. Yet in the end, the resources and predilections of each local community created suitably varied sounds, all of them legitimately Methodist, to offer praise to God.

I would like to thank Carlton Young for his gracious and helpful comments on a draft of this article. He helpfully provided several additional references and shared some of his unpublished work.

CHAPTER 7

Eucharistic Piety in American Methodist Hymnody (1786–1889)

Geoffrey C. Moore

Introduction

Methodists have always been a singing people. Louis Benson asserts that the Methodist movement "recovered the emotional fervor of the first singing of vernacular psalms by the Huguenots, and repeated the spiritual triumphs of Reformation Psalmody," permanently enriching English hymnody in the process (220). But Benson does not address the way in which Methodist hymnody shaped the movement itself. Both John and Charles Wesley understood the power of hymns to communicate theology and inculcate doctrine. And although neither brother was a systematic theologian, they penned, published, and distributed hymns on almost every conceivable Christian subject and doctrine.

John and Charles Wesley's eucharistic zeal is widely known and appreciated, and one finds no better window on their thought and theology than the collection of 166 hymns titled *Hymns on the Lord's Supper* (J. and C. Wesley 1745: hereafter *HLS*). The Wesleys "regarded the Lord's Supper as the crown of Christian worship, and held it in profoundest reverence. This book of 1745 is the witness of their desire that their followers should share their views" (Benson: 251). The collection is prefaced by John's "extract" of a seventeenth-century treatise by Daniel Brevint (1616–95), dean of Lincoln, titled *The Christian Sacrament and Sacrifice.* John Wesley did not merely appropriate Brevint's work here but sought to redirect eucharistic theology and piety away from memorialism—a view of the Eucharist that holds that it is commemorative of Jesus and that there is no "real presence" of Christ other than in a purely symbolic sense—and toward a more Catholic theology than prevailed among Anglicans. Brevint divided his treatise into eight sections, each dealing with an aspect of sacramental theology. While the collection of hymns closely parallels Brevint's structure and themes, Wesley made minor adjustments by dividing the hymns into six sections:

> Section I: As it is a Memorial of the Sufferings and Death of CHRIST
> Section II: As it is a Sign and a Means of Grace
> Section III: The SACRAMENT a Pledge of HEAVEN

Section IV: The HOLY EUCHARIST as it implies a Sacrifice
Section V: Concerning the Sacrifice of our Persons
Section VI: After the SACRAMENT

But how was such a shift appropriated by the Wesleys' followers? If one accepts the premise that "poetry, sung in public congregations, sinks into the soul; and sentiments thus imbibed are regarded by multitudes with reverence scarce inferior to that which belongs only to holy writ" (Floy: 169), then a survey of the appearance of hymns from *HLS* in American Methodist hymnbooks may reveal something about what was available to "sink into the soul." While mere frequency of printing does not establish frequency of use with any certainty, an examination of what was printed should at least reveal what was thought useful on the part of hymnbook editors and General Conferences, if not also what was believed to "have been tested by long usage, and have become indispensable for popular use" (MEC 1878: vi; see Appendix 2). To this end, the Wesleys' topical division of the hymn collection into sections (hereafter *HLS* I, *HLS* II, etc.) will play a key role in analyzing the types of hymns appropriated by the American Methodists and whether they chose to walk through the door the Wesleys opened up to a less memorialist and more sacrificial eucharistic theology. Since the doxological statement in hymns (i.e., explicit and implicit statements of praise directed toward God for his glorification; see Berger: 17–23) is found not only in the text, but also in the music itself, then the types of tunes chosen to transform these hymns into songs may be revealing, as well.

The three largest Methodist denominations from the formation of the American church in 1784 through the close of the nineteenth century were the Methodist Episcopal Church (hereafter MEC), the Methodist Episcopal Church, South (MECS), and the Methodist Protestant Church (MPC). With few exceptions, the hymns from *HLS* enter American Methodist hymnody in four groups: the first three introduced in specific hymnals, and the fourth resulting from a series of mid-nineteenth-century revisions between 1837 and 1849 associated with the various divisions in the denomination. I will consider each of these groups separately, with a representative hymn from each discussed in detail.

Group 1. *A Collection of Hymns for the Use of the People Called Methodists*

Of the eight eucharistic hymns in this collection (J. Wesley 1780), none were taken from *HLS* I or II. Three are from III and placed under headings such as "Describing Heaven." A single hymn is from IV and placed under the heading "For Believers Brought to Birth." The remaining four are from V and all placed under "For Believers Saved." Of those that were to remain in the repertory during the nineteenth century, the ones from V are placed under "Petition," "For Full Redemption," and various headings dealing with sanctification. The single hymn in this group from IV did not make a significant contribution to the repertory, for it fell out after MEC 1836. The three hymns from III migrated through various sections dealing with heaven, death, and the communion of saints. Therefore, as a result of the way the hymns in this collection were incorporated into the broader corpus of hymnody, although they were drawn from across the theological spectrum of *HLS*, none of them was ever directly associated with the Eucharist. Consequently, their eucharistic imagery was weakened or lost altogether, and their contribution to *eucharistic* theology and piety is, at the very least, questionable. None of these hymns ever appears in any future hymnbook under a eucharistic heading, a fact one could attribute to Wesley's original placement of them in the 1780 *Collection*. It should be kept in mind, as Robin Leaver points out in Chapter 3, that Wesley intended his *Collection* "merely to be used by the *Society*," where the sacraments were rarely observed, and "was never designed by him to subserve all the purposes of a Church Hymn Book" ("The New Hymn Book": 69). Thus one would not expect to find hymnody supporting eucharistic theology and piety in the 1780 *Collection*. Instead, it seems fairly clear from the multiple and frequent printings of *HLS* that it was to serve this purpose as an independent supplement.

Representative of this group of hymns is "Happy the souls to Jesus joined" (III:96). In his 1780 *Collection*, John Wesley assigned the tune SPITALFIELDS to this text. This tune is found first in Thomas Butts's *Harmonia-Sacra* and was named after one of Wesley's early London chapels (Hildebrandt: 784). SPITAL-FIELDS exhibits what Louis Benson would describe as the "old Methodist" style (see Scholes: 637; Temperley 2001), one notable characteristic of which is the frequent use of melismas (two or more notes for a single syllable) (Benson: 240). The text "Happy the souls" is included in the first American edition of *A Pocket Hymn Book* (MEC 1786; see C. Young 1993: 100–105) and carried through every edition of that book and of *The Methodist Pocket Hymn-Book* (MEC 1803).

Unlike other texts in MEC 1786, which were assigned tunes beginning with the eleventh edition in 1790, "Happy the souls" was not assigned a tune until after the appearance of James Evans's *David's Companion* in 1808. This is interesting for two reasons. First, evidence indicates that the editors of MEC 1786 had copies of Wesley's 1780 *Collection* available to them. Second, reference to certain tunes in the eleventh edition of MEC 1786 indicate that the editors had access to one of Wesley's or Butts's tune collections, since some of these tunes had not yet appeared in any American collection. These two facts suggest that the editors would have been aware of Wesley's preference for SPITALFIELDS and had access to the tune. But Evans set the text to DEVIZES, which marks the first time for this pairing, and his choice was then followed by the editors of MEC 1786. A "tune-with-extension" which received antiphonal treatment in most sources, DEVIZES became part of the core Methodist repertory for the nineteenth century (Graham: 62).

The editors of the church's first major hymnbook revision (MEC 1821) chose another antiphonal tune-with-extension, SUFFOLK. This tune did not enjoy much popularity, as it dropped out of the repertory after the 1837 edition of *The Harmonist.* In the 1836 revised and corrected edition of MEC 1821, the editors returned to the previous choice of DEVIZES. This pairing appears to have had some appeal, as "Happy the souls" was assigned DEVIZES in *Hymns for the Use of the Methodist Episcopal Church, Revised Edition with Tunes* (MEC 1857) and the *Wesleyan Hymn and Tune Book* (MECS 1860).

Any relative stability in tune-text association quickly dissipated. In the 1860 hymnbook of the MPC's eastern and southern Conferences, *Hymn Book of the Methodist Protestant Church* (MPC 1860), the editors chose to assign "Happy the souls" the tune BATH CHAPEL. The move away from an antiphonal tune-with-extension to a "plain" tune—one without text repetition and, for the most part, homorhythmic with all four parts active throughout (Graham: 19)—may have been due to the influence of Lowell Mason, discussed in Chapter 6. BATH CHAPEL appears only once in the repertory (Hill: 409). The MPC's next official hymn book to include tunes, *The Tribute of Praise* (MPC 1882), assigns the text to another plain tune, BALERMA.

The MEC and MECS moved in different directions. The MEC, in its last hymnbook of the nineteenth century (MEC 1878), assigned "Happy the souls" to William Croft's perennial favorite ST. ANNE's. The MECS demonstrated the greater influence of the revival tune by choosing HEBER (MECS 1874b, 1880). First appearing in *The Devotional Harmonist,* HEBER, with its simple melody and harmony and its dotted rhythms, represents a transition between the revival tunes of the first half of the century and the gospel tunes of its second half. MECS 1889, which was patterned after MEC 1878, followed the northern church's lead and assigned "Happy the souls" to ST. ANNE's.

Group 2. *A Pocket Hymn Book*

The group of eleven *HLS* hymns introduced in the new *Pocket Hymn Book* 5th edition (MEC 1786) constitutes the second largest to enter the American Methodist repertory. Nine of them were used to create its "Sacramental" section. Of these, four were taken from *HLS* I, five from *HLS* II. They would form the core of the "Sacramental" section for all subsequent hymnbooks of the nineteenth century. One additional hymn from II was included under "Petitions." The only hymn included in this group outside I and II was taken from VI under the heading "Praise."

Representative of this group of hymns is "Jesu, dear, redeeming Lord" (II:33). Once it entered the corpus of American hymnody in MEC 1786, it remained a rather stable part of the repertory throughout the period under consideration. It was, however, paired with nine different tunes in eleven different appearances. MEC 1786 assigned it PLYMOUTH. Although this tune may very well be based on the German hymn "Ich begehr nicht mehr zu leben," it was first named PLYMOUTH by Butts. The tune was subsequently adopted by Wesley in slightly altered form (cf. *HTI* 917c, 917d). Although it is unclear whether the reference in

MEC 1786 is to Butts's or Wesley's version—only the former was ever printed in America—both demonstrate characteristics of the old Methodist style: frequent melismatic treatment, simple harmonic motion, and a wide melodic range, usually of an octave or more.

The editors of MEC 1803 assigned the tune HARTS by Benjamin Milgrove. As found in Evans's *David's Companion,* the source from which all the tunes were drawn, HARTS (Illus. 7.1) is presented as a "4 lines 7s" tune followed by a sixteen-measure, four-phrase hallelujah. While subsequent appearances of HARTS dropped the hallelujah refrain structure and may be classified as an antiphonal tune-with-extension, Evans's version can be classified as a revival tune (Baldridge: 451). To the modern ear, its choice seems mismatched to the temperament of the text. The words evoke a tender intimacy as sinners seek to find Christ and experience his healing forgiveness in the breaking of the bread. The second and third stanzas capture this sentiment:

> In the rite thou hast enjoined
> Let us now our saviour find,
> Drink thy blood for sinners shed,
> Taste thee in the broken bread.
>
> Thou our faithful hearts prepare,
> Thou thy pardoning grace declare;
> Thou that hast for sinners died,
> Show thyself the crucified.

This scene is in stark contrast to the mood created by HARTS. The time signature Evans indicates for the tune, 2/4, is his quickest tempo marking, giving the

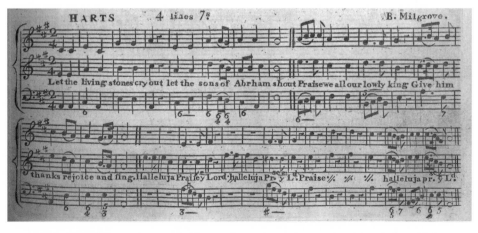

ILLUS. 7.1. Milgrove, HARTS (Evans: 35). Reproduction courtesy of the Kathryn Sullivan Bowld Music Library, Southwestern Baptist Theological Seminary.

feeling of a *gavotte* or *rigaudon* (Evans: 4). His version of HARTS is, in fact, just the sort of tune to which John Wesley objected (C. Young 1995a: 95).

And yet for early American Methodists, a tune such as HARTS may have conveyed an important aspect of eucharistic piety that was not otherwise communicated in a text like "Jesu, dear, redeeming Lord" and thus represented an important and distinct *American* stamp on Methodist hymn singing. As Lester Ruth has convincingly argued, the early American Methodist celebrations of the Eucharist that took place during quarterly meetings often involved a great deal of evangelical fervor. It was here that "the intense sensibility of God's presence led Methodists to experience what they called 'raptures' or 'ecstasies' of joy in the sacrament" (Ruth: 138). The choice of HARTS may have provided precisely the evangelical zeal needed to balance the more subdued and penitential aspects of the text. If this is the case, then it would find resonance in the preference, already demonstrated, for the more florid old Methodist style of tunes such as SPITALFIELDS, PLYMOUTH, and even to some extent DEVIZES and SUFFOLK. Further evidence for this tendency may be found in the fact that the tunes assigned to *HLS* texts in general show a higher frequency of "non-plain" tunes, that is tunes-with-extension, antiphonal tunes, and antiphonal tunes-with-extension, than the general repertory. Baldridge has shown that the number of non-plain tunes constitutes 61 percent of the total number of hymn tunes in *David's Companion* (Baldridge: 204–7). Yet of the twenty *HLS* texts assigned tunes in MEC 1786 and its subsequent *Supplement* (MEC 1808), 68 percent are assigned non-plain tunes. This difference seems to indicate a bias toward tunes in which the music's structure is more complex than that of the text, so that the text does not govern the music, as in a plain tune. Such tunes often demonstrate a wider range of emotional expression.

Any evangelical fervor the tune may have brought to the hymn, however, was quickly domesticated by the text. In each of the following series of hymnbooks for the northern church, "Jesu, dear, redeeming Lord" is set to a plain tune. MEC 1821 assigns the tune CONDOLENCE, also known as PLEYEL's HYMN or GERMAN HYMN. When the hymnbook was revised in 1836, the editors decided to assign the tune NUREMBURG (*HTI* 923a, d). Both of these tunes are in the core repertory (Graham: 89, 98) and congruent with the growing influence of the "better music" movement with their conservative harmony, syllabic text setting, and diatonic melodies in a narrow range, generally no more than an octave. In MEC 1857, "Jesu, dear, redeeming Lord" is assigned the plain tune ST. LOUIS, written by Isaac Baker Woodbury (1819–1858) for this same text. ST. LOUIS has an extremely static harmony and a melody marked to be sung "with earnestness," which may further demonstrate the growing influence of the text over the tune, as noted above. MEC 1878 assigned INNOCENTS, an anonymous tune new to American Methodism that had first appeared in *The Parish Choir*, a London monthly, in November 1850.

GEOFFREY C. MOORE

The MECS chose two different plain tunes, COSTELLOW and PUMROY, for 1860 and 1874 respectively. Of unknown authorship, COSTELLOW appears to have entered the repertory in Woodbury's *Lute of Zion*. Other than an appearance in *The Wesleyan Sacred Harp* (1854), it did not join the repertory. PUMROY first appears in MECS 1860, attributed to the compiler, Leonard C. Everett (1818–1867). With its predictable harmonic movement, pedestrian rhythm, and prosaic melody, PUMROY may be a classic example of what one reviewer of the hymnbook called tunes of "*Everett-ish* origin . . . which this compiler has attempted to foist upon the public" (Bonnell: 498–99). In MECS 1889, the southern church returned to the 1836 choice of the northern church and set "Jesu, dear, redeeming Lord" to the plain tune NUREMBURG.

While the MECS appears to have followed the lead of the northern church in moving toward more conservative plain tune settings, the MPC did not at first. It seems to have followed the earlier inclinations of Evans's choice of HART's and assigned the tune HENDON to the text. Although a nineteenth-century composition, this antiphonal tune-with-extension by Genevan French Reform hymnist Henri Abraham César Malan (1787–1864) recalls the old Methodist style, with its range exceeding an octave, intermittent two-note melismas, antiphonal voicing, and text repetition. The pairing may not have been very successful, however, for the text was assigned to PLEYEL's HYMN (CONDOLENCE) in the denomination's next hymnbook with tunes, MPC 1882.

Group 3. *Supplement to the Methodist Pocket Hymn Book*

Of the five additional hymns from *HLS* in the *Supplement* (MEC 1808), four are placed under the heading "Christ Our Passover, or The Lord's Supper." All of these hymns come from *HLS* I and II. The remaining hymn, "Jesus drinks the bitter cup," constructed from the fourth, sixth, seventh, and eighth stanzas of "God of unexampled grace" (I:21), is placed under "Redemption."

Representative of this selection is "O thou eternal victim, slain" (I:5). When Francis Asbury, the compiler of the *Supplement to the Methodist Pocket Hymn Book,* assigned it a tune he chose the plain tune WELLS. At the time, this tune was almost as popular as OLD 100TH. It entered the Methodist repertory with *David's Companion*, by which time it had already appeared in excess of 135 times in North America alone, where it remained a part of the core repertory (Graham: 126). WELLS is constructed in a straightforward ABA'B' form, with a time signature of "Ɔ," or very quick, according to Evans's preface (4). As with "Jesu, dear, redeeming Lord," the apparently mismatched affect for a text that speaks of the "bloody hue" of the sacrificial victim's vesture, whom the worshipper now views "bleeding on the tree," may be an attempt to communicate a fervor in eucharistic piety that is lacking in the text. It should also be noted that WELLS is a long-meter tune (8.8.8.8) for which the text (8.8.8.8.8.8) has been altered significantly.

The editors of MEC 1821 chose PLYMOUTH DOCK, a part of the core repertory (Graham: 99). This six-line tune (8.8.8.8.8.8) is found either with a four-line text plus extension or a six-line text, and thus allowed for the restoration of the entire text of "O thou eternal victim, slain." More than likely a nineteenth-century composition, PLYMOUTH DOCK provides another excellent example of the old Methodist style surviving at a time when preference for this style was waning and the "better music" movement was beginning to exercise influence; the persistence of such tunes in association with *HLS* texts exemplifies the observed preference for a more zealous musical expression than is immediately indicated by the text. Yet while such a choice recalls an earlier type of piety, the influence of the trend toward more staid hymnody and tunes governed by the text's affect can be seen in the slight slowing of the tempo of PLYMOUTH DOCK over time, moving from cut time in *David's Companion* to common time in *The Harmonist*.

The same trend continues to be evident in subsequent tune choices for "O thou eternal victim, slain." Indeed, by the time of the 1836 revision of MEC 1821, the preference for non-plain tunes had been reversed, with non-plain tunes representing 39 percent of those assigned to *HLS* texts, as opposed to 48 percent in the semiofficial tune book *The Harmonist*. The 1836 revision of MEC 1821 assigned MINORCA, a plain tune in 2/2 showing some affinity with the old Methodist style but much less than PLYMOUTH DOCK. In the final revision of the 1821 hymnbook, MEC 1857, the editors chose SELENA, despite the fact that PLYMOUTH DOCK remained a part of the repertory. A plain tune by Woodbury, in his *New Lute of Zion* and still part of the repertory today, SELENA eventually became associated with "Victim divine" (*HLS* IV:116), a hymn to be discussed in the next section. SELENA exhibits fairly static harmonic and melodic movement, underscored by the fact that this is an "LM 6 lines" tune, indicating that the first two phrases are repeated. In a slow 3/2, SELENA is much more contemplative than the tunes assigned earlier. *The New Lute of Zion* has it marked "with tenderness." The increasing use of slower, weightier tunes such as SELENA reinforced the tendency to abandon tunes that communicated the seemingly incongruous evangelical enthusiasm of early Methodist eucharistic piety. The choice of these more tender tunes also demonstrates the tendency to allow the tone of the text to shape the choice of tune. SELENA remained the tune of choice in MEC 1878.

While "O thou eternal victim, slain" was not picked up by the MPC, it was by the MECS, which in 1847 placed it under the heading "Mediation of Christ," despite the fact that the MEC first included it under hymns for the Lord's Supper. The first tune assigned to the text in the MECS tradition is FARNSWORTH in 1860. A plain tune of unknown origin, FARNSWORTH remained in the repertory as late as MECS 1889 but was no longer assigned to this text. Much like SELENA, it is an LM 6 tune in 3/4. The appearance of passing-tone activity in multiple parts and a range expanded past the octave, however, demonstrate a movement away from the "better music" movement. Instead of FARNSWORTH, MECS 1889 assigned the more conservative WORTH, a plain tune by Mason set in 3/2 meter with the feeling of an old psalm tune.

Group 4. Mid-Nineteenth-Century Additions

The creation of the MPC in 1828 and the MECS in 1844 brought about significant changes in Methodist hymnody during the second quarter of the nineteenth century. Having split from the MEC over issues surrounding slavery, the episcopacy, and church government, both these denominations needed to create their own hymnbooks. They did so in 1837 and 1847, respectively. In the midst of these divisions, the MEC revised its hymnbook twice: in 1836 the Book Concern issued a revised and corrected edition of MEC 1821 with a supplement added; and in 1849, at the direction of the General Conference, an entirely new book was issued, dropping the designation "A Collection of," which had been in use since Wesley published his 1780 *Collection,* in favor of simply *Hymns for the Use of the Methodist Episcopal Church* (MEC 1849). The slight change may be an indication that the Church was consciously moving away from using Wesley's *Collection* as a framework for its hymnody and seeking a broader representation of hymns. Not only did the number of hymnbooks increase during this period, but so did their size. MEC 1849 contained 1,148 hymns, almost double the number of the 1836 edition. Such a growth in the Church's hymnody is also reflected in the number of *HLS* hymns that entered the repertory.

There are seventeen new hymns from *HLS* in this group: one was added in the 1836 supplement to MEC 1821, four in MPC 1837, and twelve in MECS 1847. Seven of these twelve were included two years later in MEC 1849. Of the seventeen hymns in the group, only seven come from *HLS* I or II, an apparent indication that the churches were moving their sacramental theology in a new direction. And, in fact, seven of the remaining ten hymns were drawn from across III, IV, V, and VI and placed under some type of sacramental heading: six by the MECS and four by the MEC. The only hymn included under the heading of sacramental hymns by the MPC comes from *HLS* I.

Representative of this group is "Victim divine, thy grace we claim" (IV:116). In his unparalleled work *Methodist Hymnology* (1848), David Creamer, who served on the revision committee for MEC 1849, asserted of "Victim divine" that perhaps a better example "could not be given, nor one that would exhibit more favorably [Charles Wesley's] power to transmute the sober realities of prose into the most exalted strains of sacred song" (128). Yet of the *HLS* texts, it is one of the latest to be adopted by the American churches and, in turn, one of the quickest to depart. It is included in MECS 1847 and MEC 1849, but it is not assigned a tune until MEC 1857. Here, the 88.88.88 text is matched to the antiphonal tune BRIGHTON, most often associated with "O love divine, what hast thou done." BRIGHTON evidently enjoyed some popularity, appearing a total of seven times in the repertory (Hill: 423). A true 8.8.8.8.8.8 tune, rather than an LM tune with the last two lines repeated to accommodate a six-line text, it is composed in 2/2, and while the antiphonal treatment can vary, it is almost always present. Although it exhibits some fleeting affinity for the old Methodist style, *New Lute for Zion* has it marked "not too fast," a designation consistent with the trend to replace the older style with a more reverent musical expression. Attributed simply as "English," BRIGHTON may exhibit some folk-tune influences with its mostly stepwise motion, only occasional intervallic skips of a third, and descent of an octave to the tonic on the last phrase. BRIGHTON remains the only tune assigned to "Victim divine" in the MEC tradition, as the text is dropped from the repertory for MEC 1878.

The MECS tradition offers two tunes for "Victim divine." MECS 1860 assigns the plain tune PESCUD. This rhythmically regular tune in 3/2 meter may be precisely the kind of "Everett variety" railed against earlier—it appears only once in the entire repertory. The tune selected for MECS 1874b, BEVERLY, may not have been much more successful. In the preface the editors remark that "while the book should contain tunes suited to the great body of hymns in our standard Hymn-book, other tunes and hymns of a popular character should be inserted, to adapt the work to the wants and tastes of the Connection at large. Special pains have been taken to secure this end" (iii). Given that the antiphonal BEVERLY appears only in MECS 1874b set to "Victim divine," one may safely presume that it represents one of the "hymns of a popular character" inserted into the book in order to adapt it to the "tastes of the Connection." Whether such a conclusion is true or not, the manner in which the center portion of the tune contrasts with the outer portions gives BEVERLY a rather odd character (Illus. 7.2). The wide leaps of the opening and closing phrases lend the tune a stately air, recalling the gestures of earlier tunes such as ST. ANNE'S; the opening gesture, in fact, seems to parody the perennially popular LONDON NEW in the form adopted by John Playford (1623–1686). But the imitation in the interior antiphonal section harks back to a late-eighteenth-century antiphonal tune, and the stepwise movement in thirds and melodic sequencing between the voices recall a revival or camp-meeting tune of the early nineteenth century. It is almost as if two tunes had been put together. Whether this interruption of an otherwise august plain tune is merely an echo of a former style or a deliberate attempt to recall an earlier, more fervent piety is impossible to determine. As an antiphonal tune, BEVERLY is certainly not alone in the repertory; the MECS continued to use antiphonal tunes through the end of the century. But no other antiphonal tunes demonstrate BEVERLY's internal contrast, perhaps a faint manifestation of the apparent tension noted earlier between the evangelical ardor of some tunes and the more somber commemorative and penitential mood of texts with which those tunes were paired.

228   BEVERLY. 8,8,8,8,8,8. (1st P. M.)   (306)

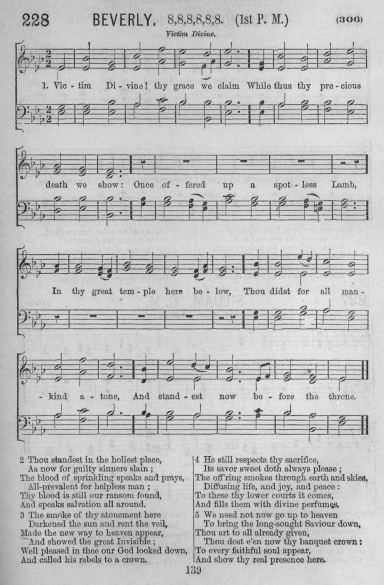

2 Thou standest in the holiest place,
   As now for guilty sinners slain ;
The blood of sprinkling speaks and prays,
   All-prevalent for helpless man ;
Thy blood is still our ransom found,
And speaks salvation all around.

3 The smoke of thy atonement here
   Darkened the sun and rent the veil,
Made the new way to heaven appear,
   And showed the great Invisible ;
Well pleased in thee our God looked down,
And called his rebels to a crown.

4 He still respects thy sacrifice,
   Its savor sweet doth always please ;
The off'ring smokes through earth and skies,
   Diffusing life, and joy, and peace :
To these thy lower courts it comes,
And fills them with divine perfumes.

5 We need not now go up to heaven
   To bring the long-sought Saviour down,
Thou art to all already given,
   Thou dost e'en now thy banquet crown :
To every faithful soul appear,
And show thy real presence here.

139

ILLUS. 7.2. BEVERLY (MECS 1874b). Reproduction courtesy of the Kathryn Sullivan Bowld Music Library, Southwestern Baptist Theological Seminary.

Wesleyan Hymnody and American Piety

These observations raise the question: Is music shaping belief, or is belief shaping music? Did the influence of the "better music" movement and the slow march toward more stoic and formal hymn tunes eventually dampen the evangelical zeal with which early Methodists approached the Eucharist, to the extent that by the middle of the nineteenth century their disposition gravitated toward memorialism? Or did the messages about eucharistic theology that Methodists were repeating over and over again in their worship eventually influence their musical choices? Certainly the trend toward more formal hymn tunes was not restricted to eucharistic hymns. The force of this movement, therefore, must be viewed as something shaping eucharistic hymns from the outside rather than the other way around. In this way it may have helped to emphasize the more somber, penitential messages that already dominated the churches' eucharistic texts. At the same time, hymn singing is more than a musical performance. It is a doxological statement that involves the profession of a text that carries a theological message. As pointed out earlier, the door the Wesleys had intended to open for their followers led to a message much broader than mere memorialism. Again, their topical division of the hymn collection will shed some important light on the questions posed here.

The hymnbook revisions of the middle of the nineteenth century seemed to offer some hope for the American Methodists to embrace the full depth of Wesleyan eucharistic hymnody and, by extension, theology. By the time MECS 1847 and MEC 1849 appeared, forty-one hymns from *HLS* had joined the repertory (25 percent of the *HLS* collection), although seven of these had already permanently dropped out of the church's hymnody. Of the remaining thirty-four hymns seventeen come from *HLS* I and II, the sections which deal with the sacrament as a memorial of Christ's suffering and death and as a sign and means of grace. Seven come from sections dealing with the sacrament as sacrifice (IV and V), and six from the section dealing with the sacrament as a pledge of heaven (III). Thus, although there is a slight bias toward the memorial and means of grace aspects of the sacrament, the collection is represented in a fairly balanced manner.

The Americans' embrace of the Wesleys' eucharistic hymnody was not to last. As we have seen, by the time the hymnbooks of the middle of the century were issued, revival tunes and non-plain tunes had already shown a marked decline in preference and "better music" formality had firmly taken hold. These musical influences supported the already firmly established eucharistic piety. When the MPC published its last hymnal of the century (MPC 1882), only eight *HLS* hymns were retained. By 1878, the MEC had dropped the count to sixteen. The MECS retained nineteen, but by the time the MEC and MECS issued their joint hymnal (MEC 1905), only one *HLS* hymn would remain, "Let him to whom we now belong" (*HLS* V:157), placed under the heading "The Christian Life: Entire

Consecration and Perfect Love." If from the beginning the genius of the Wesleys was found "precisely in the unity that they saw between a sacramental and an evangelical vision of Christianity" (Crockett: 199), then one must wonder if the American Methodists' handling of the hymns of *HLS* fostered a different eucharistic understanding.

A cursory survey of some of the liturgical practices and attitudes of early American Methodists confirms a drift away from a truly Wesleyan grounding. Although at its founding in 1784 the Church officially adopted John Wesley's *Sunday Service*, which included the celebration of communion every week, that rite was not to remain intact for very long. In 1792 the portion of the ante-communion preliminary to the offertory sentences was discarded. The communion service was divorced from the sermon and relegated to a separate part of the discipline, thus leaving the historic link between Word and Table in doubt. And, perhaps most devastating of all, the church made allowance for an elder who is "straitened for time" to omit everything except the prayer of consecration, leading to the "corruption" of the rite by ministers who freely composed their own material. (Westerfield-Tucker: 125–26.)

While the rite itself drifted toward minimalism on the one hand and extemporaneity on the other, attitudes toward the sacrament gravitated toward memorialism. Philip Gatch (1751–1834), an itinerant minister in the 1770s, copied fourteen hymns from *HLS* into his sermon outline notebook. All save one are from *HLS* I and II. If, as Ruth asserts, Gatch had "ample opportunity to spread this appreciation to other Methodists such as Bishops Francis Asbury and William McKendree, both of whom were frequent visitors to his home" (140), then he was not promoting one of the main elements that shape Wesleyan eucharistic theology: sacrifice. In fact, in 1854 MECS removed the rubrics for the manual acts, which were presumed by some to be "a mimicry of our Saviour's sacrifice—the offering of him as an unbloody sacrifice upon the altar" (Summers: 23). Thomas O. Summers was one of the leading theologians for the MECS in the middle of the nineteenth century. He made this statement in the face of Wesley's assertion in more than one hymn from *HLS;* for instance:

> Ye royal priests of Jesus, rise,
> And join *the daily sacrifice;*
> Join all believers, in His name
> *To offer up the spotless Lamb.* (III:137.1; emphasis added)

In a tradition without any systematic or normative theology outside the sermons and exegetical notes of John Wesley, the hymnic legacy that both Wesleys left behind provides an important norm, albeit hidden, that quietly shaped the identity of the community over time (Berger: 24). And the idea that hymns had a normative effect was not lost on those who shaped and used the hymnals of this earlier period. James Buckley, who would serve on the committee for MEC 1878, observed:

It is also certain that the character of the hymns read and sung by a denomination greatly influences the imagination and the language of those who use them, furnishing much of their religious vocabulary, and stamping peculiar forms of expression upon them. . . . The hymn book must be an embodiment of doctrine, in all particulars in which doctrine is connected with religious emotion. To contradict the teachings of the "Confessions of Faith" and the Catechisms in the hymns is an effectual way to change the sentiments of the people. (Buckley: 311–12)

There can be no doubt that early American Methodists had a deep eucharistic piety—countless journals, notes, and minutes testify to a great hunger for the sacrament (see Ruth: 135–45). But the form that piety eventually took was shaped by particular circumstances and resources, the hymnody of the Church foremost among them. From its formation in 1784, American Methodism chose to embrace a variety of eucharistic hymnody from the Wesleyan tradition that focused on the sacrament as a memorial of Christ's suffering and death and as a sign and means of grace. By the time the editors of Methodist hymnals tried to reshape hymnody (and thereby, presumably piety) in the middle of the nineteenth century, not only were the imaginations of American Methodists already "stamped" with a peculiar form, the language of which had sunk into their souls, but the exuberance of earlier revival tunes, antiphonal tunes, tunes-with-extension, and the like had been replaced by the staid formalism of the "better music" movement. More reverent, even weighty, tunes served to reinforce a simplified and more reverent piety. And although the last half of the nineteenth century would see the rise of the gospel tune, as far as eucharistic piety was concerned the foundation had already been firmly laid. When the various denominations came back to editing their hymnals for the last time before the turn of the century, much of the reshaping attempted in the middle of the century was edited back out.

Conclusion

John and Charles Wesley certainly understood the power of singing to shape belief. They encouraged singing in all their societies as a way to foster evangelical zeal, promote fellowship, and inculcate doctrine. Throughout their ministry, they penned and published countless tune books and hymn collections, each of which offers a window onto their thought and theology. In their tune books, such as *Sacred Melody* and *Sacred Harmony,* they helped perpetuate a style of singing eventually known as "old Methodist," which captured the energy and enthusiasm of their movement. In their 1745 collection *Hymns on the Lord's Supper,* the brothers sought to wed their evangelical movement to a rich sacramentalism and open a door onto a eucharistic theology that went beyond the commemorative and penitential aspects of prevailing Protestant theology and reclaimed some sense of the Eucharist as sacrifice.

American Methodism chose, for whatever reason, not to walk through the
door the Wesleys had tried to open by embracing the full depth of the Wesleyan
eucharistic theology. Subsequent musical choices and trends dampened any lin-
gering eucharistic zeal and reinforced confessional choices. By the time of the
third generation of its adherents, around the middle of the nineteenth century,
its character had been set: a temperament decidedly staid and simple, a creed
decidedly commemorative and penitential. The Wesleys' door remained quietly
and securely shut.

CHAPTER 8

The Musical Settings of Charles Wesley's Hymns (1742 to 2008)

Carlton R. Young

Britain

A remarkable feature of eighteenth-century British Wesleyan worship-song practice is that a divergent people of various educational, religious, social, and economic conditions was taught to sing a basic repertory of hymns, most by Charles Wesley, set to tunes in a number of meters and a variety of musical styles. People sang the same doctrine in their hymns as they heard taught in the Wesleys' sermons (Outler: 102). (Those were the days!) Methodists' essential beliefs were embodied and expressed in Wesley hymns, which in turn were ingrained in the people's hearts by the agency of music. S T Kimbrough, in his foreword to *Music of the Heart,* identifies this quality as lyrical theology, a sung theology (C. Young 1995a: xiii–xiv).

Charles and John Wesley discovered that the most effective means to create the personal and corporate memory of a heart and life filled with self-emptying love is in music of the heart—a uniting of text and music in a symphony of aesthetic emotion, musical/poetical art, and intellect, with Christ's self-giving love at the center. Therefore, they committed their lives to shaping the musical and textual memory of God's people. They formed a lyrical theology by which the faith community could remember who it was and what it was to do. Charles became the lyricist, and John, though also a poet, became the astute collector of tunes.

Methodists, preaching and singing the Wesleyan understanding of the new life in Christ, as set forth in a fourfold doctrine of grace (prevenient, justifying, sanctifying, and perfecting), continued the vital link between preaching and congregational singing, a distinguishing feature of the sixteenth-century German and Swiss reformations and of eighteenth-century English evangelicalism.

It is estimated that Charles Wesley, during his half-century career as co-founder and lyrical theologian of Methodism (1738–88), composed 6,500 hymns and sacred poems. Of these, approximately 200 were published with underlaid first stanzas (that is, printed under the music), and 500 were published with tune names attached though without music. Beginning with the fifth edition (1786) of his definitive *Collection of Hymns for the Use of the People Called Methodists,* John Wesley placed a tune name at the head of each of the 528 hymns, 480 of which were by his brother. These 194 tunes in 31 different meters may be considered John Wesley's definitive choices as settings for these hymns, especially those of his brother: all but one are found in his last tune book, *Sacred Harmony* (J. Wesley 1781b). James T. Lightwood comments, "Wesley evidently approved of the 'fixed tune' system, and would doubtless feel he had done all he could to prevent irresponsible leaders of the singing from introducing new tunes composed by themselves or their friends" (1928: 8).

Wesley's essential task as tune book compiler/publisher was to find suitable tunes for Charles's hymns, composed in an unprecedented variety of meters and rhyming schemes. During John Wesley's final years, the music market he had created began to be exploited by composers and publishers producing collections of familiar and new settings for well-known Wesley hymns, for instance those of James Leach (see Chapter 5). In the first decades of the nineteenth century, the compilers of British Methodist tune collections began the task of maintaining, improving, and adding to the impressive tune repertory established by John, who was Methodism's arbiter of taste and performance practice. Charles's sons, Charles and Samuel, upgraded the quality of the musical settings of their father's hymns. Charles the younger revised and edited his uncle's *Sacred Harmony,* adding figured bass and several new tunes (C. Wesley 1822; JN 182), and Samuel made a bold and musically interesting break with the styles of traditional and emerging Methodist tunes by composing thirty-four settings for four voices, in the twenty-six meters of the hymns in his uncle's 1780 collection (S. Wesley 1828). Samuel's request to have his tune collection published by the Methodist Book Room was turned down, so he published it at his own expense, the Book Room agreeing to sell it. Two years earlier, Samuel had made another and unexpected contribution to the music of his father's hymns. While researching in the Fitzwilliam Collection, Cambridge, he discovered a one-page manuscript of Handel tunes composed for three of Charles Wesley's hymns (S. Wesley 1826). Samuel's arrangements of Handel's tunes entered nineteenth-century Wesleyan tune books. The inclusion of Handel's setting of "Rejoice! The Lord Is King" as GOPSAL in *The English Hymnal* (1906) brought it to the attention of a wider audience, and it was subsequently included in a number of twentieth-century hymnals.

The first post-Wesley tune collection with a degree of authorization was *A Companion to the Wesleyan Hymn-Book,* published by the Wesleyan Conference Office in 1847, consisting of 228 tunes for use with the 1780 collection and its supplement (J. Wesley 1831), together with 18 psalm chants. Other Victorian tune books include Edward Booth's *The Wesleyan Psalmist* (Leeds, 1843); *The Free Methodist Tune Book* (London, 1874); and *The Bristol Tune Book* (London, 1863), with 750 tunes, expanded to 904 by 1891. A new hymnal carrying the old title, *A Collection of Hymns for the People Called Methodists,* was authorized by the Conference in 1874. The music edition (1877) was edited by three prominent non-Methodist church musicians. Henry J. Gauntlett, the designated editor, died in 1875 and was succeeded by George Cooper, organist of the Chapel Royal, who died in 1876. Edward J. Hopkins, music director of the (Anglican) Temple Church, prepared the book for the press; the committee stated in the preface that Hopkins "was not responsible for the selection of the tunes or their appropriation to the hymns." The hymnal retained a number of traditional Methodist tunes set in four-part Victorian style, as well as psalm tunes, English hymn tunes, chorales, and both familiar and newly composed Victorian-style tunes influenced by *Hymns Ancient and Modern* (London, 1861). Hymn texts were not underlaid, and texts were sometimes cross-referenced to appropriate tunes elsewhere in the book.

The music edition of *The Methodist Hymn-Book with Tunes* (1904) was edited by Sir Frederick Bridge, King Edward professor at the University of London and organist of Westminster Abbey. According to the preface, Bridge "drew largely on the work of the great composers of the last generation, and of others happily still with us, whose names are household words in Christian homes, and whose tunes have done so much to elevate popular taste in Church music." He added, "It will be of interest to state that of the [more than 600] tunes and chants included in this book 93 were composed specially for it."

Of its 991 musical settings, 192 were contributed by four composers: John Bacchus Dykes (55), Joseph Barnby (42), Arthur Sullivan (33), and Bridge himself (29). Bridge's penchant for upgrading Methodist music is seen in his retention of the sturdy sixteenth-century psalm tune WINCHESTER as the setting for "O for a thousand tongues to sing," arguably the signature hymn of Methodists, while relegating old favorites, such as a four-voice LYDIA (*HTI* 11786) and the repeating tune LYNGHAM, to an appendix of "Supplemental Tunes." The rationale is set forth in the preface: "Owing to the revived interest manifested in what are commonly known as 'Old Methodist Tunes,' the Committee has felt justified in placing in an Appendix a select number of those melodies most widely known and used. For these it must assume entire responsibility, though in connexion with them Sir Frederick Bridge has offered valuable suggestions."

The Methodist Hymn-Book with Tunes (1933) includes a greatly expanded tune repertory, much of it coming by way of *The English Hymnal,* which was the book favored by high-church Anglicans. The well-written preface includes the rationale for selecting the music of this collection, presumably prepared on behalf of the committee by its two musical advisers, a Methodist, Maurice L. Wostenholm, succeeded at his death by an Anglican, George F. Brockless. With few exceptions, the 243 Charles Wesley hymns, about a fourth of the 984 in the collection, remained contextualized in eighteenth- and nineteenth-century settings. For the first time in a Methodist collection, the tune SAGINA was matched with "And can it be that I should gain."

The 1933 edition had a remarkable half-century life span, during which the compilers of its several supplements, including the stylistically innovative *Partners in Praise* (1979), did little to diminish the pre- and post-Victorian musical captivity of Wesley's hymns. This captivity extends to the present authorized hymnal, *Hymns and Psalms* (1983). Of its 984 hymns, 203 are by Charles Wesley: they are set to 174 tunes, of which 53 (including arrangements) are from the eighteenth century, 87 from the nineteenth, and 30 composed in the twentieth. Of the latter only one, Donald Swann's FLANDERS, even faintly reflects the compilers' admirable efforts elsewhere in the volume to incorporate a variety of contemporary sounds.

This survey of musical settings of Wesley hymns in British Methodist hymnals can be summarized in these words from the preface to the 1933 collection: "The collection of 1780 was meant to serve a movement, this is to serve a church." Nicholas Temperley describes the transition thus: "[Methodists] moved more clearly in the direction of bourgeois affluence and political conservatism, which tended to be expressed in more formal music" (Temperley 2001). Conservative musical editors of recent British Methodist hymnals have tended to avoid twentieth-century-style musical settings of Wesley's hymns.

The United States

The American Methodist bishop Francis Asbury, in his so-called valedictory address of 1813, described the Methodist Church founded in 1784 in these words: "We were a Church, and no Church," prompting this comment from historian Frederick A. Norwood: "Ever since, Methodists have been trying to decide who they would be, a great church or a holy people" (132). In many respects, Norwood's comment describes the tensions within American Methodism, whose worship music developed in two distinctive locales, each with its own repertory and performance practice: (1) urban seaboard cities and settled places; (2) the expanding frontier.

In the cities, ordained clergy selected and led hymns from collections organized on Wesley's pattern of redemption (*ordo salutis*) authorized by the general Church, and the Church's bishops, following John Wesley's role in British Methodist music, were the authorities and commentators on worship music condemning the singing schools' fuging tunes. While Methodists were discouraged from singing "fuge-tunes" in the congregation, their private use was not considered sinful (*Doctrines* 1798: 122–25). This official prohibition condemned New England composers' most characteristic music and set the developing church's worship music apart from the growing popularity of singing schools. The resulting cultural and musical isolation may explain the relative dearth of Wesley hymns in two important shape-note collections, *Southern Harmony*, 1835, and *The Sacred Harp*, 1845.

The first departure from central authority was the hymnal of the African American Church founded by Richard Allen. It is not referenced to a tune collection, suggesting that the worship song of urban African Americans may have developed from an improvised fusion of English and African styles and rhythms, as J. Roland Braithwaite has pointed out (R. Allen: xlvi; see also Spencer).

On the rural frontier, a new style of Methodist worship music that joined music and dance with preaching was developed by traveling preachers and song leaders, in camp meetings that were held in cleared spaces in the wilderness, the outdoor tabernacle, and improvised meeting-houses. The revival chorus emerged as frontier Methodism's most characteristic song form, its simple repetitive melodies in contrast to the strophic hymn tune repertory in English tune books and the singing school's fuging tunes. (C. Young 1995b: 86.) Season after season, an acceptable body of words and music was formed, and it complemented and expressed the faithful's and the not so faithful's sometimes primitive—albeit unique—tastes, sensitivities, abilities, and needs. Here American Methodism's distinctive music developed without need or benefit of the Church's official collections (Westerfield-Tucker: 159–61; C. Young 1993: 54–61).

In the early nineteenth century, a unique African American variant of the camp meeting song developed in the worship of the southern plantation praise house. Here a designated or impromptu music leader, sometimes the preacher, lined out a psalm, hymn, or spiritual in call-and-response form (later known as "meter music" or "deaconing out"), then led a call-and-response sung prayer and preached-sang "within" a hymn or spiritual. This was followed by a prolonged concluding sung and danced response—the traditional African ring shout. (See Ex. 8.1 for an example of a call-and-response version of Wesley's "A charge to keep I have.")

The hymnody of the newly founded Methodist Episcopal Church, as in British Methodism, was at first usually assembled in privately published pocket hymn-books, in contrast to large collections. The bishops regarded the latter as "admirable indeed, but . . . too expensive for the poor, who have little time and less money" (MEC 1786: iii–iv). Beginning in 1790, these pocket editions included a tune name for each text, apparently with reference to Wesley's tune collections or to Butts's *Harmonia-Sacra*. Reflecting the musical activity of the John Street Methodist Church, New York City, *David's Companion* was the first attempt to produce a comprehensive tune book. It was compiled by James Evans and published in two forms, one (1808) to go with the "Methodist Pocket Hymn-Book," presumably MEC 1803; the other with the "Large Hymn Book," presumably Wesley's 1780 collection.

EX. 8.1. Spiritual, "A charge to keep I have," opening.

(See *HTI:* EvanJDC, EvanJDCM.) In 1808 the Conference gave the tune book tacit approval even though it contained examples of the fuging tunes so repugnant to John Wesley. A supplement was issued in 1820 as *Wesleyan Selection.*

Much work has been done on the tune books of American Methodism (see Graham; Yardley 1999b; Westerfield-Tucker). The first authorized tune book was *The Methodist Harmonist* (MEC 1822), cross-referenced to the 1821 hymnal, itself modeled after Wesley's comprehensive 1780 *Collection.* It was widely used both in congregations and singing schools (Yardley 1999a). By midcentury, the church's authorized hymnals had so greatly expanded that the 1849 hymnal included 1,148 hymns, 553 by Charles Wesley. This edition was the first to have a companion tune book (MEC 1857). Each tune was printed with one stanza underlaid, to be sung to any of the hymns set out on the facing page. However, the sequence of tunes was based on the length and meter of the text, not on the order in which they appeared in the parent book. The result was one of the most confusing formats in the annals of American hymnody, necessitating a special index that correlated hymn numbers in the parent book with page numbers in the music edition.

The compilers, Sylvester Main and William C. Brown, "selected for their acquaintance with our denominational taste" according to the preface, chose 306 tunes, including a good selection of fuging tunes for Wesley's hymns, such as "O happy, happy place" and "O what a mighty change," each appearing on the page with Daniel Read's LISBON; "O for a thousand tongues to sing," set to NORTH-FIELD; and LENOX for "Blow ye the trumpet, blow." The collection includes other tunes from early American collections, such as KENTUCKY and BARTIMEUS, originally CHARLESTOWN. Some tunes have traveling choruses, for instance THE VOICE OF FREE GRACE. A number of new tunes are taken from Woodbury's *New Lute of Zion* (1856). The size of this hymnal raised anew the criticism that official hymnals were more anthologies of devotional poetry than practical congregational hymnals. In the next two decades, private and denominational publishers produced a flood of songbooks intended to please those who strongly objected to both the size and the content of the official hymnal.

Compilers of the MEC 1878 began their work intending to reduce the size of the book by one-third (*Revision:* 21) but instead increased the number from 1,149 to 1,155. A total of 375 hymns were dropped, including 311 by Charles Wesley, to make room for recently composed hymns, primarily new hymns and translations from *Hymns Ancient and Modern:* in most instances the tune came with the text (Rogal). This edition featured standard evangelical tunes of the eighteenth and early nineteenth centuries, fuging tunes (mostly in domesticated versions where the imitative section has been reduced to block harmony; see Ex. 6.1), and several Sunday school melodies and gospel hymns. Lowell Mason's tunes, and his adaptations of tunes by Handel and Haydn and folk melodies of Great Britain and northern Europe, were placed alongside Lutheran chorales (in isometric form), Anglican chants (40 single and double chants), and "new and popular" four-part English parish hymn tunes by Dykes and Barnby. Wesley's "Come, thou long-expected Jesus" appeared for the first time in an American Methodist hymnal, infelicitously set to the tenor aria "If with all your hearts" from Mendelssohn's *Elijah,* and "O for a thousand tongues to sing" was set to AZMON, initiating a long and unfortunate association, compared to its settings in British Methodist hymnals.

Beginning with this collection, the content of American Methodist authorized hymnody moved from overwhelmingly Wesleyan to what may be termed Wesleyan-ecumenical. The latter developed in large urban churches constructed to accommodate burgeoning and more affluent congregations. The hymnal committee declared that "Methodism is not now, as it was at first, struggling for a foothold and recognition, or simply carrying the Gospel to the ignorant and degraded; but it sustains pastoral relations to millions, among whom are the prosperous, the cultured and the influential" (*Revision:* 42). As explained in Eben Touriée's influential introduction (reprinted C. Young 1993: 67–72), the people's worship song was now dependent on the choir and organ for support and was redefined within a tripartite worship paradigm: hymn singing, organ and choral music, and preaching. In consequence, Charles Wesley's hymns in authorized hymnals were thereafter set in musical styles reflecting urban church members' acquired and presumed tastes for "good music," and the requisite singing abilities.

MEC 1905 was jointly prepared by the MEC and MECS. It was a big book, 602 pages, 728 hymns, the size of present-day hymnals. It offered a much more scholarly selection of classical church music than did previous hymnals of either church: a goodly number of the nineteenth-century gospel songs were missing, and many new compositions by modern composers were introduced (Vernon, 1:200).

The committee's neglect of the significant gospel song repertory, to some extent necessitated by greedy demands of copyright holders, created a huge Methodist market for collections of gospel hymns, foremost *The Cokesbury Worship Hymnal* (1923), published by the MECS. The music editors were Peter Lukin, an Episcopal scholar and composer, and the Methodist literary professor and amateur composer Karl P. Harrington. They provided settings in a variety of musical styles for the texts, which had been selected by the committee without regard to appropriate tunes. Their often imaginative choices of tunes for the 102 texts by Charles Wesley include Samuel A. Ward's MATERNA for Wesley's "How happy every child of grace" and C. Hubert H. Parry's exquisite choral setting MARYLEBONE, imported from the 1904 British Methodist hymnal, for "In age and feebleness extreme." The music editors included only traditional and Victorian settings for Wesley's hymns, even though several gospel-style settings were available, such as "Jesus, the light of the world," arranged by George D. Elderkin; "Jesu, lover of my soul," set by Joseph P. Holbrook; and "Jesus! The name high over all," set by George F. Root. This was the first edition to "fix" one tune to one text. The new format with an underlaid first stanza led to complete interlining (i.e., the printing of all stanzas between the staves) in successive Methodist hymnals. Interlining renders a poem a confusion of hyphenated syllables and words, as in an anthem to be performed, rather than religious verse to be thoughtfully sung.

The compilers of MEC 1935, led by its editor, Robert G. McCutchan, loosened the stylistic gridlock by restoring American folk hymns, including a number of gospel hymns, and introducing British folk and early twentieth-century-style tunes from *The English Hymnal* (1906). However, as in the previous edition, the hymns of Charles Wesley were set to Anglo-American Victorian-style tunes whose singing rarely produced the Methodist-style music that Erik Routley would later describe as "sacred folk-song" invoking "medieval informality" (Routley 1967: 161). The committee and publisher learned an important lesson about the power of congregants' association of tune and text stored in collective memory banks, when the hymnal appeared with new harmonizations thought to be by the popular composer Van Denman Thompson replacing the original harmonies of familiar, sung-from-memory tunes. The searing, sustained uproar from preachers, pew-persons, and perennial choir-folk caused the publisher to remove the "improvements" and restore the original harmonies in subsequent printings. See Example 8.2 for an excerpt from the reharmonization of MARTYN, the hymnal's first tune for "Jesu, lover of my soul." (Compare Ex. 6.2.)

MC 1966 was the first authorized hymnal to include Negro spirituals (identified by the hymnal revision committee as "American Folk Hymns"), a Charles A. Tindley urban gospel hymn, a Native American hymn, and hymns from Asia and Africa. The musical settings for the 71 hymns by Charles Wesley were more diverse in style than those in the previous hymnal. The revision committee commissioned Robert J. Powell to set Wesley's exquisite two-stanza 66.66.88 eucharistic hymn "Author of life divine." Powell's well-crafted setting, and Lloyd Pfautsch's sturdy EUCLID for "I want a principle within," both in minor keys, are important

EX. 8.2. Simeon B. Marsh (harmonization thought to be by Van Denman Thompson), MARTYN (final section omitted here) (MEC 1935).

contributions to the music of Wesley hymns (Exx. 8.3, 8.4). The publication of the hymnal occurred during a renewed interest in Wesleyan liturgical traditions prompting a short-term but significant increase in the number of Wesley hymns sung in local churches, seminaries, and hymn festivals. The hymnal's liturgy for holy communion is a modified version of "The Sunday Service" John Wesley sent to the founding of the Methodist Episcopal Church at Baltimore in 1784, incorporating musical settings by John Merbecke from the *Book of Common Praier Noted,* 1550, which John Wesley would probably not have known or, if he did, might not have recommended singing!

This brings us to the present edition (UMC 1989), widely recognized for its stylistic inclusivity. There is something for everyone, from ancient plainsong ("Of the Father's love begotten") to Duke Ellington's religious pop "Come Sunday" and Charles Ives's classic "Serenity," plus a generous offering of gospel hymns, Negro spirituals, and global hymns. However, the musical settings of Wesley's hymns, with few exceptions, remain contextualized in eighteenth- and nineteenth-century sounds, formats, voicings, and styles. Tunes by Robert Powell and Lloyd Pfautsch premiered in the previous hymnal were not included.

The academic interest in Wesley biography, theology, and hymns, especially the five-yearly meeting of the Oxford Institute, and the two-decade preparation and publishing of *The Works of John Wesley* (now totaling twenty-six volumes), prompted the Hymnal Revision Committee to convene a Wesley consultation, consisting of British and American scholars, which selected, edited, and recom-

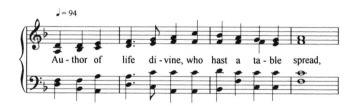

EX. 8.3. Robert J. Powell, AUTHOR OF LIFE DIVINE, opening (MC 1966). Reproduced by permission.

EX. 8.4. Lloyd Pfautsch, EUCLID, opening (MC 1966). © 1964 Abingdon Press (administered by the Copyright Company, Nashville, Tenn.). All rights reserved. Used by permission.

mended 100 Charles Wesley hymns with suggested tunes for inclusion. Decisions of the full committee, including a mandated 15 percent cut in the size of the hymnal, resulted in including only 58 Wesley hymns. Of the 42 settings for these, 40 are in four parts, the other two for unison voices: Wesley's classic "Wrestling Jacob" ("Come, O thou Traveler unknown") is set to a traditional Scottish melody, taken over from previous hymnals; and his lyrical treatise on the mystery of the Eucharist, "O the depth of love divine," set by this writer in an early-twentieth-century style (Ex. 8.5).

During the 225-year transition of American Methodism from horseback to Internet, its structure and mission moved from a religious society within a church to a freestanding church. Methodist congregational song developed in two distinct repertories. One was a populist song, largely represented by privately published popular songbooks and hymnals that featured folk hymns, Sunday school songs, and gospel hymns, some composed by Methodists, such as Fanny Crosby. The other was shaped from art music and meant to serve urban church members' musical tastes. This dichotomy was already beginning in the Wesleys' time, as Chapter 1 has shown. The music of authorized hymnals was primarily sourced from the latter until the present edition. Hymnals became worship books, consisting of spoken and sung liturgies, psalms, prayers, creeds, and hymns. All stanzas of all hymns are now underlaid. There are now fewer hymns and tunes, partly because of binding and construction considerations. Hymn content has moved away from significantly Wesleyan to Wesleyan-ecumenical (Westerfield-Tucker).

Consequently, American Methodist hymnals now share with other mainline denominational hymnals a basic core of traditional and recent hymns and their musical settings (Hawn 1996, 1997), while retaining some repertories that express their unique traditions and doctrines. British Methodists facilitated the latter by scattering the 203 hymns by Charles Wesley throughout their 1983 hymnal, which is organized according to the Christian year and topics. American Methodists, in a similarly organized hymnal, created a section with hymns expressing classic Wesleyan doctrines of grace. Of the 113 hymns in that section, only 18 are by Wesley. This proportion clearly indicates that for the committee that prepared UMC 1989, Wesley's hymns, and the tunes that come with them, have ceased to

EX. 8.5. Carlton R. Young, STOOKEY, opening (UMC 1989). ©1987 Hope Publishing Co., Carol Stream, Ill., 60188. All Rights Reserved. Used by permission.

be the most important source of Wesleyan lyrical theology. The vast majority of the hymns reflecting these doctrinal categories come from traditional and recently composed hymns. Foremost among them are the 300 hymns by Fred Pratt Green (1903–2000), in whom Erik Routley said "the genius of Charles Wesley lives again" (Routley 1979: dedication).

This conclusion is supported by an extensive study of United Methodist worship music (*Report* 2008). In one portion of the study, 1,045 pastors, music directors, and lay people in urban, suburban, and small-town churches were asked: "Approximately how many Wesley hymns have you sung in the last 12 months (yearly average)?" (*Report:* 102). Four percent replied "none"; 29 percent "1–5 hymns per year"; 25 percent "6–10"; 22 percent "11–20"; 14 percent "21–50"; 5 percent "more than 50." Thus most churches were singing fewer than 20 Wesley hymns per year; UMC 1989 contains 58 (51 with tunes), including two translations by John Wesley.

The study also shows a great divergence in opinions regarding the importance of Wesley hymns as resources for worship, theology, and identity: (1) they are important but must be adapted to more contemporary styles and rhythms; (2) they have become quaint historical artifacts that we sing out of familiarity or fondness; we no longer have a clear United Methodist identity; (3) they are so rich and varied, we can keep mining them for generations.

Recent Congregational Settings of Charles Wesley's Texts

Malcolm Williamson's *Six Wesley Songs for the Young* (M. Williamson 1963) demonstrates the possibility, if not the necessity, of creating new settings with appealing modern rhythms and harmonies for well-known hymns cemented for a century with one or more tunes. This was a concern expressed by the composer in a conversation with this writer in 1973.

These unison anthems include the playful "Rejoice, the Lord is King" and the Broadway-style "Love divine, all loves excelling." Williamson's earlier well-constructed, "considered pop," 5/4, congregational setting of Wesley's "Christ, whose glory fills the skies" (Ex. 8.6) has been included in recent non-Methodist hymnals and supplements.

Williamson's efforts may have encouraged David S. Goodall to compose his jazzy, dancing 3/2-meter New Saraband (1967) for "Ye servants of God" (Ex. 8.7), and Erik Routley to write Woodbury for "Come, O thou Traveler unknown" (1969) (Ex. 8.8), using Herbert Howells's harmonic unsettledness to provide an expressive and new tonal context for Wesley's classic "Wrestling Jacob," which had been trivialized in American Methodist hymnals by matching it to "Ye banks and braes o' bonnie Doon."

Recent attempts by British Methodists to change the musical environment of Wesley's hymns have produced several remarkably singable yet harmonically

EX. 8.6. Malcolm Williamson, "Christ, whose glory fills the skies," opening. © 1962 Josef Weinberger Ltd. Reproduced by permission of the copyright owners.

EX. 8.7. David S. Goodall, NEW SARABAND, opening. Reproduced by permission of the composer.

EX. 8.8. Erik Routley, WOODBURY, opening. © 1971 Carl Fischer Inc., New York. International copyright secured. All rights reserved. Used by permission.

challenging tunes, including Richard Bradshaw's HUTTON RUDBY (Carter: hymn 14; Ex. 8.9) and his imaginative pop setting of Wesley's unpublished three-stanza hymn on God's presence, "Far off we need not rove," last included in the 1933 hymnal. Philip Carter's collection, *Wesley Music for the Millennium* (2001), provides 56 original tunes in traditional, contemporary, and pop styles. Paul Leddington Wright has edited a collection of 17 old and new choral settings of Wesley hymns: *Praise the Lord!* (2007).

American Methodist publishers have also produced new music for Wesley's hymns, including Abingdon Press (*All Loves Excelling*) and Global Praise, a unit of the United Methodist General Board of Global Ministries (Kimbrough and Young). Abingdon's efforts include Mark Miller's Broadway-style "Love divine, all loves excelling" and this writer's bluesy "Spirit of faith, come down" (Exx. 8.10, 8.11).

The celebrated Argentinean teacher and composer Pablo Sosa comments on the theological importance of global song: "God continues to be revealed in different cultures and forms as they are touched by the Gospel, [giving] us a chance to enjoy new visions of the divine. This is one of the reasons for the unparalleled richness in church music, and particularly in congregational singing developed in the last fifty years" (Hawn, 2010: preface). Kimbrough presents this rationale for new "global" settings of Wesley's hymns: "Today [as] the Christian faith finds expression in innumerable cultures, ethnic groups, [and] languages, . . . we [can] discover new riches of inspiration and theological understanding in the Wesley hymns . . . sung to the rhythms and music idioms . . . of diverse cultures" (Kimbrough and Young: preface). Four global settings of Wesley hymns conclude this essay. "Come to the Supper," by Patrick Matsikenyiri of Zimbabwe, brings an African sound to the eucharistic invitation. No one is excluded. It reflects the parable of the king's invitation for all to come to dinner from Luke 14:16–24 (Ex. 8.12). The Taiwanese music historian and music editor I-to Loh offers a gamelan-styled, Phrygian-mode setting for "Gentle Jesus, meek and mild" (Ex. 8.13); incidentally, the same text set to a Chinese melody by Bliss Wiant, a Methodist music missionary and hymnal editor, had been included in *Hymns of Universal Praise* (Shanghai, 1936). A simple, prayerful, pentatonic setting of

EX. 8.9. Richard Bradshaw, HUTTON RUDBY, opening. Reproduced by permission of the composer.

EX. 8.10. Mark A. Miller, CAMP ALDERSGATE, opening. © 2003 Abingdon Press (administered by the Copyright Company, Nashville, Tenn.). All rights reserved. Used by permission.

EX. 8.11. Carlton Young, EMILY, opening. © 2007 Abingdon Press (administered by the Copyright Company, Nashville, Tenn.). All rights reserved. Used by permission.

EX. 8.12. Patrick Matsikenyiri, "Come to the Supper" (transcribed Mark McGurty), opening © 2001 The Charles Wesley Society, Archives and History Center, Drew University, Madison, N.J., 07940. Administered by the General Board of Global Ministries, t/a GBGMusik, 475 Riverside Drive, New York, N.Y., 10115. All rights reserved. Used by permission.

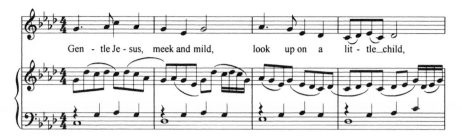

EX. 8.13. I-to Loh, "Gentle Jesus, meek and mild," opening. © 2001 The Charles Wesley Society, Archives and History Center, Drew University, Madison, N.J., 07940. Administered by the General Board of Global Ministries, t/a GBGMusik, 475 Riverside Drive, New York, N.Y., 10115. All rights reserved. Used by permission.

EX. 8.14. Li dong, Chan Hung-da and Swee Hong Lim, "Still, for thy loving kindness Lord," opening. Music © Swee Hong Lim. Administered by the General Board of Global Ministries, t/a GBGMusik, 475 Riverside Drive, New York, N.Y., 10115. All rights reserved. Used by permission.

EX. 8.15. George Mulrain (arr. Joorge Lockward), "Even now, the kingdom's near," extract from bar 5. © 2001 The Charles Wesley Society, Archives and History Center, Drew University, Madison, N.J., 07940. Administered by the General Board of Global Ministries, t/a GBGMusik, 475 Riverside Drive, New York, N.Y., 10115. All rights reserved. Used by permission.

"Still, for thy loving-kindness" (Ex. 8.14) comes from the pen of a Singaporean composer and teacher, Swee Hong Lim; while a Caribbean pastor and composer, George Mulrain, has provided a reggae setting for the previously unpublished Wesley hymn "Now, even now, the kingdom's near" (Kimbrough and Beckerlegge, 2:174), based on Luke 19:11 (Ex. 8.15).

The celebration of Charles Wesley's tricentennial in 2007 prompted a number of concerts and hymn festivals (partially listed in "Charles Wesley Tercentenary Events": 133–36). A number of these events introduced new settings of Wesley's hymns in contemporary styles, ranging from folk to rock, from "indie" to electronic.

These recent attempts to free Charles Wesley's hymns from their captivity to eighteenth- and nineteenth-century tunes and match them with twentieth- and twenty-first-century sounds and styles allow hymnal committees to consider an expanding repertory of familiar and newly discovered Wesley hymns set in pop, contemporary Christian, jazz-influenced, and global styles.

PART 2

The Wesley Musicians

CHAPTER 9

Style, Will, and the Environment

THREE COMPOSERS AT ODDS WITH HISTORY

Stephen Banfield

Hardly a Profession

The elder Charles Wesley's last known letter, dictated to his daughter in February 1788, was to a music seller who was charging him for a bill he had already paid. One may speculate as to how his musical progeny might have reacted had this happened to them. His son Charles, in a flurry of vagueness, would have had no idea whether he had paid it or not and would have looked it up in his notebook. Sam would never have paid it in the first place and would now scrounge the money from friends or wait until the bailiffs came. Sebastian would have drawn himself up to his full height and lectured the unfortunate tradesman on his impudence toward a professional of such high calling.

Their forebear's actual response was to say that he would rather pay a bill twenty times than be thought not to have paid it at all (Best: 330). What, then, happened to the famous Wesleys, in their transition from religious to musical avocations, that the gracious idealism of Charles the elder should have found its sequel in the almost picaresque narratives of foible, frustration, and general imperfection that dogged his brilliant sons and grandson? Touching as was the father's ongoing engagement with music, at this late stage of his life he had plenty else to worry about in the irreversible process of separation from the Church of England that the Methodist movement was undergoing, a movement that he and his brother had made into something changing the lives of thousands, eventually millions, and affecting the moral cast of an entire nation. One guesses he had bought the musical item for one of his sons, perhaps for Charles, who at the age of thirty might by now have been expected to be earning an independent living.

Yet the sons and grandson were indeed brilliant. What did he expect of them, and would he have been surprised to be told that Samuel and Sebastian would prove the finest English composers across the best part of a century? What do we expect of them, given the conditions under which they were laboring? What were the odds, and what did they achieve?

Critical commentary at the time and since has agreed that the odds were considerably against them, and Philip Olleson has analyzed Samuel's uneasy relationship with the musical profession in some detail (2000b). Recognizing, as does Rohr (7–12), that it was hardly a profession at all highlights the conceptual and practical gulf fixed between John and Charles Wesley's sphere of activity and degree of influence, based as these were on education, politics, and authority natural to any English gentleman of the time, and those of Charles's musical descendants. Comparable musical achievement was simply not possible in a country and period in which the art was perceived as intrinsically foreign. Travel abroad as a virtuoso might mitigate these odds, if undertaken young and especially when under aristocratic or royal patronage, because it would channel new talent into the cosmopolitan mainstream. This was the case with the flautist Andrew Ashe, about the same age as Charles the younger, and the Irish violinist, baritone, and composer Michael Balfe, Sebastian's near contemporary. (It was also the case with Thomas Attwood, a man whose modest later profile weakens the argument somewhat.) But staying at home, Charles, Samuel, and Sebastian had to settle for less fulfilled lives than those of John and Charles the elder. In any case, a musical career was always insecure. As Deborah Rohr states, a sizable proportion of professional musicians, from obscure orchestral players to top vocal stars, "ended their careers no better and in many cases worse off financially than when they started" (159).

Samuel, moreover, was born in a decade, the 1760s, curiously devoid of successful musical peers, only Cherubini, Méhul, and Dussek sharing it among internationally leading musicians. Attwood (born 1765) was his closest musical contemporary at home. These men would come to their maturity just as the *ancien régime* was crumbling and twenty-five years of European war were beginning. I myself live in a terrace of houses begun in 1791 but left unfinished at the financial collapse of two years later. "A lot of building going on, especially on the hill," Joseph Haydn remarked of its neighborhood on his visit to "Pristol" in August 1794 (Landon: 269). But the building was not going on: it had stopped, and the houses would not be completed for a generation. Regardless of his temperamental problems, one senses in Samuel a degree of self-knowledge making for chronic frustration with the time, place, and avocation to which he was tied. How else are we to square the esteem in which he was held by those who knew him with his dissatisfaction with his career? In its account of his burial, *The Times* claimed him as "one of the greatest musicians this country has ever produced" (October 18, 1837: 5), and the following year one James Rudge published a warm and detailed tribute to him in *The Penny Satirist*:

> [I] occasionally met this original character, and can [offer testim]ony to the astonishing mental powers with which he was gifted. . . . Wesley was indeed a man of no common intellectual powers; and I have been sometimes at a loss

what to admire most, his extraordinary fund of conversation or the astonish-ing extemporaneous skill with which he played the organ . . . [He was not] like many great men, who are perfect masters [in one] particular line or department, but who, in others, [possess] the simplicity of children, and all the prejudices [of the igno-]rant. Wesley was a master-spirit in music, but [not for a moment] so warped by professional predilections as not to [know the] importance, and appreciate the advantages, of other [branches] of learning and science. His infor-mation on [many topics] was rich and varied; and there was scarcely [a subject] upon which he did not charm by the brilliancy [of his talk] and instruct by the extent of his knowledge (June 9, 1838: 3 [imperfect copy]).

Here was a man clearly the intellectual heir of his father and uncle and aware of that fact, yet unable to harness his powers to commensurate status, recogni-tion, and rewards. Sometimes his attitude seems to have been resentment that he had ever been trained up for music (see the comments quoted by Olleson in Chapter 13, p. 000), at others, that he had wasted the opportunity offered him by his father to study the classics and make himself "eligible for any one of the learned Professions" (quoted in Olleson 2003: 31–32). Given his intellectual abilities and his awareness of them, and what we know about the limitations of a musical career in England at that time, these comments should be respected.

It is worth considering what Charles and Sarah's options for their sons really were. One has to sympathize with their plight, if music ousted all attempts to turn them into classically educated gentlemen, as Samuel's comment suggests and as Jackson claimed when he stated that "Charles enjoyed the advantages of a classical education, being regularly trained in a school at Bristol; but he appears to have been incapable of excelling in anything except music" (T. Jackson 1841: 345–46). On the other hand, Jonathan Barry suggests in Chapter 10 that Charles's desire to find the "best teachers" for their musical development was tempered by religious scruples. Certainly it needs to be asked why the parents did not pursue an institutional arrangement. William Boyce's offer to place Charles in the Chapel Royal was declined because his father had no thoughts of turning him into a professional musician; why, then, was such trouble taken to expose the boys' musical talents, to the point of advice or lessons from most of the leading musicians in London and a nine-year concert series attended by high society? However gentlemanly this arrangement, Wesley family finances were not sufficient to prevent Charles and Samuel from having to earn a living, and their father's age at their birth will have aggravated his and Sarah's awareness of this. Indecision seems to have played a part, for even in Bristol a secure and not inflexible path could have been determined. Had Charley and Sammy become cathedral choristers, their musical training would have been taken care of and, as Rohr points out (62), university residence could have followed, for they would have been taught the classics at choir school. This would have turned them into gentlemen, the status enjoyed by their father but sometimes flouted by Samuel's personal behavior, perhaps because in his case it could neither be assumed nor denied. The other vocational route, economically prudent and therefore arguably more responsible, would have been a formal musical apprenticeship. But this would have stamped the boys for trade rather than gentility, one possible reason why their parents chose instead an equivocal middle path. Other reasons may have included profound ambivalence about music, mixed with pride in talent; financial caution; progressive and affectionate notions of children's upbringing within a family environment; and, most disturbing if responsible for the shift from divinity to music as the Wesleys' family line, concern over whether or not Methodism would remain within the Church of England. Everything about the boys' upbringing suggests a policy of "wait and see" on their parents' part. The most obvious alternative to music as their livelihood would have been Anglican ordination—unless Methodists by then were no longer within the Church.

Charles Wesley the Younger

Children can be uncannily aware and exploitative of adult weakness, and it is not impossible that Samuel's rebelliousness was a reaction to parental temporizing. If so, it is easier to explain Samuel's disaffection than the modesty of Charles's musical profile as an adult. In considering Charles, there are two incumbent factors. First we must correct notions of failure, his reception history having hitherto undervalued him. Second, we must interpret his character and motivation.

Charles composed steadily throughout his life. At 185 works, his catalogue (see Appendix 1) may be only a third of the size of Samuel's (Kassler and Olleson 2001: 573–676), but it is respectably varied in genre and scope. Moreover, he published a noticeably larger proportion of it. There are in addition lost works of some substance, such as the oratorio *Elijah* (JN 29), predating Mendelssohn's treatment by more than twenty years (B. Matthews: 1112); a setting of Addison's "The spacious firmament on high" for voices and instruments (JN 30), mentioned by Samuel in his reminiscences (*Lbl* Add. 27593: 145r.); and the *Ode on the Death of Dr. Boyce* to words by his father (JN 122): these would almost certainly have enhanced his reputation. Samuel admired the *Ode,* written, he thought, "in a delightful Style" and containing "several interesting Airs, and three splendid and highly wrought Choruses." He considered it "much to be regretted that it has remained unpublished," already missing when he referred to it in 1836 (31r.).

But what is undeniable is that Charles became musically more conservative as he got older. As early as 1784, when only twenty-six, he was lamenting, "My two Masters have not left their fellows behind them" (Wainwright: 68), which refers to Boyce and Kelway, both of whom had died within the previous five years. This makes it hardly surprising that even his youthful works modulate stylistically between baroque and *galant,* though not indiscriminately: in his organ voluntaries and concertos, for example, the decorative sensibility of the newer style tends to be drawn on in slow movements, while fast ones, including his splendid fugues, remain bluff and Handelian. No. 6 of his Six Voluntaries (JN 23) offers an example, the concerto allegro of this extensive seven-movement work (opening, Ex. 9.1a) being very much in the baroque concerto vein, while the Larghetto is more classical in gesture (Ex. 9.1b—note the slower-moving, less assertive harmonies, the contrast between rhythmically unsupported slow and fast notes in bar 1, and the simpler texture, in two or three parts, among other features). Not only that, but the Larghetto exploits the contrasts of sonata form, with a new subject in the dominant migrating through the texture a little way into the movement (Ex. 9.1c).

Charles was a fine melodist, and at his best could command freshness and wit, whether in the assertive contours of a minuet (Quartet No. 2 in D from JN 9) or the military march theme and variations from the sixth of his organ concertos (JN 5), where the tune is announced first on wind only, flutes and timpani having

EX. 9.1. Charles Wesley, Organ Voluntary, JN 23/6 Allegro moderato and Larghetto, extracts.

been held in reserve for this last movement of the last concerto in the set (Ex. 9.2). Nor did he shun vocal virtuosity, well to the fore in verse anthems such as *I will lift up mine eyes,* JN 52 (1778), and his concert aria "Placido zeffiretto" of 1783 for soprano, oboes, muted violins, and continuo (JN 161). These show a young but not juvenile composer luxuriating in fashion, like his sister with her accident-prone shoes (see p. 159). Yet even here he might not submit entirely but prefer to work in two styles at once, along the lines of Samuel (as Peter Holman points out on p. 198). In *I will lift up mine eyes,* as in the organ voluntaries, he retains what feels like the moral security of the late baroque in an Allegro preceding the soloist's real showpiece, the minuet section "The Lord shall preserve thy going out and coming in," not intended for church performance (for which he provided a more demure alternative). In the opening section of the anthem he appears at times to reach further back, toward Purcell (whom he had been studying with Kelway a few years previously), in his use of dotted notes and angular minor-key inflections.

That in Charles's case such style modulation represented lack of confidence rather than independence of mind, or a forward-looking historicism, is strongly suggested by his later misgivings about the contemporary musical idiom. These he must have voiced in a letter to Samuel in 1806 for the latter to have replied thus: "Haydn & Mozart must be heard often before they are thoroughly understood, (as it strikes me) even by those who have heard *much* Music of more *gradual* Modulation; but I do think, that when the Ear & Mind become perfectly habituated to their rapid Successions of Harmony, the Feast is rich indeed" (January 15, 1807, in Olleson 2001: 44). By the early 1820s he had given up trying to understand anything current, referring to "these degenerate days" and mourning John Christopher Smith and John Stanley as though they had died only yesterday (Wainwright: 73, 77).

EX. 9.2. Charles Wesley, March Pomposo (opening), Organ Concerto No. 6.

Charles was not alone in using the musical style of the past as a literal starting point in composition for church usage, almost as though it represented the
theological authority of a text on which disquisition could then be based. As late
as 1831, Samuel's Bristol friend Edward Hodges (1796–1867) wrote a verse anthem,
"A Loyal Prayer," in the form of theme and variations, where the jaunty triple-
time theme, in three-bar phrases, sounds fully Purcellian but the variations, for a
progressively larger number of voices, add cumulative passagework in their organ
accompaniment until it sounds like a Mozart concerto. Perhaps the 1830s were the
last decade in which the scholarly connoisseurship of the organ loft could expect
to maintain an independence of aesthetic tradition in the face of the vehement
politics of congregations and clergy and the musical fashions that would reflect
them throughout the remainder of the nineteenth century and beyond. Hodges
himself would come under pressure to modernize his music when he emigrated
in 1838 to New York, where the critic George Templeton Strong found its idiom,
also represented by the improvisations of Hodges's son, "prosy," "ponderous,"
"wooden," and on one occasion indistinguishable from that of "some austere
English composer of the reign of Edward VI" (Ogasapian: 122, 152, 166). Whether
or not it was a phenomenon peculiar to their period, English organists such as
Charles Wesley and Edward Hodges came perilously close to disqualifying themselves as composers when measured by Julian Johnson's stricture: "No significant
composer of art music has ever written in a manner that was completely unaware
of what has already taken place in music. There are no significant 19th-century
composers writing music in a thoroughly baroque idiom, as if they were still in
the 17th century" (100).

Part of the difficulty in assessing the musical achievements of both Charles
and Samuel is that in their own day they were admired more as executant stylists
on the English organ than as composers. Kollmann singled out Charles along
with Samuel as pre-eminent among English organists in 1812 (*Quarterly Musical
Review* 1:21). Charles's fame as a Handel performer elicited the comment by "C.
T." in 1818 that "few, if any, have ever surpassed him in giving upon that noble
instrument, the organ, the full and characteristic expression to his music. . . . he
touches every note with life and spirit, and calls forth all the latent beauties of his
favorite author. He feels with all the soul of HANDEL" (*Quarterly Musical Magazine
and Review* 1:283); and as late as 1831, demonstrating a new organ for the Brighton
Pavilion in the London workshop of its builders Flight and Robson, "the veteran
organist" played Handel "with as much feeling and enthusiasm as distinguished
the performances of his earlier days" (*Morning Chronicle,* March 18, 1831: 3).

Samuel enjoyed an unsurpassed reputation for extemporization, and his exceptional ability here has posed three problems. First, it gave him less incentive
to write down and publish finished compositions to be marketed independent
of the effect of his own impromptu performance. Second, it almost certainly

made his compositional aims less architecturally conformist than they would otherwise have been (and this also applies to works by Sebastian such as the "Choral Song" for organ). Third, it distanced his output from the very instrument he unwittingly promoted, the C-compass organ with independent pedal board necessary for playing the works of J. S. Bach. As a result of this last impediment, what ought to have been Samuel's major contribution to the canon, his twelve Op. 6 voluntaries (KO 621) published singly and then together in two sets between 1801 and 1817, have never become widely known. Francis Routh points out that they have the scope of sonatas, which is true, though they are not really within that genre, never starting with an allegro, never casting a movement beyond the tonic (or very rarely, relative) major or minor, and always containing a fugue. They are, alas, unplayable on a modern organ, and Routh's own edition of 1982–83 effectively constitutes an arrangement, as Alyson McLamore recognizes (2006: 448). Players and audiences nowadays are reluctant to embrace an artifact based on such a degree of textual interference, though admittedly that has not stopped Mozart's late F-minor fantasia for mechanical clock from becoming a classic.

It would be easy to conclude that Charles was unwilling to take aesthetic risks in his music, and that those of Samuel worked brilliantly when improvised but transferred unsatisfactorily to paper. The truth will require more careful seeking out, both here and in commentary to come once the outputs of both composers begin to be properly known. It may be that Charles's early virtuosity rendered him unaware of his own capabilities. He cannot have been a lazy performer if, as Samuel maintained in 1836, he played Domenico Scarlatti "with such Spirit, Energy, Taste and Precision as always to astonish as well as captivate his Hearers" and left "no Artist in any Degree comparable to himself in the perfect Command of that justly esteemed, elegant and elaborate Composer" (*Lbl* Add. 27593: 26v.). Yet where is the influence of those "very original . . . Compositions" on his own sonatas? If any composer could have minimized for Charles the painful distance between baroque and classical, let alone romantic, it was surely Scarlatti. Perhaps there is something of his dash and fire in the sudden explosion, thirteen bars in, of *forte* octaves in the first movement of his F-minor keyboard sonata of 1781 (JN 18), followed up as they are by a scale from the top of the keyboard, strong diatonic dissonances, and a trill effect borrowed from bar 3 (Ex. 9.3). But however he may have performed the passage, one works hard to construe these gestures as the adventurousness of a great musical mind.

There are nevertheless surprises in Charles's output, and more will come to light. Delightful ones occur in his cantata *Caractacus* of December 1791 (JN 130), setting part of William Mason's dramatic poem to music. Quite what attracted him, and indeed three other composers, to the druidic legend of Brutus of Troy bringing the harp to Anglesey is anybody's guess (though his mother was Welsh), but such stuff was popular enough at the time. He duly introduces the instrument

EX. 9.3. Charles Wesley, Sonata in F Minor, JN 18, first movement from bar 13. Reproduced by permission of Special Collections, Bridwell Library, Perkins School of Theology, Southern Methodist University.

into a solo aria celebrating the fact, "Hail thou harp of Phrygian frame," scored for "cembalo e Harpa senza orchestra" (though not in the Phrygian mode!). Other colorful touches have preceded this in the duet "Welcome, gentle train," in which, sung by Charles's favorite combination of two intertwining sopranos, the persistent rain of north Wales is eulogized as "Dews of Peace and dews of Innocence," followed by droplets on two violins and pizzicato bass. Granted, Handel had done this sort of thing fifty or sixty years earlier.

The temptation is to treat Charles's compositional preferences as the indulgences of a gentleman amateur and forget that he was a top professional, at least insofar as he enjoyed a royal appointment. Advertisements of the time make the most of this, be they for an organ concerto at the Theatre Royal, Haymarket, performed and presumably composed by him, which had "never yet been played but before their Majesties," or for a teacher of French and music who begged leave "to observe, she is recommended by Mr. Charles Wesley, organ-performer to his Majesty" (*The Times,* February 6, 1804: 1; June 15, 1820: 1). He was favored by both George III and the Prince of Wales, the latter appointing him organist-in-ordinary. If, as Rohr points out, royal patronage "conferred enormous social and professional prestige, which translated into other engagements as performers and teachers," we cannot view Charles as anything less than the "dedicated and professional musician" Carlton Young has begun to discover underneath his negative posthumous press (Rohr: 42; C. Young 2007: 32).

But Thomas Jackson's image of the ineffectual dandy not "able to dress himself without assistance" remains (1841: 346), not least because his emollient personality contrasts so strongly with that of his fiery brother. Regardless of what their actual music might tell us, this has led to an understanding of Charles's character as feminized where Samuel's remains firmly masculine. And effeminacy was the concomitant to musicality most chronically feared by the English (Rohr: 17–21). Precisely what Charles the elder meant when he tried to steer his son away from the "nest of hornets" that was the Hanoverian court is not now to be known. But had Charles the younger been born a century or more later, everything about him, from his love of soprano duets and lifelong residence with mother and sister to the gloves in Russell's 1776–77 portrait (see p. 155), would suggest the identity, unfulfilled or otherwise, of a socially compliant gay man. The question historians have to consider is the extent to which such formations of identity can be projected back into earlier periods for an explanation of character, behavior, motivation, and—perhaps most important—reception. There seem to be two schools of thought, a structuralist one that nominalizes homosexuality into something period- and culture-specific beyond which our own conceptualization of it is irrelevant and misleading, the other believing that the feelings and therefore to some extent the tokens of men desiring men are of *longue durée*—that is, applicable over a long period within a particular civilization (see Haggerty). I incline to the latter view. In the very nature of the case, evidence of Charles's possible orientation is not likely to appear, but to my mind that makes speculation incumbent on us if we are to do him justice.

Samuel Wesley

No such mystery surrounds the private life of Samuel, which not even Methodist commentary, the source of virtually all consideration of his brother from Jackson onward, could ignore. (Charles the elder's biography has also been largely treated within a Methodist framework, downplaying the last, family-oriented thirty years of his life—see Lloyd 2007a.) If anything, it will have unduly influenced expectations of his music as similarly fitful, eccentric, uncontrolled, unbalanced, and oppositional or marginal to the cultural norms of his time and place. But perhaps some of these epithets really are applicable. Certainly he does not often compose standard sonata structures. It is worth seeing what he does instead, and whether the compensations are architecturally sufficient.

The Grand Duet, KO 604 (1812), is "an enormous three-movement sonata lasting for around fifteen minutes, and can probably lay claim to being his greatest work for the organ" (Olleson 2003: 302). The first movement mixes elements of concerto, sonata, and ternary form while lacking real obeisance to any of these. A tuneful A section of sixteen bars extended sequentially to nineteen is hardly a ritornello, for its later tonic return comprises the unique and important moment of a sonata recapitulation; yet this recapitulation occurs little more than halfway through the movement. This self-contained A section is followed by a succession of two contrapuntal motifs (B, C) more in line with the forms of vocal polyphony, but these are capped by a jaunty dotted-note figure (D) that sounds like the closure of a larger A section. A triplet motif (E) is then introduced for extended sectional contrast, and it continues until the tonic return. Rather than a sonata, this moment might suggest a large ternary form were the return of A not so early and so varied, giving way to two new motifs (F, G) arising from the first introduction of sixteenth-notes, these continuing for some time until dotted notes finally re-emerge to signal overall completion, though the codetta figure D is never repeated. This makes for a movement really of four sections of alternately greater and lesser length: 1. (A, B, C, D), 2. (E, C), 3. (A, F, B, C), and 4. (G, C). In its unorthodox way, this is a balanced structure, and Wesley ensures that motif C appears once in each section, in the dominant, dominant, tonic (as if a second subject under recapitulation), and relative minor. Nowhere in the movement does he settle in the dominant or anywhere else, though paradoxically he moves toward it in the recapitulation of B rather than its initial statement. One may feel it a weakness that a movement of this length lacks such an arrival point, but he makes up for it in a slow movement full of intricate classical detail, its exposition moving at leisure from F to C major, complete with dominant second subject, though even here he considerably varies his recapitulation, omitting the second subject before matching up the two sections again with their closing theme.

The closing double fugue is enormous, and one marvels at Wesley's ability to maintain energy, invention, and thematic relatedness, none of these flagging for a moment, without any block repetition, though he relies a good deal on sequence. These must have been the qualities in his improvisations that so impressed his hearers. He himself had no idea how he did it: "Sir," he once replied to an "opulent Individual" who thought the secrets could be sold, "as soon as ever I myself know and can explain to you the Nature of my Extemporaneous Faculty, I will teach you for nothing" (*Lbl* Add. 27593: 129). The fugue, not far short of three hundred bars in length, repeats the formal illusion of the first movement, in which a shorter proposition gives way to a larger one. At first it seems to entail a four-part exposition followed by three middle-section subject entries (in the tonic, relative minor, and mediant). But these together turn out to be the first stage of an argument in which the second, roughly from bars 100 to 218, comprises a development breaking up the theme into smaller units and inversions interspersed with free sequence. Only once is it put back together again, in a third stage of the movement, when it is augmented over a massive dominant pedal that nevertheless evaporates before a frivolous motif and fanfare-like new tune that sounds like a melodic quotation.

Wit thereby has the last word, Haydn's aesthetic capping Bach's, suitably enough given the sociable occasion the first performance must have been. Wesley himself performed the duet with his friend Vincent Novello at the close of his benefit on June 5, 1812, when the audience must have emerged smiling into Hanover Square with their minds relieved, if only for a moment, of thoughts about war with America and France, the recent assassination of their prime minister, and the maneuvers of Wellington in Spain and Napoleon toward Russia.

For great music may be in counterpoint to great events. Not that Wesley kept aloof from the world around him. Official posts and major assignments may scarcely have come his way, but there is ample evidence that this man of "no common intellectual powers" was alive to music's capacities and obligations as a mirror of the public sphere. Above all, he had the imagination to bring opposites or apparently unrelated elements together into a vision seen as meaningful, unique, and, once he had accomplished it, necessary. His engagement with vernacular music in the secular works offers powerful examples of this. In his most important chamber work, the F Major Violin Sonata written for Salomon in 1797 (KO 508), the rondo theme arrives with a sharp intake of fresh air after the ornate sensibility of the slow movement, and it is Celtic air, with the unmistakable humor of a fiddler's jig. For all their folkloric rondos and Scotch song arrangements, Haydn, Mozart, and Beethoven do not sound like this, especially when, on its ninth appearance eight bars from the end, Wesley sanctimoniously reharmonizes the tune as though belatedly trying to redeem its manners for the drawing room (Ex. 9.4).

If he is attempting to link contradictory worlds, the piano rondos take the process much farther. To select two of them, "The Widow Waddle" and "Kitty Alone and I," KO 728 and 732 (Temperley 1985: 105–10, 141–49), both seem to turn him into a Hegelian romantic seeking a synthesis of opposites, in the one case of the low with the high, in the other of the past with the present, to produce respectively a humorous catharsis of everyday life and a distinctive, idiosyncratic future for English musical style. In "The Widow Waddle" one gets a sense of Wesley's

EX. 9.4. Samuel Wesley, Violin Sonata in F, KO 508, rondo theme on final appearance. Reproduced by permission.

private and scholarly lives blending into a picaresque agenda of rare musical risk. Dedicated to the great clown Joseph Grimaldi and published around 1808, it is based on a song by William Reeve that Grimaldi sang in *The Cassowar* in August 1807. Things turn out badly for the suitor who marries the widow "who kept a tripe and trotter shop in Chickabiddy Lane," for before long "They'd words and with a large cow heel she gave him such a wipe, / And he return'd the compliment with half a yard of tripe." A hiatus in the couple's hostilities, either when they are bound over to keep the peace or as Tommy lies dazed in the shop with a "join stool" about his head, is presumably depicted in a cross-rhythmic passage presaging ragtime, before a headlong presto suggests inevitable re-engagement and the moral to be drawn, the former with potent levels of diatonic dissonance (four adjacent scale degrees sounding simultaneously), the latter as the tune breaks up into Beethovenian fragments dying away against its own augmentation. Wesley had been at a particularly low ebb through ongoing marital estrangement that March when he wrote to Charles about his sacrifice of peace to "one of the most unworthy of all Mortals" (Olleson 2001: 51); less than two months later, Horn's edition of Bach fugues, including the "Dorian," with its unprecedented levels of diatonic dissonance, was published ("Chronology," 16), and if it is difficult to point to any precise textual concordance or indeed the exact moment in 1807 when Wesley began to study Bach's fugues (Olleson 2001: 75), tripe, trotters, and Bach are undoubtedly blended in this extraordinary piece.

"Kitty Alone and I," dating from 1830, includes, if anything, stronger Bachian sequences of rich seventh chords chromatically decorated. But there is a stranger element too, for the Scottish folk tune is one of those oscillating between a minor tonic and the major chord a tone below it, and this modal conundrum Wesley strikingly explores, whether in the almost schizophrenic passage contrasting a *lento* minor sequence with a sudden *tempo primo* shift to the parallel G major immediately counteracted with a chord of F major (Ex. 9.5a), or in the next *lento* interpolation, a solemn incantation reversing the cycle of fifths out of a foreign chord of A flat major (Ex. 9.5b), far ahead of this gesture's late-nineteenth- and twentieth-century usage. In these and the other piano rondos, Wesley shows himself a true original, and it would be gratifying to be able to group him with the English creative visionaries of his period—William Blake, Samuel Palmer, Edward Calvert. Perhaps, worked in a limited medium and away from the cosmopolitan pressures of fashion, that is indeed where these compositions belong. Undoubtedly he represents a musical tradition of dissent in a way that his brother Charles could only dream of, if he did even that.

It will be obvious to any listener or performer that in these pieces Wesley is drawing on more than one musical language. Insofar as this entails dialogue between them, hybridity, and transformation, the procedure bears consideration as Bakhtinian heteroglossia: a popular patter song responds to Bach, an old country dance suddenly exchanges modes or confronts an echo of monastic

a)

b)

EX. 9.5. Samuel Wesley, Rondo, "Kitty alone and I," KO 732, extracts.

plainsong. Mikhail Bakhtin claimed: "It is precisely the diversity of speech, and not the unity of a normative shared language, that is the ground of style," in an article demonstrating how diversity of utterance gives triumphant artistic life to the portrayal of London—essentially Wesley's London—in the work of Charles Dickens (Bakhtin: 203). With Dickens the heteroglot novel triumphs; it "revels in variety and conflict" and "is skeptical of all languages that assume they are the only voice of truth, a claim to exclusive privilege that Bakhtin calls the 'lie of pathos.'" To "the languages of all who hold power and are well set up in life" it opposes "the language of the merry rogue" (Clark and Holquist: 292). Heteroglossia exploits "the conflict between 'centripetal' and 'centrifugal,' 'official' and 'unofficial' discourses" within speech, every utterance containing within it "the traces of other utterances, both in the past and in the future" (Morris: 248–49).

If Wesley projects his musical materials in an analogous way, he is responding just as he should to the foreignness of musical culture in London. But this does not mean that he is ignoring the essentially dramatic nature of the postclassical idiom of his period. Insofar as his music is pantomimic of an individual, a frame of mind, or a situation, it brings him closer to a mimetic—that is, a theatrical—conception of music's capabilities than his parents and uncle would have been comfortable with.

Yet music for the stage was the one medium he never attempted, and it was of course the medium that in his day aroused the greatest contention and might reap the highest financial rewards—contention because of the British musical theater's domination by Italian opera and because of perceptions of immorality or degeneracy attaching to its practitioners, high rewards because of its secure position nevertheless at the peak of fashion and culture. Anybody with a streak of independence and dissent would have a hard time reconciling the practicalities of successful composition for the theater with the demands of their art, and it would be another hundred years or more, in the figures of Ethel Smyth and then Benjamin Britten, before English composers would come fully to terms with the equation.

Paradoxically, had Wesley enjoyed less of a freelance existence from his boyhood onward and been more institutionalized within the Anglican networks of the metropolis, he might have gained theater experience and brought that moment forward. A number of his contemporaries, and his own son Sebastian, did gain such experience as Chapel Royal choristers or young adults, though none consolidated it for posterity. Attwood wrote music for over thirty stage works in the 1790s and beyond, many while serving as organist of St. Paul's cathedral and composer to the Chapel Royal. William Hawes had a finger in almost every musical pie in London. John Goss had a theatrical success with *The Serjeant's Wife* in 1827. The young Walmisley was wanted for the English opera, according to Arthur Coleridge in the first edition of *Grove*, but chose Cambridge and the organ loft instead.

Sebastian Wesley

Walmisley was four years younger than Sebastian Wesley. What was at stake when both of them turned their backs on a career in the theater? For Sebastian too was offered, through Hawes, his former choirmaster, the chance of such a career, working in the pit of the English Opera House (whose productions included English-language versions of recent Continental operas) in the late 1820s and early 1830s. Horton recognizes that "the experience he gained during these years had a considerable bearing on his subsequent development as a composer. Not only did he become fully conversant with the contemporary early romantic idiom, but he also experienced the use of music in a dramatic context" (2004: 24; see also Horton 2002: 230). Most important, his one known theatrical assignment as a composer, dating from 1832, was for a melodrama, *The Dilosk Gatherer*. (One of the seventeen music cues is actually "help! Murder!" [*Lbl* Add. 33819].) Here the youthful composer was forced to associate music with raw, immediate emotion depicted in brief, telling strokes, and the results, several portions of which are reproduced in Horton 1999, were most fruitful. He had above all to think in terms of instantly established contrasts of character and situation, but also to consider long-term connections, for at least five recurrent motifs are generated.

Two years later, at a similar age, Richard Wagner must have been learning the same techniques on the road with Bethmann's theater company.

The young Samuel Wesley had hated London and moved to a village near St. Albans for as long as he could. It seems that Sebastian was equally impatient with the city that could have offered him a lifetime's musical career second to none, however unpredictable, in or out of the theater, and perhaps made him into the one composer of the nineteenth century who, with his "ability to create music of . . . emotional power" already displayed in *The Dilosk Gatherer* (Horton 2004: 25), finally would have broken through the barrier separating English talent from operatic success. For in the very month that *The Dilosk Gatherer* took the stage, he was the successful candidate for the organistship of Hereford cathedral. "Painful and dangerous is the position of a young musician who, after acquiring great knowledge of his art in the Metropolis, joins a country Cathedral," he very soon discovered (1849: 11), having exiled himself to one provincial situation after another for the rest of his life. And it must be emphasized that his was not a typical organist's career: many, possibly most, cathedral practitioners of his period came from regional dynasties and stayed put in the same post for up to half a century, like John Davis Corfe at Bristol or Zechariah Buck at Norwich. Sebastian was not doing the expected or natural thing.

Many vestiges of Sebastian Wesley's "other" career lie hidden in the anthems, especially at both chronological ends of his output. While still a chorister, he had repeatedly sung for George IV at the Brighton Pavilion, and on one occasion in 1823 Rossini was present as a fellow performer. Is it not a Rossinian *stretto*, repeated as it is, that concludes the late anthem *Let us now praise famous men* (Ex. 9.6)? In an early one, *Blessed be the God and Father*, Peter Horton hears the dominant seventh chord immediately preceding the allegro of Weber's *Oberon* overture echoed in the one Wesley places at a similar juncture (personal communication); certainly this anthem can be understood formally as an Introduction, Aria, and Allegro, the concert allegro at the words "But the word of the Lord endureth for ever" starting as if with an exhilarating military tutti antiphonally answered by woodwind, to which string *coups d'archet* are added. Wesley's most outstanding rhetorical repetition may owe something to *Oberon* too. The heady, almost narcotically heightened effect of the extra return of the second half of the second subject at the end of Weber's overture is comparable with that of Wesley's *O Lord, thou art my God* when the triumphant moment of homophonic assertion, after fugal treatment, that "this is the Lord; we have waited for him, and he will save us" (Ex. 9.7) is set to unforgettable melody and harmony not just immediately reiterated but returning as if in continued ecstasy twenty-four bars later.

This is one of the great moments of English music. As Temperley writes, "It seems to express the Church of England's awakening from long slumber" (1981: 199). But its full contextual meaning is not easy to grasp, and this chapter concludes with an attempt to reconcile Sebastian Wesley's flawed career and genius with both the musical demands of his century and the theological passions of his

EX. 9.6. Sebastian Wesley, *Let us now praise famous men*, extract.

EX. 9.7. Sebastian Wesley, *O Lord, thou art my God*, extract. © The Musica Britannica Trust. Reproduced by permission of Stainer and Bell Ltd, London, England, from Musica Britannica, volume 57. www.stainer.co.uk.

forebears. On the one hand, it is easy to miss the stylistic and generic coordinates of such passages as those described earlier as metropolitan residue amid all the fugues and hymns. Yet there are many further examples to remind us that long after he had left London, Wesley continued to study the musical romantics, or at least to think like them. Mendelssohn, in particular *Elijah,* surely informs much of the conception and detail of *Ascribe unto the Lord,* and this influence is especially noticeable in its orchestral version. The parenthetic first entry of the voice in "I have been young and now am old" of 1848 (reproduced in Horton 2004: 214) is pure Schumann, the technique grafted onto a theme with the serenity of the second subject of Mendelssohn's *Hebrides* overture. But as with other Wesleys, Sebastian remains so completely his own man that it is difficult to judge how much he continued to hanker after the secular musical developments of his time and how much he was content to work within the artistic contingencies of sacred texts and liturgies. In particular, there are two respects in which he might or might not be considered a willing servant of God and the Church in the troubled tradition of his grandfather and great-uncle.

The first raises again the question of whether the organist's improvisatory technique and hence aesthetic, which he possessed in abundance, represented for him a sufficient functional norm of an artisanal kind: his trade, not a profession where composition was concerned. As with his father, such a representation seems not to do justice to a strikingly individual approach to compositional structure, borne out by the tangential relationship with sonata form of his C major/minor orchestral Allegro, which Horton suggests was the first movement of a symphony never completed. The material is firmly post-Beethovenian, and the constant shifting between tonic major and minor is comparable with Schubert's usage, though it sounds quite different from Schubert. Schumann's piano concerto is foreshadowed in one particular passage of chromatics (quoted in Horton 2004: 79 as Ex. 2.11b; see also Horton 2002: 234), and Berwald is brought to mind by the freshness of some of the diatonic dissonance. At first sight, as criticized by Horton (78–81), the movement remains tonally earthbound and unbalanced as a sonata form. On closer study, Wesley is creating a variant form of his own, in which over a substantial span of more than three hundred common-time bars every block of agglomerated musical units appears twice except for a short development section, but not in the expected ways. The higher-level form is A B C D B C X D A in more or less proportionate sections, with X as the unique development. If A, B, and C are first subject, transition, and second subject, with the second subject in E flat (the conventional relative major if C minor is taken as its tonic), then section D articulates the form's idiosyncrasy, for it begins like an exposition repeat, soon prefers development, and then prepares the repeat of B and C, but with C this time in some kind of a dominant (G minor/B flat major). There is a sense here of sonata-form reversal, as though we had heard the recapitulation before the exposition and both before the development (compare this with Samuel's procedure in the Grand Duet). More striking is the fact that Wesley also reverses his lower-level material within the final A section.

The second question is a larger one. The overall form of Wesley's multisectional anthems is no easier to grasp than that of the "Symphony," and they often present risks of musical pacing. William Gatens, as noted by Horton (2004: 90), finds them to have "a remarkable coherence, for which a satisfactory explanation is elusive" and seeks the answer "more in the large-scale aesthetic gesture than in . . . conventional focuses of analytical attention." In each of his three greatest works, the Exeter anthems of 1836–40 (*Let us lift up our heart, O Lord, thou art my God,* and *To my request and earnest cry*), there are moments when Wesley seems to withdraw from achieved musical movement, moments all the more striking when preceded by a fugue, a texture that will always have a rhythmic continuum based on its established proposition. The simplest example occurs at the end of another anthem, *Wash me throughly.* This is surely one of the most perfect short pieces of the nineteenth century. Yet after a spectacular display of intellectual form—three diminished-seventh chords a major third apart like teardrops accompanying the A theme's recapitulation above dominant pedal; the B section's fugue theme now combined with the A theme; the A theme inverted—Wesley entirely abandons the sad, waltzlike rhythmic movement of this desperate petition. It would have made much better musical sense for the final two iterations of "and forgive me all my sin" to have retained the half-note/quarter-note rhythm of the previous ones, for the work's musical climax occurs within one of them. But again and again he will end a work with a derhythmicized gesture of submission, as though human agency can do no more: for all the sinner's lullaby-like craving for God's comfort in *Wash me throughly,* he must relinquish his feelings, abandon his will, and leave the rest to grace.

The aesthetic is thus ultimately determined not by music but by the rhetoric of speech, of prayer and sermon, of theology. He was a less rebellious churchman than he may have seemed. In purely musical terms, there are passages and tempo ratios in the Exeter anthems that simply do not work by analogy with concert composition, all the more strikingly because of the huge scale of musical movement and climax surrounding them. The most extreme example is perhaps where the beautiful (and very secular-sounding) main theme of *To my request and earnest cry* returns, now in 6/4, for the third time. If, as Horton suggests (S. S. Wesley 1990: 167), it is to arise proportionately out of the preceding chorale-like section, the latter has to be extremely slow. Conversely, if the magnificent opening section of *Let us lift up our heart* is to have sufficient dynamism to maximize the musical drama of the motif that emerges at the words "doubtless thou art our father," it must be, or become, a good deal faster than Wesley's tempo marking of 116 quarter-notes to the minute, and then the subsequent fugue at "Oh that thou wouldst rend the heav'ns" will be truly passionate, at a pace of urgent speech rhythm. The young John Stainer's recollection of how fast Wesley wanted "As for the gods of the heathen" in *Ascribe unto the Lord* is useful here (Horton 2004: 224–25; Dibble 2007: 31–32). At other moments, Wesley will establish, in the organ part or through the rhythmic lattice of contrapuntal voice writing, motoric support for slower notes, only to withdraw it suddenly. One may wonder whether this is sometimes notational shorthand for a momentum that would have continued in his improvised organ accompaniment, but the purely vocal instances suggest otherwise. It is, rather, as though the listener's mind is after a while to be drawn away from the worldly movement of music to contemplation and petition that lead to silence and the discipline of waiting. What makes the end of *O Lord, thou art my God* so humanly satisfying is that for once a complex fugue is not only allowed to continue motorically without withdrawal, but is trumped by Wesley's spectacular series of worldly gestures, including a solitary, very modern instance of triplet quarter-notes. On this occasion the Church triumphs on earth, here and now, in this world. But none of the great Wesleys would want to risk complacency by taking such a vision for granted, or go with the flow for more than a moment.

CHAPTER 10

Charles Wesley's Family
and the Musical Life of Bristol

Jonathan Barry

The Bristol Context and Family Narratives

When Thomas Chatterton satirized a typical Methodist in January 1770, he claimed that he "Could sing One hundred Hymn by rote / Hymns which will sanctify the throte / But some indeed composed so oddly / Youd swear twas bawdy Songs made godly" (Chatterton, 1:446–47). At that date, Chatterton (1752–1770) was one of four child prodigies living in Bristol, the others being Hannah More (born 1745), and, of course, Charles (born 1757) and Samuel (born 1766) Wesley. All four were brought up in England's second city, which, with about fifty thousand inhabitants, was at the height of its importance. Although celebrated then (and since) largely for its economic prosperity and political weight, Bristol was also a very active cultural center, with a whole range of artistic and literary activity aimed both at its own citizens and at the fashionable visitors to its Hotwells, a major summer rival to nearby Bath. It was also home to a diverse and dynamic religious culture. It had perhaps the strongest congregations of old Dissent (Presbyterian, Baptist, and Quaker in particular) outside London, and, from 1737 onward, it formed the western center both of Methodism and of other branches of the wider evangelical movement (Barry 1988, 1991a, 1993a, 1997). Charles and Sarah Wesley had a home in Bristol from 1749 to 1778, and it was their main residence from 1756 to 1771, after which their son Samuel remained there until 1776 while father and son Charles were based in London (Rack 2004a, 2004b).

This chapter will try to tease out the significance of this Bristol period in the life of Charles Wesley's family by exploring the relationship, both positive and negative, between the musical and religious cultures to which the family were exposed. It will also consider how the attitudes of the Wesleys, especially as they affected the musical education of the two boys, mirrored wider concerns in Bristol culture regarding the relationship between the secular, even "bawdy," world of music, and the religious and moral values of the "godly." As I have shown elsewhere (Barry 2005), the very different careers of those other child prodigies, Chatterton and More, can

profitably be compared in this context. Here I hope to demonstrate that the boys'
life in Bristol also throws light on the family's ideals in music and religion, and,
by focusing on the Bristol context, to enhance the accounts of the musical careers
of the younger Wesleys offered recently by Lloyd (1998) and C. Young (2007).

There are two main sources for the musical education and activity of Charles
the younger and Samuel in Bristol. These are Charles the elder's account of his
two sons, reproduced in the Thomas Jackson edition of his journal (C. Wesley
1849, 2:140–55), and Samuel's manuscript reminiscences held in the British Library (*Lbl* Add. 27593), extensively quoted by Winters and Lightwood (1937): for
the latter source I will quote from Lightwood. Beyond that, there are occasional
references in letters, and a few mentions in the Bristol newspapers, although the
infrequency of these demonstrates the extent to which Charles the elder was
fulfilling his policy of keeping his sons (and indeed himself) out of the public eye.
Occasionally visitors to the house give us an additional insight. On November
5, 1761, the Bristol accountant and Wesleyan follower William Dyer noted in his
diary (as summarized by him later): "Visited Charles Wesley and heard wife play
and sing hymn tunes on the spinet she being noted for singing and for music.
One of the children, a child in petticoats, a kind of prodigy for music being able
to play a tune on the spinet without having learned the notes, but would hit
upon a tune merely by a surprising genius for music" (*BRcl* 20095: November 5,
1761). This brief comment encapsulates several key themes that emerge from the
longer accounts. Apart from the emphasis on young Charles's talent, not only
prodigious but also natural rather than learned, we find the stress on his mother's
own musical skills and influence and, of course, the centrality of hymns to the
domestic music making.

The importance of Sarah's influence is emphasized in all the accounts. She had
received a good education in music and singing in Brecknockshire as part of the
gentry family of Marmaduke Gwynne. When he was converted to Methodism
by Howell Harris, he clearly became a patron of Methodist music. For example,
Edward Godwin dedicated his *Hymns,* printed at Bristol in 1747, to "Marmaduke
Gwyn Esq.," as a patron who was very fond of hymns. Charles's account describes
the two-year-old Charles playing tunes based on what his mother sang (or what
he heard in the streets), and how she used to play the harpsichord to him, before tying him to a chair so he could also play (C. Wesley 1849, 2:140). Samuel
noted that his mother had very considerable vocal talent, played prettily on the
harpsichord and sang sweetly, especially Handel's oratorios. He claimed that his
father considered that his sons had music by their mother's side (Lightwood 1937:
14–15). It is perfectly reasonable, of course, to take this statement at face value, but
one may wonder whether it also reflects a certain distancing of Charles from his
sons' musical skills, both in terms of gender and also perhaps in terms of religious
significance. Or, put more positively perhaps, it was well within the proper sphere
of a mother, especially such a devout and devoted mother as Sarah, to educate

her sons to a love for, and skill in, music, which ideally would reflect her own subordination of that musical skill to the interests of both family and religion.

The Choice of Teachers

The stress on Sarah's influence also has to be understood in the context of the boys' natural precocity, and the extent and nature of their formal musical education. This theme dominates Charles's account of the boys' music making. As we have seen, when under three years old, Charles was said to play a tune readily and in just time and with true bass "without study or hesitation" (2:140). His talent was identified by the Bristol organist Edmund Broderip (not John Broderip, as assumed by Lloyd), who "heard him in petticoats and foretold he would one day make a great player" as he played "*con spirito*," but he was "left to ramble on" until nearly six (Lloyd 2004: 181). Even then, when given a music master, they chose an obscure organist called Edmund Rooke, "a man of no name but very good-natured who let him run on *ad libitum,* while he sat by more to observe than to control him." This was despite the fact that another Bristol organist, Nelme Rogers, "the oldest organist in Bristol" was his "first and very great friend," often setting him upon his knee and making him play to him, "declaring he was more delighted to hear him than any of his scholars or himself" (C. Wesley, 2:141).

The reason Charles then gives for not providing his first son with a better formal education is how costly it would have been to get him "the first masters" or purchase the necessary music. This was probably a factor, since music teachers were certainly expensive and the Wesley family not wealthy. But there also seems to be a note of pride in Charles's statement that, without hope of a benefactor to provide support, his son went on "with the assistance of nature" until ten. "Then Mr Rogers told me it was high time to put him in trammels," so the boy was sent first to Mr. Granville at Bath and then to various "London masters," until he returned to Bristol in March 1770. Then, Charles is at pains to tell us, he asked Joseph Kelway whether "he should not have Mr Br[oderip] to my son. He answered 'no, he can learn nothing from B., tho B. may from him'" (2:142–49).

A similar theme, though less fully articulated, is found in his account of his younger son's early talent. Samuel was playing tunes when two years, eleven months old, mostly picked up from the street organs. While his brother was playing he used to stand by "with his childish fiddle scraping and beating time." He taught himself to read and write at four to five years old from various oratorios, and he composed a great deal of music of his own for oratorios before he was six. Although Broderip apparently also took a great interest in him, he learned to play by note between six and seven from "Mr. Williams a young organist of Bristol," but during his year under Williams it was hard to say "which is the master and which the scholar," as he chose what music he learned and often played extempore. He also taught himself the violin, admittedly assisted by a soldier for six weeks, before he had twenty lessons from the professional violinist Mr. Kingsbury. (2:152–55; Lightwood 1937: 20–21.)

Why this family reluctance, both to make use of professional musicians and to acknowledge that they might have done much to assist the early flowering of the two boys? No doubt family pride and the narrative power of natural genius played a major part, just as the problems of finance were certainly real. But was there also a family decision to choose lesser masters who lacked the influence, or perhaps the capability, to educate the boys in musical directions that might have challenged the family's ideals and values? A parallel is offered by a remark of the Moravian minister in Bristol in his diary on December 23, 1766, commenting on how Sammy Fripp, one of the children of a wealthy tobacco cutter, "lately began to learn on the harpsichord by his father's desire from a worldly master one Mr Combe [Coombes; see p. 146]—surprising what dangers this exposes him to" (*BRu*: Diary of Single Brethren, 1766).

If we consider again the various Bristol masters who are named, an interesting pattern emerges. (The information about them and other matters in the ensuing paragraphs was, unless otherwise stated, found in the *Bristol Journal, Bonner and Middleton's Bristol Journal, Bristol Weekly Intelligencer, Felix Farley's Bristol Journal*, Hooper, and the Bristol Record Office sources listed in the Bibliography.) Edmund Broderip, a leading member of the west country musical dynasty of Broderips, had been educated (at the expense of Lady Betty Germain) by Francesco Geminiani and Thomas Kelway. His Bristol friend John Malchair claimed that "no one but his master Kelway could touch Scarlatti like him. The Londoners heard him with admiration" (Hooper: 113, 160; *Ob* MS. Mus.d.32; Lynan, wrongly claiming Edmund taught the Wesley brothers). Although he never advertised his teaching services in the newspapers, he taught harpsichord and singing to the young Mary Robinson, later the Prince of Wales's mistress "Perdita" (M. Robinson: 14–15). Broderip was not only organist of several of the parish churches (St. James, Temple, and the Mayor's chapel), but also performed regularly at concerts and balls in various venues and was the first organist at the Assembly Room, opened in 1756 on Prince Street, for which he supplied the organ. He represented not just the most expensive and fashionable face of Bristol music, but also the closest alliance between the religious foundation of music making (his church positions) and the secular world of fashion. These came together, for example, in the regular concerts held for the Sons of the Clergy "feasts" (in aid of the families of Anglican clergy), Bristol's equivalent of the Three Choirs Festival, which he often organized.

The tensions between these two worlds could be expressed in many ways. For example, organists were accused of neglecting their church duties for more lucrative work: in 1771 the Temple vestry rebuked Broderip for not attending as often as he ought and for sending inferior deputies. Organists were also criticized for the style of their playing. Although Chatterton published one poem praising Broderip's "excellent performance on the organ" (1:168), in several others he attacked his playing, and in a letter of January 1770 he contrasted him unfavorably with John Allen, a regular organist at his beloved St. Mary Redcliffe, claiming he lacked real taste, indulging instead in over-ornamentation, tickling the fancy or providing empty amusement by offering airs "stolen from Italian operas" (1:425, 516–17, 640). It is certainly clear that Broderip was very effective at maximizing his own reputation through ensuring a high profile in both religious and secular events and that he shared his musical skills and repertory across both worlds. So, even though he was a pillar of both the Church and the musical establishment in Bristol, his very public and self-aggrandizing career management may have appeared to the Wesleys to offer precisely the model they wished to avoid for their sons.

By contrast, as Charles stressed, Edward Rooke was a man of little reputation. Despite being organist of the cathedral temporarily in 1756, of All Saints from 1759, and then of the cathedral from 1769 until his death in 1773, he appears little in the newspapers or musical press, although benefit concerts were held for him both at the Assembly Room and at Cooper's Hall (another ballroom and concert venue). He was a singer as well as an organist, singing in the cathedral choir from 1759 to 1762 and at his benefit concerts. According to an advertisement in 1759 he offered home lessons on the harpsichord, and two years after his death an auction included "all his harpsichords and spinets."

Even greater obscurity surrounds David Williams, the chosen master for Samuel. Samuel's own reminiscences confirm that Williams was his only master on the harpsichord and "taught me with great attention for some years." He acknowledges his "justness and precision" but also echoes his father's account in claiming that Williams allowed him to choose his own music (Lightwood 1937: 20). Williams succeeded Rooke as organist of All Saints in 1772, although he had presumably been in Bristol since at least 1767, when he was married at St. James church, and in 1768 he obtained the freedom of the city (allowing him to vote) as the husband of a cordwainer's daughter. It is tempting to suppose that she may have been the "Mary Williams organist" living in St. James churchyard who appears on the Wesleyan membership list for Bristol in 1783: this would imply that David was chosen by the Wesleys as a co-religionist. The same list also includes a "Grace Rooke" in James Street, who may have been a widow or daughter of Edward Rooke, so religion may have affected both choices (Kent: 123, 121), assuring the Wesleys that these particular organists were less likely to corrupt their sons.

If family trust was the key factor, it is less clear how it excluded the choice of Nelme Rogers. Why, if he was young Charles's "best friend," was he not asked to teach him? Maybe it was a matter of age. He was indeed Bristol's oldest organist, having first held a church post at All Saints in 1715, and also serving St. James, Christchurch, and in particular St. Mary Redcliffe, where he was organist from the time the new organ was built (1727) until his resignation in 1772 (although John Allen must have often deputized for him there prior to his own appointment in 1772). However, for about twenty years until the late 1740s, Rogers had also taught dancing to private families and at a dancing school in the Guildhall, so he may also have seemed too much part of the world of fashion.

It is worth adding that there were plenty of other organists in Bristol during this period from whom teachers could have been chosen. Rooke was preceded as cathedral organist by Edward Higgins and George Coombes. Higgins, who came to Bristol in 1759 from Salisbury and was also a vicar choral in Dublin, quit his cathedral post in 1765 but remained in Bristol, dying in King's Square in 1769. He was also a singer, performing in *Acis and Galatea* at the Assembly Room in 1765. In 1759 he advertised that he instructed gentlemen and ladies in music on the harpsichord, violin, violoncello, and guitar, as well as in singing, for the usual price of £6 6s per annum if waited on, or £4 4s in the boarding schools. Presumably these prices were too high for the Wesleys, or else Higgins's active involvement in the concert life of the city put them off.

George Coombes, the "worldly master" of Sammy Fripp in 1766, had two periods as the cathedral organist (1756–59 and 1765–69), having come to Bristol from Wimborne in Dorset, and was also All Saints organist in 1756–58. Like all the cathedral organists, he was expected to instruct the choristers, but he was also paid for two years as a "singing man," that is, an adult member of the choir. In 1757 he advertised that he taught young ladies on the harpsichord and learners on the guitar and would attend ladies in the countryside, and he was involved in a dispute in 1767 with a singing man he had instructed.

Reference has already been made to John Allen, organist and "music master" (his occupation when freed as a joiner's son in 1774), "nicknamed 'Thumbs' as playing upon the great organ [of St. Mary Redcliffe] had changed all his fingers" (*BRro*, Bristol Infirmary Biographical Memoirs, 1:f.54). He is mentioned by Samuel in a letter of 1773 as calling at their house (Lightwood 1937: 21). William Bayton, Broderip's former pupil, was active in concerts and as a composer of secular music and songs from about 1770, but he never obtained a church living, which may help explain why he appears in the 1775 trade directory as "nurse, organist"! (Sketchley: 6). Finally, Rice Wasborough (or Wasbrough), freed as a barber-surgeon's son in 1774, began playing at St. Augustine and at St. Peter in 1771–72 and was being favorably compared with Broderip in 1773, before eventually becoming cathedral organist in 1781.

The Politics of Religious Music in Bristol

The prominence of the church organists in the public musical life of Bristol reflects the success with which the Anglican Church, through investment in organs and architectural improvements, had established its place in the polite culture of the period (Barry 1993a: 202–4). This success may, in turn, have ensured the relative stagnation of the nonconformist societies in the decades after 1720, by attracting the polite classes back into church: a report of the opening of the new organ at St.

Peter in 1772 commented on the presence of many nonconformists, even Quakers, in the packed church, confirmed by a poem on the same event.

But this alliance of religion and fashion had its own problems. The music of organs and elaborate chanting and intoning in the cathedral tradition was distrusted by many as a popish element, compared to the simple metrical psalm singing of parish churches. Defenders of complex music, such as Arthur Bedford (vicar of Temple in the early eighteenth century), had first of all to establish the scriptural warranty for the music they favored. As we have already seen, there could be tensions between the demands of church work and secular activity, leading to questions about how far the true interests of religion became sacrificed to commercial demands and secular values: these issues were highlighted by Bedford and remained sensitive (Barry 1993a: 201, 204–6). But there was also the matter of whether this particular form of music met the needs of the whole congregation or the full range of church activity. Was fashionable organ music, while attracting a polite congregation, perhaps preventing the churches from reaching ordinary people, or from meeting the demand for a more intense and participatory religious experience?

Significantly, this question became focused on the issue of singing. Despite the building of organs, the Anglican churches (and their rivals in old Dissent) had retained the traditional method of congregational singing (with the parish clerk giving out the line) and generally the old tunes. It was widely recognized that a major attraction in the new evangelical revival, deployed not just by the Methodists but also by Baptist and other Calvinist evangelicals, was the new manner of hymn and psalm singing. This new approach involved the congregation far more intensely and utilized lively tunes often borrowed from secular ballads or operas: Chatterton's "bawdy songs made godly."

Chapters 1 and 4 have considered the impact of this development within the Methodist movement and the place of the Wesleys within it. Suffice it to note here that numerous Methodist hymnbooks were published in Bristol by Wesley's printers, first two of the Farley family (Felix and his widow, Elizabeth) and then William Pine (Barry 1991b, 1993b; see also Chapter 3). Charles and John's publishing, in which their hymns were central, lay at the heart of their income. John had used the value and profits of his books to persuade the Gwynnes to allow Sarah to marry Charles, and it was the profit from one of his hymn publications that allowed Charles to buy his Bristol house (J. Wesley 1975, 26:347; C. Wesley 1849, 1:46).

In addition to the Wesleys, Methodist authors in Bristol included Edward Godwin, Joseph Humphreys, John Thomas, and William Williams (the last two aiming at the Welsh market). In 1756 Robert Williamson published another collection in Bristol, under Moravian auspices. The Bristol Moravians purchased an organ in 1756 and in early 1757 began to buy children's hymnbooks, before in 1769 urging all their "brothers and sisters" that, when the new hymnbooks arrived, they "never come to chapel without them so that they may join in the singing without the brother's giving out the line" (*BRru* Moravian Collection, Committee Minutes: August 20, 1756; January 9, 1757; July 30, 1769). George Whitefield's Tabernacle chapel in Bristol also regularly bought hymnbooks from 1767 onward, ordering twenty-five at a cost of £2 10s in 1775, and in 1774 they appointed John Price as a singing master "to teach the singers" at £4 per annum.

However central it was to Bristol Methodism, the development of hymn singing had a much wider impact on churches of all kinds, which responded vigorously to the Methodist challenge. The most active group in exploiting the potential of the hymn were the Baptists. Hymn singing was a well-established tradition among Bristol Baptists by the early eighteenth century, but it was greatly encouraged by the emphasis on congregational hymn singing of their dynamic minister Benjamin Foskett, who started an academy in Bristol (later called the Baptist Education Society, and forerunner of Bristol Baptist College), whose pupils included Benjamin Beddome (Hayden: 28–29, 35–36, 152, 231, 269–97; Sharpe). Among its clergy and teachers were a number who wrote hymns, including John Beddome (father of Benjamin), John Needham, and Caleb Evans, who published one of the Baptists' earliest hymn collections in 1769 in collaboration with his former pupil John Ash.

But the influence of hymnody spread far beyond such evangelical leaders. Many lay people were also drawn to hymn writing: a considerable number of the poems published in the newspapers were called hymns, and devout young Christians such as Mary Stokes (later Dudley) wrote hymns on their spiritual condition (Chatterton, 1:4; Dudley: 7–8). Many of the music collections advertised for sale by Bristol booksellers were psalm and hymn settings, and these were presumably played by the devout when making music at home on Sundays (e.g., Butterworth: 4–5). Hymns were printed for a meeting at the city workhouse in 1767, and Christmas Day 1770 was celebrated in several parishes with hymns sung from specially printed sheets (*Hymns Sung; Hymns for Christmas Day*).

As Temperley has shown, the revived interest in congregational singing at this period was reflected not just in hymns, but also in new emphasis on the singing of psalms, which were acceptable to many Anglicans and Presbyterians who were dubious about hymns. In 1769 Edmund Broderip's brother John, organist at Wells cathedral, published his *Psalms, Hymns and Spiritual Songs*. By the 1770s, many of the parish churches were buying new versions of the psalms for congregational use. In the *Bristol Journal* of March 7, 1772, the Bristol music seller Naish advertised a volume, under the title "Divine Music," which was eventually published in London as *Twenty Psalm Tunes in Three Parts . . . sung . . . at the Cathedral and most other Places of Worship in Bristol* (*HTI* #TPT). The music was composed by the late cathedral organist Coombes and others. Intriguingly, the British Library copy of this volume belonged to Samuel Wesley, probably as a youngster, and it includes some keyboard fingering and organ registration added by him. In a letter of 1773, the seven-year-old Samuel reports that "last Sunday I played a psalm at St. James' church" (Lightwood 1937: 21)—perhaps using this book? Later eighteenth-century Bristol organists produced similar publications, and Hooper has noted the popularity of metrical psalmody during this particular period (271–80).

The fullest account of that renewed popularity comes in the records of the Lewin's Mead Presbyterian congregation, which at this point contained many of the leading merchant families. In 1758 they proposed "to introduce a better manner of singing psalms in public worship." The ministers were to preach suitable sermons to recommend the people to "this delightful act of worship in singing forth the praise of God" and "making melody not only in their hearts but with their voices," especially asking the females to join "in a concert so divine." The aim was to be achieved partly by paying the clerk to instruct *gratis* any young people or others who wished to learn to sing (initially £10 per annum, reduced to £7 in 1762), and partly by abandoning singing by line in favor of singing from books. In order to achieve this, the church had to purchase enough books for all the poor (150 books at a cost of £13), while expecting the prosperous to buy and bring their own. Even this assumed that all the congregation could read, and reluctantly the church made the concession to illiteracy of singing each hymn or psalm twice, once before the sermon according to the old method, and once after by the book (*BRro* 6687).

The Position of Handel

The final theme that runs through the family narratives is the significance of a particular brand of music, epitomized by the figure of Handel and his oratorios. Charles noted that any master they chose for Charles the younger had to be an admirer of Handel, "as my son preferred him to all the world." His two favorite authors before he was ten were Handel and Corelli, and the choice of Granville of Bath was because he was "an old friend of Handels." During the next four years in Bath and London his influences were "Handel, Corelli, Scarlatti and Geminiani," and he had a "particular bent to church musick, especially oratorios" (2:142–44). There are only two recorded instances of the young Charles playing in public in Bristol. One was a harpsichord concerto at a benefit concert for a violinist (Mr. Morgan) in 1769 at the Assembly Room (presumably the performance for which his father was reprimanded by two Bristolians in 1769 [Lloyd 1998: 27]), but the other was *Messiah* in the cathedral in 1774, at which Master Charles Wesley played a concerto on the organ between the acts (*Bristol Journal*, January 28, 1769; March 12, 1774; Lightwood 1937: 4). There were only two Bristol subscribers to a series of Handel oratorio publications in the early 1770s (*Jephtha* in 1770, *Israel in Egypt* in 1771, *Saul, Joshua*, and *Judas Maccabaeus* in 1773): one was "Charles Wesley junior," the other Henry Burgum (see p. 151). Samuel taught himself to read words from the oratorio of *Samson* and by five "had all of *Samson* and *Messiah* by heart." As already noted, he remembered his mother singing Handel's oratorios. In the 1773 letter he reports: "I have learnt Handel's water piece today and some of the Highland Laddie" (Lightwood 1937: 21). In a satirical poem of 1776 he observed: "I question if their worships know / The Odds 'twixt me and Handel" (Lightwood, 1937: 38–39).

It would seem clear that for the Wesley family, Handel's music in general, and his oratorios in particular, provided the ideal blend of musical excellence with religious edification, allowing full engagement of both voices and instruments. Interestingly, in this respect at least their preferences are closely matched in the public world of Bristol music. For all those seeking to reconcile the worlds of church music and public concert making, Handel's oratorios became the perfect compromise. Anthems and oratorios by Purcell, Handel, and Boyce (whose *Solomon* was performed at the Assembly Room on December 17, 1759) were used in concerts, and even on the stage, as well as in church performances (Hooper). It was noted of Broderip that "he extracted organ parts from the most famous choruses of Handel and played them in a most masterly style" (*Ob* MS. Mus.d.32). Handel's *Messiah* was performed at the opening of the new Assembly Room in 1756, and *Judas Maccabaeus* the next year when the new organ (Broderip's) was unveiled. In 1763 Broderip conducted another *Messiah* at the Assembly Room (Dean: 472–73; Collins: 44–46; newspaper sources).

A newspaper article by "Philalethes," prompted by the 1756 opening, welcomed the proper use of music for its first purpose of religion, although noting that it was "often prostituted to wicked and wanton purposes." He suggested that it become "an established rule" for there to be a performance of "so solemn a piece of sacred musick" at each "high festival of the church," but he feared that such religious purposes would be neglected and the new assembly room used only for entertainment and diversion. Its organizers should ensure it was constantly used for religious piety, "not just consecrate it with a sublime piece of musick and afterwards banish it from the place." Music, like that of David or the new Jerusalem, could not only take away the cares of the world, but also mend hearts and instruct in religious truths. Those who prevented this and would "rather pervert it by confining it solely to the more fashionable use of love and gallantry, solely to humor the depraved taste of the age, will banish from their Assembly many who would gladly join in any instructive or innocent entertainment." The following week a further correspondent, "Laicus," praised not only the excellent performance, the elegance of the room, and the conduct of the occasion, but also the "serious disposition" of the audience "as such a solemn occasion giving glory to our God requires, that the whole assembly rising from their seats seemed with their whole hearts to join in the heavenly song." But again there was a warning tone in the final statement that "I think we may be well assured no light and wanton strains, no French or Italian soft airs, will ever afford such solid, rational delight, such secret joy and satisfaction, as every well-disposed heart must certainly have felt in a very sensible manner on this occasion" (*Felix Farley's Bristol Journal,* January 10 and 17, 1756).

Apart from Handel's famous performances of *Messiah* at the Foundling Hospital beginning in 1750, the only one given in a sacred building in his lifetime was that at Bristol cathedral in 1758. As we have seen, another was mounted in Easter 1774, supported by Charles the younger. A printed list of the music for that performance survives (*BRro,* Bristol Infirmary Biographical Memoirs, 3:61). There are no records of similar performances in Bristol's parish churches in this period, though the neighboring church of Keynsham (home of the Brydges family, friends of Handel) was used for this purpose several times after 1750, with Bristol musicians playing a major part (Johnstone 2008: 118; and newspaper sources). Handel's oratorios were used both at the musical "feasts" of the Sons of the Clergy and at the opening of the new chapel run by Lady Huntingdon's Connexion in Bristol. Both John Wesley and William Dyer were impressed at the effect of the 1758 oratorio on the crowded audiences at the cathedral. This was the only musical event that Dyer recorded having attended, and he noted that "a great multitude assembled to see and hear this great performance of sacred music, sung by men and women of unhallowed lips" (J. Wesley 1975–, 11:161; *BRcl* 20095: August 17, 1758).

Yet, as Dyer's rather equivocal tone signifies, even Handel performances stood uneasily between the hallowed and the unhallowed. The 1774 performance at the cathedral degenerated into violence as people competed for seats: in Dyer's words, "a riot took place, and many of the ladies lost their caps, muffles etc." (March 31, 1774). In the newspaper controversy that followed about who was responsible for the disturbances, blame for poor organization was widely placed on Henry Burgum, the Handel-worshipping pewterer. He is now best known as one of Chatterton's patrons, for whom Chatterton constructed a false pedigree, but at the time he was notorious in Bristol for his attempts to run a series of musical events and other charitable occasions, which led eventually to his bankruptcy through neglect of his business. To his numerous critics this was only to be expected since, as one of the critics of the 1774 riot put it, Burgum might "cut a worthy figure among his brother tradesmen, but should learn not to go beyond his last" (Meyerstein: 136, 149–50; *Bristol Journal,* April 2 and 9, 1774). A series of rival subscription concerts was dogged by mutual accusations that those running them were not genteel or knowledgeable enough to organize such matters (Barry 1985a: 194–95; newspaper sources). The public world of the concert was inevitably part of that hierarchical world of wealth, education, and fashion from which both John and Charles Wesley felt generally alienated and from which they hoped to protect Charles's children. By limiting their musical education, and following the ideal domestic combination of hymns and Handel offered by Sarah, the Wesley family sought the best possible reconciliation between music and religion.

Beyond Family Concerns

There remains the question of how far the two boys shared the concerns of their family. Were they content to be kept away from the public life of Bristol music and to develop their music in the protected setting of their house? Here we may note again the occasional hints of another world of "street" music influencing the boys, with the two-year-old Charles picking up tunes heard in the street, and Samuel at the same age picking up tunes mostly "from the street-organs" (C. Wesley 1849, 2:140, 152). This reminds us that Bristol's musical soundscape included work- and drinking-based music, built on the simpler music of fiddles and drums, accompanying the maritime and industrial trades of the city or filling the taverns and clubs, which enjoyed vigorous traditions of toasting and harmony singing. Then there was another world of civic culture, with regular processions and events accompanied by music, notably that provided by the wind and string instruments of the city waits (Barry 1985a: 221–28).

We also have several versions of a "serio-comic epistle in verse" supposedly written by Samuel (though copied down by his father), recording his disappointment at being initially invited to perform publicly in Bristol and then turned down on grounds of age. One version clearly refers to the 1774 cathedral concert described above, suggesting that Charles's organ concerto replaced a planned performance by Samuel. Another, apparently a couple of years later, states that the occasion of the verse was "On being advertised, *as a child,* to play before the Worshipful the Mayor and Corporation at a City Feast, and afterwards declined." In both, Samuel complains playfully about being treated as a child, noting ironically his evident lack of the "solidness" or "judgement" of Henry Burgum, or the "steadiness" or "gravity" of another of the organizers, Thomas Lediard ("Liddy," to rhyme with giddy).

> Excusing their contempt they say
>   (Which more inflames my passion),
> I am not grave enough to play
>   Before the Corporation.
>
> To those sweet city waits, although
>   I may not hold a candle
> I question if their worships know
>   The odds 'twixt me and Handel.

In one version he also compares himself to the organists:

> With Bristol-Organists not yet
>   I come in competition
> But let them know I wou'd be great
>   I do not want ambition

Recording his high-spirited resentment of his "rash despisers," he threatens revenge unless compensated with an (expensive) Stainer violin:

> Nothing shall, sir, appease my rage
> At their uncouth demeanor
> Unless they prudently assuage
> Mine anger with A Steyner.
> (Baker 1962: 324–26)

Judging by the poem's strong (if playful) sense of personal worth, even "ambition," to be judged superior to the limited talents of the musical amateurs of Bristol, it is tempting to think that, for all his parents' efforts, Samuel Wesley had more in common with fellow prodigy Thomas Chatterton than with the latter's stereotypical Methodist!

CHAPTER 11

Pictorial Precocity

JOHN RUSSELL'S PORTRAITS OF
CHARLES AND SAMUEL WESLEY

Peter S. Forsaith

Introduction

In the Duke's Hall of the Royal Academy of Music, London, hang two large full-length oil portraits of Charles Wesley's sons Charles and Samuel (Illus. 11.1 and 11.2). They are undated but are by the evangelical artist John Russell, a friend of the Wesley family. That of Samuel was exhibited at the Royal Academy in 1777 and engraved by William Dickinson in 1778, suggesting that the pictures were painted around 1776 or 1777. Charles would have been about twenty, Samuel nine.

Both are set in a musical context: Charles, dressed as a young man about town, sits nonchalantly beside a harpsichord, half leaning on it. Samuel, in red coat and breeches, stands at a desk, writing music. His oratorio *Ruth,* composed at the age of eight, leans against the desk, and an organ is in the background. Clearly, the paintings are a pair: of equal size (160 × 105 cm [63" × 41.5"]) and identically framed (the framing seemingly contemporary with the pictures). The furniture and carpet that appear in both are probably Russell's studio interior; they appear also in two Russell portraits of a cleric, probably Martin Madan, and his wife dating from 1771 (Christie's, London, April 26, 1985, lot 94). But the key question is: why were these two grand pictures painted, and what do they signify? In order to address those questions we need to examine the circumstances.

The Wesley family moved to London in 1771, predominantly, it seems, for the boys' musical education (Olleson 2007: 131). Yet there was another, subtler adjustment taking place: while Charles the elder had always been comfortable among "polite" company (in a way John Wesley was not) and cultivated friends from musical and artistic circles as well as from evangelical society drawing rooms, he had remained active among Methodists who were generally from a lower level of society. Based in Bristol while itinerant between there and London, he could keep these aspects of his life in balance. His move to the new and fashionable suburb of Marylebone may have seemed pretentious to some Methodists. As his friend John Fletcher, vicar of Madeley, Shropshire, warned him in October of that year:

ILLUS. 11.1. Charles Wesley the younger (Royal Academy of Music). Oil portrait by John Russell. Reproduced by permission of the Royal Academy of Music and Norman Lebrecht.

ILLUS. 11.2. Samuel Wesley as a boy (Royal Academy of Music). Oil portrait by John Russell. Reproduced by permission of the Royal Academy of Music and Norman Lebrecht.

You have your *enemies* as well as your brother, they complain of your *love for musick, company,* fine *people, great folks,* and of the *wane of your former zeal & frugality.* I need not put you in mind to cut off *sinful appearances, you were taught to do* this before I knew anything of the matter: Only see you abound more and more to stop the mouth of your adversaries [and] your jealous friends. My Xn. Love to your household & Sally. (*Eg,* Box 2.1; Forsaith 2008: 185.)

Fletcher, who was godfather to Sally Wesley and often included a special greeting to her when writing to her father, seems to have been more understanding than critical of Wesley's move, and his perception was probably accurate: in fact, little had changed but appearances. Charles Wesley was always among the cultural elite by virtue of his education, at Westminster School and Oxford, and his Anglican orders. His son Samuel, on his deathbed, apparently reminded his son, "Remember, the Wesleys were all gentlemen and scholars" (T. Jackson 1873: 232). But the move to London made that more evident. Although frugal, Wesley lived well and enjoyed the finer things of life as he could, including art. It would not have been out of character to have an up-and-coming (evangelical) artist to paint his family's portraits for their new home. While some Methodists may have had scruples about art, this varied with different sectors of the movement: John Wesley's societies were often drawn from the lower strata of society, while the likes of Lady Huntingdon or Lord Dartmouth wore their coronets and prayed, as the poet Cowper put it. It is impossible at this time to draw real distinctions between Anglican Evangelicals and "Methodists," although some would doubtless disapprove in principle on the grounds that pictures were a luxury item, while in the context of their buildings the absence of decoration was consistent with the second commandment.

John Russell and His Earlier Work

Charles Wesley had probably met the artist John Russell some years previously. Russell (1745–1806) was from the market town of Guildford, some thirty miles southwest of London, where his father was a printer and became mayor. The family had been in the town since at least 1509; they were established and prominent. The young John Russell showed an aptitude for drawing and was apprenticed to a leading London artist, Francis Cotes, from about age fifteen. By 1767 he was working on his own—suggesting a seven-year apprenticeship. He attended the recently founded Royal Academy schools from 1770, when he won a gold medal for a drawing, and eventually became one of the leading British portrait artists of the late eighteenth century. His most characteristic work (and the majority of his output) was in "crayons" (pastels); in 1772 he published *Elements of Painting with Crayons,* which went to several editions and which he revised and enlarged in 1777. He was appointed crayon painter to the king in 1790.

However, in 1764 Russell had experienced an evangelical conversion under the ministry of Madan. His newfound religious zeal did not sit easily with his professional life, and his determination to spread the faith lost him clients, who came to be painted, not to be preached at. He was thrown out of Lord Cowdray's house, Midhurst Park, for attempting to convert his Catholic staff. In 1768 he noted that he thought the people of Guildford would be glad to see him drowned in the river (Rhodes).

He was thus faced with a difficult prospect in establishing the sort of studio clientele necessary to build a successful career, although he had useful contacts through his own family (despite their disapprobation of his religious views) and through his in-laws following his 1770 marriage to Hannah Faden, daughter of a leading London map- and printmaker. So the first few years of their marriage were spent in poverty. Four of their first five children died in infancy, Russell could not afford to buy shoes, and in 1774 he faced imprisonment as a debtor. But around the mid-1770s his career developed, and the inheritance of a small estate in 1781 put the years of penury behind him.

One promising source of patronage was among supportive evangelicals whom he painted, including George Whitefield (c. 1770), (probably) Martin Madan (1771), the young William Wilberforce (1770), and Lady Huntingdon (several portraits, 1772–73, including a curious full-length one in biblical costume for Whitefield's "orphanage" near Savannah, Georgia). This constituency could be double-edged, as some urged him to abandon painting and become a preacher: Lady Huntingdon tried to persuade him to attend her seminary at Trevecca, Wales. But although he did speak at meetings, he remained clear that art was his vocation—and indeed his pulpit, for by his pictures he was able to promulgate his religious views. His "fancy pictures" of children (usually a posed set scene) particularly carry a moral message of innocence in a world of temptation, and his later fascination with the moon is rooted in his theological understandings of God and nature (A. Matthews).

In the early 1770s, when he was struggling, he painted portraits of Charles Wesley's family. Four of the five survive, in addition to the two later, larger portraits that are the subject of this chapter. That of Charles the elder (see Chapter 2, Illus. 2.1) is at the Museum of Methodism, City Road, London; those of Charles's wife Sarah, of Charles the younger, and of Samuel are at Charles Wesley's House, Bristol. Not without some difficulty, Charles also persuaded John Wesley to have Russell take his picture. The original or an early copy (see Illus. 1.1) is at Kingswood School, Bath (Ward and Heitzenrater: 303). These earlier portraits of Charles the younger and Samuel—quite different from the later ones, although also showing them engaged in musical activity—present some questions. That considered to be of Charles, signed "John Russell 1771," relies for identity on the apparent age of the sitter and the facial likeness with his mother. In its provenance, for example when sold through Christie's (London, November 30, 1917; May 15,

1936) or Bonhams (London, December 21, 1961), it has generally been referred to as of Charles, but that is not conclusive.

The picture of Samuel is more problematic. While there is some facial likeness to the later Russell portrait, he is portrayed playing a violin or viola left-handed. As in the later picture he is wearing a scarlet suit, with a medallion pendant from the waistcoat. It is neither signed nor dated, and its provenance prior to coming into the ownership of the New Room, Bristol (at an unknown date probably between 1930 and 1970), is not known. The medallion is identical to one known to have been awarded to William Crotch (1775–1847), another musical prodigy, but whether that was unique to Crotch is also unclear. It has indeed been suggested that the portrait is of Crotch rather than Wesley (Snowman: 234–45), but the evidence is so far circumstantial.

There was also a portrait of Charles's daughter Sally, which is now lost: it was available to Marshall Claxton for his "Holy Triumph" of John Wesley's deathbed, exhibited at the Royal Academy in 1844. Sally was not musical but was artistic: John Russell taught her to draw. Her humorous caricature of her father coming from preaching in Bristol is a tribute both to her own graphic abilities and her sense of humor, as well as to Russell's tutelage. She depicts herself as a fashionable young lady, being criticized by serious-minded Methodists (*Mu* DDWes 1/62).

Charles Wesley was paternally cautious about his children's fashionable habits, writing to Sally in 1777 after a fall caused by her "narrow fashionable heels . . . Providence saved you from a like accident at Guildford. Beware the third time!" (Tyson: 354). He wrote a corrective poem for Charles (quoted T. Jackson 1873: 228):

> "Take time by the forelock," is old Charles's word;
>   "Time enough," quoth his son, with the air of a lord;
>   "Let the vulgar be punctual; my humour and passion
>   Is to make people wait, or I can't be in fashion."

Russell's later portrait showed just this side of young Charles, foppishly dressed with an air of disdain, although years later Thomas Jackson commented on his "genteel poverty" (1873: 227).

The Two Later Portraits

Eighteenth-century portraiture, if not formulaic, involved accepted cultural specifics in its processes and its products, which have been described and analyzed extensively elsewhere (Piper 1992; Pointon 1993; Vaughan 1999). Engaging a painter was a contractual business between the client (usually the sitter but, in the case of child portraits, parents or patrons) and the artist. The viewer was the third party in the transaction, as the response of family, friends, and the public at large was critical to the appreciation not only of the picture, but of the sitter's and artist's reputations. Although the artist would make his (or her, for there were female artists) interpretation of the sitter, it was ultimately to the client that they deferred (Pointon). So, for instance, when John Wesley was painted in 1789 by George Romney, by then the leading London portraitist, a decision about an engraving was left to Mrs. Tighe, who paid for the picture (Telford 1931, 8:115; Forsaith 2004).

Compositional conventions were also coded. How a person was painted sent messages about them. Samuel Wesley, for instance, is shown *contrapposto*, standing with his right leg crossed over his left—a pose probably derived from a classical statue in the Uffizi Gallery, Florence, thought to be of Mercury. The sitter is thus associated with the qualities of the visual allusion—if Mercury, then the messenger of the gods (appropriate to a musician) and a child prodigy (Haskell: 266–67; Meyer).

However, there may be more to be read from this canvas. In 1774, just prior to his move to London, Thomas Gainsborough showed in Bath a picture of the musician Johann Christian Fischer, a gifted German oboist who had been in Britain since 1768 and would later marry Gainsborough's daughter. It bears some strong resemblances to Russell's portrait of young Samuel. Fischer is also depicted in "Mercury" pose, clad in a scarlet suit, and composing music, quill in hand. Gainsborough's picture was not commissioned but probably painted as a display piece to advertise the artist's talents. It would hang in his studio, and possibly Russell saw it in London. Russell's picture of Samuel Wesley may almost be said to mimic Gainsborough (Sloman: 100–105). If this is so, the implications are clear: that not only was there a classical allusion, but Wesley was also being associated with a virtuoso musician.

An artist's studio was not merely a working space but served as a gallery does today: a place where polite society might come to see who was being painted or be seen themselves and view the artist's "show" pictures. The choice of such pictures was a careful matter, since the artist needed to advertise the versatility of his capabilities. The two later pictures of the Wesley boys suggest that Russell may have been demonstrating that he could both model on the antique and be original, for the picture of young Charles is not so obvious in its connotations. It is unclear from which classical statue the pose might be derived, and if he was again drawing on Gainsborough, it is difficult to see which picture may have been his model. While his brother's picture indicates musical industry, this one conveys a message of studied leisure, if not indolence, on Charles's part. The sitter has clearly little intention of playing the instrument against which he is so nonchalantly leaning: his left hand is gloved, his right holding his hat. It is as if he is about to go out rather than be busy at his music.

In its poised repose it is not dissimilar to Gainsborough's *Blue Boy* of 1770 (painted partly as a challenge to Reynolds's aversion to using blue) and indeed seems stylistically linked more to "fancy paintings" of children than to adult portraits. Arguably this is the more eye-catching picture of the two, a composition less cluttered than that of Samuel and using light pastel colors to emphasize the fluid diagonal axes. But its apparent unrelatedness to other portraiture might indicate that Russell composed a truly original picture, which depends on no prototype for its formula. Paired with a painting that clearly does derive from both classical model and fashionable practice, could it be indicative of Russell wishing to demonstrate his virtuosity in two contrasting styles?

Although much of Russell's output, and his characteristic work, is in pastels, he worked in oils earlier in his career, and many of his portraits of evangelicals and their families from that time are in that medium. Although oils tend to give a harder treatment, their use may not have been a deliberate comment on evangelicals but imply simply that he moved over to pastels only as his career developed. Some of his oils coloring reflects his use of pastels.

There thus seems a weight of probability that these portraits were showpiece pictures, either for the artist's studio or for the sitters' family, or perhaps for both. The provenance is ambiguous: although the Royal Academy of Music received the paintings through Samuel Wesley's son, Matthias Erasmus Wesley (1821–1901), it holds an invoice of January 6, 1891, for Matthias's purchase of them from the London dealer Colnaghi for £189 (R. J. B. Walker, 1:543). Earlier Colnaghi records do not survive. If descent was through the Wesley family, it could be surmised that even if they hung for some years in Russell's studio, they also hung in the Wesleys' house, possibly even in the concert room in which Charles and Samuel performed.

The Marylebone House and Its Concert Room

Records of the series of subscription concerts given by the Wesleys in their home at 1 Chesterfield Street, Marylebone, between 1779 and 1787 indicate "audience numbers for individual concerts between twelve and sixty-two, with attendances typically in the forties and fifties. The subscribers and their guests came from a wide cross-section of society," including Lord Mornington, Dr. Johnson, and General Oglethorpe (Olleson 2003: 22; see also Kassler and Olleson: 24ff.). John Russell senior, the artist's father, attended at least once. Yet was the Wesleys' concert room of sufficient capacity to accommodate an audience of that size? It seems unlikely that the people of rank who attended would have been content to find themselves cramped together like a crowd in a Methodist meeting house, however different were attitudes to personal space then.

The lease of the house to which the family moved piecemeal in 1771, and where they continued to live into the nineteenth century, was given to Charles Wesley by Mrs. Gumley, a member of the aristocratic evangelical circle that possibly extended to Lord Chesterfield (Schlenther: 57–58; Welch: 73–75). While Charles Wesley's home at Charles Street, Bristol, survives, as does John Wesley's in City Road, London, the Marylebone house was demolished around 1860 and only a sketchy likeness remains (Illus. 11.3). It depicts a two-bay dwelling, with four stories and possibly a small "area," suggesting a basement as well. A surviving block plan in the archive of the Howard de Walden and Portman Estates, Ltd., London, shows that 1 Chesterfield Street was 22'1" wide and 30'3" deep.

Marylebone had been a small outlying village, but from the early eighteenth century was progressively developed with larger houses in the squares and more modest dwellings in the side streets. Much of the land was owned by the Dukes of Portland, whose family names are commemorated in those squares and streets (including Cavendish, Harley, and Welbeck). Although built prior to the standard "rates" laid down by the 1774 London Building Act, it would most likely have conformed to a similar pattern. Two upper floors would comprise the bedrooms, while domestic utilities would have been at basement level (and a washhouse is shown in the yard). Typically the staircase was placed against the sidewall of

ILLUS. 11.3. Charles Wesley's Marylebone home (Telford 1927: 159).

the house and toward the rear, with entrance and minor reception rooms on the ground floor and the main living space on the first floor, above the noise and smell of the street.

This *piano nobile* would consist of front and back rooms, possibly separated by folding doors so that it could become a single space, large enough for a domestic concert, in this case probably approaching six hundred square feet. But how might such a room be decorated? Pictures, in a Georgian architectural setting, do not form an incidental addition to interior space but are integral to the space, and therefore to the activities within that space. The portrait especially had a symbolic and actual value within the life of a family. The notion of a division between private and public space had not developed, and pictures conveyed a sense of the values, loyalties, heritage, and interests of the family. So a concert room might be hung with likenesses of appropriate composers or musicians, most likely as engraved prints, but canvases of the principal performers would be far from out of place.

In more modest times such paintings might be considered a form of brazen self-advertisement, but in an eighteenth-century context that was hardly so. To promote the prestige of the young Wesley musicians performing in their home, it would have been quite in keeping to have fine portraits of them adorning the room, a visual accompaniment to their music.

However, this scenario must remain hypothetical as long as the early history of these paintings is unknown. If they were, as does seem quite probable, a pair of showpiece pictures, they may equally have hung nearby in Russell's studio, for from 1770 he lived at 7 Mortimer Street, Cavendish Square, later moving to Newman Street, both places within a mile of Chesterfield Street—although if they were painted by 1777, when the portrait of Samuel hung at the Royal Academy, Russell may well have wanted to replace them with more recent work. It is intriguing to ponder that while they hang together now in a rather greater performance space, it is only a short distance not only from where they were originally painted, but from where they may have hung as their sitters made music beneath them.

The author wishes to acknowledge the assistance of Richard Bowden, archivist; Howard de Walden and Portland Estates Ltd., London; and Janet Snowman, archivist, Royal Academy of Music, London.

CHAPTER 12

Harmony and Discord in the
Wesley Family Concerts

Alyson McLamore

Beginning in January 1779, Charles Wesley started opening his home to audiences in order to present the first of a series of sixty-four concerts featuring his two talented sons, Charles and Samuel, as performers and composers. The lease of the house, at 1 Chesterfield Street, Marylebone, London, had been the 1770 gift of Mrs. Martha Colvil Gumley, a supporter of Charles Wesley. Over the subsequent nine years of performances, Wesley documented a wide range of statistics pertaining to the series. In particular, he made lists: of the subscribers and their payments for each season, of the subscribers who attended each evening's performance, of the people who came in lieu of or as guests of the subscribers, of the repertory, of all the performers and the amount each person was paid, of the nightly expenses, and of the concert and household expenditures that were debited against the profits from each season (McLamore 2004). In short, he left behind a remarkable cache of data. As far as eighteenth-century concert life is concerned, there is simply nothing like it.

Questions about the Concerts' Administration

For scholars today, this detailed legacy is certainly to the good. Nevertheless, for every bit of factual information that can be gleaned from the seemingly thorough records, there are also questions that can be raised, subtexts that can be revealed, and presumptions that must be challenged. As if the data were viewed through a prism, each new angle can present a new perspective on the concerts and often reveals a new source of friction. In fact, when we look more closely at some of the complicated tensions and pressures that surrounded the Wesley concerts, it's a wonder that the boys could make a go of the series at all.

This chapter briefly examines several of the frictions and unanswered questions that surround these concerts. The most practical are those pertaining to the operation of the venture, beginning with the ticketing policies. A comparison of the proposal for the first year of the concert series (*Mu* DDCW 8/21: 3) with the first draft of the proposal for the second year (25–26) reveals some interesting differences:

[1779]
It is Proposed by Mess[rs] Cha. & Sam. Wesley To have every other Thursday at their own House in Ches[ld] st. Marybone [:] An Entertainment of (chiefly) their own Music, consisting of Overtures, Concerto's, Quartettos[,] Trios, Duets (particularly for Two Organs)[,] Solo's, Extempore Lessons on the Harpd. & Voluntaries on the Organ[.] The Price for 6 Concerts 3 Guin[s]. The Number of Subscribers 14[.] The Music begins while y[e] Clock is striking Seven. The First Concert on Thursday January 14. 1779.

[1780, draft 1]
Proposals For a Subscription Concert By Mess[rs] Wesley At their own house in Chesterfield Street, Marybone: When a Convenient Room will be fitted up against the Next Season, to contain Fourscore Persons. The Number of y[e] Subscribers Threescore. No person admitted without a Ticket. The Music—1 That of Handel Corelli Scarlatti & Geminiani. 2 The most Excell[t] of a later date[.] 3. Their own; consisting of Overtures, Concerto's, Quartettos, Trios, Duets (partic. for 2 Organs)[,] Sonatas[,] Solo's[,] Extemp. Lessons on y[e] Harpd & Voluntaries on the Organ[.] The Price to Subscribers 7 Concerts for 3 Guineas. Each subscriber is desired when hindered from attending, to send a Friend; ~~only giving previous notice~~ The Concert begins every Thursday Evening Exactly at Seven & is over by Ten[.] Such of the First Subscribers (Or Others) as chuse to subscribe to This Concert will be pleased to give in their Names.

[1780, draft 2]
Proposals (mended) for a 2[d] Subscr[n] Concert &c. The Music 1 That of H. C. G & S[.] 2. The most excellent of a later date[.] 3. Their own; consisting of Overt[s.] &c. The N[o] of Subscribers 3 score[.] The Price 3 Guin[s] for 7 Concerts[.] Any Subscriber hindered from attending is permitted to send a friend[.] The Music begins every other Thur Exactly at 7. & is over by Ten[.] The First Concert will be on Thur January 20. 1780

In the first year, a goal of fourteen subscribers was set, and Wesley's records indicate that although the family started the season with twelve subscribers, an additional sixteen people paid for a subscription the second evening. Attendance wavered from a low of twelve people the first night to a high of thirty-two the second evening; the first year of concerts ended with a satisfying thirty-one people in attendance on the final night (McLamore 2004: 80–82). The Wesleys set their subscription target much higher the second year: after announcing that they would fit up the concert room to accommodate "fourscore Persons," they limited the subscribers to "Threescore." (They never quite hit that target, although they did attract more than fifty subscribers to their third season.) Then a new stipulation was added: "No person admitted without a Ticket." Anyone who has ever been responsible for running an organization knows that alterations to rules and guidelines are almost always reactionary: one does not bother to change the wording unless there has been a problem. We have to wonder just why Wesley felt it necessary to add this caution to the subscription announcement. Similarly, at the bottom of the first page of his proposal he wrote, "Each Subscriber is desired, when hindered from attending, to send a Friend," although he scored through the final stipulation: "only giving previous notice." Clearly, the Wesleys wanted to fill the seats in the concert room, but had there been some problem with gatecrashers?

Another difference in wording between the two proposals hints at a second possible problem with what today could be called crowd management. In 1779: "The Music begins while ye Clock is striking Seven." The following year the announcement reads, "The Concert begins every Thursday Evening Exactly at Seven & *is over by Ten*" [emphasis added]. Did the Wesleys suffer from hangers-on who just wouldn't go home? More likely, the stipulation was included to help manage vehicular traffic, as was the case in 1759 when the Castle Society announced, "No Coaches are to return for their Company till after Nine o'Clock." The Castle Society advertisement also warned that coaches would not be permitted to wait on certain nearby streets during the concert, nor could the company use a particular side-street entrance (*Public Advertiser,* February 26, 1759). In a similar fashion, the Wesleys' reference to a specific ending time may have been intended to guide coachmen.

There is yet another discrepancy between the first two proposals that may again be an effort to counteract a precedent, begun in the first season, that had contradicted the announced intentions for the 1779 series, for reasons that have never been explained. The 1779 proposal offered six concerts for three guineas, while in 1780 seven were to be presented for the same three-guinea price. The second year may seem like the better bargain for subscribers, but in actuality, *eight* concerts had been presented during the first season rather than the stipulated six. No discussion among the Wesley family members seems to have survived that explains the reason for this deviation from the initial plan, but the result was a sizable increase—a third more than promised. The following year's specification of seven concerts was perhaps an effort to rein in the expectations of those who might have been hoping for eight. It is possible that extra concerts were more common than we know, judging by a letter written by Wesley's wife, Sarah, to their daughter Sally, dated May 13, 1786. We can detect a hint of proprietary pride in Sarah's letter, although it also alludes to another source of tension stemming from the concerts:

> Yesterday we had a fuller musick Room than you have seen since the alteration of it, 54 I reckon'd, (*a very few* of whom had not constant seats)—no inconvenience was mention'd by any—for it was *free* from *expence,* however we thereby co[ul]d

know what number cou'd be accom[m]odated when they subscribe. One Musical Lady of Mr. Barnards introducing desir'd to have her Name put down, who said of all the Musick she attended Yr Bros. excell'd. (*ATu* Box 3, item 24)

This otherwise undocumented May 12 performance was not part of the actual subscription series, and Sarah's letter raises a new question: if the music room was fuller than Sarah had seen "since the alteration of it," we are prompted to ask: *what* alteration? The 1786 records contain a sixteen-shilling expenditure for a carpenter (*Mu* DDCW 6/58), but there is no information as to what the carpenter actually built or remodeled. In fact, as Peter Forsaith pointed out in Chapter 11, very little is known about the size and design of the Wesleys' music room in Chesterfield Street.

A separate expense, contained in the same list, is a payment to the carpenter for "chair-mending," at 14s. 6d. (Evidently, there had been considerable chair breakage.) Perhaps it was these repairs that allowed most people in the audience to have "constant seats," as Sarah states, implying that the Wesley audiences had previously been somewhat ambulatory, as seems to have been the case at many fashionable concerts and routs (McVeigh: 61).

On the other hand, some organizations required more respectful audience behavior; the Castle Society went so far as to fine those who talked or moved about during the performance (McVeigh: 62). Demand for chairs may have waxed and waned as latecomers arrived and other audience members left early, although the clearly published starting and ending times for the concerts were perhaps intended to discourage such freedom of movement. It is also possible that the May 12 performance was a daytime "open house" performance, which the Wesleys seem to have offered at various times over the years. For instance, the Earl of Dartmouth wrote to Wesley on January 29, 1781, that he was grateful for the invitation to the "morning concert" and would attend when he was able but would come alone to reduce the crowding (*Mu* DDWes 1/91). In any event, despite the chair shortage, Sarah noted that because it was a free concert, "no one had complained of inconvenience" over the seating problem, which suggests that people *had* complained at some evening performances—perhaps a further small hint of friction.

Sarah Wesley's Role

In general, Sarah was frustratingly silent concerning the concert series, and little more is known about her actual involvement with the endeavor. She apparently took some degree of maternal pride in the display of her offspring's talent. Moreover, she could be viewed as genetically responsible for much of that musical ability; Samuel explained, "My Father used to say of my Brother and me, 'The Boys have Music by the Mother's Side,' meaning that *he* had no claim to any of the

Talent which she certainly possessed." It is unclear how much Sarah welcomed—
or encouraged—the concerts as a way to promote her sons, but certainly she
must have appreciated the income generated by the series; Wesley's accounting
records reveal numerous expenditures on behalf of the family, far beyond the
immediate expenses of the concerts themselves. Despite Sarah's musicality, she
seems never to have participated in any performance, even though Sally sang on
two occasions in the nine-year series (McLamore 2004: 94), but Sarah and Sally
both applied concert income toward new kerchiefs, caps, shifts, gowns, gloves,
powder, aprons, and ribbons, and Sally's hair was dressed on a regular basis
(97–100). Perhaps the ladies of the Wesley family were expected to serve as social
hostesses for the concerts, but there is no evidence of such a role in the surviving
documentation. Moreover, Wesley made it clear that the concerts kept *him* very
busy: he apologized to John Langshaw, writing, "Till [the concerts] were over, I
could not get an hour for answering You" (Wainwright: 32). It is difficult to know
what the expectations would have been for Sarah, since the operative practices
of other private series seem to have varied somewhat in format. Performances
in the two most prominent private series, the "Sunday Concerts" (also called the
"Nobility Concerts") and the "Ladies Concerts," rotated through various private
houses; nevertheless, the occasional newspaper reference to one or the other of
these series almost always cited a female house owner or hostess. Elaine Chalus
notes, "[Private] social events were considered to be largely [women's] preroga-
tive," and more than one gentleman recorded his engagements in his personal
diary by referring to his hostess rather than his host (Chalus: 679). However,
although the concerts are mentioned frequently within the surviving Wesley
family correspondence, there is not a single instance in which a writer describes
a performance as taking place "at Mrs. Wesley's" or in language to that effect;
instead, the concerts are credited to Charles or (more frequently) to his sons.

Even if it were Wesley rather than his wife who publicly welcomed the subscribers to the concerts, could Sarah have been the private driving force behind
the continuation of the concerts during the last few seasons? As early as November 1783, Wesley lamented, "I am quite weary of our Concerts . . . It is not
yet settled, whither [*sic*] we shall have a Concert this year or not" (Wainwright:
64). Wesley's phraseology makes it clear that he could not (or did not feel that
he could) make a unilateral decision, and equally clearly, he ended up being
outvoted in the matter. After three more seasons, John Wesley had been led (presumably by his brother) to believe that the concerts were ending after the 1786
season (Kassler and Olleson: 30), but again Charles was overruled—by whom?
We can imagine that Sarah prized the concerts' value—not only as a showcase
for her sons, but for the financial stability that they offered the entire family;
did she therefore lobby for their continuation when her husband's enthusiasm
began to wane as he approached his eightieth year? Perhaps Sarah was indeed
the primary motivator, although there are hints that she was sometimes less

practical about money than she might have been: in 1787 Wesley complained to Sally that her mother never seemed to think about the problems of paying for lodging in Bristol, and earlier that month he told Sally that her mother was "inconsiderate" (*Mu* DDWes 4/20, 4/12). Without further evidence, Sarah's degree of participation and enthusiasm must remain as conjecture, just as there is no known documentation that reveals the familial negotiations concerning the perpetuation of the series from year to year.

The Musical Repertory

Another area of tension was the concert repertory itself. England, by the 1780s, had a thriving concert life, with musical tastes that were beginning to coalesce around particular types of music. One of the most polarized distinctions was between the "ancients" and the "moderns." The ancients appreciated and promoted the older baroque repertory of Handel and Corelli, while the moderns favored new, "never-before-heard" pieces, often advertised as "just printed," or even "in manuscript," implying a very high degree of exclusivity. (See Chapter 14 for further discussion.) The debate between the ancients and moderns was extensive and, to modern readers, at least, often highly entertaining. There were some pacifists, such as John Marsh, who argued in 1796, a decade after the Wesley family concerts had ceased,

> by blending . . . the ancient and the modern styles in one performance, the effect of each of them will be improved. A piece of ancient music, in which the harmony chiefly predominates, will certainly be heard with double pleasure by all lovers of harmony, immediately after a modern piece, in which the harmony is subordinate to the melody. In like manner, a good modern piece will seem to have a greater degree of brilliancy, and appear to greater advantage, after one in which classical accuracy is more attended to than general effect.

Marsh added a confidential aside, saying, "I also cannot help thinking that modern amateurs are far more tenacious of the old style of writing than the composers themselves would have been, had the modern style been introduced in their days" (Cudworth: 160).

Beginning with the second year of their concert programming, the Wesleys tried to sail that middle passage between ancient and modern repertories, thereby making a distinct change from the more restricted range of pieces that had been offered the first season. The 1779 announcement had claimed that the concerts would consist "of (chiefly) their own Music," while the 1780 series promised music in three categories: first, "That of Handel, Corelli, Scarlatti, & Geminiani," second, "The most Excellent of a Later date," third, music composed by the Wesley brothers themselves. The difference between the two concert proposals is not merely a matter of more detailed advertising. The repertory listings for the first season make it evident that 1779 had presented music solely from categories 1 and 3, so the second season's promise of music of a "later date" represented a significant change. The proposal for the third season, 1781, made the polarized repertory even more explicit; Wesley now described the first category as "What is called The Ancient" (*Mu* DDWes 7/41):

[1781]
PROPOSALS FOR A Third Subscription Concert, By Messrs. CHARLES and SAMUEL WESLEY, *In Chesterfield-Street, Marybone.* THE CONCERT To begin JANUARY 25, 1781, *And to be continued every other THURSDAY Evening, precisely at Seven o'Clock.* The MUSIC performed, will be 1. What is called The Ancient: especially that of HANDEL, CORELLI, GEMINIANI, and SCARLATTI. 2. The most Excellent, of a later Date. 3. Their Own, of every Kind; particularly Voluntaries on the Organ, Extempore Lessons on the Harpsichord, and Duets for Two Organs. The Price, THREE GUINEAS for SEVEN CONCERTS. *No Person admitted without a Ticket.* Such Persons as desire to subscribe, will be pleased to send their Names. and Places of Abode, to N° 1. *Chesterfield-Street.*

Certainly, as a marketing ploy, this shift in the breadth of offerings must have been intended to attract the widest possible audience. However, it may also reflect a bit of a schism within the Wesley household. As discussed elsewhere, Samuel was considerably more receptive to modern styles than his father and brother.

There are aspects to the Wesley concert programming that pose a further question, defying some of the expectations we might hold today, but it is unclear whether or not these elements reflect familial tension. For example, despite the formidable religious output of the boys' father and uncle, not a single hymn is to be found in the repertory of any of the sixty-four subscription concerts that are detailed in Wesley's records. A small handful of hymns *was* offered in a separate concert series that the boys organized for Lady Horne in 1780, which shows other repertory differences as well, but presumably those contrasts were a reflection of the hostess's taste rather than that of the Wesley boys. It is certainly the case that oratorio excerpts are found within the Wesley programs, but in truth the English approached oratorios in a rather less devotional manner than did their peers in, say, Lutheran Germany. Nevertheless, we are left to wonder about what sort of musical distinctions the two boys were maintaining by including sacred works by Handel but none based on texts by their own relatives. Were the younger Wesleys deliberately trying to establish a separate sphere of expertise apart from their older kinfolk?

Moral and Social Tensions

The sense of purpose that might have driven some of the concert programming can be extended to the justifications for the concert series itself, reflecting another area of concern (or indeed, several areas). Wesley's oft-quoted "Reasons for letting my Sons have a Concert at home" (*Mu* DDWes 4/65) was a private manifesto alluding to various implied sources of tension, some of which Philip Olleson explores at greater length in Chapter 13:

My Reasons for letting my Sons have a Concert at home are

I. to keep them out of harm's way: the way (I mean) of *bad Music & bad Musicians* who by a free Communication with them might corrupt both their Taste and their Morals.

II. That my Sons may have a safe and honourable Opportunity of *availing themselves* of their musical Abilities, which have cost me *several hundred pounds.*

III. That they may enjoy their full right of *private Judgment,* & likewise their *Independency*: both of which must be given up if they *swim with the Stream* & follow *the Multitude.*

IV. To improve their Play & their Skill in Composing: as they must themselves furnish the principal Music of every Concert. Altho' they do not call their Musical Entertainment *a Concert. It is too great a Word.* They do not presume to rival the *present great masters* who excel in the variety of their Accompaniments. All they aim at in their concert music of 4 [orchestral] *parts is Exactness.*

If they excel in any degree it is in Composition and Play. Here then they chiefly exert themselves, as sensible that "many accompaniments *may hide and cover bad Play,*" but that the *fewer* the accompaniments are, Good Play is the more conspicuous.

The points of controversy are fairly wide-ranging. Wesley suggests that the home concerts were for the boys' safety: that out in the world they might encounter "bad Music and bad Musicians," items that might "corrupt both their Taste and their Morals." Undoubtedly, the attitudes regarding ancient versus modern music must have driven some aspects of Wesley's views concerning good or bad music, but the issue of bad musicians and morality is more intriguing—and harder to isolate. Of course, Wesley was not the first father to be concerned about life in London; one recalls Leopold Mozart's declaration, "I will not bring up my children in such a dangerous place (where the majority of the inhabitants have no religion and where one only has evil examples before one). You would be amazed if you saw the way children are brought up here; not to mention other matters connected with religion" (Anderson: 56).

Although Mozart was talking about religion in London as a whole, tension over the issue of worship—and appropriate behavior for men of God (and their children)—certainly overshadowed the Wesley concerts. While an observer today might be surprised at how little sacred music the concerts contained, Methodist contemporaries were somewhat shocked that Wesley would allow his sons to participate in such a secular endeavor. As early as 1771 he had been warned by John Fletcher that certain other Methodists (Wesley's "enemies") were criticizing his "*love for musick, company,* fine *people,* [and] *great folks.*" Wesley's declaration anticipated the objections that he himself knew would be raised against the enterprise. He argued that the concerts' controlled environment protected the boys' morality, that it made financial sense to recoup the expensive musical training the boys had received, that it would foster their independence, and that it was really much too modest an undertaking to warrant the term "concert." (This is the only time that Wesley tried playing that particular humble card: the term "concert" permeates all of his and everyone else's subsequent references to the series.) Just before the second season, the prominent Methodist Society member Thomas Coke alluded to the presence of internal tensions that he deplored: "I looked upon the Concerts which [Charles Wesley] allows his sons to have in his own house, to be highly dishonorable to God; and himself to be criminal, by reason of his situation in the Church of Christ; but on mature consideration of all the circumstances appertaining to them, I cannot now blame him" (*Arminian Magazine* 13 [1790]: 50–51). It would be very interesting to know just what "circumstances" weighed the most with Coke; it is perhaps the case that he grew to appreciate the significant musical talent that each boy possessed and could no longer fault Wesley for promoting their abilities as best he could. Perhaps Wesley had revealed to Coke the extent to which the concerts contributed to the household budget—income that was of critical importance to a barely solvent preacher. Nevertheless, on December 22, 1781—shortly before the fourth season of concerts—Wesley downplayed the potential profit of the series, telling John Langshaw that "[Charles the younger] and Sam ... dont expect to get by [the concerts] much more than Reputation and increase of Skill," adding, "What more ought we to wish than Content with food & raiment" (Wainwright: 56). Of course, if Sarah Wesley truly was a behind-the-scenes force in lobbying for the concerts, Coke might have recognized the inevitability that Wesley would have to yield to her efforts.

Coke was not the only Methodist to express (reluctant) acceptance of the family enterprise. The boys' uncle, John Wesley, made a specific effort to attend some of the performances and even brought some Methodist ministers with him on one occasion, saying, according to Samuel, "I do this, to shew that I consider it no Sin" (*Lbl* 27593: 3; see also *Mu* DDWes 6/57, summarized in Kassler and Olleson: 555). Nevertheless, the issue of propriety was far from settled in John's mind. In 1789—two years after the concerts had ceased, and a year after Wesley had died—John published a letter from his brother written in 1779. Charles had declared: "I am clear, without a doubt, that my sons concert is after the will and order of Providence. It has established them as musicians, and in a safe and honorable way." John footnoted this with a tart rejoinder: "I am 'clear' of another mind" (*Arminian Magazine* 12 [1789]: 387).

Despite his lasting misgivings, John Wesley's occasional presence at the concerts was an appreciated gesture of family solidarity in the face of the criticism from fellow Methodists. Wesley's recognition of John's magnanimity is evident in the list of attendees at the January 25, 1781, performance (the date of John's first visit); he followed John's initials with an exclamation mark ("Mr. J. W.!"), emphasizing the visit's significance (*Mu* DDCW 8/21: 51). It is also through John Wesley that we can recognize the balancing act that had to be maintained by the concert series: that of social class and the perceived right to pursue leisure activities. It is important to note that these performances at home were *not* purely private affairs; they were not casual, informal gatherings around the fireside for friends and neighbors to enjoy a hodge-podge of pieces played by the two boys. Instead, the Wesleys sold tickets and tried to limit admission only to those who had purchased them, or to the guests of those subscribers. They did not always know the identity of their audience members, as they would have if the concerts had been fully private, invitation-only gatherings. They advertised many of the concerts in prominent London newspapers. They tried to maintain strict starting and ending times. They hired professional musicians, some of whom were highly visible in London's concert life, to fill their orchestra. It is true that an occasional amateur would join the band, such as Lord Mornington, who participated inter-mittently, but this seems to have been very much the exception rather than the rule. Of course, presenting the concerts at home, rather than in one of the increas-ing number of dedicated public music venues, meant that there would be those who disparaged the domestic undertaking as an amateur endeavor (although it certainly allowed Wesley to dodge the restrictions of English licensing laws). A writer for the *Morning Chronicle* dismissed the series as a "hedge concert, at a dancing-master's room, in one of the new streets leading to the fields" ("Musi-cal Intelligence," *The Morning Chronicle*, February 4, 1785). (The reference to "a dancing-master's room" is not clear; it may have been the writer's own misun-derstanding, or simply a generic reference to this sort of semi-private venue.) At the same time, the anonymous author clearly was aware of the concerts; even in disparaging them, he gave them some degree of legitimacy. Regardless, though, of the future consequences that would result from the boys' musical training, the concerts were conducted in the most polished manner that the young prodigies could manage.

The professionalism and social aspirations of the concerts are clarified through the comments of John Wesley. After his first visit, he noted in his diary, "I spent an agreeable hour at a concert at my nephews, but I was a little out of my element among lords and ladies. I love plain music and plain company best" (Curnock, 6:34). It is clear that this was *not* just a gathering of the boys' friends and sup-porters. It was a mix of social classes that mirrored the mixture occurring in London's higher-profile events and was thus privy to the tensions that were ac-companying the growth of English concert life. Public concerts were still a fairly new phenomenon, and there were those who sought to restrict the experience solely to the upper classes. Letters to the editor were published in newspapers, detailing the risks of making such entertainments available to young apprentices who would spend long evenings out and would then be useless in the counting house the next day, or to young women who might fall prey to rakes (see, for instance, editorials in the *London Chronicle*, March 25 and 31, 1766; April 15, 1766; and May 9, 1767). Other people wrote letters wondering why middle-class merchants should be *excluded* from polite and refined pleasures; one asked, "What set of men contribute so much to the support of Government? Who supply us with the necessities and elegancies of life from the most remote regions of the globe?" (*Lloyd's British Chronicle,* April 16, 1766). The Wesley concerts managed to attract a wide social range of audience members; people with titles were regular supporters, but so were people from other walks of life. Wesley customarily used audience members' names in his attendance lists, but on occasion some were unknown to him, and his descriptions of these nameless attendees are sometimes telling. For instance, on May 2, 1782, he recorded that "A Gentleman" accompanied Lord Fortescue, while he designated a second unknown man as "a Gent.—Humble" (*Lam* MS-L: 43). It is apparent that the semi-private nature of the Wesley concerts, which attracted both aristocrats and members of the middle class, placed the series right in the centre of this have/have-not controversy and the changing English social milieu.

A Marginalized Endeavor

A final issue concerning the Wesley concerts has been their place in posterity. Wesley's diligent records are relatively scattered today, and they are best known through an incomplete nineteenth-century copy transcribed by Samuel's daughter Eliza and long held by the British Library (*Lbl* Add. 35017). The library catalogued Eliza's transcription as a "Register of juvenile concerts given by the brothers Charles and Samuel Wesley" (Hughes-Hughes: 382). The designation "juvenile" was rather unfortunate, for it subtly marginalized the endeavor. Moreover, it is not an entirely accurate designation: true, Samuel was only twelve when the concerts began (he turned thirteen the day before the fourth performance), but his brother was already twenty-one years old—an age at which many of London's professional musicians had been long established—and Samuel, too, would be twenty-one before the final year of concerts had ended. Certainly, the regrettable catalogue description gives only a small hint of the riches the document contains, so that its wealth of primary-source data has been frequently overlooked.

Beyond the carefully documented statistics, however, the Wesley concerts have much to teach us about English life in general. The Wesleys' nine years of domestic music making were a stew of conflicting texts and subtexts, juxtaposing sacred and secular, ancient and modern, and "good" and "bad" music against a backdrop of both professional and amateur presentation to a sometimes uncomfortable mix of social classes. In short, the concerts were a nexus where idealism maintained a wary coexistence with pragmatism, where harmony fought to survive among discord.

CHAPTER 13

Father and Sons

CHARLES, SAMUEL, AND CHARLES THE YOUNGER

Philip Olleson

It is hard to overestimate the impact on the lives of Charles Wesley and his wife Sarah of having first one, and then two, musical child prodigies in their family. We should be aware of one important meaning of *prodigy* as "an unusual or extraordinary thing or occurrence; an anomaly; something abnormal or unnatural" (*OED*). By definition, child prodigies are out of the ordinary: the effect that they have on their families is inevitably profound, and their upbringing presents their parents with major challenges. Not all parents, and not all child prodigies, are able successfully to cope with these challenges. As is all too apparent from present-day and historical examples, many child prodigies fail to achieve their full potential, and many grow up to be unhappy and unfulfilled, if not actually psychologically damaged by the experience.

The Boys' Upbringing

The approach of Charles and Sarah Wesley to their children's upbringing and musical education was principled, well thought-out, and responsible (see Olleson 2007). (I assume here that Sarah was fully involved in decisions about the upbringing of the children, even though contemporary biographical accounts are silent on her precise role and frame their discussions solely in terms of her husband.) By the standards of the time, Charles was a liberal father, subscribing to modern views on the rationality of the child, attempting to engage with his children, and providing them with opportunities for play and recreation. At the same time, he set them high standards, expected a great deal from them, and could be stern with them when their behavior failed to meet his expectations. All this can be seen in the following reproving letter he addressed to the seven-year-old Samuel, in response to some undisclosed but no doubt minor act of childhood naughtiness:

> Come now, my good friend Samuel, and let us reason together. God made you for Himself, that is to be ever happy with Him. Ought you not, therefore, to

serve and love Him? But you can do neither unless He gives you the power. Ask, (He says Himself) and it shall be given you. That is, pray Him to make you love Him: and pray for it every night and morning in your own words, as well as in those which have been taught you. You have been used to say your prayers in the sight of others. Henceforth, go into a corner by yourself, where no eye but God's may see you. There pray to your heavenly Father who seeth in secret: and be sure He hears every word you speak, and sees everything you do, at all times, and in all places.

You should now begin to live by reason and religion. There should be sense even in your play and diversions. Therefore I have furnished you with maps and books and harpsichord. Every day get something by heart: whatever your mother recommends. Every day read one or more chapters in the Bible. I suppose your mother will take you now in the place of your brother, to be her chaplain, to read the psalms and lessons, when your sister does not . . .

Foolish people are too apt to praise you. If they see anything good in you they should praise God, not you, for it. As for music, it is neither good nor bad in itself. You have a natural inclination to it: but God gave you that: therefore God only should be thanked and praised for it. Your brother has the same love of music much more than you, yet he is not proud or vain of it. Neither, I trust, will you be. You will send me a long letter of answer, and always look on me both as your loving father, and your friend. (*Mu* DDWes 4/70)

For all the concern revealed in this letter, Wesley may have found difficulty in expressing his love for his children. Writing in 1754 to Sarah in response to her criticisms of his undemonstrativeness to their first son, John (1753–1754), he said: "Why, I love him as well as you do. Only you make the most of a little love, by showing it, and I make the least of a great deal, by hiding it" (Baker 1948: 13). It is easy to see how he may have continued this tendency as a matter of deliberate policy with Charles and Samuel, and how it may have had a thoroughly unhealthy effect on them. Aware of the amount of attention they were receiving from other quarters, he would naturally have wanted to avoid any possibility of their becoming proud and conceited and would therefore have taken good care not to overpraise them. But combined with the heavy burden of expectation that he laid on them, this reticence may have led them to feel that they could never do enough to please him and consequently to low self-esteem.

In addition, we should not forget that Wesley had come to fatherhood late: he was forty-five at the birth of his first child, John; at the birth of Charles, the first to survive infancy, he was fifty, and at Samuel's he was fifty-eight. At the beginning of the family concerts in 1779 he was seventy-one, and by their end he was nearly eighty. This large difference in age between him and his children must have had an impact on his relationship with them in the form of a distance and remoteness that would have been less had he been younger.

As the movement's co-founder and its most prolific and distinguished hymn writer, Wesley had an extremely prominent position within Methodism. He was also well known in wider London society. Unlike his brother John, he was a naturally gregarious man, and his social circle included not only Methodists, but also actors, musicians, and men of letters. This on occasion aroused the criticism of fellow Methodists, worried about the potential damage such worldly behavior might do to the reputation of their movement. Wesley's links to music and the theater were undoubtedly to his advantage in educating his sons and meant that he was easily able to secure the best teachers for them (see, however, Chapter 10). But these same links made him distinctly unusual among Methodists. Typically, Methodists regarded secular music with suspicion and disapproval. They had, of course, a strong musical tradition in their worship, but they tended to be censorious of music that was not directly used in worship or as an aid to devotion. Any music connected with the theater was very firmly disapproved of, and even secular vocal music and instrumental music were suspect. As we read John Wesley's 1779 treatise "On the Power of Music" (J. Wesley 1781a), we are aware of a general failure to recognize the value of music except insofar as it could be used for worship. Although Charles did not subscribe to these views, they were bound to be a fruitful and ongoing source of tensions between him and other members of the Methodist community that must have been very apparent to his sons.

Such differences inevitably crystallized in the question of how the children's musical education should proceed. Wesley's policy appears to have been straightforward: in accordance with the precepts of the Parable of the Talents, to ensure that they had the chance to develop their skills to the full. Accordingly, he had them taught by professionals and ensured that they had every opportunity to play with professionals. This was in part the rationale for the family concerts, discussed in Chapter 12.

With this background and these opportunities, it might be thought that their natural career progression was to go on to earn their livings as professional musicians. But this is probably not how it appeared to Wesley, and he would have had grave misgivings about the suitability of music as a career for his two sons. As already noted in Chapter 9, music scarcely qualified as a profession at all in the eyes of many—certainly in comparison with the "learned" professions of the church, medicine, and the law—and professional musicians were typically low in status, badly paid, and insecure. No gentleman would have been happy with the prospect of his children becoming musicians, and Wesley would have been no exception.

What to do with the boys, therefore, was a major problem, given that their abilities seemed to indicate their future careers so clearly. Wesley had realized this as early as 1769, when he wrote to a correspondent, Eleanor Laroche, who had criticized him for allowing Charles to play in concerts, "I always designed my son for a clergyman. Nature has marked him for a musician: which appeared from his earliest infancy. My friends advised me not to cross his inclination. Indeed I could not if I would. There is no way of hindering his being a musician but cutting off his fingers" (*Mu* DDWes 4/70). A possible solution, it might be thought, would have been for his sons to have entered some more "respectable" area of music, such as that of the cathedral close and organ loft. But the Anglican cathedral positions were usually filled by those who had received their musical education within the Church of England, first as choristers and then in assistant organist positions, and it would not have been easy for an outsider to break into this world. As it happened, a possible opening for Charles presented itself in early March 1788 when the organist's position at St. George's Chapel, Windsor, became vacant. Charles was interested in the post, and because of his links with the court he would have been a strong contender, but his father strongly disapproved of the idea and forbade him to apply (see Olleson 2003: 37). In the case of Samuel, his Roman Catholic associations would in any case have counted strongly against him in any application he made to an Anglican cathedral or parish church.

At the time, the family concerts must have seemed to offer an inspired solution to the problem of providing the best possible musical opportunities for the two sons. But the ethos of the concerts can only have had the effect of sending out distinctly mixed messages to them, conveying at the same time their father's support for their musical education and his doubts about music as a suitable employment. This ambivalence can clearly be seen in his well-known "Reasons for letting my Sons have a Concert at home" (see p. 171).

Problems about the eventual outcome of the musical education of Charles and Samuel were not the only ones to confront the Wesley family in the 1780s. Another major issue was Samuel's rebelliousness. This, very much a Wesley family trait, and almost a defining characteristic of Samuel's personality, first came to the fore in his adolescence, manifesting itself by various forms of revolt from the values and norms of his family and class. Two striking examples—although we should take care not to see them solely in these terms—were his love affair with Charlotte Louisa Martin and his involvement with Roman Catholicism (Olleson 2003: 24–33).

Perhaps more important, and bound up with every aspect of Samuel's behavior in a way that is singularly difficult to disentangle, was his mental illness. It is clear that there was a strain of depressive illness in the family that went back at least to Samuel's paternal grandfather and also afflicted his father. In Samuel's case, the evidence points strongly to bipolar affective disorder or manic depression, which had its first manifestations during his adolescence (see Goodwin and Jamison; Jamison).

Charles and Samuel's Subsequent Attitudes to Music

The subsequent musical careers of the two sons were very different, reflecting differences in their personalities and in their responses to their musical education. In the case of Charles, the experience seems to have removed from him any desire to put his musical talents to full use. Although by all accounts an exceptionally fine keyboard player, he appears rarely to have performed at public concerts. Where he made most impression was at court: he played at the private concerts of George III and Queen Charlotte at Windsor, where Fanny Burney heard him in July 1785 (Dobson, 2:395), and was for many years private harpsichordist to the Prince of Wales (later Prince Regent and King George IV). Having been a prolific composer at the time of the family concerts, he later composed less and became more thoroughly conservative. This lack of adventurousness was paralleled in his private life. After the death of his father in 1788, he continued to live with his mother and his younger sister Sally until each of them in turn died, in 1821 and 1828 respectively; it is clear that it was Sally, and not Charles, who assumed the role of head of the family. In his later life, he was a figure of mild eccentricity and otherworldliness (see Lloyd 1998). He held organists' appointments at several chapels and parish churches, but his restricted professional activity as a performer can be seen as arising from a general timidity and lack of ambition, and from a refusal to engage with the rough-and-tumble of the world of professional music making. It can also be seen as a refusal to compete with his more flamboyant and successful younger brother. (See also Chapter 9.)

The case of Samuel was quite different. From his earliest years, his attitude to his musical gifts appears to have been one of ambivalence. Although his father refused to exhibit him in public as a child, he was nevertheless taken around to various family friends and acquaintances by his godfather Martin Madan and was required to perform to them. Another child might have been pleased and gratified by the attention and praise that he received, but Samuel was not, saying that he had felt humiliated by it. He had resented his father's behavior in allowing Madan to carry him around "like a raree show" (i.e., a spectacle), adding: "this soured my temper toward him at an early age. I contracted a dislike of my father's conduct, which grew with my growth, and strengthened with my strength" (T. Jackson 1841: 357). It is notable, too, that after the end of the final series of family concerts in 1787, by which time he was twenty-one, Samuel's next step was not to enter the music profession, but to spend the next few years in—as far as we can tell—aimless drifting. The flow of his compositions, so abundant during the time of the family concerts, slowed to a trickle, and he appears to have made no attempt to perform in public. Perhaps relevant here is his recollection, recorded by Thomas Green many years later, that at the time of the Handel Commemoration Festival in 1784 he had been seized with a "nervous horror against music" that caused him "torment and pain" (1838/2: 468).

It is clear that Samuel's adolescence was a time of considerable mental turmoil, when there was a great deal more than music occupying his mind. Most important over the period was probably his complicated relationship with Roman Catholicism, which progressed from an initial fascination with the music of Catholic worship to a deeper involvement and culminated in 1784 in his conversion. Disenchantment with Catholic doctrines followed within a relatively short time, but Wesley retained a lifelong love for the music and liturgy of the Church, and in particular for Gregorian chant. In addition, there was his love affair with Charlotte Martin, which had begun in 1782 when he was sixteen and she was twenty-one or twenty-two. It continued in the teeth of family disapproval, if not downright opposition, on the grounds of what the family saw as Charlotte's worldliness and general unsuitability, to the point ten years later when, still unmarried, they decided to set up house together. As can readily be imagined, both the Roman Catholic involvement and the continuing relationship with Charlotte, the overtly physical nature of which Samuel made no attempt to conceal (and which on occasion he openly flaunted), were additional sources of tension between Samuel and his family. To these was added a general wildness and unruliness of behavior that included staying out to all hours, drunkenness, and physically abusing servants.

As I have argued elsewhere (Olleson 2003: 30–31), what we know from accounts of Samuel's frequently extreme behavior during this period suggests the first manifestations of the hypomanic phase of the manic-depressive illness from which he was to suffer for the remainder of his life. There is less information about any depressive episodes at this time, but they can be surmised from the clear evidence of such phases later in his life and from the almost complete drying up of his compositions in the late 1780s, once the stimulus of writing for the family concerts was no longer present. And in July 1789 we find him writing to his mother from Bramfield, Hertfordshire, in terms that suggest that he had suffered some sort of collapse, from which he was now convalescing:

> Everything here is as comfortable as can be. I have much Attention paid to me, am very quiet, and the People are remarkably neat and exact: but it is the sort of Situation which no one but he who loves Retirement as well as I would perhaps be contented in: I came hither for that end, principally; and that end is answered.
>
> I hate public Life: I always did; and it was a cruel Mistake in my Education, the forcing me into it.
>
> But it may have had one good Consequence, that of making me very willing to quit a World which till I knew, I might have valued. (*Lbl* Add. 35012: 5)

What is most significant here is Samuel's statement that his education had "forced" him into music. This is a theme he returned to during his later life, with varying degrees of emphasis and apportionment of blame among his father, the cruel trick of fate that had cursed him with musical abilities, and himself.

Samuel was inclined to feel that his musical abilities were more of a curse than a blessing and that they had kept him from doing anything more valuable. Specifically, he felt that had things been different, he could have been a classical scholar. This was a view he continued to hold until late in his life. In March 1829, aged sixty-three, he commented:

My Mind is not that of a *mere* Musician: I have (from a Boy) been a Lover of more of the Alphabet than the seven incipient English Letters, & had I not been an idle Dog, under the Instruction of my classical Father (whose Loss is by me daily felt, *more than 40 years since its Occurrence*) I might long ago have been well qualified to bandy Latin & Greek along with Parr & Porson [two celebrated classical scholars]. My *Trade* is Music, I confess; & would to Heaven it had only been destined for mine Amusement, which would certainly have been the Case, had I availed myself of the Advantages which were offered me in Juvenescence, of rendering myself eligible for any one of the learned Professions; but it was (it seems) otherwise ordained; & I was to attend only to the Cultivation of *one* Talent, which *unluckily cost me no Trouble to do:* had there been any up-Hill Work for me in Music, I should soon enough have sacrificed it altogether. (*Lbl* Add. 31764: f. 28)

This harks back to a passage in a letter to his father of August 1785:

You have often told me that I should like to be a Scholar without taking the pains which are necessary for it, but I hope this is not exactly the State of the Case: if you recollect that *one pursuit is a great deal for one person* but two are much more difficult: Music employs a *great deal of my Time* which I would gladly change for Study, and whatever you may think, I would willingly devote double my Time to the latter, but as I was born with a Trade not a Fortune in my hands it is necessary to make the most of it.

There is little doubt but that I may understand *Latin perfectly within three years with I suppose* moderate application; whether I shall ever have *Time to master Greek* is a Question, but if I had no other business than Study there would be little or no probability of my dying a Dunce.

If I do I shall have no one to blame, not even myself, for nothing but Music prevents my close application, and that must not be thrown aside till my Purse is fuller than at present, which I see no very promising Symptoms of, but as many persons of equal and superior Merit to me are in a much worse Situation, this consideration ought to make me content. (*Mu* DDWF 15/2)

As this shows, Samuel appears at this time to have had difficulty in acknowledging the value and worth of his own musical abilities. We have already seen one aspect of this in his later statement that the cultivation of his talents had cost him no effort, with the clear implication that in consequence he did not value them. We can also readily understand, in the light of this and his earlier remarks about being carried about as a child "like a raree show," his deep-seated unease about the whole business of public performance, and a sense of resentment against his father for having encouraged him in it. For Samuel, endowed with natural abilities that he did not value and a low sense of self-esteem, it must have been easy to see himself at times as little better than a circus artist, entertaining his audiences with trivial performances that demeaned both himself and them. From here it was only a short step to despising and hating himself for wasting his time by performing, and his audiences for their shallowness and gullibility in being taken in by him. This was not a healthy attitude for a performing musician, and one that was in the long term not sustainable by any artist who wished to maintain a measure of self-respect. It seems likely that it was this that played a large part in his decision in early adulthood not to enter the music profession.

In fact it was not until the late 1790s, ten years after reaching his majority, that Samuel started to develop a public career as a performer. About his activities during the intervening period little is known, but enough to suggest that he made a modest income through giving individual music lessons in schools (an activity he hated but that was readily available to him and paid reasonably well) and was working through a variety of personal crises, religious, educational, and developmental, in which longer or shorter periods of depression, of varying degrees of severity and duration, were no doubt implicated.

From this perspective, Samuel's inactivity of the late 1780s and 1790s is wholly explicable. However, by the time he made his long-delayed entry into public musical life in the late 1790s, he appears to have come to a reasonably satisfactory accommodation with himself on the nature of his own musical talent, and on music as a way of making a living. This accommodation continued through a long career that brought him considerable celebrity as a performer, composer, and lecturer on music. His letters to his fellow musicians, characterized by wit, enthusiasm, and exuberance, are those of a man comfortable in his role and thoroughly at ease in the company of those with whom he spent his professional life. Notwithstanding subsequent bouts of depression, some of them serious and extended, he was able to manage his continuing mental health problems and the legacy of his early upbringing sufficiently well to construct a viable public career in music that continued until a final bout of depression forced his retirement in 1830.

CHAPTER 14

Samuel Wesley as an Antiquarian Composer

Peter Holman

The English Interest in Old Music

It is well known that Samuel Wesley was interested in and engaged with old music throughout his career. Until the eighteenth century, music was essentially a novelty that barely outlived the composers who created it, though England was the first place where a cumulative and permanent concert repertory in the modern fashion developed (Weber). Organizations devoted to old music, such as the Academy of Ancient Music and the Madrigal Society, revived sixteenth- and seventeenth-century madrigals and motets, while the classics of particular genres, such as Handel's oratorios, string concertos by Corelli and Geminiani, Henry Purcell's theater music, or pre–Civil War cathedral music, remained in the repertory alongside more modern works. Thus by the 1770s, when Samuel had his formative musical experiences, English musical life was distinctive in European terms in its engagement with the past, though that engagement was consistent with other areas of English cultural life, as we will see.

Samuel encountered a good deal of old music as a child. Corelli and Handel were favorites of his elder brother Charles, who remained an ardent Hande-lian throughout his life. Samuel's earliest musical education was listening to and participating in his brother's music lessons with Joseph Kelway; he memorized Handel's oratorios *Samson* and *Messiah* before he was five and composed his own oratorio, *Ruth*, before he was six, though he was only able to write it down when he was eight. The music publisher Robert Bremner introduced Samuel to much earlier music when he showed him the Fitzwilliam Virginal Book, which he owned at the time; Samuel quickly mastered difficult passages "which none of the harpsichord masters could execute," though he objected to "liberties" taken by the composers (Barrington: 289–300; C. Wesley 1849, 2:330–38; Olleson 2001: 84–88, 130; Olleson 2003: 5, 10, 218, 251–52).

Given this background, it is not surprising that the domestic concerts Charles and Samuel gave between 1779 and 1787 included songs by Purcell; orchestral

183

ILLUS. 14.1. Samuel Wesley as an adult. Portrait by John Jackson, R.A., c. 1815–20.
© National Portrait Gallery, London.

music by Corelli, Geminiani, and Handel; and vocal numbers by Handel. However, they also performed pieces in the modern *galant* style by John Christian
Bach, Felice Giardini, and others. Thus the brothers had a foot in both of the two
main camps of London's concert life. The old music they performed was similar
to that espoused by the Academy of Ancient Music and the Concerts of Ancient
Music (which only performed music more than twenty years old), while the
modern Continental style was particularly associated with the famous concert

series put on by J. C. Bach with Charles Frederick Abel (Doane: 76–83; Hawkins; McLamore 2004; McVeigh; Matthew; Weber: 56–74).

Samuel was clearly associated with musicians in the Bach-Abel circle: he appeared aged eleven with other musical prodigies at Hickford's Room on May 20, 1777, in a concert promoted by J. C. Bach (McLamore 2004: 74–75). Daines Barrington recorded that Abel "wrote him a subject," presumably for an improvisation; that Wilhelm Cramer "took a great liking to him, and offered to teach him the violin, and played some Trios with Charles and him"; that Samuel told him one day that he had practiced "Three or four hours; which Giardini had found necessary," presumably as a teacher or advisor; and that he had "been at Bach's concert," where he was "much satisfied with the compositions and performers" but criticized them for playing four successive pieces in the same key (Barrington: 297, 303). Barrington added: "I have heard him [Wesley] frequently play extemporary lessons, which, without prejudice to their musical names, might have been supposed to have been those of Abel, [Mattia] Vento, [Johann] Schobert, and Bach." Wesley's fragmentary "Sketch of the State of Music in England, from the Year 1778 up to the Present" includes an apparently firsthand account of the Bach-Abel concerts, a rare source of information about these exclusive events (*Lbl* Add. 27593).

Thus the position adopted by the Wesley brothers (though one suspects it reflected Samuel's taste more than Charles's) was similar to that adopted by the diarist and amateur composer John Marsh in his 1796 essay "Comparison between the Ancient and Modern Styles of Music" (Cudworth), or that articulated by the Colchester amateur musician Thomas Twining, writing to Charles Burney on May 18, 1776, about the Concerts of Ancient Music, then just formed:

> I never heard or read of anything so completely absurd as the Concert you tell me of. If the institution had been to mix old pieces with new to have a concerto of Corelli, Geminiani, &c., every night, &c., I shou'd not have been angry; for I confess I think compositions of that age & stamp do not deserve to be quite discarded; the less so, as there is nothing of the same kind (I mean *full* concertos not *obligati*) to be substituted for them in modern music. Nor shou'd I have grumbled if solo pieces had been limited; for I have found myself cloyed with a concert composed of such performances, tho' excellent; one likes, sometimes, to hear *music,* as well as to hear *playing.* But to exclude modern music, &c., is such an absurd piece of childish retaliation, such a sulky *bouderie!* never heard anything like it! (R. S. Walker: 114–15)

Repeated bouts of depression prevented Samuel from developing a consistent long-term performing career, though he seems to have maintained this moderate aesthetic position as an adult. Thus he played a Handel organ concerto during the first performance of his Ode to St. Cecilia (KO 207) at Covent Garden on February 22, 1799, and the one surviving program from a series of concerts he gave with his brother at the Tottenham Street Rooms during the 1802 season shows that Handel (the overture to *Atalanta* and an arrangement for two organs of the final chorus of *Esther*) was mixed with modern music by Mozart, Dussek, Cimarosa, the promoters themselves, and others. From about 1808, much of his energy was spent promoting the music of J. S. Bach. For instance, he performed music by Bach in his annual benefit concerts at the Hanover Square Rooms on June 11, 1808 (keyboard "preludes and fugues"), June 3, 1809 (the motet *Jesu, meine Freude* with Latin words, and an organ trio sonata), May 19, 1810 (part of *Jesu, meine Freude*, a sonata for violin and harpsichord, and an organ trio), April 27, 1811 (a sonata for violin and harpsichord, and "Solo, Violin," played by Salomon), and June 5, 1812 (Vincent Novello's arrangement for organ duet and orchestra of the Prelude in E flat, BWV 552). In a lecture given at the Royal Institution, probably in March 1828, he described an ideal public concert that mixed Handel, concertos by Corelli or Geminiani, a chorus by J. S. Bach, and "some first-rate Glee, or Madrigal, or a Cantata of Purcell, or Canzonet of [John] Travers [1703–58]" with modern operatic music and "one of Haydn's, Mozart's, or Beethoven's best Symphonies" ("Chronology"; Edwards: 654–55; *Lbl* Add. 35014; Kassler and Olleson: 62; *Morning Chronicle*; Olleson 2003, 2004.)

Wesley also made editions and arrangements of old music, some published, others remaining in manuscript. His arrangements for keyboard duet of "He gave them hailstones" from Handel's *Israel in Egypt* appeared at the time of the family concerts, though he only began to publish on a large scale once he began to promote Bach's music. He collaborated with Charles Frederick Horn (1762–1830) in editions of the 48 Preludes and Fugues (c. 1808–30) and the organ trio sonatas "adapted for three hands upon the piano forte" (c. 1809–11), and published three of the Six Little Preludes (BWV 933–35) off his own bat (1812–13). Publications of other composers included anthems by William Croft and Maurice Greene in 1809, an arrangement (c. 1816) of the *Macbeth* music, then thought to be by Matthew Locke but actually written by Richard Leveridge in 1702. He also planned editions of the Credo from Bach's Mass in B Minor and antiphons from William Byrd's *Gradualia* (in 1825–26), though they never materialized (Fiske; Kassler 2004b, 2004c; Kassler and Olleson: 689–98; Olleson 2004: 308–10; Olleson and Palmer, esp. 53–60; Tomita 2004a, 2004b).

Antiquarian Composition in Wesley and His Predecessors

Wesley's interest in old music went far beyond performance, arrangement, and publication. It also profoundly affected his attitude to composition. It was customary in England at the time to use conservative idioms for genres associated with the Church, such as the anthem and the organ voluntary, or those posthumously dominated by Handel, such as the oratorio and the organ concerto. Thus Wesley's Morning and Evening Service in F (1824) was heavily influenced by Restoration services, particularly Purcell's in B flat and Blow's in G; both of these had been published in Boyce's *Cathedral Music* (1760–73), so Wesley would have known them from childhood. The *Harmonicon* review of Wesley's published score described a discord in the doxology of the Jubilate Deo as "in an extremely bare, crude, state, and to our ears very cacophonous, though Dr Blow [John Blow, 1648–1708] might have enjoyed it much," and also objected to the false relation at the end of the same movement. Wesley quoted twice from Purcell's service in his lengthy reply to the review, pointing out that it included a rather similar false relation. (*Literary Chronicle,* June 6, 1825: 377–80; Olleson 2003: 170–82, 245–47.)

Wesley clearly thought that the contemporary neglect of Purcell's service was paralleled by the hostile reception and subsequent neglect of his own. He wrote to Novello on June 10, 1830, that "Henry Purcell's immortal Church Service in B flat is very rarely (if ever) sung at St. Paul's Cathedral, at Westminster Abbey or at the Chapel Royal; whereas all the harmless and hackneyed Chords of [Charles] King and [James] Kent are in Constant Request at the Cathedrals all over England" (Olleson 2001: 450–51). His service was neglected for similar reasons: it is longer, more difficult, more adventurous in its harmony, and more complex in its counterpoint than most Anglican church music of the late Georgian period. He must have recognized, as did others (including Mozart, when writing his Mass in C Minor), that counterpoint was a much more satisfying and appropriate idiom for choirs than the homophonic and largely syllabic writing mostly used in church music in Catholic parts of Germany and central Europe, and taken up in England through the influence of Haydn's masses and works such as Mozart's "Ave verum corpus" (Temperley 1961: 314–15; 1981, esp. 183–87). Purcell was clearly an important model for Wesley. Novello wrote that his songs "Gentle Jesus, meek and mild," KO 128 (1808), and "'Twas not the spawn of such as these," KO 312 (1825), were respectively "worthy of Purcell himself" and "a most admirable imitation of Henry Purcell's style," and added that his style "strongly resembled that of Purcell, with a mixture of Mozart, Handel, and Sebastian Bach in it" (Olleson 2003: 249, 280). Wesley always placed Purcell and Thomas Arne (1710–1778) "in the first rank of our native composers," according to an article published shortly after his death ("Professional Memoranda": 113).

In secular music, part songs and glees also carried conservative expectations, particularly because examples were often written for organizations concerned with the revival of early vocal music, such as the Madrigal Society, the Glee Club, and the Concentores Society (Robins 2006). They often offered prizes for glees and catches, encouraging composers to conform to their stylistic and ideological concerns. Thus Wesley's "O sing unto mie roundelaie," KO 233 (1812), was written for a competition run by the Madrigal Society for a piece "after the manner of madrigals of Bennett, Wilbye, Morley, Ward, Weelkes, Marenzio and others" (Olleson 2003: 128). He did not win, but his entry is remarkable for its command of the renaissance madrigal idiom, with contrapuntal points associated with each phrase of the text, detailed word painting, an imaginative use of the combinations offered by the five voices, and a modally inflected harmonic idiom including *tierces de Picardie*, elongated cadences using the 5-3, 6-4, 5-4, 5-3 formula, and a change halfway through from tonic minor to major recalling Wilbye's "Adieu, sweet Amaryllis" (Olleson 2003: 273). For this exercise in musical antiquarianism, Wesley appropriately set one of Thomas Chatterton's fake "Thomas Rowley" poems by a supposed fifteenth-century Bristol author; it is the first verse of one of the minstrel's songs in "Ælla: A Tragycal Enterlude" (Chatterton, 1:210). As a well-educated person interested in literature, Wesley would have known that Chatterton had been suspected of forgery ever since the 1780s, so he probably chose the text tongue in cheek. Philip Olleson suggested that he did not win the prize because he was not prepared to write "out-and-out pastiche," but in fact "O sing unto mie roundelaie" is a more convincing essay in the madrigal style than the piece that won, William Beale's "Awake, sweet muse."

Wesley was not the first English composer to be interested in old music or to write in a self-consciously antique style. Purcell copied out pre–Civil War anthems and edited them for performance, and wrote contrapuntal consort music that referred back to the sixteenth century. Johann Christoph Pepusch (1669–1752), a German-born musician who settled in England, inspired a group of musicians associated with the Academy of Ancient Music to collect, study, and imitate renaissance vocal polyphony, and he wrote contrapuntal four-part settings of the psalms "Beatus vir" and "Laetatus sum"; the former was performed at the Academy on December 19, 1734, and on several subsequent occasions. Boyce's *Cathedral Music* had its origins in materials collected by Maurice Greene (1696–1755), who also wrote modal five-part anthems, probably for the academy (Cook, 2:200–202; Holman 1994: 84–85; Johnstone 1975; Shay and Thompson: 33–46).

Among Pepusch's followers was John Keeble (1711–1786), who advised Charles Wesley on his elder son's musical education, though the most important composer among them was Benjamin Cooke the younger (1734–1793), who wrote madrigal-like glees such as "In the merry month of May" (1775) and "Fair Susan did her wifehode well mayntayne" (entitled *Susannah and the Two Elders*, 1771), the latter a setting of a Chaucer imitation by Matthew Prior and thus a possible model for "O sing unto mie roundelaie." Cooke also applied Pepusch's interpretation of Greek music theory to the composition of orchestral anthems and other concerted music, producing by accident or design an approximation to the Restoration idiom, with its expressive word setting, intense passing dissonance, and rapid modulations (Eggington: 143–87, 319–39; Olleson 2003: 8).

Cooke was ideologically committed to the cause of old music, yet in his large-scale works there is often a disparity between the conservative style of the choruses and the more modern style of the vocal solos (Eggington: 166–67). English composers were not alone in using what we might call "stylistic diversity." It can be found, for instance, in those sacred vocal works of J. S. Bach such as the Mass in B Minor that have *stile antico* fugal movements as well as arias in a modern operatic style. It was also an important feature of Italian eighteenth-century church music. To take an obvious example well known in eighteenth-century England, Pergolesi's *Stabat mater* has movements in a modern, expressive style alongside *stile antico* fugues in the *alla breve* idiom. Wesley's engagement with Catholicism and the Catholic chapels in London in the 1780s seems to have brought him into contact with a good deal of Latin church music, either written in London by Charles Barbandt, Samuel Webbe and others, or imported from Italy. His own Latin church music is extremely diverse, ranging from simple solos, duets, and trios, probably written for the Catholic chapels in the 1780s, to the complex contrapuntal double-choir motets *Deus majestatis intonuit*, KO 23 (1799), *Dixit Dominus*, KO 26 (1800), and *In exitu Israel*, KO 43 (1810). The first two were apparently inspired by Neapolitan double-choir pieces rather than Bach's double-choir motets, though he is known to have possessed a volume of "Bach's Mottets" in 1814—presumably the 1803 Breitkopf edition (Olleson 2000a; 2001: 216–17; 2003: 230–44).

Wesley and Stylistic Diversity: The Vocal Works

Wesley used stylistic diversity in three extended Latin works, *Missa de Spiritu Sancto*, KO 3 (1784), *Ave maris stella*, KO 15 (1786), and *Confitebor tibi, Domine*, KO 20 (1799, but not performed until 1826) (Olleson 1999, 2003 *passim*). In *Ave maris stella*, scored for two sopranos, strings, and continuo, the first three movements are largely in the *galant* style, while the last is in a conservative idiom using contrapuntal gestures involving a constantly repeated plainsong phrase and a running bass expressing rapidly moving baroque-style harmonies (Ex. 14.1). In the other two works the distinction is between the contrapuntal choruses, occasionally based on plainsong, and the solo airs, written in an up-to-date style. An obvious reason for this disparity is the development of vocal technique during the eighteenth century. Baroque solo vocal technique, exemplified by Handel, used a relatively small range with passagework largely confined to simple runs and arpeggios. By the 1760s, Italian singing teachers had expanded the ranges used, particularly for sopranos, and had introduced much more demanding writing, such as the rapid triplets in arpeggio patterns and the wide leaps used in "The soldier tir'd of war's alarms" from Thomas Arne's *Artaxerxes* (1762), a soprano display piece for much of the nineteenth century. Writing of this sort goes naturally with *galant* orchestration, with its simplified harmonies and enriched scoring using horns and other wind instruments to reinforce the strings in what German scholars call the "Bläserorgel" or "wind organ" (Spitzer and Zaslaw: 464–67).

Arne was the first English composer to get to grips with the *galant* style and was therefore an important early exponent of stylistic diversity, though he tended

Spiritoso (Cantus figuratus super Tono Octavo)

EX. 14.1. Samuel Wesley, "Vitam praesta puram" from *Ave maris stella*, KO 15,
bars 1–19. www.primalamusica.com. Reproduced by permission.

to use it for characterization in theater works, as in *Artaxerxes,* where the major
characters (including Mandane, who sings "The soldier tir'd") mostly have demanding, richly scored airs in the *galant* style, while those for the minor characters
are more conservative and are simply scored. Arne's one surviving oratorio, *Judith*
(1761), is rather a surprise in that much of the choral writing is as modern as the
solos, though there are some Handelian fugal sections, including one in the *alla
breve* style, "O Lord our God, whose mighty arm" (Smither: 257, 261–90; Zöllner:
95–112). In this respect, Wesley seems to have been influenced more directly by

Thomas Linley the younger (1756–1778), in particular by his short oratorio *The Song of Moses* (1777), performed by the Wesley brothers for Lady Horne on March 17 and 19, 1780 (McLamore 2004: 113). Its splendid choruses are Handelian, and "Praise be to God, and God alone," with its *cantus firmus*-like theme, is clearly indebted to the section "I will sing unto the Lord" in "Moses and the children of Israel" from *Israel in Egypt*. By contrast, the airs are mostly in the *galant* style, such as the delicious "Thou, as thy mercy hath decreed," with its slow-moving harmony, its divided violas doubled at the octave by flutes, and its virtuoso passagework for the soprano in triplets, doubtless influenced by "The soldier tir'd." Even the arch-modernist J. C. Bach wrote Handelian choruses in his oratorio *Gioas, rè di Giuda* (1770), presumably in an attempt to please English oratorio audiences.

Wesley partly conformed to this tradition in *Confitebor tibi, Domine*. The great soprano solo "Fidelia omnia mandata ejus," probably written for Gertrud Elisabeth Mara in 1799 and sung by Mary Ann Paton in 1826, is a full-blown sonata-pattern aria in the Mozartian march style with flutes, oboes, horns, and strings. It runs to 270 bars, demands a range of nearly 2½ octaves (a–d'''), and takes the singer through a varied menu of late-eighteenth-century virtuosity, including spectacular runs, staccato arpeggios up to top notes, sudden changes of register, and little decorative turns. By contrast, there is a fine five-part *alla breve* choral fugue, "Mandavit in aeternam," and the concluding chorus, "Sicut erat in principio," uses free counterpoint based on several rather Purcellian minuet-like themes. However, two of the other choruses, "Magna opera Domini" and "Virtutem operum suorum," are more advanced than the Handelian archetype. The former contrasts a fugue subject with a more modern answering phrase pairing voices in thirds, while the *furioso* orchestral accompaniment of the latter, much of it in unisons and octaves, disguises the fact that the voices have a good deal of conventional counterpoint. The quartet "Memoriam fecit" is based on a rhythmicized plainsong theme but is completely modern in its harmonic style and orchestration. Most people would never know that it is based on plainsong had not Wesley pointed out the fact in his autograph score. Wesley seems to be moving here beyond the conventional contrasts between old and new in separate movements, incorporating both elements into a single movement. The device achieved its most characteristic form in his later instrumental works, where he combined elements of J. S. Bach's idiom with modern sonata patterns.

Before discussing those instrumental works, we should consider Wesley's other mature large-scale work, the *Ode to St. Cecilia*, KO 207 (1794), a setting of "Begin the noble song," a poem by his grandfather and namesake (Olleson 2003: esp. 48, 57–59, 252–54). In this work Wesley reached beyond the obvious model, Handel's *Ode for St. Cecilia's Day* (1739), to Purcell. Purcell's St. Cecilia odes, "Hail, bright Cecilia" and "Welcome to all the pleasures," were not available in print in the eighteenth century, though three of his other odes, "Celebrate this festival," "Great parent, hail," and "Of old when heroes thought it base," ap-

peared around 1790 in Benjamin Goodison's abortive collected edition (King).
Purcellian movements in Wesley's ode include the air "Numbers, Cecilia, soft as
those," with its minuet-like themes and simple syllabic writing for solo soprano
and choir, the contrapuntal trio "How various, Music, is thy praise," based on
a descending chromatic sequence, and "'Tis here, a sacred vestal, Music turns,"
with its archaic choral writing and Purcellian alternation between voices and
instruments (Ex. 14.2). Not all the numbers are so conservative, though it is
striking that all of the solo vocal writing is relatively straightforward, avoiding
the extended techniques already discussed.

EX. 14.2. Samuel Wesley, "'Tis here, a sacred vestal, Music turns" from
Ode to St. Cecilia, KO 207, bars 59–64.

Stylistic Diversity in the Instrumental Works

Wesley's first major instrumental work to use stylistic diversity is the Symphony in B flat Major, KO 409, probably written for the 1802 concert already mentioned. The delightful symphonies he wrote for the family concerts show that he had mastered the *galant* idiom while still a child. This work is much more ambitious and serious, and it takes Haydn's London symphonies as a point of departure. Wesley wrote in his reminiscences that Salomon's concerts in 1792, 1794, and 1795 formed "a grand Epoch of new musical Excellence by the Introduction of Haydn and his inimitable Symphonies into this Country." He attended them "very frequently, and received both Pleasure and Advantage in listening to a fine Band of the best vocal and instrumental Performers so judiciously selected and so ably and skilfully conducted" (Olleson 2003: 222). We learn from another passage that he was at the first performance of Haydn's Symphony No. 98 in B flat Major on March 2, 1792.

Wesley was the only native English composer who mastered Haydn's late symphonic style properly; John Marsh's rather trite Symphony in D Major (1796) shows how elusive the idiom could be. However, he was not content with mere imitation. He used a typical Haydn orchestra (two flutes, two oboes, two horns, two bassoons, and strings with timpani), Haydn's formal patterns (though with no slow introduction to the first movement), and much of Haydn's musical language, including sophisticated and wide-ranging harmonic patterns, though he followed J. C. Bach or Mozart in his florid solo writing for wind instruments and also incorporated elements of the contrapuntal baroque style. Haydn used a great deal of counterpoint in his late instrumental music, though mainly in the form of motivic conversations, akin to the contrasted ideas given to characters in the ensembles of contemporary Italian operas (Schroeder: 78). Interestingly, the one Haydn London symphony without a slow introduction, no. 95 in C minor (1791), is also the only one with a movement (the Finale) that combines formal fugal writing with the sonata pattern; perhaps it was Wesley's immediate model (Landon: 515–18). Wesley used contrapuntal writing almost obsessively in the outer movements of his symphony. In both, the main theme is discussed contrapuntally throughout, not just in the development section, as in many eighteenth-century symphonies. This makes them largely monothematic and leaves the homophonic second subjects rather isolated. There is a good deal of ingenious counterpoint: at one moment in the first movement, fragments of the theme are heard simultaneously with simple and decorated inverted forms, creating numerous false relations (Ex. 14.3).

Wesley also used baroque harmonies and melodic types to give his symphony a serious and rather antique flavor. The Finale's main theme is harmonized with a baroque-style running bass, and its second subject has a hymnlike character, though with a chromatic inflection that makes it sound oddly Mendelssohnian

EX. 14.3. Samuel Wesley, Symphony in B flat, KO 409, Allegro, bars 67–72 (Schwarz). Reproduced by permission.

(Ex. 14.4). Similarly, the Minuet and Trio are full of baroque harmonies and melodic patterns, and there are a few bars at the beginning of the second section of the trio where a combination of busy counterpoint, cross accents, and a particular deployment of wind instruments brings Mendelssohn or even Berwald irresistibly to mind (Ex. 14.5). The Andante is more conventional on the surface, using Haydn's favorite mixture of sonata and variation patterns, though it does not sound at all like Haydn, and the listener only gradually realizes this is because it is largely a study in three-bar phrases (Ex. 14.6). Again, the avoidance of regular four- and eight-bar phrases suggests music of a much later period, when such tactics had become more common. It is a measure of Wesley's skill as a composer that this extraordinary movement always sounds natural and logical.

Mendelssohn is not likely to have been influenced by or even to have known Wesley's symphony, though the two men did meet shortly before Wesley's death in 1837. What they had in common was a fascination with old music. Both were involved in performing and promoting it and therefore wished to engage with it in their own music. In Wesley's case, this has traditionally been seen as part of

EX. 14.4. Samuel Wesley, Symphony in B flat, KO 409, Vivace molto, bars 61–66 (Schwarz). Reproduced by permission.

EX. 14.5. Samuel Wesley, Symphony in B flat, KO 409, Minuetto (Vivace), bars 56–62 (Schwarz). Reproduced by permission.

EX. 14.6. Samuel Wesley, Symphony in B flat, KO 409, Andante, bars 1–12 (Schwarz).
Reproduced by permission.

the collective failure of English musicians to keep up with the times, though critics and historians have applauded similar things in nineteenth-century German
music, such as Beethoven's *Grosse Fuge* and the overture *Die Weihe des Hauses,*
Spohr's *Historische Sinfonie,* or Mendelssohn's *Reformation Symphony.* In Wesley's
case, the decision to use elements of the baroque style in genres not particularly
associated with it (such as the symphony, chamber music, and piano music) was
clearly a deliberate choice: as we have seen, he had completely mastered the *galant* style as a child.

I would like to suggest that, in embracing musical antiquarianism, Wesley and
his English contemporaries were in advance of composers in Continental Europe.
Their interest in old music should be seen as part of a fashionable pre-romantic
interest in the past in many areas of eighteenth-century British culture, expressed
in such things as the revival of Gothic architecture, the mock-antique poetry of
James Macpherson (as "Ossian") and Thomas Chatterton, the Gothic novel, the
trend toward historical accuracy in painting and in the theater, and, perhaps
most important, the development of antiquarian scholarship (Lipking; Langford,
esp. 473–76; Sweet). In music, as in other fields, Britain led the way in historical
research. Thus Boyce's *Cathedral Music* was the first printed anthology of old
music; John Mainwaring's *Memoirs of the Life of the Late George Frederic Handel*
(London, 1760) was the first full-length biography of a composer; the first comprehensive music histories were by Sir John Hawkins (1776) and Charles Burney
(1776–1789); and Samuel Arnold's *The Works of Handel* (1787–97) was the first
collected edition of a single composer. (For further discussion, see Duckles.)

Seen in this light, Wesley's later obsessive engagement with the music of J. S. Bach is not so remarkable or unexpected, particularly since other prominent English musicians at the time were also enthusiasts, including Salomon, Clementi, and William Crotch ("Chronology"). An early attempt to incorporate Bach into his own music was fairly crude: he inserted the D-major fugue from the 48, Book 1, into his Organ Concerto in D Major, KO 414 (1800), then revised it for a performance at the Tamworth Festival on August 22, 1809, played first as a keyboard solo and then in an orchestral arrangement (Olleson 1993; 2003: 96–97, 288–89). By 1809, Bach was already beginning to influence Wesley's musical idiom, particularly in his solo keyboard writing. Good examples in his solo harpsichord and piano music (in which, as a secular genre, elements of the Bach style stand out more clearly than in the organ music) are the fugue on a theme of Salomon from the Sonata in D Minor, KO 705 (c. 1808), *The Christmas Carol*, KO 718 (c. 1815), and the Fugue in D Major, KO 736 (1825).

"The Christmas Carol, Varied as a Rondo," KO 718, using a variant of the tune now known as "God rest you merry, gentlemen," includes fugal writing, rapid Bachian passagework often outlining chromatic harmony, with ninths and other strong dissonances, and, at one point, an appearance of the theme in augmentation, like a chorale prelude (Ex. 14.7). Olleson suggests that the fugue of KO 705 does not reflect Wesley's enthusiasm for Bach but is instead "in the austere, gritty manner that characterizes so many fugues by composers of the late Classical period" (2003: 317–18). However, the "gritty manner" itself was derived at least partly from Bach, as for instance in Mozart's Fugue in C Minor, K426, 546/2, for two pianos or strings. Temperley aptly observes that in the Fugue in D Major (1828, KO 736), Wesley imitated "the severe passage-work and diatonic dissonance of the late baroque idiom, which he sometimes takes to extremes of harshness," and suggests that its "abrupt, downright ending can be taken as a rebuke to all the decadence of the modern schools of pianism, which Wesley thought of as coming from the Continent" (1985: xvi).

EX. 14.7. Samuel Wesley, *The Christmas Carol*, KO 718, bars 164–75.

There is similar writing in the Trio in D Minor/Major, KO 826, for three pianos (1811). Wesley wrote that he had been inspired to compose it after encountering Mozart's Sonata in D Major for two pianos (*Lbl* Add. 35014: 36), though it is not very Mozartian in style. A more obvious model would have been Bach's two concertos for three harpsichords. They were not readily available in England until they were published in the *Bachgesellschaft* edition in 1885, though Wesley would have known about them from the list of works in Johann Nikolaus Forkel's 1802 biography of Bach. An English translation of Forkel, which Wesley and Charles Frederick Horn planned to publish, existed as early as 1808 (Kassler 2004a). Wesley's Trio is concerto-like in its interplay among the three instruments, though it has a sonata-like structure, laid out in two extended movements. A short, slow introduction in D minor leads to the D-major Presto assai, a large-scale sonata movement dominated by Bachian "two-part invention" writing. There is not much formal counterpoint, but the harmonic writing, with rising and falling sequences and walking basses, is solidly baroque in style, as is the thematic material. By contrast, Mozart's sonata is in an elegant classical idiom, with varied melodic writing supported by repeated-note bass lines or simple cadential progressions. Wesley's second movement, an Andante grazioso, is organized in an unusual way. It begins as a set of variations, again on a baroque-style theme, but there is a middle section in D minor. Shortly after the variations resume with the return to D major, the theme is transformed into a lilting Pastorale in 6/8. Again, there are few points of contact with the Mozart sonata, except possibly in some of the details of the decoration in the second movements of both works. The Trio for three pianos is not an isolated experiment: we find a similar mixture of classical patterns and baroque musical language in the Trio in F Major for two flutes and piano, KO 514 (1826), and in the relatively well-known Grand Duet in C Major, KO 604 (1812), for organ four hands, which ends with a large-scale barnstorming fugue rather than a rondo or a set of variations (see pp. 130–32 for an analysis).

Summary

Wesley's unusually diverse compositional style was in part a reflection of London's uniquely eclectic musical life. As a child he was able to experience the best modern music at the Bach-Abel concerts as well as several centuries of old music at the Concerts of Ancient Music, mixing the two repertories together in the family concerts. He used both styles with assurance in his early music, but as an adult he began to see the possibilities of combining them in large-scale works, following the precedent established by Arne, Cooke, and Linley, among others. However, he seems to have been the first person to combine old and new in single movements. In his later instrumental works he showed his enthusiasm for J. S. Bach by combining elements of Bach's contrapuntal musical language with large-scale classical patterns. Stylistic diversity of this sort was an expression of London's advanced cultural life, where the past had been discovered and embraced in most intellectual and artistic fields earlier than in other European centers. Samuel Wesley's fruitful engagement with the past certainly anticipated similar things in Mendelssohn, Schumann, and other nineteenth-century German composers and produced a number of fine, distinctive works that deserve to be better known today.

I am grateful to William Davies, Peter Lynan, and Simon McVeigh for access to unpublished materials, and to Harry Johnstone, Philip Olleson, and Nicholas Temperley for their helpful comments on a draft of this paper.

CHAPTER 15

The Anthem Texts
and Word Setting of
Sebastian Wesley

Peter Horton

Sebastian Wesley and Received
Textual Practice in Anthems

Open any collection of anthems composed for cathedral or Chapel Royal use by a composer active between the late seventeenth and early nineteenth centuries and the likelihood is that the texts will have been taken from the book of Psalms. Thus twenty-nine of William Croft's *Thirty Select Anthems* of 1724 are settings of verses from the Psalms, as are thirty-five of Maurice Greene's *Forty Select Anthems* and thirteen of William Boyce's *Fifteen Anthems* of 1780. As one progresses through the century, the proportion of non-psalm texts gradually increases: four out of sixteen in the posthumously published *Sacred Music* of Thomas Attwood (1765–1837) and six out of seventeen in the similar collection of Thomas Attwood Walmisley (1814–1856). Indeed, by the middle of the nineteenth century, psalm texts were poised to become a minority, forming fractionally over half the texts—eighteen out of thirty-five—in the anthems of Samuel Sebastian Wesley and rather fewer than half, only seventeen out of forty, in the works of his contemporary John Goss (1800–1880). In the anthems of Goss's successor as organist of St. Paul's cathedral, John Stainer (1840–1901), they form an even smaller proportion of the total, an aspect of his work that has yet to be examined in full detail. Neither of Stainer's modern biographers makes more than passing comments on his choice of texts (Charlton; Dibble 2007); only William Gatens discusses the matter in any depth (Gatens: 184–88).

My purpose, however, is neither to conduct a survey of nineteenth-century anthem texts, nor to chart the steady rise of the New Testament as a source of texts for musical setting, fascinating as both would be. Rather, it is to look at the strikingly individual practice of that master of mid-nineteenth-century sacred music, Samuel Sebastian Wesley. It is a subject that has already been touched upon in my book on Wesley, and it has also been covered by Gatens and by Nicholas Temperley (1981). But it is worth revisiting because of what it tells us

ILLUS. 15.1. Samuel Sebastian Wesley, 1849 (Royal College of Music). Oil portrait by William Keighley Briggs. Reproduced by permission of the Royal College of Music.

about Wesley's idiosyncratic approach to anthem composition and about possible influences on his work. A brief glance at his background will help to put his work into its historical context.

Born in 1810, Wesley was the first child of his father Samuel's second, illegitimate, family with his former housemaid Sarah Suter. Despite a remarkably distinguished religious pedigree, Sebastian's upbringing was anything but conventional. Not only was his father a victim of bipolar disorder and in consequence unable to work and hence earn during the worst phases of his illness, but, as far as Samuel's mother and siblings were concerned, he had also placed himself beyond the pale by deserting his wife and children (Horton 2004: 3–4). In consequence, there was virtually no contact between Samuel and Sarah's children and the other members of the Wesley family. Indeed, after the failure of a plan by several of Samuel's friends and his sister Sally to send seven-year-old Sebastian to be educated, free of charge, near Manchester, Sally felt able to wash her hands of the matter:

> Having thus discharged the Duties of Humanity, and our Efforts being defeated, the matter ends: poor Sams children are likely to be involved in the Misfortunes of their Father, and probably may live to be sad memorials of his mispent Youth. We would have rescued this poor Boy, and given him a chance of becoming a good Member of Society, & shall therefore have no Self-reproaches. (*ATu* OBV1: 85)

Not long after this scheme had fallen through, an alternative future beckoned for Sebastian following his acceptance as one of the children (choristers) of the Chapel Royal, St. James's palace, London. Here he would remain under the stern charge of William Hawes, master of the children, for over eight years, taking part in the chapel services and experiencing for himself the riches of the Anglican cathedral music tradition. The repertory was dominated by services and anthems dating from the late seventeenth and eighteenth centuries, in other words by the works of composers who would naturally have turned to the Psalms for most of their anthem texts. Indeed, some three-quarters of the anthems included in the 1826 edition of the Chapel Royal wordbook set verses from the Psalms (Pearce 1826).

But there was one significant exception, John Stafford Smith (1750–1836). Appointed one of the two joint organists in 1802, he had published a collection of anthems in 1793 which were not only "Intended to exhibit a closer Analogy than usual between the Accent of Speech, and the Melody of Song," but also set verses from a much wider variety of sources than was customary, a practice hitherto found in oratorios but rarely in anthems (J. S. Smith). Smith's anthems include settings of the Beatitudes, words from the books of Proverbs and Ecclesiasticus, and several selections from Isaiah. What is of particular interest is the way in which he combined verses from different sources in a manner that uncannily prefigures Wesley's. The most extreme example is *Horrible is the end of the unrighteous generation,* whose text is assembled from ten discrete sections from the

Wisdom of Solomon, Ecclesiastes, Joel, II Chronicles, Psalms 25 and 79, and the Litany. But of greater significance in the present context is his anthem *Trust ye in the Lord*. It uses Isaiah 26:4 and Habbakuk 3:17–18, exactly the same selection that Wesley would himself use in his *Trust ye in the Lord* (c. 1835). Given that Wesley followed Smith in changing "Yet I will rejoice" to "Yet will I rejoice," it is difficult to believe that this was entirely coincidental, though it should be noted that he saw no reason to imitate Smith's change of "the fields shall give no wheat" to "the field shall yield no meat"!

While Stafford Smith's example may have inspired Wesley to look more widely for his anthem texts, it was surely his own sensitivity to words, combined with a firm knowledge of the Bible, that led him to assemble such individual selections of verses. But before examining these in detail we must consider two interrelated topics: Wesley's emergence as a composer of church music in the early 1830s and the place of anthems in his compositional output. Despite his long association with sacred music at the Chapel Royal, when Wesley left the choir in 1826 it was to embark on a varied career that over the next few years would embrace Sunday positions as a parish church organist, work as pianist and "conductor of the chorus" at the English Opera House, the post of organist at the Lent Oratorio Concerts, teaching, occasional organ recitals, and composition. His early output consisted largely of solo songs, music for piano and organ, and choral and orchestral music (Horton 2004: 23–34). His primary aim as a composer was to gain recognition in the concert hall and theater, not the Church. Indeed, had it not been for his unexpected move to Hereford as cathedral organist in September 1832, it is questionable whether he would have become the man we remember today: the composer of sacred music par excellence. But there can be no doubt that his banishment to the provinces directly contributed to the composition of his first major anthem, *The wilderness and the solitary place*. Written to commemorate the reopening of the enlarged cathedral organ, it was first heard on November 8, 1832, and immediately stamped Wesley as a composer to be reckoned with. From this point on, church music and more particularly the anthem gradually achieved a position of pre-eminence in his output. When, many years later, he prepared some autobiographical notes, he wrote that "My published 12 Anthems is my most important work," significantly drawing attention to "the manner in which the words are expressed" (*Lbl* Add. 35019: 124–25).

Tradition and Innovation in *The wilderness*

When Wesley turned to church music in the 1830s, the principal forms in use, settings of the canticles ("services") and anthems, had undergone little external change for over a century, with composers still writing verse anthems, full-with-verse anthems, and full anthems whose formal outlines would have been recognized by Purcell and his successors. (A verse anthem opens with a "verse," a section to be sung by single voices to a part; a full-with-verse anthem opens and closes with movements for full choir but includes movements for verse ensemble; a full anthem is scored for full choir throughout.) Wesley himself, although radical in some respects, was content to build on the work of previous generations and simply took over the anthem forms as he found them, adapting or developing them as necessary. *The wilderness,* for example, is a traditional verse anthem, while a majority of its successors are of the full-with-verse type, but sometimes, as in *Blessed be the God and Father* and *Trust ye in the Lord,* with a novel slant.

Many writers have pointed out that Wesley's more radical side found expression through the bold use of a contemporary musical idiom—new wine in old bottles. This chapter explores a less familiar aspect of his originality: the fashioning of idiosyncratic anthem texts. It is first encountered in *The wilderness,* which sets verses from Isaiah 35, some of which, probably unbeknown to him, had earlier been used by his uncle Charles Wesley (JN 90). Although all the verses are taken from the same chapter, he selected only those that served his purpose, cutting out what Temperley has described as "dead or perfunctory passages" (Temperley 1981: 195; see also Gatens: 139). In this context it is instructive to compare his text with the one set nearly thirty years later by John Goss (see Table 15.1). Goss's setting was commissioned by the dean and chapter of St. Paul's cathedral after Wesley had turned down their request to borrow a set of copies of his own setting. His self-defeating action was apparently motivated by their earlier refusal to subscribe to his collection of anthems (*Lbl* Add. 35020: 57v.).

The two most striking differences are the considerably greater length of Goss's text (albeit for a shorter work) and Wesley's ruthless excision of incidental details that would obscure rather than illuminate the message he wished to convey. Take, for example, verses 8 and 9, where he clearly considered the dual references to a "highway" and a "way" to be unnecessary. Likewise with the references to the "wayfaring men" and lions, however picturesque the imagery. Both composers omitted verse 7. It is not, I think, too fanciful to argue that his early experience at the English Opera House could have demonstrated to him the virtue of concise, direct expression. No less importantly, his feeling for words ensured that he avoided the pitfall of setting a text so short that its meaning would be weakened by too much repetition. (See, for example, the treble solo "For this our heart is faint" in Walmisley's anthem *Remember, O Lord,* which consists simply of the two phrases "For this our heart is faint, for these things our eyes are dim.") There is also another, hidden difference between the two texts: Wesley had chosen his own words, Goss's had been selected by W. C. Fynes Webber, succentor of St. Paul's cathedral.

The text of an anthem is not, of course, complete in itself, but merely one half of a musical composition, and there are equally striking differences in the way the two composers set the opening words. While Wesley used a measured,

TABLE 15.1. Text of *The wilderness:* comparison of Wesley with Goss

	Wesley (1832)	Goss (1861)
vv. 1–2	The wilderness and the solitary place shall be glad for them, and the desert shall rejoice and blossom as the rose. It shall blossom abundantly, and rejoice with joy and singing.	The wilderness and the solitary place shall be glad for them, and the desert shall rejoice and blossom as the rose. It shall blossom abundantly, and rejoice even with joy and singing; the glory of Lebanon shall be given unto it, the excellency of Carmel and Sharon; they see the glory of the Lord, and the excellency of our God.
v. 3		Strengthen ye the weak hands, and confirm the feeble knees.
v. 4	Say to them of a fearful heart, Be strong, fear not: behold, your God, even God, He will come and save you.	Say to them that are of a fearful heart, Be strong, fear not: behold your God will come with vengeance, even God with a recompense; He will come and save you.
v. 5		Then shall the eyes of the blind be opened, and the ears of the deaf shall be unstopped.
v. 6a	Then shall the lame man leap as an hart, and the tongue of the dumb sing.	Then shall the lame man leap as an hart, and the tongue of the dumb shall sing.
v. 6b	For in the wilderness shall waters break out, and streams in the desert.	For in the wilderness shall waters break out, and streams in the desert.
vv. 8–9	And a highway shall be there: it shall be called The way of holiness; the unclean shall not pass over it, but the redeemed shall pass there.	And a highway shall be there, and a way, and it shall be called The way of holiness; the unclean shall not pass over it, but it shall be for those: the wayfaring men, though fools, shall not err therein. No lion shall be there, nor any ravenous beast shall go up thereon, it shall not be found there; but the redeemed shall walk there.
v. 10	And the ransomed of the Lord shall return, and come to Zion with songs, and everlasting joy upon their heads; they shall obtain joy and gladness. And sorrow and sighing shall flee away.	And the ransomed of the Lord shall return and come to Zion with songs and everlasting joy upon their heads; they shall obtain joy and gladness, and sorrow and sighing shall flee away. Amen.

stately rising melody for solo bass, from which he developed a movement of some substance, Goss was content to treat them as an unmeasured *recitativo secco.* Likewise, while Goss's "timeless" music could have been written at almost any time from the mid-eighteenth century onward, Wesley's imaginative organ accompaniment and decorative chromaticism place his anthem firmly in the early nineteenth century (see Ex. 15.1).

WESLEY

GOSS

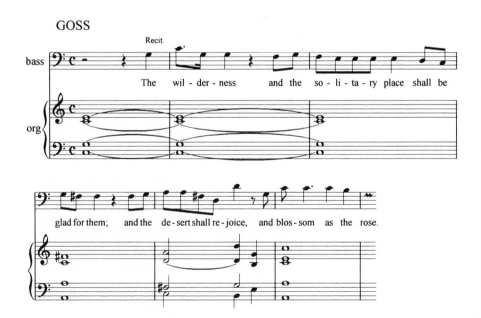

EX. 15.1. Comparison of the openings of Sebastian Wesley's and John Goss's *The wilderness.*

Broadening Textual Strategies

Another early anthem based on verses from a single biblical source is *Blessed be the God and Father,* written for use on Easter Day 1834, with a text from I Peter 1. Here we see Wesley taking more extreme liberties with his chosen verses and, in a manner reminiscent of Stafford Smith, treating the Bible as a quarry from which phrases could be taken and reused, often in a slightly different context. Note particularly verses 17, 22, and 23, where he extracted a single idea from each verse and, in verse 23, immeasurably strengthened the impact (in a musical context) by cutting the end, which enabled him to conclude with the powerful words "by the word of God" (Table 15.2).

From the mid-1830s, Wesley increasingly followed the practice of building up texts from a wider range of sources. A typical example is *O Lord, thou art my God,* begun in 1836 (Table 15.3). Here he drew on Isaiah 25 (as set by Purcell in his anthem of the same name), Psalm 33, I Corinthians, and the Wisdom of Solomon to create an appropriate text for an extended five-movement full-with-verse anthem. The verses from Isaiah (which are interpreted as looking forward to the coming of Christ) are assigned to the three movements for full choir—the first, third, and fifth. Those from the other sources provide a commentary on the ideas expressed in the Isaiah verses. (Stainer would later use a similar pattern in *And Jacob was left alone,* in which verses from Isaiah recounting Jacob's

TABLE 15.2. Text of *Blessed be the God and Father*

I Peter, chapter 1	
v.3	Blessed be the God and Father of our Lord Jesus Christ, which according to His abundant mercy hath begotten us again unto a lively hope by the resurrection of Jesus Christ from the dead.
v.4	To an inheritance incorruptible, and undefiled, *and* that fadeth not away, reserved in heaven for you.
v.5	Who are kept by the power of God through faith unto salvation ready to be revealed in the last time.
v.15	But as he which hath called you is holy, so be ye holy in all manner of conversation;
v.17	*And if ye call on the Father, who without respect of persons judgeth according to every man's work,* pass the time of your sojourning here in fear:
v.22	*Seeing ye have purified your souls in obeying the truth through the Spirit unto unfeigned love of the brethren,* see that ye love one another with a pure heart fervently:
v.23	Being born again, not of corruptible seed, but of incorruptible, by the word of God, *which liveth and abideth for ever.*
v.24	For all flesh is as grass, and all the glory of man as the flower of grass. The grass withereth, and the flower therof falleth away.
v.25	But the word of the Lord endureth for ever. *And this is the word which by the gospel is preached unto you.*
	Amen

Note: Wesley's omissions are marked in italics.

TABLE 15.3. Text of *O Lord, thou art my God* compared with the original verses

	As set by Wesley	Original verses
Isaiah 25, v. 1	O Lord, thou art my God; I will exalt thee, I will praise thy name; thy counsels of old are faithfulness and truth; thou hast done wonderful things.	O Lord, thou art my God; I will exalt thee, I will praise thy name; thou hast done wonderful things; thy counsels of old are faithfulness and truth.
Isaiah 25, v. 4	For thou has been a strength to the poor and needy in his distress[, a refuge from the storm, a shadow from the heat].*	For thou has been a strength to the poor, a strength to the needy in his distress, a refuge from the storm, a shadow from the heat, when the blast of the terrible ones is as a storm against the wall.
Psalm 33, v. 21	For our heart shall rejoice in him, because we have trusted in his holy name.	For our heart shall rejoice in him, because we have trusted in his holy name.
Psalm 33, v. 22	Let thy mercy, O Lord, be upon us, according as we hope in thee.	Let thy mercy, O Lord, be upon us, according as we hope in thee.
Isaiah 25, v. 8	He will swallow up death in victory; and the Lord God will wipe tears from off all faces; the rebuke of his people shall he take away from off all the earth: for the Lord hath spoken it.	He will swallow up death in victory; and the Lord God will wipe away tears from off all faces; and the rebuke of his people shall he take away from off all the earth: for the Lord hath spoken it.
I Corinthians 15, v. 53	For this mortal must put on immortality	For this corruptible must put on incorruption, and this mortal must put on immortality.
I Corinthians 15, v. 34	Awake to righteousness, and sin not; for some have not the knowledge of God.	Awake to righteousness, and sin not; for some have not the knowledge of God: I speak this to your shame.
Wisdom 3, v. 9	They that put their trust in him shall understand the truth.	They that put their trust in him shall understand the truth: and such as be faithful in love shall abide with him: for grace and mercy is to his saints, and he hath care for his elect.
I Corinthians 15, 51-52	We shall not all sleep, but we shall all be changed, in a moment, in the twinkling of an eye, at the last trumpet.	Behold, I shew you a mystery; We shall not all sleep, but we shall all be changed, In a moment, in the twinkling of an eye, at the last trump: for the trumpet shall sound, and the dead shall be raised incorruptible, and we shall all be changed.
Isaiah 25, v. 9	And in that day it shall be said, Lo, this is our God; we have waited for him, and he will save us; this is the Lord; we have waited for him, we will be glad and rejoice in his salvation.	And in that day it shall be said, Lo, this is our God; we have waited for him, and he will save us; this is the Lord; we have waited for him, we will be glad and rejoice in his salvation.

* The bracketed words were originally included by Wesley but omitted from the revised version of the anthem published in 1853.

dream are interspersed with ones from Charles Wesley's hymn "Come, O thou traveller unknown.")

The book of Isaiah, with its prophesies of the coming of Christ, seems to have been a particular favorite with Wesley early in his career, and he made use of it in seven anthems. Indeed, advertisements for his first, abortive attempt in 1836 to publish a collection of *Six Anthems* announced that the words were "selected from the Prophet Isaiah" (see *Woolmer's Exeter and Plymouth Gazette,* February 6, 1836: 2). A later and better-known anthem to draw on Isaiah was *Thou wilt keep him in perfect peace,* completed in about 1851. Once again the text—a slightly odd compilation of verses from Isaiah 26, Psalm 139, I John 1, Psalm 119, and the Lord's Prayer—has received little comment, but it begins to make sense in the light of a note on the score, "To follow the Collect 'Lighten our Darkness'" (S. S. Wesley 1853: 44), which had limited practical effect since this was the normal place for an anthem in evensong. The core message of the anthem thus lies not in the opening and closing phrases, which merely set the scene, but in the central section beginning, "The darkness is no darkness with thee" (see Table 15.4). Here indeed is a continuation of the theme of the collect ("Lighten our darkness . . . and defend us from all perils and dangers of this night"), which Wesley in turn followed with the words from I John ("O let my soul live, and it shall praise thee") and the doxology from the Lord's Prayer ("For thine is the kingdom, the power and the glory"). To conclude, he returned to the gravity of the opening words and music, whose contemplative beauty and arching melody, as Erik Routley observed, seem "so exactly to describe the shape of a spacious cathedral interior" (Routley 1968: 167). It is a remarkably apt description, as Wesley is surely first and foremost creating a mood, a musical impression, such as that which greeted a visitor to Leeds parish church in 1843, who recorded, "As we entered the porch, the rich swell of the organ fell on our ear, mingling with the full and clear tones of the choir, and our soul felt at once the divine influence of the sacred minstrelsy—our thoughts and aspirations mounted towards the throne of God" (*Leeds Intelligencer,* October 14, 1843: 7).

Although this is not the place to discuss purely musical matters in any depth, it must be noted that Wesley, unlike many other nineteenth-century church music composers, was rarely guilty of distorting his texts to fit regular musical phrase lengths or rigid formal schemes. Instead, he allowed his texts to help shape the musical structures, using thematic and tonal means to construct musically satisfying, largely through-composed movements. Gatens has indeed suggested that in his anthems "the musical and textual conceptions developed simultaneously in the composer's mind" (139), a process that largely precludes the imposition of a ready-made structural pattern. And probably unbeknown to Gatens, there is documentary evidence to support such a theory. One of the few anthems for which a manuscript draft survives is *Cast me not away from thy presence* (1848). The manuscript reveals how he changed the text from the Prayer Book version of Psalm 51 (derived from the Great Bible of 1540) to the King James version while

TABLE 15.4. Text of *Thou wilt keep him in perfect peace*

	Text as set by Wesley	Original verses
Isaiah 26, v. 3	*Thou wilt keep him in perfect peace, whose mind is stayed on thee.*	Thou wilt keep him in perfect peace, whose mind is stayed on thee: because he trusteth in thee.
Psalm 139, v. 11	The darkness is no darkness with thee, but the night is as clear as the day: the darkness and the light to thee are both alike.	Yea, the darkness is no darkness with thee, but the night is as clear as the day: the darkness and light to thee are both alike.
I John 1, v. 5	*God is light, and in him is no darkness at all.*	This then is the message which we have heard of him, and declare unto you, that God is light, and in him is no darkness at all.
Psalm 119, v. 175	O let my soul live, and it shall praise thee.	O let my soul live, and it shall praise thee: and thy judgments shall help me.
The Lord's Prayer	For thine is the kingdom, the power, and the glory, for evermore.	For thine is the kingdom, the power, and the glory, for ever and ever.
Isaiah 26, v. 3	*Thou wilt keep him in perfect peace, whose mind is stayed on thee.*	Thou wilt keep him in perfect peace, whose mind is stayed on thee: because he trusteth in thee.

Note: Portions used with the rondo theme marked in italics.

composition was in progress. Why he did so is another matter, but one possible explanation is that he preferred the stronger translation of verse 12, "Restore unto me the joy of thy salvation," to the slightly less forthright "O give me the comfort of thy help again."

Personal and Specific Considerations in the Choice of Texts

The text of *Cast me not away* also provides a good illustration of a theme that runs like a thread through many of Wesley's most inspired anthems: an impassioned plea for forgiveness and salvation. While the reasons behind this are uncertain, it is surely no coincidence that he appears to have inherited a tendency to depression from his father, as well as a "difficult" temperament that often led to strained personal relationships followed by genuine remorse for hasty actions. The later 1850s was a time when his depression, although far less severe than his father's, came to the fore. Remarkably, three of his five sons also showed signs of mental instability, with two taking their own lives and the third spending half his life in an asylum after feeling suicidal (Horton 2004: 285–87). Although Wesley rarely harbored ill will for long, he did bear grudges against several perceived or potential professional rivals, notably Henry Gauntlett and George Elvey, and also came to view two successful former pupils, George Garrett and William Spark, with suspicion.

Most of Wesley's anthems were written between 1836 and 1850, a time that spanned two periods—the later 1830s and the later 1840s—in which he was particularly frustrated by his working conditions at Exeter cathedral and Leeds parish church respectively. The circumstances behind the composition of *Cast me not away* and a companion work, *The face of the Lord,* were, however, rather different. Both date from 1848 and demonstrate how personal matters can sometimes intrude into the public sphere. On December 23, 1847, Wesley broke his right leg and was laid up for six months in the village of Helmsley, and it was during his convalescence that he wrote the two anthems, each of which contains a pointed reference to his accident: "the bones which thou hast broken," accompanied by searing diatonic dissonance, in *Cast me not away,* and "He keepeth all his bones; not one of them is broken" in *The face of the Lord.* Another anthem containing a powerful prayer for forgiveness is *To my request and earnest cry,* which sets the final section of Psalm 119 in the *New Version* paraphrase by Nahum Tate and Nicholas Brady. Dating from the late 1830s, it is unusual on several counts: it is Wesley's only anthem to have a wholly metrical text; only one verse, 173, is omitted from the selected portion of the psalm; the order of the remainder is unchanged; and very few alterations or omissions are made.

Wesley's choice of the *New Version* was in itself decidedly unusual, in that metrical versions of the psalms—principally *The Whole Book of Psalms* (1562) by Thomas Sternhold and John Hopkins, known as the "Old Version," and *A New Version of Psalms* by Tate and Brady (1696)—were primarily sung in parish churches and had no regular place in cathedral worship. But while this circumstance might both account for the fact that there were no recorded performances of the anthem during his lifetime and explain his decision to withhold it from publication (despite having planned to publish it in 1840), it fails to elucidate his reasons for selecting such a text (for a fuller account see Horton 2004: 105–6).

Only two other anthems include sections of metrical verse. When Wesley published *Let us lift up our heart* in his collection of *Anthems* in 1853, the words of "Thou judge of quick and dead," with which it concludes, were not attributed to his grandfather but to "Bishop Wilberforce's Metrical Version" (S. S. Wesley 1853: 218). Why? Was he unaware who wrote them, or did he consider it politic, at a time when hymns were still viewed with suspicion in some quarters of the Church of England, to disguise their non-scriptural (and Methodist) origin? But that is as nothing in comparison with his use of verses by John Milton in *By the word of the Lord.* The anthem dates from 1854 and was written to celebrate the opening of the new organ in Winchester cathedral, where it received a solitary performance on June 3. It remained unpublished until 2010 (see S. S. Wesley 2010). Its text includes a typical Wesley amalgam from Psalm 33 (King James version),

Job 38, and Nehemiah 9, but with the addition of verses from *Paradise Lost*. Was it, as seems likely, the first Anglican anthem to set verses, albeit ones in praise of music, by Milton? As Table 15.5 illustrates, it also contains some extreme examples of Wesley's practice of extracting a nugget of gold and discarding the remaining "dross," most notably in the two verses from Nehemiah.

Two extended anthems from the same period as *By the word of the Lord* are *Ascribe unto the Lord,* probably written in 1851 for the Church Missionary Society's annual service in Winchester cathedral, and *Give the king thy judgments,* composed to celebrate the marriage of the Prince of Wales in 1863. Both have texts used earlier by eighteenth-century composers. John Travers (c. 1703–1758) simply set the complete text of Psalm 96, verses 7–13, adding only an Amen at the end. Wesley selected about half the words of verses 7–10, added some phrases from earlier verses, then turned to contrasting verses from Psalm 115 that contain scornful references to the "gods of the heathen" and celebrate God's strength. By so doing, he transformed *Ascribe unto the Lord* from a generalized affirmation of divine power and call to thanksgiving to one specifically designed to promote missionary work. *Give the king thy judgments,* whose text had been used straightforwardly by Croft and Boyce, provides a further illustration of Wesley's broadening of a text through the incorporation of verses from another psalm—in this instance Psalm 128, with appropriate references to the wife and children of the "king's son." It also demonstrates his use of two versions of the same psalm in one work: verses 1 and 2 of Psalm 72 are from the Prayer Book translation, the remaining verses (Psalm 72, verses 4, 7, 15, 18, 19, and Psalm 128, verses 2–7) from the translation in the King James Bible (1611). Wesley also freely rearranges the order of the verses and makes a number of omissions.

Difficulties with an Assigned Text

The common denominator to all the anthems discussed so far is that their texts were chosen by Wesley himself. In 1873, however, he was invited to write an anthem for use on founder's day at Clifton College, Bristol, and, apparently for the first time, found himself having to set words not of his own choosing: *Let us now praise famous men* (Ecclesiasticus 44). Brief quotations from his correspondence with the school's organist, W. F. Trimnell, were later published in *The Musical Times* ("Clifton College": 240) and provide a rare example of comments on a work in progress:

> My reason for not liking to set the words . . . is this, I don't like much solo singing in church . . . I hope I have not left out any words. One word I know I have; but I did not think it mattered, or I would have put it in. It is the word "for," in ver. 14 [Ecclesiasticus 44]. Oddly enough, Handel left out that word in his set-

TABLE 15.5. Text of *By the word of the Lord*

	Text as set by Wesley	Original verses
Psalm 33, v. 6 (Bible)	By the word of the Lord were the heavens made;	By the word of the Lord were the heavens made; and all the host of them by the breath of his mouth.
Psalm 33, v. 9	he spake, and it was done; he commanded, and it stood fast.	For he spake, and it was done; he commanded, and it stood fast.
Job 38, v. 7	The morning stars sang together, and all the sons of God shouted for joy.	When the morning stars sang together, and all the sons of God shouted for joy?
Paradise Lost, Book 5, line 165	Him first, him last, and without end	Him first, him last, him midst, and without end
Nehemiah 9, v. 6	Thou, thou art Lord alone; thou hast made heaven, the earth, and all that is therein, thou preservest them all;	Thou, even thou, art Lord alone; thou hast made heaven, the heaven of heavens, with all their host, the earth, all things that are therein, the seas, and all that is therein, and thou preservest them all; and the host of heaven worshippeth thee.
Nehemiah 9, v. 5	Blessed be thy glorious name, above all praise and majesty.	Then the Levites, Jeshua, and Kadmiel, Bani, Hashabniah, Sherebiah, Hodijah, Shebaniah, and Pethahiah, said, Stand up and bless the Lord your God for ever and ever: and blessed be thy glorious name, which is exalted above all blessing and praise.
Paradise Lost, Book 5, lines 160–65	Speak ye who best can tell, ye Sons of Light, for ye behold him, and with songs And choral symphonies, Circle his Throne rejoicing, ye On Earth, in Heav'n join all ye Creatures to extol Him. Speak ye who best can tell, Speak Angels, for ye behold him, Him first, him last, him midst and without end. Join all ye living creatures, join all to extol him.	Speak ye, who best can tell, ye Sons of Light, / Angels, for ye behold him, and with songs / And choral symphonies, Day without Night, / Circle his Throne rejoicing, ye in Heav'n; / On Earth join all ye Creatures to extol / Him first, him last, him midst, and without end.
Psalm 33, v. 13–14	The Lord looketh down from Heaven, from the place of his habitation he looketh upon all the inhabitants of the earth.	The Lord looketh from heaven; he beholdeth all the sons of men. From the place of his habitation he looketh upon all the inhabitants of the earth.
Psalm 33, v. 12	Blessed is the nation, whose God is the Lord; and the people whom he hath chosen for his inheritance.	Blessed is the nation, whose God is the Lord; and the people whom he hath chosen for his inheritance.
Psalm 33, v. 21	Our heart shall rejoice in him, because we have trusted in his holy name.	For our heart shall rejoice in him, because we have trusted in his holy name.
Psalm 33, v. 22	Let thy mercy, O Lord, be on us.	Let thy mercy, O Lord, be upon us, according as we hope in thee.

ting of the verse. It occurs in one of his Chandos Anthems [actually the Funeral Anthem for Queen Caroline], and used to be sung at Royal Funerals. I did not think I should ever have set words which are all about mankind . . .

I now send the second anthem I have composed to the words—the difficult words you gave me. I assure you they have proved a hard task. I am pleased with what I send, and hope it will suit your young warblers.

Three points stand out, all relating to the text. The first is his asserted dislike of solo singing, which is particularly interesting in the light of his earlier cultivation of extended solo arias in *The wilderness* (1832), *Trust ye in the Lord, O give thanks unto the Lord* (both c. 1835), *O Lord, thou art my God, Let us lift up our heart,* and *To my request and earnest cry* (all c. 1836-40). However, a comment in the notes he made for the lectures on church music given at the Collegiate Institution, Liverpool, in 1844 reveals that his views on the appropriateness of solo singing in church were already changing (Horton 2004: 190). Secondly, there is his usual omission of words. Thirdly, his doubts about setting "words which are all about mankind": the final paragraph refers to the fact that after his first attempt (later published as edition "B") proved too difficult for the boys, he had subsequently completed a second, easier setting (misleadingly published as edition "A").

Interesting as they are, Wesley's comments nonetheless pose further questions: why did he find the words so difficult, and why, in his opinion, did some demand solo singing? Although we will probably never know the answer to the first question, one reason could simply have been the fact that he had neither chosen nor shaped them himself, and therefore felt in duty bound to set them without alteration. But the comment that he had never expected to set words "which are all about mankind" suggests a further possibility: Wesley's approach to anthem writing was very much a personal one, but these words were essentially a public utterance, and it was perhaps for this reason that he felt less comfortable with them.

Why he considered that verses 8–10 ("There be of them that have left a name behind them, that their praises might be reported") demanded a solo voice is simply not clear. This was not, however, the first time that he had expressed his unhappiness with the use of solo voices in church music. In the notes for his lectures on the history of church music at the Collegiate Institution in Liverpool in the 1840's he had written:

Solo singing in the Church, I confess, I do [not] think should be much encouraged. I do not think it should be absolutely prohibited, but the portions of the service set apart for music are meant to be the voice of the people, and altho' perhaps our music should not altogether be restricted to Chorus, still I think the Solo should be a rare exception, and in almost every instance so mixed with chorus that the individuality of the Singer may [not] attract that attention to himself which belongs solely to the sense of the words, and for a higher purpose. (*Lcm* 2141f: 18v., 25r.)

While the breadth of Wesley's anthem texts would be more than matched by that of John Stainer, the latter's anthems (dating from the 1860s to the 1890s) rarely employ the type of textual amalgam so typical of Wesley. Thus while Stainer, whose personal opinion of Wesley was not high (Dibble 2007: 103–4), felt free to curtail sentences, omit words, and combine verses from different sources, he never did this as systematically or as ruthlessly as Wesley. Indeed, the latter's practice was so individual that few other composers have been tempted to set the majority of his anthem texts. One exception is *Thou wilt keep him in perfect peace*, whose opening verses (and sometimes more) were used for anthems by no fewer than forty-nine composers in the years up to 1980 (*CPM*, 56: 283–84). One of the most interesting settings is that by Charles Lee Williams (1853–1935), Wesley's successor but one at Gloucester, who used some two-thirds of Wesley's text but failed to capture the spacious beauty of his work. Williams also followed Wesley very closely in his own setting of *Cast me not away*.

Conclusion

The use of a broader selection of biblical verses was a natural development, but turning to non-biblical texts was a more radical innovation. Wesley's still bolder practice of altering his chosen texts challenged another part of the conservative theological inheritance that the inspired words of the Bible were not to be tampered with. It recalls John and Charles Wesley's introduction of man-made hymns, reflecting a similar readiness to confront and, if necessary, change received opinion. And in this, as with the stylistic revolution he inaugurated in the anthem, Sebastian showed himself to be a true pioneer and a true bearer of the Wesley name.

CHAPTER 16

The Legacy of Sebastian Wesley

Stephen Banfield and Nicholas Temperley

Restricted Dissemination

How influential was Samuel Sebastian, the last of the great Wesleys? It is today easy to argue that he was the finest English composer of the early Victorian period, on the basis of originality, expertise, and passion viewed across his output as a whole. The commanding technique conveying exceptional emotion in an anthem such as *Wash me throughly* helps focus Wesley as an important cultural conduit of his time. With the confidence, individuality, and sense of mission of his family forbears, he was fully aware of this position and as a young man acted on it decisively, most notably in his second provincial position at Exeter. The three large-scale Exeter anthems are astonishingly broad and powerful. Yet they were not influential, for the tragic reason that they were never published as intended.

Announced they certainly were, and *Trewman's Exeter Flying Post* was full of them in the weeks leading up to their intended appearance in 1840: this city was to be proud of its romantic young composer, still only thirty years old. The subscription list was published on September 17 and included "Mr M. F. Liszt," Liszt having done the concert rounds of Exeter, Sidmouth, Exmouth, and Teignmouth the previous month. A week later, readers were reminded that "Dr. Wesley of this city, is about to publish a most valuable work, consisting of six of his own splendid anthems," and on October 15, alongside a glowing account of Wesley's opening of a new organ in Sheffield earlier in the month, the anthems were announced as "in course of publication by Mr. Hannaford," Peter Hannaford being the local bookseller. Then the trail went dead, and the volume never appeared.

Years later Wesley wrote that the plates had suffered destruction in a fire at the engraver's house (Horton 2004: 87).

One wonders whether this was the truth. If insufficient subscribers were the real or an additional problem, the stress laid upon this ambitious visionary, who had lost a daughter earlier in the year and was about to see his creative offspring reviewed by Henry Smart in *The Musical World,* makes his vicious physical attack on two of the Exeter choirboys on September 26 a little more understandable, though no less unforgivable. For *visionary* is the only word that would seem to do justice to the final movements of *Let us lift up our heart, O Lord, thou art my God,* and, above all, *To my request and earnest cry.*

It needs to be emphasized how up-to-date was Wesley's style in the later 1830s and how fresh its full impact at this point would have been, especially coming from the provinces. The snappy dotted rhythms of the final tutti in *O Lord, thou art my God* may remind us of the close of Part I of Mendelssohn's *Elijah,* but *Elijah* dates from the following decade. Mendelssohn had, however, closed his setting of Psalm 42, *As pants the hart,* with something similar, and echoes of that work's strikingly waltzlike opening seem palpable in the 6/4 sections of Wesley's *To my request and earnest cry,* unless they share some common source of influence. Psalm 42 had been among the very first of Mendelssohn's sacred works to be published in England, by J. Alfred Novello in 1838. Wesley must have assimilated it rapidly if it left its mark on his anthem; his harmonic treatment, moreover, makes Mendelssohn's sound rather pallid. Nor had Beethoven been dead more than a decade when Wesley wrote the last movement of *Let us lift up our heart,* a D-major epilogue of touching depth and originality doubtless indebted to Beethoven's keyboard style. "I ever regret leaving Exeter," Wesley stated later in life, and the aspiration we might sense here to an English pastoral idiom—transcendence vouchsafed beside the waters of Exe—eighty years in advance of Vaughan Williams's patented version causes us to regret it too, consoled a little by the fact that he was at least buried there in a cemetery above the river. As for the "overwhelming" final movement of *To my request and earnest cry* (Horton 2004: 106–8), culminating in almost sexual exhaustion, it was first published in 1990. How many performances has it yet had? Have we really begun the job of assimilating Wesley the romantic?

Wesley, unlike Stainer, Sullivan, and possibly Stanford, was never a fashionable composer, and it is telling that when, on August 9, 1890, William Thomas Best (1826–1897) included his "Andante cantabile" in the opening recital on the Sydney Town Hall organ, then the largest instrument in the world, it was reviewed in the *Sydney Morning Herald,* somewhat unenthusiastically, as being "by the once famous Samuel Sebastian Wesley" (August 11: 6). Against this, such was the nature of the British cultural diaspora in the nineteenth and earlier twentieth centuries that any long-term musical practitioner with pupils or a steady audience at home would in the course of time be heard and quite likely imitated in the farthest corners of both the formal empire and the more informally constituted anglophone world, including, up to a point, the United States. The worldwide Anglican communion chose its organists from a home-grown surplus until well after World War II, and Wesley, aware of it or not, was responsible like other senior institutional figures for a spread of musicians across the globe.

Pupils or associates at one or more removes emigrated to or were taken up in India, South Africa, Australia, New Zealand, Canada, and the United States.

Some of Wesley's chants and a hymn tune may have been sung in India before they were well known in Britain, for his Winchester articled assistant George Mursell Garrett (1834–1897) became organist of Madras Cathedral in 1854, where two years later he produced *The Madras Psalter*, "fully believed to be the FIRST Psalm Tune Book ever Published in India," as proudly though incorrectly noted in a footnote to its preface. This contains two of Wesley's chants (as well as three by his father), plus one of his hymn tunes, ROSS, in its first publication.

Posthumous Opinions

It is open to question whether Samuel Sebastian's reputation in his lifetime as a performer and composer exceeded that of his father. Opinion is divided among historians today as to which was the greater of the two. But there is no doubt that Sebastian's public reputation as a composer has proved the more durable. A number of his major compositions have remained in continuous use until the present time, which cannot be said of his father (let alone his uncle). This despite the fact that Sebastian carried the burden of being a Victorian.

The early twentieth century saw an unusually strong movement against Victorian cultural values, culminating in the reactions to the cataclysm of World War I. In music the Victorians themselves had tended to belittle native efforts, and their successors spoke of a "dark age" or of a "land without music" (Temperley 1999). The "English musical renaissance," whose beginning is usually assigned to about the year 1880, looked to English folk song and sixteenth-century music, and to recent Continental secular music, for fresh inspiration. After 1918, Victorian composers of secular music (Arthur Sullivan excepted) were fast heading for oblivion.

But the innate conservatism of the Church put on the brakes a little. Church music was, in fact, the one area in which Victorian music survived with some continuity into the twentieth century. Anthems and services, as well as hymn tunes, were protected by the habit and affection brought on by long familiarity, and by the unchanging daily or weekly routines that did not exist in other branches of musical life. Of course Sebastian Wesley was, above all, a church musician. Peter Horton has recently drawn proper and overdue attention to his accomplishments in other fields (Horton 2004). But it was only by virtue of his music for choirs, congregations, and the organ that his fame endured. And his hymn tunes are represented in the popular mind today by only two examples, AURELIA and HEREFORD, for reasons explained by Erik Routley (1968: 195–232).

Ernest Walker (1870–1949), in an authoritative history of English music published in 1907, attributed the generally low level of Victorian church music to "foreign influences." He did praise Wesley, but with a somewhat mealy mouth:

> His genius was not capable of taking wide views, and his style is always—using the term in no derogatory sense—somewhat feminine in character; temperate,

cultured, devotionalness is its aim, and it lives and moves and has its being in the cathedral chancel. But while we are bound to recognize that Sebastian Wesley's music, even at its best, lacks the full measure of that indefinable universal appeal beyond the bounds of race and creed that we find in the work of the great men, and in the handful of best things of his father, yet there is not the least doubt that he is one of the very foremost names in English artistic history in the nineteenth century. (E. Walker: 265)

But even as his contemporaries sank from view, Wesley seemed to loom larger as an exception to the decadence that some perceived in Victorian church music generally. Charles Stanford (1852–1924), a leading composer of the "renaissance" and a prolific writer on musical subjects, was brutally dismissive of the Dykes/Barnby/Stainer generation that followed Wesley, saying that their hymn tunes "degrade religion and its services with slimy and sticky appeals to the senses" (1914: 310). But elsewhere he said that Wesley "had a genius for choral writing, and a grasp of new harmonic effects which were new to his day. His two anthems, *The wilderness* and *Let us lift up our heart,* although written to suit the limited conditions of a Cathedral service, show an independence of thought and a mastery of climax which was well above the heads of his listeners" (1916: 301). This is a noteworthy tribute from a man who has himself been identified as one of those who "finally halted" the "steady decline in English church music" (Long: 368).

Surprisingly, the strongest endorsement came from a relative outsider, Edward Dannreuther (1844–1905), the German pianist and writer who had settled in England in 1863 and had been a forceful champion of Wagner and Liszt. Though not himself deeply involved in church music, he wrote an ardent appreciation of Wesley's anthems for *The Oxford History of Music,* published in 1905: "There is nothing in the range of modern religious music more sincerely felt than, for example . . . *Wash me throughly. . . .* The best examples of S. S. Wesley contain an expression of the highest point up to that time reached by the combination of Hebrew and Christian sentiment in music. They are well worthy of comparison with Mendelssohn's psalms, with the best things in Spohr, and with the *Beatitudes* of Liszt and César Franck" (290, 297; quoted Horton 2003: 119–20).

Approval by a prominent German authority was a rare accolade for an English composer in that age and carried enormous weight. For instance, Hans Richter's championship of *The Dream of Gerontius* in 1900 and Richard Strauss's positive reaction to the work in 1902 are held by some to have been a principal factor in establishing Elgar's pre-eminence in Britain (Kennedy: 100–101). Similarly, Dannreuther's praise of Wesley may well have emboldened the English critic and historian H. C. Colles (1879–1943) to heighten his appreciation in a perceptive essay published in 1910. He questioned "whether another instance can be produced of an artist whose own work was so consistently good and whose influence on his successors was so fatal." He even likened Wesley to Wagner for his devotion to a single musical medium, and for his "capacity for making theoretical advocacy and practical demonstration run in double harness." But he dismissed the attempt to compare Wesley's style with that of Continental composers as "really a futile one," and like Stanford he had no patience for "the sickly inanities of the men who have copied Wesley's weaker characteristics" (Colles: 131–33).

Edmund H. Fellowes (1870–1951), who was in many ways the protagonist in the revival of early English music, was equally hard on Wesley's mid-Victorian successors, such as Joseph Barnby and John Stainer, when late in life he came to write a history of cathedral music. Like Walker, he was inclined to attribute their ineptitude to the influence of Spohr and Gounod (Fellowes: 221–31). But he was concerned to correct a "general misunderstanding that Victorian church music was of a very inferior quality, tainted with sentimentalism." He made the startling claim that "a great revival took place in the early years of Victoria," and the hero of this revival was Sebastian Wesley (203).

Later historians have tended to go still further in assessing Wesley's exceptional standing. In 1940 the anonymous author(s) of *Forty Years of Cathedral Music* called him "incomparably the greatest anthem-writer of the 19th century" (15n1). H. Watkins Shaw (1911–1996), after heaping praise on Wesley's "richness and color as well as resourceful inventiveness and expression," concluded that "his great anthems had no real successors (except Parry's *Hear my words*); but the more superficial aspects of the Service in E were not without imitators, as likewise some of his harmonic characteristics, which unhappily proved fatally attractive to the second-rate" (Shaw: 721–22). Like Colles, Shaw gives no examples of this supposedly unhappy influence. Percy Young (1912–2004) called Wesley "the one church musician of the period touched with genius" (460). Kenneth R. Long (1920–1972) conceded that John Goss, Thomas Attwood Walmisley, Frederick Ouseley, and other "minor composers" had "managed to keep the torch of true cathedral music burning, sometimes fitfully, often dimly," but he saw Wesley as standing far above all these, "the most important church musician since John Blow" (Long: 339). John Caldwell (b. 1938) is prepared to label Wesley "the most considerable of all the 19th-century composers of cathedral music," although "not by any reasonable yardstick a 'great composer'" (2:238–39).

An entirely different viewpoint has been adopted by William J. Gatens, who is chiefly concerned with rescuing Wesley's maligned contemporaries from their disgrace. He identifies a series of composers (Thomas Attwood, Walmisley, Ouseley, Stainer, and Barnby) as the true exponents of the proper meaning, value, and dignity of the cathedral service, as rescued by high-church ecclesiology in the Victorian period. He sees Wesley as "a romantic, but one set in an environment largely uncongenial to romanticism," and, while admiring the quality of his music, regards him as an outsider to the true succession (Gatens: 128–46). The greatest difference between Gatens's position and that of most other writers concerns the value of Victorian cathedral music in general. He agrees with them about the exceptional nature of Wesley's music.

Reception since Wesley's Time

How did Wesley's reputation as an exceptional Victorian play out in practice? Passing over the lists of recommended music issued by various authorities and self-appointed advisers, we can turn to some records of actual performance. Over a period of more than a century, a series of investigations has been conducted to determine the frequency of performance of anthems and services in British cathedrals and choral foundations. The 1898 survey was carried out by Fellowes, with the assistance of Percy Buck (*Ob* Tenbury 1482), and in 1938 the Church Music Society sponsored a second survey (Tenbury 1483) and published a summary of both (*Forty Years of Cathedral Music*), adding a third in 1958 (*Sixty Years*); the Friends of Cathedral Music brought these up-to-date in 1986 (*Eighty-Eight Years*). We have followed these with a modest unofficial questionnaire, covering both the choral foundations of the United Kingdom and a sample of Anglican churches in the United States and other parts of the world. The results are summarized in the tables that follow. However, each survey covered a different selection of cathedrals and other choral foundations. Therefore, in order to trace changes over time in the relative popularity of the different services and anthems, it is necessary to use percentages rather than the raw number of places.

Only three service settings by Wesley are relevant: the great Service in E Major completed at Leeds and published in 1845; the Short Service in F Major published in 1869; and the "Chant Service," also in F, published in 1855 (see Horton 2004: 336–37, nos. B1, B6, and B4a). Since evening services were by far the most often sung, we have directed our attention to evening services only (Magnificat and Nunc Dimittis). Table 16.1 shows the number of cathedrals, colleges, and other choirs that reported to each of four surveys, and the percentage of those places at which each of the three services was regularly performed. (The 2008 survey did not include questions about services.)

The figures show, somewhat surprisingly, that as far as evening services are concerned, the height of Wesley's popularity was reached in 1938, sixty years after his death, after which there was a steep decline. They also indicate that in the earlier twentieth century, the Short Service in F was much more frequently sung than the Service in E, universally regarded as one of his greatest works. This preference could well have been due to the much greater length and difficulty of the latter. The relatively insignificant Chant Service came into its own as choirs declined in size, availability for rehearsal, and financial support.

In 1898 the seventeen services more popular than Wesley's were the work of twelve composers. Six were men of the past: Henry Aldrich, Samuel Arnold, William Boyce, William Croft, Orlando Gibbons, and James Nares; three were approximate contemporaries: John Goss, Henry Smart, and James Turle; and three were younger composers: George Garrett, Francis Gladstone, and Charles Stanford, the first two being Wesley pupils. In 1938 Wesley in F was outperformed

TABLE 16.1. The popularity of Wesley's services in British choirs

Year of survey	1898	1938	1958	1986
Number of places reporting	58	34	54	75
Percentage of places at which Wesley's services were in repertory				
Wesley in E	*27*	*76*	*56*	*31*
Wesley in F	*45*	*85*	*56*	*15*
Wesley in F (chant)	*0*	*0*	*28*	*16*
Number of services by other composers that were more popular than Wesley's most popular one				
	17	4	22	67

only by Stanford in B flat, Walmisley in D Minor, Gibbons in F, and (Charles Harford) Lloyd in E flat.

In 1958 the compiler of the published report, W. K. Stanton, still listed Wesley's services in E and F among twenty-one "Perennials," but they were outranked in that list not only by Gibbons, Goss, Stanford, Tallis, and Walmisley, but (more surprisingly) by Samuel Arnold's Evening Service in A. The other Victorians had receded, while several post-Wesley works such as Harwood in A flat, Noble in B Minor, and Wood in E flat had outstripped him. New, simpler types of evening service for unison voices, men only, boys only, or "fa-burden," were rapidly gaining ground. By 1986 these trends had gone much further, with many twentieth-century composers in the forefront (*Sixty Years:* 11–14; *Eighty-eight Years:* 16–37).

The story is similar with regard to anthems. "There is certainly no diminution in the ubiquitousness of S. S. Wesley's anthems," as the 1938 report concluded (*Forty Years:* 25). Indeed, 1938 again represents the summit of their popularity, as Table 16.2 plainly indicates. No fewer than twenty-six complete anthems were in the repertory at that time, and the three all-time favorites—*Blessed be the God and Father, Thou wilt keep him in perfect peace,* and *Wash me throughly from my wickedness*—were being sung at more than 90 percent of the places surveyed. One anthem now regarded as belonging in the top tier of Wesley's output, *To my request and earnest cry,* is barely represented in the table, for the simple reason that it was not available in its entirety until reconstructed by Peter Horton for Musica Britannica (S. S. Wesley 1990).

Wesley's anthems took part in the general decline in the performance of Victorian cathedral music after World War II; many, as can be seen, fell out of the repertory altogether. Table 16.3 shows how many anthems by Wesley were performed in ten or more places. For 1958 and 1986 this figure is compared with the corresponding number for other leading composers (that comparison is not available for 1898 or 1938). (Of course, Brahms wrote no anthems in the strict sense: *anthem* in this case means any piece of choir music, regardless of origin or text, that functioned as an anthem at matins, evensong, or communion.) The

TABLE 16.2. The popularity of Wesley's individual anthems

Year of survey	1898	1938	1958	1986	2008 UK	2008 World
Number of places reporting	52	37	54	75	13	18
Anthem (or excerpt)	Percentage of places in which it was performed					
All go unto one place	6	16	---	1	0	0
Ascribe unto the Lord	48	68	56	28	46	27
O worship the Lord	2	5	---	0	0	0
The Lord hath been mindful	0	19	---	20	8	6
Blessed be the God and Father	90	97	87	88	85	67
Love one another	0	0	---	8	0	0
Blessed be the Lord God of Israel	10	0	---	0	0	0
Blessed is the man that feareth the Lord	0	5	---	0	0	0
Cast me not away from thy presence	17	62	61	41	23	11
God be merciful unto me	12	16	---	0	0	0
I am thine, O save me	6	11	---	5	0	0
I will arise	4	5	---	0	0	0
I will wash my hands	2	3	---	0	0	0
Let us lift up our heart	8	27	57	4	0	0
Be not wroth	6	8	---	0	0	0
O may we thus ensure	0	3	---	0	0	0
Thou, O Lord God, art the thing that I long for	6	14	---	1	0	0
Thou judge of quick and dead	38	51	---	7	0	6
Let us now praise famous men	0	3	---	0	0	0
Lord of all power and might	4	0	---	0	0	0
Man that is born of woman	6	3	---	0	0	0
O give thanks unto the Lord	17	30	33	4	8	0
Who can express	2	8	---	8	15	6
O God, whose nature and property	2	14	---	0	0	0
O how amiable are thy dwellings	8	5	---	0	0	0
Blessed are they	21	19	---	0	0	0
O Lord my God	63	76	43	8	23	17
O Lord, thou art my God	4	11	---	0	0	6
And in that day it shall be said	2	0	---	1	0	0
For our heart shall rejoice in him	2	5	---	0	0	0
For this mortal must put on immortality	10	8	---	0	0	0
He will swallow up death in victory	10	21	---	0	0	0
Praise the Lord, O my soul	31	54	28	5	8	6
Lead me, Lord	13	46	44	36	58	7
The face of the Lord is against them	13	24	---	0	0	0
The Lord redeemeth the souls of his servants	10	3	---	0	0	0
The Lord is my shepherd	19	35	19	5	0	0
Thy loving kindness	2	3	---	0	0	0
The wilderness and the solitary place	65	70	48	31	38	27
Thou wilt keep him in perfect peace	50	95	87	76	77	89
To my request and earnest cry	0	0	---	0	8	0
Wash me throughly from my wickedness	44	92	80	68	85	78
Wherewithal shall a young man cleanse his way	0	3	---	0	0	0
With my whole heart	0	0	---	0	8	6

Note: Three dashes indicate that the anthem was listed in less than ten places out of fifty-four, but the exact number is not recorded; hence 0–17%.

TABLE 16.3. The popularity of Wesley as a composer of anthems

Year	No. of anthems in the normal repertory at ten or more places				
	By Wesley	By others			
		from the top downward		born between 1780 and 1840	
1958	12	Byrd	16	Mendelssohn	7
		Wood	14	Goss	6
		Purcell	11	Ouseley, Stainer	3
		Stanford	11	Sterndale Bennett	2
		Gibbons	9	Brahms, Cornelius, Dvořák, César Franck, Pearsall, Steggall, Walmisley	1
1986	8	Byrd	22	Mendelssohn	4
		Purcell	10	Goss, Schubert	2
		Gibbons	10	Brahms, Ouseley, Sterndale Bennett, Walmisley	1
		Tallis	10		
		Stanford	9		

figures indicate that while anthems by other early- to mid-Victorian composers were fast disappearing during the later twentieth century, Wesley's held their position relatively well.

The three favorites, along with *Cast me not away*, were chosen in 1965 for inclusion in *The Treasury of English Church Music*, designed as a representative selection for choirs (Knight and Read: iv). Clearly, however, there has been a continuing decline in performance of some of the larger-scale works; in many cases, excerpts from them have been preferred, most notably "Lead me, Lord" from *Praise the Lord, O my soul.* (It is also possible that some of the longer anthems reported were not performed in full.)

The decline in performance does not necessarily indicate a diminution of Wesley's eminence as a composer of anthems. The last century has shown a steady drop in the frequency of fully choral services. By 1986, choral matins had virtually disappeared, and not one English cathedral offered daily choral evensong (*Eighty-Eight Years*: 8–10). Many foundations have had to give up maintaining choirs capable of performing (for instance) an eight-part chorus such as occurs in some of Wesley's larger anthems. One cathedral choirmaster reports that Wesley is performed less than many other composers, "but this does not reflect my view of his music—merely the absence of a choir able to perform most of his works. I generally only have trebles and basses on a Sunday at evensong—we only sing on Sundays anyway."

At the same time the body of musical compositions acceptable as anthems has broadened greatly, to include Catholic motets in Latin by early English composers (never heard in Anglican services in 1898); excerpts from oratorios; sacred compositions by Palestrina, Bach, Haydn, Mendelssohn, and many other foreign composers; and simpler pieces such as hymns and carols. Indeed, some choir directors have lost any idea that there is a distinctive Anglican repertory that might be given preference. Paul Brough, of All Saints, Margaret Street, illustrates this point: "With a choir that sings just Sundays and Feasts it means that some 230 pieces are sung each year: so from the whole corpus of Western Church Music 1000 to 2008, for a composer to have 3 regular slots out of 230 is quite an accolade." If Wesley is competing not only with all the anthem composers who have preceded or followed him, but with every composer of church music in the world, it is not surprising to find that his relative prominence is not what it was in Victorian times.

In the 2008 survey, respondents were asked to "estimate Wesley's ranking among all composers with respect to frequency of performance at your establishment." Not all were able to answer, but according to those who did, Wesley's ranking in British cathedrals ranged from twelfth to fiftieth. In contrast, no fewer than four out of seven American respondents, as well as one from Australia, ranked Wesley sixth in frequency. This unexpected result, though based on too small a sample to be conclusive, suggests that Wesley, like his contemporary Hector Berlioz, is now more highly esteemed abroad than in his home country.

Influence

Wesley's style was so individual that it would be difficult to pin its specific influence on his lesser pupils and grandpupils. Garrett, who soon returned from India, later edited Wesley's organ works for Novello. He can sound a little like Wesley in his church music when exercising sequence, broad melody, and elegant harmonic rhetoric; the Services in D and E flat and some of the anthems exhibit these qualities. But overproduction for an insatiable market easily turned such talents generic, as in Garrett's *Harvest Cantata* (1889), a work that traveled as far as Canada, first performed there, according to *The British Daily Whig* (September 12 1892: 1), on September 25, 1892, in Sydenham Street church, Kingston, Ontario—one of the oldest Methodist congregations in upper Canada. *The Song of the Redeemed* by George Benjamin Arnold (1832–1902) is a little more up-to-date than this but not much more distinctive, despite being "the first work ever composed for an American vested choir by any musician of note abroad," as the *New York Times* proclaimed (April 12, 1891: 11) at its premiere by the choir of St. James, Madison Avenue. Arnold was another of Wesley's pupils, indeed his immediate successor as organist and choirmaster at Winchester cathedral, a post he held until his death.

Conversely, one of Wesley's favorite diatonic dissonances, heard in the first line of the hymn tune Hereford and the last of Aurelia and consisting of a 6/3 triad on the subdominant with suspended ninth and seventh, was so thoroughly assimilated into the Victorian sacred idiom that it was hardly noticed when A. E. Floyd (1877–1974), an Arnold pupil and assistant at Winchester long

EX. 16.1.   A. E. Floyd, Three Church Preludes, No. 2, opening.

after Wesley's death, used it in the second of his *Three Church Preludes* for organ (Ex. 16.1), published in Australia in 1945. Floyd had also trained under A. H. Mann at King's College, Cambridge, and held various other English posts before emigrating in 1915 to become director of music at St. Paul's cathedral, Melbourne, where he remained for thirty-two years, becoming a much-loved radio speaker as well as performer (Burk). Despite these broader connections, he never missed an opportunity to affirm his Wesleyan lineage, and when making in January 1941 a transcription for the organ of Samuel Wesley's "Old English Melody" arrangement of June 1806, perhaps on his mind as Britain dealt with the Blitz, he inscribed it "to the memory of my old master, Dr. G. B. Arnold . . . successor to S. S. Wesley, and a steadfast upholder of the English Cathedral tradition." However widespread its use, the gentle dissonance pinpointed in Example 16.1 is still recognized as quintessentially Anglican, for Howard Goodall retails it in his title music for the TV series *The Vicar of Dibley* (1994–2007). Goodall knows his Wesley: he was a chorister at New College, Oxford, returning to the city as a music undergraduate under Simon Preston at Christ Church, whose choir later recorded the theme.

Garrett's Cambridge pupil Hugh Blair (1864–1932), who became organist at Worcester cathedral in 1895, did emulate Wesley's style (Horton 2004: 323), possibly more than another of Wesley's own pupils, Francis Gladstone. Two further links might be followed up in the persons of William Coulson Tregarthen (1856–1942) and Thomas Tallis Trimnell (1827–1897), both nurtured in Bristol. Tregarthen, brother of a celebrated Cornish naturalist, studied as a teenager with Wesley in Gloucester from January to October 1875 before emigrating only three years later to South Africa, where he remained. But notwithstanding a respectable musical career there, he appears to have published no church music beyond a few hymn tunes (Malan). Trimnell, who was the brother of Wesley's editor W. F. Trimnell, settled in New Zealand, becoming a leading figure (Thomson: 215). Wesley would have been gratified to know that on Easter Sunday in Wellington in 1895, to take an example, Garrett's Jubilate in F rubbed shoulders with Trimnell's new evening service in E flat and his own *Blessed be the God and Father* at the pro-cathedral of St. Paul (*Wellington Evening Post,* April 15, 1895: 2).

Wesley's most pervasive influence worldwide, however, beyond the continued currency of a handful of his anthems and hymn tunes, will have been through a longer if slower channel, the style of the two English composers most indebted to him, Parry and Walton. Hubert Parry (1848–1918) was a bright and impressionable teenager home from Eton for the vacation when Wesley first appeared in Gloucester in 1865, and Wesley treated him more like a young colleague than a potential pupil. Parry's diary over the next few years (Horton 2004: 261–70, 287) indicates repeated exposure and undoubted influence, beginning with Wesley's *Ode to Labour* (see Horton 2004: 253 for a music example with a busy texture that recalls Parry) and including Wesley's organ improvisations in the cathedral.

Whether or not consciously following Wesley's practice, it was in the treatment of diatonic dissonance that Parry passed on an English idiom. Jeremy Dibble has illustrated this at length in an important article (1983) in which he categorizes Wesley's procedures, as when for example "a comparatively slow rising bass line supports a series of . . . double suspensions . . . for the space of three bars before subsiding" (59). One might trace this peculiarly English predilection right back to a short passage in John Wilbye's madrigal "Draw on, sweet night" of 1609 (Ex. 16.2), where it is perhaps significant that the one moment at which six different notes are sounding is on a Wesleyan subdominant with 9–8 and 7–6 suspensions. Wesley could have come across Wilbye's madrigal if hired out as a chorister to the Madrigal Society in London by his master William Hawes, though his adult participation in the Devon Madrigal Society appears not to have encompassed it (information from James Hobson). Dibble amply demonstrates Parry's use of similar dissonance, citing *I was glad* in addition to many non-liturgical and secular instances.

William Walton (1902–1983) was a chorister at Christ Church, Oxford, and the year before he died he chose Wesley's *The wilderness* for the first of his *Desert Island Discs* as a guest on the well-known radio program of that name (Plomley: 282). Moments of diatonic dissonance in Walton's biblical settings frequently suggest Wesley's influence, perhaps the most striking of them at the recapitulation of the opening theme of his a cappella anthem *Set me as a seal upon thine heart* (1938), a wedding gift to a friend, with its semitonal clash of a suspended C♯ against D and E (Ex. 16.3). Walton's romantic intensity is a match for Wesley's

EX. 16.2. John Wilbye, "Draw on, sweet night," extract.

EX. 16.3. William Walton, *Set me as a seal
upon thine heart,* extract. © Oxford University
Press 1938. New edition © 1999. Reproduced by
permission. All rights reserved.

not only here, where the intimacy befits the occasion with its text from the Song
of Solomon, but also in the much broader Old Testament canvas of desolation
and exultation explored in his cantata *Belshazzar's Feast,* premiered in Wesley's
city of Leeds in 1931. Contours and clashes in the triple-time counterpoint of the
"By the waters of Babylon" section are in places distinctly reminiscent of those in
Wesley's *Wash me throughly* (Ex. 16.4). A quite different congruence of technique
is suggested when, at the joyful end of the spectrum, Walton sets up a motoric
background that in due course can simplify or drop out as the choral foreground
takes flight. In *Belshazzar's Feast* he does this between cues 62 and 64 and again
refocuses between teeming detail and sublime simplicity at cue 74; less virtuosic
but comparable moments from Wesley were mentioned in Chapter 9.

Perhaps it was inevitable that Wesley and Walton would exhibit similarities a
century apart. Both harnessed the power of romantic harmony within formidable
contrapuntal contexts, Walton in places benefitting from the development of jazz.
Jazz was an idiom that would have been unimaginable to Wesley. But it arose
partly from the same contexts of personal religious feeling and expression that
he himself lived and worked to express in his output and that his grandfather
and great-uncle had done so much to awaken and empower in vast numbers of
people of different races across the western Protestant world and eventually across
the globe.

We express our gratitude to Martin Holmes for providing a detailed report on *Ob* Tenbury
1482–83. We also wish to thank those who responded to our questionnaire, and Martin
Holmes, Simon Lindley, and Roger Wilkes for their assistance in organizing the survey.

WESLEY

WALTON

EX. 16.4. Comparison of extracts from Sebastian Wesley's *Wash me throughly* and William Walton's *Belshazzar's Feast*. *Belshazzar's Feast* © Oxford University Press 1931. Reproduced by permission. All rights reserved.

Appendix 1

CATALOGUE OF COMPOSITIONS BY CHARLES WESLEY THE YOUNGER

John Nightingale

This catalogue comprises all known compositions of Charles Wesley (1757–1834), extant and lost. Within each of the four main sections, works are grouped by genre in estimated chronological order, with undatable works arranged alphabetically at the end.

Information is presented as follows. Number; title or description, with lost works in square brackets (author of text where known). Scoring; key; date (of publication when preceded by publisher's or series name); subtitle; individual, institution, or occasion for which written. Location of manuscript(s). Any cross-reference.

Entries containing multiple works represent preexisting groupings by the composer, with the exception of **13–16, 31–37, 47,** and **50,** which have been grouped here for convenience. In scorings, instruments and voices in parentheses in group entries feature in only some works in the group; those in single entries are optional alternatives. Alternatives indicated by the composer are shown with a forward slash, as in "org/hpsd." Instruments and voices in square brackets are not indicated in the source but implied. In vocal works, voice parts clearly intended as solos are listed first, in lowercase.

Unless otherwise stated, manuscripts are autograph. All works published in Wesley's period were issued in London. With minor exceptions, reprints and publications issued after 1850 are not included; further details of, and in some cases materials for, recent editions may be obtained from the author, john.nightingale9@btopenworld.com.

Library sigla

BRcl	Bristol: Central Library
Cfm	Cambridge: Fitzwilliam Museum
DAu	Dallas: Bridwell Library, Southern Methodist University
Lam	London: Royal Academy of Music
Lbl	London: British Library
Lcm	London: Royal College of Music
Mu	Manchester: John Rylands University Library
Ob	Oxford: Bodleian Library
SM	San Marino, Calif.: Huntington Library
Wc	Washington, D.C.: Library of Congress
Wgu	Washington, D.C.: Leon Robbin Collection, Georgetown University Library, Special Collections Research Center

I: *Instrumental Works*

CONCERTOS

1. **Six(?) concertos for organ.** Org solo, 2fl 2ob 2hn 2vn va vc cb. [No. 1?] D, 1775, rev. 1780; no. 5, E flat, publ. as Op. 2 [**5**], no. 6; remainder lacking. *Lbl* Add. 35018

2. **Six concertos for organ or harpsichord.** "Second Sett 1776." Org(/hpsd) solo (2fl 2ob bsn 2tr timp) 2vn va bass; g, A, d–D, G, E, d–D. *Lcm* 4023. No. 1/ii rev. as **23** no. 3/iii

3. **Six concertos for organ or harpsichord.** "A Third Set. London 1778." Org/hpsd solo, 2ob (2hn) 2vn va vc cb; d, E, F, C, g–G, D. *Lbl* Add. 35018. Nos. 1, 3–6 publ. as Op. 2 [**5**], nos. 1, 2, 4, 5, 3

4. [**Six concertos for organ or harpsichord, Op. 1.** Selected from **1–3** by 1779 (*European Magazine,* June 1784: 449)]

5. **Six concertos for organ or harpsichord, Op. 2.** d, F, D, C, g–G, E flat. From 3/1, 3/3–6, 1/5 with added timp part; Bremner, 1781

6. [**Concerto for organ and harpsichord.** Perf. 1782–85, Marylebone (*Lam* MS-L [Wesley])]

7. **Concerto grosso in seven parts.** 2ob 2hn 2prin vn 2rip vn va vc cb; c; Bremner, c. 1784; ded. 2nd Earl of Dartmouth

8. [**Concerto for bassoon.** Perf. 1787, Marylebone (*Mu* DDCW 9/15)]

ENSEMBLES

9. **Six string quartets.** 2vn va vc; F, D, E flat, E, B flat, F; Johnston, c. 1778; ded. William Boyce

10. [**Quintet for oboe and strings.** ob 2vn va vc; perf. 1778, home of Mrs. Hervey (*Mu* DDCW 8/21)]

11. [**Trio for oboes.** 2ob hpsd; perf. 1780, Marylebone (*Mu* DDCW 8/21)]

12. **Sinfonia.** 2ob 2hn 2vn va bass; E flat. *Lcm* 4024 (inc.)

SOLOS

13. **Fugue subjects, sketches etc.** Keyboard; various; by 1774. *Lcm* 6070

14. **45 three-part fugues.** Keyboard; various; by 1774; numbered. *Lcm* 6070

15. **16 two- and three-part fugues.** Keyboard; various; by 1774; unnumbered. *Lcm* 6070

16. **2 two-part canons.** Keyboard; C, C; by 1774. *Lcm* 6070

17. **Minuet fragment.** Instrumentation unspecified; d; ? mid-1770s. *Lbl* Add. 31763

18. **Sonata for harpsichord.** f–F; 1781. *DAu* Spec.Coll.MM2

19. **Three sonatas for harpsichord, Op. 4.** D, G, E flat; c. 1783 (Birchall, c. 1790); ded. Miss Cholmondeley

20. **God save the King with variations.** Org/hpsd; C; Dale, Proud, 1798; ded. Miss Horten

21. **Gavotte with variations.** Pf; B flat; Bland and Weller, 1815; ded. Miss Harvey; theme is finale of Handel's Overture to *Ottone*

22. **Air with variation[s].** Pf/hpsd; E; ? by 1816 (Lonsdale,?1865); ded. Princess Charlotte of Wales. *Lbl* Add. 63817 (air only, not autograph)

23. **Six voluntaries.** Org/pf; D, d–D, g–G, G, a–A, C; Bland and Weller, by 1818; no. 6 ded. Miss Liddell. No. 1/v is March from **147**; no. 3/iii is rev. of **2** no. 1/ii

24. **Sonata.** Pf; c; Weller, 1818; ded. Mrs. Span

25. **The Sicilian Mariner's Hymn with variations.** Pf; F; Birchall, by 1819; ded. Hon. Miss Tonge

26. **A Favorite Waltz by Mozart with variations.** Pf; C; Proud, 1820; ded. Lady Isabella Turnour

27. **German Air with variations.** Keyboard; G. *Lcm* 4024

II: Sacred Vocal Works

WORKS FOR CHORUS AND ORCHESTRA

28. **Begin the high celestial strain** (Elizabeth Rowe). sst, SATBB, 2fl 2ob 2bsn 2vn va vc cb org; B flat; 1789. *Lcm* 4019

29. **[Elijah.** 1824 (Kassler and Olleson: 417; B. Matthews: 1112)]

30. **[The spacious firmament on high** (Joseph Addison). Instruments and voices. Cited by Samuel Wesley (see p. 124)]

SERVICE MUSIC AND CHANTS

31. **32 double chants.** SATB; various; by 1774; untexted. *Lcm* 6070

32. **10 Gloria Patri settings, through-composed.** SATB, [org]; various; by 1774; the first eight numbered 2–9. *Lcm* 6070

33. **4 Jubilate settings, through-composed.** SATB, [org]; various; by 1774. *Lcm* 6070

34. **2 Magnificat settings, through-composed.** SATB, [org]; various; by 1774. *Lcm* 6070

35. **4 Nunc Dimittis settings, through-composed.** SATB, [org]; various; by 1774; the first without Gloria Patri. *Lcm* 6070

36. **8 Sanctus settings, through-composed.** SATB, [org]; various; by 1774. *Lcm* 6070

37. **13 single chants.** SATB; various; by 1774; untexted. *Lcm* 6070

38. **Te Deum, through-composed.** SATB, [org]; D; by 1774. *Lcm* 6070

39. **Sanctus.** (i) SATB, [org]; E flat; 1778. (ii) SSAATTB, [org]; E flat. (iii) SSAATTBB, 2ob 2bsn 2vn 2va bass org; E flat; 1803. Birchall, not traced; for St. George's Chapel, Windsor. (i) *Lbl* Add. 35039, (ii) *SM* HM486, (iii) *Lbl* RML 23.g.16

40. **Te Deum.** saatb, SSAATTB, org; E flat; 1786. *SM* HM486

41. **Kyrie.** SAATB, org; a; 1788. *SM* HM486

42. **Nunc Dimittis.** satb, SSATB, org; D; 1788. *SM* HM486

43. **Te Deum.** sssatb, SSAATBB, 2ob bsn 2hn 2tr timp 2vn va vc cb org; D; 1789. *Lcm* 4019 (inc.)

44. **Gloria Patri.** SATB, bsn 2hn timp 2vn org; D; 1801; "For the Rev: Mr. B's Church." *Lam* 190

45. **Jubilate.** ssatb, SSATB, org; C; 1821; for John Turner. *Ob* Tenbury 1351
46. **Te Deum.** ssatb, SSATB, org; C; 1821; for John Turner. *Ob* Tenbury 1351
47. **6 double chants.** SA(A)TB, [org]; E flat, a, A, d, B flat, D. *SM* HM486 [1–5],
    Lbl Add. 35039 [1], 35038 [6]
48. **Jubilate.** aatb, SSAATTB, [org]; E flat. *SM* HM486
49. **Kyrie.** SATB, [org]; E flat. *SM* HM486
50. **6 single chants.** SATB, [org]; E flat, c, E flat, E, D, b. *SM* HM486

ANTHEMS

51. **O God, my heart is ready.** satb, SATB, org; d; 1775. *SM* HM486
52. **I will lift up mine eyes.** ss(tt), SATB, org; A; 1778; ded. Lord Le Despencer
    (Sir Francis Dashwood, Bart.). *Lbl* Add. 31754 (includes alternative setting of
    final verse for liturgical use)
53. **I will thank thee, O Lord and king.** ss(a)t, SATB, org; e; 1778. *SM* HM486
54. **My soul hath patiently tarried.** sat(t)b, SATB, org; B flat; 1782 (Page,
    Harmonia-Sacra, 1800); for Rev. Benjamin Mence. *SM* HM486. 3 choruses as
    org solos in *Cathedral Voluntaries* (ed. Vincent Novello, 1831)
55. **Hear my prayer, O Lord.** ss, SATB, org; g; 1783; for Bristol cathedral. *Lbl*
    Add. 35039, *SM* HM486, *Lcm* 4019
56. **O worship the Lord in the beauty of holiness.** (i) ssb, [org]; E flat; 1787
    (Birchall, c. 1789). (ii) ssb, SATB, org; E flat; Novello, 1875. (i) *SM* HM486
    without acc.; authorship of Gloria Patri, present only in (ii), uncertain
57. **Save, Lord, and hear us.** saa, SSATB, vc org; D; 1787–88. *SM* HM486
58. **O Lord, grant the king a long life.** ss, SATB, vc org; d-D; 1788; "For His
    Majesty." *SM* HM486
59. **God is our hope.** sa, SATBB, 2ob bsn 2tr timp 2vn va vc cb org; d; 1789. *Lbl*
    Add. 31754
60. **Lord, remember David.** ss, SSAATTB, ob bsn 2vn va bass org; e; 1789
    (Hackett, *The National Psalmist,* 1842 [opening duet, with org]). *Lcm* 4019
61. **O Lord, I have heard thy speech.** atb, SATB, org; D-d; 1789. *SM* HM486,
    Lcm 4019
62. **Not unto us, O Lord.** ss(at)b, SATB, org; G; 1790. *Lcm* 4019
63. **Let heav'n, earth, sea their voices raise.** SATB, ob 2vn bass org; D; 1791.
    Lcm 4019; probably the final chorus of a larger work
64. **O pray for the peace of Jerusalem.** ssatb, SATB, org; E flat; ?1791. *Lcm* 4019
65. **Thy hands have made me.** ssb, SATB, org; E flat; 1791. *Lcm* 4019
66. **Oh that my head were waters.** saab, SATB, bsn org; d; 1793. *Lbl* Add. 31754
67. **Thou shalt guide me with thy counsel.** (a)ttb, SATB, org; E flat; 1796. *SM*
    HM486
68. **Thou hast girded me with strength.** b, SATB, 2ob 2bsn 2tr timp 2vn va bass
    org; d-D; 1797. *Lbl* Add. 31754, *SM* HM486 (extended version of opening air,
    with org)
69. **O sing unto the Lord a new song.** satb, SATTB, 2ob 2bsn 2hn 2tr timp 2vn
    va bass org; C; 1799. *Lbl* Add. 31754 (includes additional, SATB, [org] setting
    in A of "Let Israel rejoice," with Amen)

70. **Blessed Lord, who hast caused all holy scriptures.** SATBB, org; E flat; 1802. *Lam* 190

71. **O Lord almighty, God of Israel.** ssatb, SATB, org; g–G; 1803. *Lcm* 4019

72. **Lord God of armies, hear our prayer.** SATB, [org]; a; 1805; "Loyal Prayer . . . at the request of a Friend." *Lbl* Add. 35039

73. **Lord, we beseech thee.** SATB, org; F; 1812; for Joseph Smith. *Wc* ML96. W487 Case

74. **Almighty God, who hast given thine only son.** satb, SATB, org; e; 1814; for Joseph Smith. *Lbl* Add. 35038, *Mu* DDWes 9/14 (B part only), *Wc* ML96.W487 Case

75. **Behold, I bring you glad tidings.** s, SATB, org; G; 1820 or 1821. *Lbl* Add. 35038

76. **Arise, O Lord.** ss, SATB, org; d-F. *Lcm* 4019

77. **Awake, put on strength.** (ssa)ttbb, SATB, org; C. *Lcm* 4019

78. **Blessed be God.** satb, SATB, org; g–G. *Lam* 190

79. **Bring unto the Lord.** sa(a)tb, SATB, 2ob 2bsn 2tr timp 2vn vc cb org; D–d. *Lbl* Add. 31754

80. **God be merciful unto us.** aat, SSATB, org; a–A. *Lbl* Add. 31754

81. **Grant, we beseech thee.** SATB, [org]; D; Hackett, *The National Psalmist*, 1842; uncertain attribution

82. **Hallelujah, Amen.** SATB; D. *SM* HM486; assumed to be the concluding section of a larger work

83. **Let not the wise man glory.** satb, SATB, org; G. *Lcm* 4019

84. **Lord, thou art become gracious.** ssatb, SSATB, 2ob 2bsn 2tr timp 2vn va vc cb org; G-C. *Lbl* Add. 31754

85. **O sing unto the Lord a new song.** sab, org; F. *Lcm* 4019

86. **Praised be the Lord who helpeth us.** aab, SAATB, org; C. *Lbl* Add. 31754

87. **This God is our God for ever and ever.** 1v, [org]; A. *SM* HM486

88. **Thou art my king, O God.** s(a)tb, SATB, org; E. *Lcm* 662

89. **Wherewith shall I come.** ssatb, SATB, org; g-G. *Lcm* 4019

90. **The wilderness.** ss, SATB, org; F; "for a Private harmonic Meeting." *Lam* 190

Let Israel rejoice: *see* **69**

HYMNS AND POEMS

91. **On the Crucifixion of Our Lord.** s, org; d; 1775; for James Hutton. *SM* HM486

92. **Six Hymns . . . with a hymn by the late Dr. Boyce.** 1v, [org]; printed for the author, c. 1795 (*HTI* 7185–9, 18667); ded. Mrs. Tighe
    1. **Thron'd in thine essential glory** ("Mr. J. K."). D; 1786. *Ob* Tenbury 621 (extended), *SM* HM486 (SAATB, org)
    2. **Oh for new strength to praise the Lord** ("the Honble Mrs. M."). F. *SM* HM486
    3. **To God our strength sing loud and clear** (John Milton). EPWORTH; E flat. *Lbl* Add. 31754

4. **In Christ my treasure's all contain'd.** B flat. *Lcm* 4021 (in the hand of Samuel Wesley)

5. **If death my friend and me divide** (C. Wesley the elder). E flat

6. **Broken the man of grief appears** (C. Wesley the elder). a

93. **The Lord my pasture shall prepare** (Addison, after Ps. 23). 1v, org; E; 1802 (Page, *A Collection of Hymns*, 1804) (*HTI* 10745). *Lbl* Add. 35038

94. **Rejoice, the Lord is king** (C. Wesley the elder). HIGHBURY; 3vv., fig bass; D; Nodes and Bowcher, *A Selection of Psalm and Hymn Tunes*, 1803 (*HTI* 10150)

95. **When I survey the wondrous cross** (Isaac Watts). CRUCIFIXION; 3vv., fig bass; E flat; Nodes and Bowcher, *A Selection of Psalm and Hymn Tunes*, 1803 (*HTI* 10136)

96. **All hail the pow'r of Jesu's name** (Edward Perronet). [SB]; D; Cahusac, by 1814; ded. Sir Egerton Leigh, Bart.; "Hymn on the Resurrection in the Collection of the Right Honble Countess of Huntingdon"

97. **How sweet the name of Jesus sounds** (John Newton). KING'S WESTON; 1v., [org]; F; J. S. Holmyard, *The Psalms, Hymns and Miscellaneous Pieces, as sung at the Episcopal Chapel of the London Society for Promoting Christianity, amongst the Jews*, c. 1820 (*HTI* 17215)

98. **Lift up your heads in joyful hope** (anon., 1760). 1v, [org]; C; 1821; "X.M. [Christmas] Hymn . . . for the New Church St. Marylebone." *Lcm* 4024

99. **Hark, the sacred minstrel plays.** 1v, cembalo; C. *Lbl* Add. 31754

100. **Jehovah reigns, let all the earth** (Tate and Brady, after Ps. 97). ST. ALBAN'S; 1v, [org]; D. *Lbl* Eg. 2512 (in the hand of Matthew Cooke). Opening phrase as **92** no. 3

101. **Lord, save me for thy glorious name** (Tate and Brady, after Ps. 54). ARUNDEL; 1v, [org]; d. *Lbl* Eg. 2512 (in the hand of Matthew Cooke)

102. **With joy we meditate the grace** (Watts). 1v, [org]; e. *SM* HM486

103. SUBMISSION. SATB; D. Hawkes 1833

Easter Psalm Elaborations and related works (most or all for Robert Glenn, music master of Christ's Hospital; texts by Rev. Arthur William Trollope (**104–120**), Rev. John Greenwood (**121**); see Jeans. *Lbl* Add. 35038–9)

104. **Sing, ye redeemed of heaven.** ss, org; A (inc.); only partly autograph; [1814]

105. **Who is that blest of heaven.** ss, SS, org; e–E; 1815

106. **Bitter is the orphan's tear.** ss, SS, org; a; 1816

107. **Child of sorrow, cease repining.** ss, SSB, org; a–A; 1817

108. **Great God, when on a guilty land.** ss, org; g–G; [1817]

109. **Hither all that glads the mind.** ss, SS, org; D; 1817

110. **Sweet are thy pleasures, mem'ry, when the mind.** ss, SS, org; C–G; 1817

111. **Sweet are the notes whose magic sounds can charm.** s, SS, org; G; 1818

112. **When to the throne of heav'n's almighty Lord.** ss, SS, org; g–G; 1819

113. **Dwells there in scenes of grief alone.** ss, SS, org; g–G; 1820

114. **Pillow'd on earth low lay the father's head.** ss, SS, org; g–G; 1820

115. **What is the life of man? In ev'ry stage.** ss, SS, org; g–c; 1822

116. **Not the rapt seraph's tongue.** ss, SS, org; g–G; 1823

117. **To all his works thro' nature's boundless space.** ss, org; c–C; 1824
118. **Where, in what hallow'd spot doth peace reside.** ss, org; C; 1825
119. **Now is mercy's work completed.** ss, SS, org; c–C; 1826
120. **Lord of life, thine ear inclining.** ss, SS, org; a–C; 1827
121. **When first Jehovah at thy dread command.** ss, SS, org; C; 1828

III: Secular Vocal Works

ENSEMBLES (ACCOMPANIED)

122. **[Ode on the Death of Dr. Boyce ("Father of harmony, farewel!")** (C. Wesley the elder). [?, ch, orch]; 1779–80. Only text survives; performers included five named singers (ssatb) (*Mu* DDCW 8/21)]
123. **The western sky was purpled o'er** (William Shenstone). [st], 2fl 2ob 2hn 2vn va bass; E; 1781. *Lbl* Add. 31753. No. 1 of **Three Cantatas**; *see also* **126, 163**
124. **May kind attendant angels wait** ("Miss [Sarah] Wesley"). 2vv, cembalo; F; 1782 (Napier by 1791); "A Favorite Duet." *Lcm* 4019 (includes additional, solo setting, to different music, of two further verses of text)
125. **Now I know what it is to have strove** (Shenstone). (i) [TT]B; e; 1782. (ii) [TT]B, cembalo/pf; e; Birchall, 1807; "Pastoral Glee." (i) *Lcm* 4019, (ii) *Lam* Mfilm RP37
126. **Shepherd, wouldst thou here obtain** (Shenstone). [st], keyboard; A; ?1782. *Lbl* Add. 31753. No. 2 of **Three Cantatas**; *see also* **123, 163**
127. **Ode on the Birthday of Portia ("Let statesmen hail with venal joy").** s, SS, 2fl 2ob 2hn 2vn va bass; G; 1786. *Wgu*
128. **Thou who shalt stop where Thames' translucent wave** (Alexander Pope). SATB, keyboard; E; 1787, publ. "at the request of Mrs U[?]" (not traced); glee. *Wgu*
129. **In gentle slumbers.** SSB, vc cembalo; e; 1789. *Lcm* 4019. *See also* **166**
130. **Caractacus: cantata** (William Mason). ssb, SSATB, 2ob 2bsn 2hn hp cembalo 2vn va vc cb; g–G; 1791. *Cfm* Mu. 714
131. **On the bank will we happy recline** (William Gilbert). [st], keyboard; G; Millhouse, after 1796; "Presented to a Nobleman on his Marriage"
132. **Elegy to the Memory of the Late Mr. Jonathan Battishill ("Weeping o'er thy sacred urn")** (Ambrose Philips). (i) SATB, vc org. (ii) SATB, pf; e–E; n.p., 1801. (i) *SM* HM486
133. **Mildly beam'd the queen of night** (Thomas Penrose). (i) SAB, keyboard; E flat; 1801. (ii) SSB, vc pf; E flat; Dale, 1801; "Glee on the Moon." (i) *Lcm* 662, (ii) *Lcm* 4019
134. **Come hither, ye nymphs of the plain** ("by a Young Lady"). (i) ATB, vc cembalo; a; Birchall, by 1806. (ii) SSB; e; Birchall, by 1806; "A Favorite Elegy"
135. **Farewell, the fields of Irwan's vale** (John Langhorne). SSB, pf; F; after 1811; glee "for the Royal Harmonic at Bath (Grand Gala Night)." *Lcm* 4024
136. **Methinks by all my tender fears** (Shenstone). [tt], cembalo/pf; E flat; Birchall, by 1819; "A Favorite Duet"
137. **The Twelfth of August ("Let's be merry, sing, and play")** (Hannah More).

[st], SAB, keyboard; C-c-C; between 1819 and 1827 (Cadell, 1827); ded. Sir Alexander Johnston; relates to abolition of domestic slavery in Ceylon, effective August 12, 1816

138. **Ode on War and Peace.** ss, pf; f, F; Proud, by 1820; Ode on War ("Hark, 'tis dire war's terrific yell"): solo; Ode to Peace ("How diff'rent far the flowery field"): duet

139. **At Charlotte's tomb.** (i) s, [pf]; d. (ii) ss, pf; d; Birchall, 1820; "Dirge." (i) *Lcm* 4019, (ii) *Lbl* Add. 35038, *Lcm* 4024; in memory of Queen Charlotte, wife of George III

140. **Come, all ye youths** (Thomas Otway). SATB, vc keyboard; g. *Lcm* 4019

141. **Come, all ye youths** (Otway). sab, SATB, 2fl 2vn va bass; B flat. *Lcm* 4019

142. **Here resignation pensive, sad.** 2vv, keyboard; d–D; Canzonetta. *Lbl* Add. 31754, *Lcm* 4019

143. **Music that doth our senses charm.** SSAB, vc keyboard; F; glee. *Wgu*

144. **My time, O ye muses** (John Byrom). [tt], keyboard; A; "Pastoral." *Lcm* 4019

145. **O thou, great source of every good** ("Miss Bowdler"). SSAB, keyboard; d; glee. *Lbl* Add. 31754

146. **She sat and sung, the rocks resound her lays** (Pope). 2vv, cembalo; G. *Lcm* 4019

147. **To the Memory of Handel ("Not one of all his progeny").** t, SATB, 2ob 2bsn 2hn 2tr timp 2vn va bass org; D. *Lbl* RML 21.h.4. March rev. in **23** no. 1

Three Cantatas: *see* **123, 126, 163**

ENSEMBLES (UNACCOMPANIED)

148. **Cruel fair one, turn and see me languish.** (i) SSB; d–D. (ii) SAB; d-D; 1782; glee "for Rev Mr. Meyer of H. M. Chapel & St. Paul's." (i), (ii) *Lcm* 4019; second section *Lcm* 4024

149. [**Hey diddle diddle.** ssb; by 1806; glee; for Bath Harmonic Society; only text survives]

150. [**Oh glad is the morn** (W. L. Bowles). ssabb; 1806; glee; for Bath Harmonic Society; ded. Lady Sophia Poulett; only text survives]

151. **Tho' gentle sleep death's near resemblance wears.** SAB; E; Birchall, by 1806, Novello, 1843 arr. SSATTB; "A Favorite Serious Glee"; ded. Sir Joseph Andrews, Bart. Novello arr. *Lbl* Add. 65460

152. [**We dwell in shady groves.** ssb; by 1806; glee; for Bath Harmonic Society; only text survives]

153. **How sleep the good and brave.** SSB; e; 1809 (Birchall, ?1809); "Dirge"; ded. George Hardinge Esq., H. M. Attorney General, in memory of George Nicholas Hardinge, Captain, R. N. *Lam* 184

154. [**In Arno's Vale.** By 1826; glee; perf. as illustration during Royal Institution lectures by Samuel Wesley (Kassler and Olleson: 444, 464)]

155. **Canon obligate in Three Parts ("Hic jacet in tumba Rosa mundi")** (anon., inscription on tomb of Rosamund Clifford). 3vv; G; texted. *Lbl* Add. 35038

156. **Lo, the pride of the village is dead.** (i) ?ATB; e. (ii) SSB; d; glee. (ii) *Lcm* 4019, (i) not traced
157. **Ye southern breezes, gently blow** (Edward Moore). ATB; G. *Lcm* 4019

Come hither, ye nymphs of the plain: *see* **134**
Now I know what it is to have strove: *see* **125**

SOLOS (ALL ACCOMPANIED)

158. **Fly swift, ye western gales.** s, 2fl 2hn 2vn va bass; G; 1778; "(Aria di Bravura) (on the approach of Spring)." *Lcm* 4024
159. **Perhaps it is not love** (Shenstone). [t], cembalo/pf; D; 1782 (Birchall); rev. (i) by 1791, (ii) 1806 (SATB; E) "at the request of Miss Sharp"; "A Favorite Ballad." *Lcm* 4024; (i) *Lam* 1237 (not autograph), (ii) *Lcm* 1122 (not autograph)
160. **Eight Songs, Op. 3.** 1v, pf; Bremner, c. 1784
    1. **O'er desert plains; and rushy meers** (Shenstone). D
    2. **Ye streams if e'er your banks I lov'd** (Shenstone). E flat
    3. **To thee a sigh I now convey.** B flat
    4. **Yes these are the scenes where with Iris I stray'd** (Shenstone). E flat
    5. **Ah Damon see the fatal hour.** F
    6. **What shepherd or nymph of the grove.** g
    7. **The lovely Delia smiles again** (Shenstone). A
    8. **O'er moorlands and mountains rude barren and bare** (John Cunningham). E flat
161. **Placido zefferetto.** s, 2ob 2vn bass; B flat; 1783; aria. *BRcl* B.16120
162. **Son qual nave.** s, 2ob 2hn 2vn bass; D; 1783; aria "for a Private Concert." *BRcl* B.16119
163. **The sun was sunk beneath the hills** (John Gay). [t], ob 2vn bass; E; 1783. *Lbl* Add. 31753. No. 3 of **Three Cantatas**; *see also* **123, 126**
164. **The voice, the breath of rosy May** (Mrs. Cowley). [s], cembalo; G; 1784; Sonnet. *Wgu*
165. **Ah, wherefore do the envious fates** (Richard Dyer). [t], 2vn va bass; g–G; 1786. *Lcm* 4019 (2 MSS), "(add. song) Timon to Eucharis"
166. **In gentle slumbers.** 1v, 2vn bass; B flat; ?1787. *Wgu. See also* **129**
167. **The god of love had lost his bow.** [t], 2fl 2ob 2bsn 2hn 2vn va bass; C; 1787; cantata "for Mrs. B . . . at the request of [Rev]. Antony Shepherd." *Wgu*
168. **To the wild woods I tell.** [t], keyboard; E flat; 1790; sonnet. *Lcm* 4019
169. **Sleep, shade of care** (James Trebeck). 1v, keyboard; e; 1807. *Lcm* 4024
170. **When Delia on the plain appears** (George, Lord Lyttleton). [t], pf; C; Birchall, by 1811; ded. Miss Phillips
171. **The Willow** ("Who is she from yonder green willow") (Emma Lyon). 1v, keyboard; F–f–F; Bell, *La Belle Assemblée*, 1812; "A Ballad"
172. **Oh! heav'nly sympathy** ("from the celebrated novel of The Wedding Day"). 1v, pf; G; Goulding, D'Almaine, Potter, by 1820; "at the request of a Lady." *Lcm* 4019, "Air in the Wedding Day"

173. **Regret ("When forc'd to part from those we love")** (Miss Pye). 1v, pf; E;
     Shade, by 1820; "A Ballad"
174. **Zamasta's Song ("Welcome to our lonely land")** (Robert Elly, from *The
     Cossack*). 1v, keyboard; G; Clementi, by 1820
175. **Adieu perhaps for ever.** 1v, keyboard; G. *Lbl* Add. 31753
176. **Bred on plains or born in valleys** (Shenstone). s, 2fl/ob 2hn 2vn va bass;
     G; "Pastorale"; relates to imprisonment of Princess Elizabeth, Woodstock,
     Oxfordshire, 1554. *Lcm* 4019
177. **Haste, Lorenzo, haste away** (Shakespeare: *The Merchant of Venice*). s,
     keyboard; D. *Lcm* 4019
178. **How sweet with innocence to rove.** [t], keyboard; F. *Lbl* Add. 31753
179. **I have heard her with sweetness unfold** (Shenstone). [t], keyboard; E flat;
     sonnet. *Lbl* Add. 31753

At Charlotte's tomb: *see* **139**
Ode on War: *see* **138**

IV: Arrangements and Editions

180. **William Boyce: Hymn, "Servant of God, well done."** 1v, [org]; G. In **Six
     Hymns** (as a seventh) (*HTI* 7190); *see* **92**
181. **Giuseppe Sammartini: Concerto grosso, Op. 8, no.1.** Arr. org/pf with opt
     vn part (2-stave redn); g; Birchall, 1820; "As performed at the Concerts of
     Antient Music"
182. **John Wesley, ed.: *Sacred Harmony*.** 1v, keyboard; 1821 (Blanshard, 1822); 120
     hymn tunes, "carefully revised and corrected"
183. **George Frideric Handel: *Alexander Balus, King of Syria*.**
     1. **Chorus of Asiates: "Flush'd with conquest," act 1, sc 1.** SATB, orch (2-
        stave redn, untexted); D. *Ob* Tenbury 621
     2. **Solo and chorus of Israelites: "Ye servants of the eternal King," act 3,
        sc 5.** t, SATB, orch (2-stave redn, partly texted); g. *Ob* Tenbury 621
184. **Handel: *An Occasional Oratorio*, pt 2: "Prepare the hymn" (conclusion
     of B solo and ch: "To God our strength").** SATB, orch (2-stave redn,
     untexted); D. *Ob* Tenbury 621
185. **Domenico Scarlatti: Thirty Sonatas,** hpsd/pf; Birchall, 1800; ed from MSS
     owned by 7th Viscount Fitzwilliam

Unattributed and Unidentified Works

The posthumous sale of Wesley's music library held at the Phillips Auction Rooms in
New Bond Street, London, on July 13, 1835, included, as lots 112–58, forty-seven items
listed under the heading "The Original Compositions in MS of Mr. Charles Wesley."
Only eight of these, however, are positively identifiable as known compositions by
him. A further eight lots clearly contained works by other composers and must be
assumed to have been either manuscripts owned by Wesley or his own manuscript
transcriptions of these works. Of the remaining thirty-one lots, only five include

reference to specific titles, viz. *The Misanthrope,* dated 1785, an *Ode,* dated 1795, and three undated items, *Ode to Sebastian Bach, The Dedication of the Temple of Solomon,* and *The War Song.* Kassler and Olleson (608) tentatively assign a work titled *The Misanthrope* to Charles's brother Samuel on the strength of two late-nineteenth-century references, but without relevant source material or indeed any further evidence of these works, no firm attribution of any of them can yet be made. The rest of the lots are described only in unspecific terms, with titles such as "anthems," "organ music," or "various compositions," which may or may not include works already listed in this catalogue.

Additionally, the surviving registers of the concerts presented by Charles and Samuel Wesley at the family home in London between 1779 and 1787 indicate many performances of similarly unidentifiable Charles Wesley compositions, notably overtures, sinfonias, and organ duets, as well as unspecified concertos, quartets, and voluntaries, at least some of which are probably among those already listed.

Appendix 2

The African Methodist Episcopal Church (1816–)

AMEC 1898   *The African Methodist Episcopal Hymn and Tune Book*. 2nd ed. Philadelphia, 1898.

The Methodist Church (1939–68)

MC 1966   *The Methodist Hymnal*. Nashville, 1966.

The Methodist Episcopal Church (1784–1939)

MEC 1786   *A Pocket Hymn Book*. 5th ed. New York, 1786.

MEC 1803   *The Methodist Pocket Hymn-Book*. Philadelphia, 1803.

MEC 1808   *A Selection of Hymns from Various Authors*. New York, 1808.

MEC 1821   *A Collection of Hymns for the Use of the Methodist Episcopal Church*. New York, 1821.

MEC 1822   *The Methodist Harmonist*. New York, 1822.

MEC 1833   *The Methodist Harmonist*. 2nd ed. New York, 1833.

MEC 1836   *A Collection of Hymns for the Use of the Methodist Episcopal Church*. New York, 1836.

MEC 1849   *Hymns for the Use of the Methodist Episcopal Church*. New York, 1849.

MEC 1857   *Hymns for the Use of the Methodist Episcopal Church*. (With tunes.) New York, 1857.

MEC 1867   *The New Hymn and Tune Book*. New York, 1867.

MEC 1878   *Hymnal of the Methodist Episcopal Church*. New York, 1878.

MEC 1905   [with MECS] *The Methodist Hymnal*. New York, 1905.

MEC 1935   [with MECS and MPC] *The Methodist Hymnal*. New York, 1935.

The Methodist Episcopal Church, South (1844–1939)

MECS 1847   *A Collection of Hymns for Public, Social and Domestic Worship*. Nashville, 1847.

MECS 1851   *Songs of Zion*. Nashville, 1851.

MECS 1860   *The Wesleyan Hymn and Tune Book*. Nashville, 1860.

MECS 1874a   *Songs of Zion*. Nashville, 1874.

MECS 1874b   *A Collection of Hymns and Tunes for Public, Social and Domestic Worship*. Nashville, 1874.

MECS 1880   *The New Hymn and Tune Book.* Nashville, 1880.

MECS 1889   *Hymnbook of the Methodist Episcopal Church, South.* Nashville, 1889.

The Methodist Protestant Church (1828–1939)

MPC 1829   *A Compilation of Hymns.* Baltimore, 1829.

MPC 1837   *Hymn Book of the Methodist Protestant Church.* Baltimore, 1837.

MPC 1859   *Hymn Book of the Methodist Protestant Church.* Baltimore, 1859.

MPC 1860   *Hymn Book of the Methodist Protestant Church.* Springfield, Ohio, 1860.

MPC 1871   *The Voice of Praise.* Pittsburgh, 1871.

MPC 1882   *The Tribute of Praise.* Pittsburgh, 1882.

MPC 1901   *The Methodist Protestant Church Hymnal.* Pittsburgh, 1901.

The United Methodist Church (1968 –)

UMC 1989   *The United Methodist Hymnal.* Nashville, 1989.

BIBLIOGRAPHY

Manuscripts and Archives

ATu Atlanta: Manuscript, Archives, and Rare Book Library, Emory University. John Wesley Collection.

BRcl Bristol: Central Library. 20095 (William Dyer's Diary).

BRro Bristol: Bristol Record Office. All Saints vestry minutes.
   Bristol Infirmary Biographical Memoirs.
   Christchurch churchwardens' accounts.
   St. Augustine churchwardens' accounts.
   St. James parish registers.
   St. James churchwardens' accounts.
   St. John Baptist churchwardens' accounts.
   St. Mary Redcliffe churchwardens' accounts.
   St. Stephen churchwardens' accounts.
   Sts. Philip and Jacob churchwardens' accounts.
   Temple churchwardens' accounts.
   Temple vestry minutes.
   6687 (Lewin's Mead: [1] minutes, [2] cashbook).
   04026 (Great Audit Book).
   04264 (Common Council proceedings and Corporation vouchers).
   04359 (Burgess books).
   35841 PT/F/1a (Tabernacle cashbook).

BRu Bristol: University Library. Moravian Collection. Diary of Single Brethren, 1766; Committee Minutes, 1756–69.

Cfm Cambridge: Fitzwilliam Museum. Samuel Wesley, letters.

Eg Evanston, Ill.: United Library, Garrett Evangelical-Theological Seminary. John Wesley Papers.

Lam London: Royal Academy of Music. MS-L (Wesley).

Lbl London: British Library. Add. 27593 (Samuel Wesley, "Reminiscences").
   Add. 31764 (Samuel Wesley, letters).
   Add. 33819 (Sebastian Wesley, *The Dilosk Gatherer*)
   Add. 35012 (Samuel Wesley, letters).
   Add. 35014 (Samuel Wesley, lectures).
   Add. 35017 (Samuel Wesley, letters).
   Add. 35019 (Sebastian Wesley, autobiographical notes).
   Add. 35020 (Sebastian Wesley, various items).

Lcm London: Royal College of Music. 2141f (Sebastian Wesley, lecture notes).

Mu Manchester: John Rylands University Library. Methodist Archives.

Ob   Oxford: Bodleian Library. Mus.d.32, unfoliated (John Malchair papers).
      Tenbury 1482 (survey of cathedral music, 1898)
      Tenbury 1483 (survey of cathedral music, 1938)
PRlro Preston: Lancashire Record Office. DDX. 1468 Acc. 4986 box 5 (Moses Heap, "The
      Occasional").

Printed Materials and Dissertations

Addington, Stephen. *A Collection of Psalm Tunes.* 3rd ed. [the earliest extant]. London, 1780. (AddiSC 3)

All Loves Excelling: New Tunes to Familiar Charles Wesley Texts. Nashville, 2007.

Allen, Richard, ed. *A Collection of Hymns & Spiritual Songs.* Philadelphia, 1801. Facsimile repr., ed. J. Roland Braithwaite. Philadelphia, 1987.

Allen, William Osborne Bird, and Edmund McClure. *Two Hundred Years: The History of the Society for Promoting Christian Knowledge.* London, 1898.

Anderson, Emily, ed. *The Letters of Mozart and His Family.* 3rd ed. London, 1985.

Asbury, Francis. *A Selection of Hymns from Various Authors: Designed as a Supplement to the Methodist Pocket Hymn-Book.* New York, 1808.

Ash, John, and Caleb Evans. *A Collection of Hymns.* Bristol, 1769.

Attwood, Thomas. *Sacred Music.* London, 1852.

Avison, Charles. *An Essay on Musical Expression . . . with Alterations and Large Additions.* London, 1775.

Baker, Frank. *Charles Wesley as Revealed by His Letters.* London, 1948.

———. *The Representative Verse of Charles Wesley.* New York, 1962.

———, ed. *The Works of John Wesley.* 34 vols. (In progress.) Oxford, 1975–.

———. *Charles Wesley's Verse: An Introduction.* 2nd ed. London, 1988.

———. *A Union Catalogue of the Publications of John and Charles Wesley.* 2nd ed. Stone Mountain, Ga., 1991.

———. "The Texts of *Hymns on the Great Festivals.*" In John Frederick Lampe, *Hymns on the Great Festivals, and Other Occasions: A Facsimile of the First Edition,* ed. S T Kimbrough, 21–30. Madison, N.J., 1996.

Bakhtin, Mikhail. "Heteroglossia in the Novel." In Simon Dentith, ed., *Bakhtinian Thought: An Introductory Reader,* 195–224. London, 1995.

Baldridge, Terry L. "Evolving Tastes in Hymntunes of the Methodist Episcopal Church in the Nineteenth Century." PhD thesis, University of Kansas, 1982.

Barber, Robert. *The Psalm Singer's Choice Companion.* London, 1727. (BarbRPSCC)

Barrington, Daines. *Miscellanies.* London, 1781.

Barry, Jonathan. "The Cultural Life of Bristol, 1640–1775." DPhil thesis, University of Oxford, 1985. (1985a)

———. "Piety and the Patient." In Roy Porter, ed., *Patients and Practitioners: Lay Perceptions of Medicine in Pre-Industrial Society,* 145–76. Cambridge, 1985. (1985b)

———. "The Parish in Civic Life: Bristol and Its Churches, 1640–1750." In Susan Wright, ed., *Parish, Church and People: Local Studies in Lay Religion, c. 1350–1750,* 152–78. London, 1988.

———. "Provincial Town Culture 1640–1780: Urbane or Civic?" In Joan H. Pittock and Andrew Wear, eds., *Interpretation and Cultural History,* 198–234. Basingstoke, 1991. (1991a)

———. "The Press and the Politics of Culture in Bristol, 1660–1775." In Jeremy Black and Jeremy Gregory, eds., *Culture, Politics and Society in Britain 1660–1800*, 49–81. Manchester, 1991. (1991b)

———. "Cultural Patronage and the Anglican Crisis: Bristol c. 1689–1775." In John Walsh, Colin Haydon, and Stephen Taylor, eds., *The Church of England c. 1689–c. 1833: From Toleration to Tractarianism*, 191–208. Cambridge, 1993. (1993a)

———. "Methodism and the Press in Bristol 1737–1775." *Wesley Historical Branch Bulletin* 64 (1993): 1–23. (1993b)

———. "Bristol as a 'Reformation City' c. 1640–1780." In Nicholas Tyacke, ed., *England's Long Reformation*, 261–84. London, 1997.

———. "Chatterton, More and Bristol Cultural Life in the 1760s." In Alistair Hayes, ed., *From Gothic to Romantic: Thomas Chatterton's Bristol*, 20–35, 126–29. Bristol, 2005.

Bayly, Lewis. *The Practice of Piety*. 3rd ed. [the earliest extant]. London, 1613.

Beaumont, John. *Four Anthems . . . To Which Are Added Sixteen Psalm or Hymn Tunes*. London, [?1793]. (BeauJFA)

———. [A proposal to publish *The New Harmonic Magazine* by subscription. London, 1795–1801.] (*UC 9)

———. *The New Harmonic Magazine, or Compendious Repository of Sacred Music*. London, 1801. (BeauJNHM)

———. *A Treatise on Lowness of Spirits . . . Likewise His Experience and Travels*. London, 1809.

Beaumont, Joseph. *The Life of the Rev. Joseph Beaumont*. London, 1856.

Benson, Louis F. *The English Hymn: Its Development and Use in Worship*. Richmond, Va., 1915. Repr. 1962.

Berger, Teresa. *Theology in Hymns? A Study of the Relationship of Doxology and Theology According to a Collection of Hymns for the Use of the People Called Methodists*. Trans. Timothy E. Kimbrough. Nashville, 1995.

Best, Gary. *Charles Wesley: A Biography*. Peterborough, 2006.

Betjeman, John. "The Wesleys: BBC Radio Four, Sunday 3 August 1975." In Stephen Games, ed., *Sweet Songs of Sion: Selected Radio Talks*, 43–55. London, 2007.

Blumhofer, Edith. *Her Heart Can See: The Life and Hymns of Fanny J. Crosby*. Grand Rapids, Mich., 2005.

Bonnell, John Mitchell. "Sacred Music." *Quarterly Review of the Methodist Episcopal Church, South (1847)* 15 (1861): 498–510.

Bowmer, John C. *The Sacrament of the Lord's Supper in Early Methodism*. London, 1951.

Boyce, William. *Fifteen Anthems*. London, 1780.

Bradley, Ian C. *Abide with Me: The World of Victorian Hymns*. Chicago, 1997.

Brekell, John, and William Enfield. *A New Collection of Psalms Proper for Christian Worship*. Liverpool, 1764.

Bretherton, F. F. "John Wesley and Professor Liden, 1769." *Proceedings of the Wesley Historical Society* 17, no. 1 (1929): 1–4.

Brewer, John. *The Pleasures of the Imagination: English Culture in the Eighteenth Century*. London, 1997.

Broadwood, Lucy, and J. A. Fuller-Maitland. *English County Songs*. London, 1893.

Browne, Simon, ed. *Hymns and Spiritual Songs*. With tune supplement, *A Set of Tunes in 3 Parts*. London, 1720. (*TS Bro a)

Buckley, James Monroe. "The Hymn Book of the Methodist Episcopal Church." *Methodist Review* 58 (1876): 309–23.

Burchell, Jenny. *Musical Societies in Subscription Lists: An Overlooked Source*. Michael

Burden and Irena Cholij, eds., *A Handbook for Studies in 18th-century English Music*, vol. 9. Oxford, 1998.

Burk, Ian. "A Tradition Transplanted and Nurtured: The Contribution of A. E. Floyd to Cathedral and Church Music in Australia, 1915–1947." PhD thesis, University of Melbourne, 2005.

Burney, Charles. *An Account of the Musical Performances in Westminster-Abbey and the Pantheon . . . in Commemoration of Handel.* Dublin, 1784.

Butterworth, Maria. *Portraiture of a Father.* N.p., 1859.

[Butts, Thomas, ed.] *Harmonia-Sacra.* London, [c. 1754]. (ButtTHS a)

Caldwell, John. *The Oxford History of English Music.* 2 vols. Oxford, 1991, 1999.

Carter, Philip, ed. *Wesley Music for the Millennium: Contemporary Tunes for Charles Wesley's Hymns.* Bristol, 2001.

The Catalogue of Printed Music in the British Library to 1980. Ed. Laureen Baillie and Roger Balchin. 62 vols. London, 1981–87. (*CPM*)

Cennick, John. *Sacred Hymns for the Use of Societies . . . Generally Composed in Dialogue.* London, 1743.

Chalus, Elaine. "Elite Women, Social Politics, and the Political World of Late Eighteenth-Century England." *The Historical Journal* 43 (2000): 669–97.

Chapman, David M. *Born in Song: Methodist Worship in Britain.* Peterborough, 2006.

"Charles Wesley Centenary Events." *Proceedings of the Charles Wesley Society* 2 (2006–7): 119–36.

Charlton, Peter. *John Stainer and the Musical Life of Victorian Britain.* Newton Abbot, 1984.

Chatfield, Mark. *Churches the Victorians Forgot.* Ashbourne, Derbyshire, [1979].

Chatterton, Thomas. *The Complete Works of Thomas Chatterton*, ed. Donald S. Taylor. 2 vols. Oxford, 1971.

"Chronology of the English Bach Awakening." In Michael Kassler, ed., *The English Bach Awakening*, 1–33. London, 2004.

Clark, Katerina, and Michael Holquist. *Mikhail Bakhtin.* Cambridge, Mass., 1984.

Clarke, Martin V. "John Wesley and Methodist Music in the Eighteenth Century: Principles and Practice." PhD thesis, Durham University, 2008.

"Clifton College and Its Music." *Musical Times* 46 (1905): 240.

A Collection of Psalms and Divine Hymns. London: Joseph Downing, 1727.

Colles, H[enry] C. "Samuel Sebastian Wesley." Repr. from *The Times*, July 2, 1910. In Colles, *Essays and Lectures*, 131–35. London, 1945.

Collins, Emanuel. *Miscellanies in Prose and Verse.* Bristol, 1762.

Cook, Donald F. "The Life and Works of Johann Christoph Pepusch." 2 vols. PhD thesis, King's College, London, 1982.

Cotton, John. *Singing of Psalms a Gospel-Ordinance.* London, 1650.

Crawford, Richard, ed. *The Core Repertory of Early American Psalmody.* Madison, Wisc., 1984.

———. *The American Musical Landscape.* Berkeley, Calif., 1993.

Creamer, David. *Methodist Hymnology.* New York, 1848.

Crockett, William R. *Eucharist: Symbol of Transformation.* New York, 1989.

Croft, William. *Thirty Select Anthems.* London, 1724.

Cudworth, Charles L. "An Essay by John Marsh." *Music and Letters* 36 (1955): 155–64.

Curnock, Nehemiah, ed. *The Journals of the Rev. John Wesley, A.M.* 8 vols. London, 1909–16.

Curwen, J. Spencer. *Studies in Worship Music* [1st series]. London, 1880.

Dannreuther, Edward. *The Romantic Period.* The Oxford History of Music, vol. 6. Oxford, 1905.

David, Hans T., and Arthur Mendel, rev. Christoph Wolff. *The New Bach Reader.* New York, 1998.

Davie, Donald. "The Classicism of Charles Wesley." In Davie, *Purity of Diction in English Verse,* 70–81. London, 1967.

Dean, Winton. *Handel's Dramatic Oratorios and Masques.* London, 1959.

The Devotional Harmonist. New York, 1849.

Devotions in the Ancient Way of Offices. London, 1706. (HickGDAW)

Dibble, Jeremy. "Hubert Parry and English Diatonic Dissonance." *British Music Society Journal* 5 (1983): 58–71.

———. *John Stainer: A Life in Music.* Woodbridge, 2007.

The Divine Musical Miscellany. London, [1754]. (#DMM)

Doane, Joseph. *A Musical Directory for the Year 1794.* London, 1794. Repr. 1993.

Dobson, Austin, ed. *Diary and Letters of Madame d'Arblay (1778–1840).* 6 vols. London, 1905.

The Doctrines and Disciplines of the Methodist Episcopal Church of America. 10th ed. Philadelphia, 1798.

Duckles, Vincent. "Musicology." In N. Temperley, ed., *The Romantic Age 1800–1914.* Athlone History of Music in Britain, vol. 5. London, 1981.

Dudley, Mary. *The Life of Mary Dudley.* London, 1825.

D'Urfey, Thomas. *Wit and Mirth: or, Pills to Purge Melancholy.* London, 1719.

Dutton, W. E., ed. *The Eucharistic Manuals of John and Charles Wesley Reprinted from the Original Editions of 1748-57-94.* London, 1871.

Dyer, Rev. Mr., late of Plymouth, ed. *A Collection of Psalms and Hymns for Social Worship.* London, 1767.

E[dwards], F. G. "Bach's Music in England." *Musical Times* 37 (1896): 585–87, 652–57, 797–800.

Eggington, Timothy J. "Benjamin Cooke (1734–1793), Composer and Academician." PhD thesis, Goldsmiths' College, London, 2008.

Eighty-Eight Years of Cathedral Music 1898–1986. Winchester, 1994; Addendum, Winchester, 1995.

Eliot, Thomas Stearns. "The Music of Poetry." In Eliot, *On Poetry and Poets,* 26–38. London, 1957.

Eskew, Harry, and Hugh T. McElrath. *Sing with Understanding: An Introduction to American Hymnology.* 2nd ed. Nashville, 1995.

Etwas vom Liede Mosis, des Knechts Gottes, und dem Liede des Lammes. 2 parts. London, 1753, 1754.

Evans, J[ames Harington]. *David's Companion.* New York, 1808. (EvanJDC a)

Everett, L. C., ed. *The Wesleyan Hymn and Tune Book.* Nashville, 1860.

An Extract of the Minutes of Several Conversations . . . between the Preachers Late in Connection with the Rev. Mr. Wesley. London, 1796.

An Extract of the Minutes of Several Conversations . . . between the Preachers Late in Connection with the Rev. Mr. Wesley. London, 1800.

Fawcett, John. *A New Set of Sacred Music.* London, [c. 1811]. (FawcJS1)

———. *A Second Sett of Psalm and Hymn Tunes.* London, [1813–14]. (FawcJS2)

———. *A Third Sett of Psalm and Hymn Tunes.* London, [1818–19]. (FawcJS3)

———. *A Seventh Set of Hymn Tunes.* Leeds, 1830.

———. *The Vocal Instructor, or Young Musician's Companion.* London, 1830.

———. *The Harp of Zion.* London, [c. 1834].

———. *A Set of Sacred Music.* 2nd ed. London, [1837].

———. *The Voice of Harmony.* [London?], [c. 1850?].

Fellowes, Edmund H. *English Cathedral Music from Edward VI to Edward VII.* London, 1941.

Fiske, Roger. "The Macbeth Music." *Music and Letters* 45 (1964): 114–25.

Floy, James. "The Methodist Hymn-Book." *Methodist Review* 26 (1844): 165–206.

Forsaith, Peter. "The Romney Portrait of John Wesley." *Methodist History* 42 (2004): 249–55.

———. *Unexampled Labours: The Letters of John Fletcher.* Peterborough, 2008.

Forty Years of Cathedral Music. Church Music Society Occasional Paper No. 13. London, 1940.

Freylinghausen, Johann Anastasius, ed. *Geist-reiches Gesang-buch.* Halle, 1704.

Frost, Maurice. "Harmonia-Sacra. By Thomas Butts I." Hymn Society of Great Britain and Ireland, *Bulletin* 3, no. 4 (1952): 66–71.

Gambold, John. *A Collection of Hymns of the Children of God in All Ages.* London, 1754.

Gatens, William. *Victorian Cathedral Music in Theory and in Practice.* Cambridge, 1986.

Gauntlett, Henry John. "English Ecclesiastical Composers of the Present Age." *Musical World* 2 (1836): 113–20.

Gill, Frederick C. *Charles Wesley: The First Methodist.* London, 1964.

Godwin, Edward. *Hymns for Christian Societies.* Bristol, 1744.

———. *Hymns for the Lovefeast.* Bristol, 1746.

———. *Hymns.* Bristol, 1747.

Goodwin, Frederick K., and Kay Redfield Jamison. *Manic-Depressive Illness.* New York, 1990.

Goold, Madeline. *Mr. Langshaw's Square Piano.* London, 2008.

Graham, Fred Kimball. *With One Heart and One Voice: A Core Repertory of Hymn Tunes Published for Use in the Methodist Episcopal Church in the United States, 1808–1878.* Lanham, Md., 2004.

Green, Richard. *The Works of John and Charles Wesley: A Bibliography.* 2nd ed. London, 1906.

Green, Thomas. "Diary of a Lover of Literature." In *The Gentleman's Magazine*, 1834–39, various pagination.

Greene, Maurice. *Forty Select Anthems.* London, 1743.

Haggerty, George. "Male Love and Friendship in the Eighteenth Century." In Katherine O'Donnell, ed., *Love, Sex, Intimacy and Friendship between Men, 1550–1800*, 70–81. Basingtoke, 2007.

Hamilton, J. Taylor, and Kenneth G. Hamilton. *History of the Moravian Church: The Renewed Unitas Fratrum, 1722–1957.* Bethlehem, Pa., 1967.

Handel, George Frideric. *Harmonia Sacra.* London, [c. 1754]. (ButtTHS a)

———. *The Fitzwilliam Music Never Before Published: Three Hymns, the Words by . . . Charles Wesley*, ed. Samuel Wesley. London, 1826.

———. *The Complete Hymns and Chorales.* Facsimile edition with an introduction by Donald Burrows. London, 1988.

Harwood, Edward. *A Set of Hymns and Psalm Tunes.* London, [1781]. (HarwES1)

———. *Vital Spark, or the Dying Christian*, arr. J. Tidswell. London, 1877.

Haskell, Francis. *Taste and the Antique: The Lure of Classical Sculpture, 1500–1900*. London, 1981.

Hatchett, Marion J. *A Companion to the New Harp of Columbia*. Knoxville, Tenn., 2003.

Hatfield, James Taft. "John Wesley's Translations of German Hymns." *Proceedings of the Modern Language Association* 11 (1896): 171–99.

Hawkes, Thomas, ed. *A Collection of Tunes . . . Adapted to the Hymns in Use by the Wesleyan Methodist Societies*. Watchet, 1833.

Hawkins, James. *An Account of the Institution and Progress of the Academy of Ancient Music*. London, 1770. Repr. Cambridge, 1998.

Hawn, C. Michael. "The Consultation on Ecumenical Hymnody: An Evaluation of Its Influence in Selected English Language Hymnals Published in the United States and Canada since 1976." *The Hymn* 47, no. 2 (April 1996): 26–37.

———. "'The Tie That Binds': A List of Ecumenical Hymns in English Language Hymnals Published in Canada and the United States since 1976." *The Hymn* 48, no. 3 (July 1997): 25–37.

———, ed. *New Songs of Celebration Render*. Chicago, 2010.

Hayden, Roger. "Evangelical Calvinism among Eighteenth-Century British Baptists." PhD thesis, University of Keele, 1991.

Heitzenrater, Richard P., and W. Reginald Ward, eds. *Journal and Diaries III (1743–54)*. The Works of John Wesley (ed. Frank Baker), 20. Nashville, 1988.

Hildebrandt, Franz, Oliver A. Beckerlegge, and Frank Baker, eds. *A Collection of Hymns for the Use of the People Called Methodists*. The Works of John Wesley (ed. Frank Baker), 7. Oxford, 1983.

Hill, Douglas E. "A Study of Tastes in American Church Music as Reflected in the Music of the Methodist Episcopal Church to 1900." PhD thesis, University of Illinois, 1962.

Hirst, Thomas. *The Music of the Church, in Four Parts*. London, 1841.

Hogwood, Christopher. "Thomas Tudway's History of Music." In Christopher Hogwood and Richard Luckett, eds., *Music in Eighteenth-Century England: Essays in Memory of Charles Cudworth*, 19–48. Cambridge, 1983.

Holman, Peter. *Henry Purcell*. Oxford, 1994.

———. "Lampe, John Frederick." In Stanley Sadie and John Tyrrell, eds., *The New Grove Dictionary of Music and Musicians*. London, 2001.

Hooper, J. G. "A Survey of Music in Bristol." MA thesis, University of Bristol, 1963. Revised version (1963). (*BRcl* 23031)

Horton, Peter. "The Unknown Wesley: The Early Instrumental and Secular Vocal Music of Samuel Sebastian Wesley." In Bennett Zon, ed., *Nineteenth-Century British Music Studies*, 1:134–78. Aldershot, 1999.

———. "Modulation Run Mad." In Jeremy Dibble and Bennett Zon, eds., *Nineteenth-Century British Music Studies*, 2:223–34. Aldershot, 2002.

———. "'The Highest Point up to That Time Reached by the Combination of Hebrew and Christian Sentiment in Music.'" In Peter Horton and Bennett Zon, eds., *Nineteenth-Century British Music Studies*, 3:119–34. Aldershot, 2003.

———. *Samuel Sebastian Wesley: A Life*. Oxford, 2004.

Hughes-Hughes, Augustus. *Catalogue of Manuscript Music in the British Library*. 3 vols. London, 1909.

Hulan, Richard Huffman. "Camp-Meeting Spiritual Folksongs: Legacy of the 'Great Revival in the West.'" PhD thesis, University of Texas at Austin, 1978.

Humphreys, Joseph. *Sacred Hymns*. 3 parts. London, 1743–64.

Hutton, James, ed. *A Collection of Hymns, with Several Translations from the Hymn-Book of the Moravian Brethren.* London, 1742. Appendix, 1744; part 2, 1746; part 3, 1748.

———. *The Tunes for the Hymns in the Collection with Several Translations from the Moravian Hymn-Book.* London, [c. 1744]. (#TH)

Hymns for Christmas Day 1770. Bristol, 1770.

Hymns Sung at St. Peters Hospital 1767. Bristol, 1767.

Ingalls, Jeremiah. *The Christian Harmony: or, Songster's Companion.* Exeter, N.H., 1805. Facsimile edition, ed. H. Wiley Hitchcock, with an introduction by David Klocko. New York, 1981.

Ingham, Benjamin. *A Collection of Hymns for Societies.* Leeds, 1748.

———. *Diary of an Oxford Methodist,* ed. Richard P. Heitzenrater. Durham, N.C., 1985.

Jackson, George Pullen. *White Spirituals in the Southern Uplands.* Chapel Hill, N.C., 1933.

Jackson, Thomas. *The Life of the Rev. Charles Wesley, M.A.* London, 1841.

———. *Recollections of my own Life and Times.* London, 1873.

Jacobi, John Christian. *Psalmodia Germanica.* Parts 1, 2. London, 1722–25. (JacoJPG1–2)

Jamison, Kay Redfield. *Touched with Fire: Manic-Depressive Illness and the Artistic Temperament.* New York, 1993.

Jeans, Susi. "The Easter Psalms of Christ's Hospital." *Proceedings of the Royal Musical Association* 88 (1962): 45–60.

Johnson, Julian. "The Old, the New, and the Contemporary." In Johnson, *Who Needs Classical Music? Cultural Choice and Musical Value,* 91–110. Oxford, 2002.

Johnstone, H. Diack. "The Genesis of Boyce's *Cathedral Music.*" *Music and Letters* 56 (1975): 26–40.

———. "Claver Morris." *Journal of the Royal Musical Association* 133 (2008): 93–127.

Julian, John. *A Dictionary of Hymnology.* 2nd ed. London, 1907. Repr. 1957.

Kassler, Michael. "The English Translations of Forkel's *Life of Bach.*" In Kassler, ed., *The English Bach Awakening,* 169–209. Aldershot, 2004. (2004a)

———. "The Bachists of 1810: Subscribers to the Wesley/Horn Edition of the '48.'" In Kassler, ed. *The English Bach Awakening,* 315–40. Aldershot, 2004. (2004b)

———. "The Horn/Wesley Edition of Bach's 'Trio' Sonatas." In Kassler, ed. *The English Bach Awakening,* 417–29. Aldershot, 2004. (2004c)

Kassler, Michael, and Philip Olleson. *Samuel Wesley (1766–1837): A Source Book.* Aldershot, 2001. (KO)

Kelly, Thomas. *A History of Adult Education in Great Britain.* Liverpool, 1962.

Kennedy, Michael. *Portrait of Elgar.* London, 1968.

Kent, John, ed. "Wesleyan Membership in Bristol 1783." In *An Ecclesiastical Miscellany,* Bristol and Gloucestershire Archaeological Society, Records Section Publications 11 (1976): 103–32.

Kilvert, Francis. *Kilvert's Diary 1870–1879,* ed. William Plomer. London, 1946.

Kimbrough, S T. "Charles Wesley and Biblical Interpretation." In Kimbrough, ed., *Charles Wesley: Poet and Theologian,* 106–136. Nashville, 1992.

Kimbrough, S T, and Oliver Beckerlegge. *The Unpublished Poetry of Charles Wesley.* 3 vols. Nashville, 2001.

Kimbrough, S T, and Carlton R. Young, eds. *Songs for the World: Hymns by Charles Wesley.* New York, 2001.

King, Alec Hyatt. "The First 'Complete Edition of Purcell.'" *Monthly Musical Record* 81 (March–April 1951): 63–69.

Klocko, David. "Jeremiah Ingalls's *The Christian Harmony: or, Songster's Companion*." PhD thesis, University of Michigan, 1978.

———. Introduction to Jeremiah Ingalls, *The Christian Harmony: or, Songster's Companion*, facsimile edition, ed. H. Wiley Hitchcock. New York, 1981.

[Knibb, Thomas.] *The Psalm Singers Help*. London, [c. 1760]. (KnibTPSH a)

———. *The Psalm Singers Help* [c. 1765]. (KnibTPSH b)

[Lampe, John Frederick.] *Hymns on the Great Festivals, and Other Occasions*. London, 1746. Facsimile edition, ed. S T Kimbrough. Madison, N.J., 1996. (#HGFOO)

Knight, Gerald H., and William L. Reed. *The Treasury of English Church Music*. 5 vols. London, 1965.

Landon, H. C. Robbins. *Haydn in England, 1791–1795*. Haydn: Chronicle and Works, vol. 3. London, 1976.

Langford, Paul. *A Polite and Commercial People: England, 1727–1783*. Oxford, 1989.

Laqueur, Thomas. *Religion and Respectability: Sunday Schools and Working Class Culture, 1780–1850*. New Haven, Conn., 1976.

Leach, James. *A New Sett of Hymns and Psalm Tunes*. London, [1789]. (LeacJNS a)

———. *A Second Sett of Hymns and Psalm Tunes*. London, [c. 1794]. (LeacJSS a)

———. *A Collection of Hymn Tunes and Anthems*. London, [1798–]. (LeacJCHTA)

Leaver, Robin A. "Charles Wesley and Anglicanism." In S T Kimbrough, ed., *Charles Wesley: Poet and Theologian*, 157–75. Nashville, 1992.

———. "Lampe's Tunes." In John Frederick Lampe, *Hymns on the Great Festivals, and Other Occasions: A Facsimile of the First Edition*, ed. S T Kimbrough, 31–44. Madison, N.J., 1996.

Levitin, Daniel J. *This Is Your Brain on Music: The Science of a Human Obsession*. New York, 2007.

Lightwood, James T. *Methodist Music in the Eighteenth Century*. London, 1927.

———. *Stories of Methodist Music: Nineteenth Century*. London, 1928.

———. *The Music of the Methodist Hymn-Book*. London, 1933.

———. *Samuel Wesley, Musician: The Story of His Life*. London, 1937.

Lipking, Lawrence. *The Ordering of the Arts in Eighteenth-Century England*. Princeton, N.J., 1970.

Lloyd, Gareth. "Charles Wesley, Junior: Prodigal Child, Unfulfilled Adult." *Proceedings of the Charles Wesley Society* 5 (1998): 23–35.

———. "Charles Wesley (1757–1834)." *ODNB* 58: 181–82. Oxford, 2004.

———. "Charles Wesley and His Biographers." In Kenneth J. Newport and Ted A. Campbell, eds., *Charles Wesley: Life, Literature, and Legacy*, 1–17. Peterborough, 2007. (2007a)

———. *Charles Wesley and the Struggle for Methodist Identity*. Oxford, 2007. (2007b)

Long, Kenneth R. *The Music of the English Church*. London, 1972.

Lynan, Peter. "Broderip, William (1683–1727)," *ODNB* 7:769. Oxford, 2004.

Lynch, Elizabeth Kurtz. "John Wesley's Editorial Hand in Susanna Annesley Wesley's 1732 'Education' Letter." *Bulletin of the John Rylands Library of the University of Manchester* 85 (2003): 195–208.

Mackerness, Eric D. *Somewhere Further North: A History of Music in Sheffield*. Sheffield, 1974.

[Madan, Martin, ed.] *A Collection of Psalms and Hymns*. London, 1760.

———. *A Collection of Psalm and Hymn Tunes . . . To be had at the Lock Hospital*. [3rd ed. London], (1769). (✱LHC A c)

Malan, Jacques P. "Tregarthen, William Coulson." In Malan, ed., *South African Music Encyclopedia*, 4:382–85. Cape Town, 1986.

Marti, Donald B. "Rich Methodists: The Rise and Consequences of Lay Philanthropy in the Mid-19th Century." In Russell E. Richey and Kenneth E. Rowe, eds., *Rethinking Methodist History*. Nashville, 1985.

Martin, Dennis. *The Operas and Operatic Style of John Frederick Lampe*. Detroit Monographs in Musicology 8. Detroit, 1985.

Matthew, James E. "The Antient Concerts, 1776–1848." *Proceedings of the Musical Association* 33 (1906–7): 55–79.

Matthews, Antje. "John Russell (1745–1806) and the Impact of Evangelicalism and Natural Theology on Artistic Practice." PhD thesis, University of Leicester, 2005.

Matthews, Betty. "Charles Wesley on Organs." *Musical Times* 112 (1971): 1007–10, 1111–12.

Maxfield, Thomas, ed. *A Collection of Psalms and Hymns*. London, 1766.

McCutchan, Robert Guy. *Our Hymnody: A Manual of the Methodist Hymnal*. 2nd ed. New York, [1942].

McLamore, Alyson. "'By the Will and Order of Providence': The Wesley Family Concerts, 1779–1787." *Royal Musical Association Research Chronicle* 37 (2004): 71–220.

———. "Various Compositions by Samuel Wesley." *Notes* 63 (2006): 440–49.

McVeigh, Simon. *Concert Life in London from Mozart to Haydn*. Cambridge, 1993.

[Mead, Stith.] *A General Selection of the Newest and Most Admired Hymns and Spiritual Songs Now in Use*. Richmond, Va., 1807.

The Methodist Hymn-Book with Tunes. London, 1904.

The Methodist Hymn-Book with Tunes. London, 1933.

Meyer, Arline. "Re-Dressing Classical Statuary: The Eighteenth-Century 'Hand-in-Waistcoat' Portrait." *The Art Bulletin* 77 (1995): 45–63.

Meyerstein, E. H. W. *The Life of Thomas Chatterton*. London, 1930.

Miller, Edward. *Dr. Watts's Psalms and Hymns, Set to New Music*. London, [1800].

———. *Sacred Music . . . Intended as an Appendix to Dr. Watts's Psalms and Hymns*. London, [c. 1800].

Miller, William Edward. *David's Harp*. London, [c. 1803]. (MillWDH)

Minutes of Several Conversations, between the Rev. John Wesley, A.M. and the Preachers in Connection with Him. London, 1779.

Minutes of Some Late Conversations, between the Reverend Mr. Wesley, and Others. London, 1766.

Minutes of Some Late Conversations, between the Rev. Mr. Wesleys, and Others. London, 1768.

Minutes of Some Late Conversations between the Reverend Messieurs John and Charles Wesley, and Others. London, 1770.

Minutes of the Methodist Conference. London, 1862.

Morgan, John. *A Brief Account of the Stockport Sunday School*. London, 1838.

Morris, Pam, ed. *The Bakhtin Reader: Selected Writings of Bakhtin, Medvedev, Voloshinov*. London, 1994.

Nagler, Arthur Wilford. *Pietism and Methodism*. Nashville, 1918.

Nettl, Bruno. "Music," section III/5, "The Function of Music." In Stanley Sadie and John Tyrrell, eds., *The New Grove Dictionary of Music and Musicians*. London, 2001.

"The New Hymn Book." *Quarterly Review of the Methodist Episcopal Church, South (1847)* 2 (1848): 69–131.

Newman, William S. *The Sonata in the Classic Era.* Chapel Hill, N.C., 1963.

Newport, Kenneth J., and Ted A. Campbell, eds., *Charles Wesley: Life, Literature, and Legacy.* Peterborough, 2007.

Noble, Yvonne. Introduction to *Twentieth Century Interpretations of the Beggar's Opera: A Collection of Critical Essays,* ed. Yvonne Noble. Englewood Cliffs, N.J., 1975.

Norwood, Frederick A. *The Story of American Methodism.* Nashville, 1974.

Novello, Vincent. *The Surrey Chapel Music.* London, [1847].

Nuelsen, John L. *John Wesley and the German Hymn.* Trans. Theo Parry, Sydney H. Moore, and Arthur Holbrooke. Calverley, 1972.

Ogasapian, John. *English Cathedral Music in New York: Edward Hodges of Trinity Church.* Richmond, Va., 1994.

Olleson, Philip. "The Tamworth Festival of 1809." *Staffordshire Studies* 5 (1993): 81–106.

———. "Samuel Wesley and the *Missa de Spiritu Sancto.*" *Recusant History* 24 (1999): 309–19.

———. "The London Roman Catholic Chapels and their Music in the Eighteenth and Early Nineteenth Centuries." In David Wyn-Jones, ed., *Music in Eighteenth-Century Britain,* 101–18. Aldershot, 2000. (2000a)

———. "Samuel Wesley and the Music Profession." In Christina Bashford and Leanne Langley, eds., *Music and British Culture, 1785–1914,* 23–38. Oxford, 2000. (2000b)

———. *The Letters of Samuel Wesley: Professional and Social Correspondence, 1797–1837.* Oxford, 2001.

———. *Samuel Wesley: The Man and His Music.* Woodbridge, 2003.

———. "Samuel Wesley and the English Bach Awakening." In Michael Kassler, ed., *The English Bach Awakening,* 251–313. Aldershot, 2004.

———. "Charles Wesley and His Children." In Kenneth G. Newport and Ted A. Campbell, eds., *Charles Wesley: Life, Literature, and Legacy,* 124–40. Peterborough, 2007.

Olleson, Philip, and Fiona M. Palmer. "Publishing Music from the Fitzwilliam Museum, Cambridge: The Work of Vincent Novello and Samuel Wesley in the 1820s." *Journal of the Royal Musical Association* 130 (2005): 38–73.

Outler, Albert C. *John Wesley's Sermons: An Introduction.* Nashville, 1994.

The Oxford Dictionary of National Biography, ed. H. C. G. Matthew and Brian Harrison. 60 vols. Oxford, 2004. (*ODNB*)

The Oxford English Dictionary. 2nd ed. 20 vols. Oxford, 1989. (*OED*)

Partners in Praise. London, 1979.

Pattison, Samuel. *Original Poems, Chiefly on Divine Subjects.* Manchester, [1790?].

Pearce, Thomas, ed. *A Collection of Anthems Used in His Majesty's Chapels Royal and Most Cathedral Churches in England and Ireland.* New ed. London, 1826.

Piper, David. *The English Face.* 2nd ed. London, 1992.

Plomley, Roy, with Derek Drescher. *Desert Island Lists.* London, 1984.

Pointon, Marcia. *Hanging the Head.* New Haven, Conn., 1993.

Porter, Samuel. *Plain and Easie Directions for Psalm-Singing.* London, 1700.

Practical Discourse of Singing in the Worship of God. London, 1708.

"Professional Memoranda of the Late Mr. Samuel Wesley." *The Musical World* 7 (1837): 81–93, 113–18.

Rack, Henry D. *Reasonable Enthusiast: John Wesley and the Rise of Methodism.* 3rd ed. Peterborough, 2002.

———. "Charles Wesley (1707–1788)." *ODNB* 58: 175–80. Oxford, 2004. (2004a)

———. "Sarah Wesley (1726–1822)." *ODNB* 58: 180–81. (Oxford, 2004). (2004b)

Ramsden, William, ed. *Hymns on the Nativity: Also New Year's Day, Love Feast, and the Passion, to the Trinity.* York, 1775.

Report of the Joint Music Study Committee of the General Board of Discipleship and the United Methodist Publishing House. Nashville, 2008.

The Revision of the Hymn Book of the Methodist Episcopal Church: Report of the Committee to the Bishops. New York, 1878.

Rhodes, Iris C. *John Russell R. A.* Guildford, 1986.

Roberts, Richard Owen. *Whitefield in Print.* Wheaton, Ill., 1988.

Roberts, Thomas. *Hymnology: A Dissertation on Hymns.* Bristol, 1808.

Robins, Brian, ed. *The John Marsh Journals.* Stuyvesant, N.Y., 1998.

———. *Catch and Glee Culture in Eighteenth-Century England.* Woodbridge, Suffolk, 2006.

Robinson, Mary. *Memoirs of Mrs. Robinson.* London, 1803.

Rogal, Samuel J. *Guide to the Hymns and Tunes of American Methodism.* New York, 1986.

Rohr, Deborah. *The Careers of British Musicians, 1750–1850: A Profession of Artisans.* Cambridge, 2001.

Routley, Erik. *The Church and Music.* London, 1967.

———. *The Musical Wesleys.* London, 1968.

———. *An English-Speaking Hymnal Guide.* Collegeville, Minn., [1979].

Ruth, Lester. *A Little Heaven Below: Worship at Early Methodist Quarterly Meetings.* Nashville, 2000.

S—, J—, organist. "Remarks on Public Singing." *Arminian Magazine* 14 (1791): 101–4.

Sacred Harmony [ed. Samuel Jenkins]. New York, 1848.

Sankey, Ira D. *Christian Endeavor Hymns.* Boston, 1894.

Schlenther, Boyd S. *Queen of the Methodists.* Durham, N.C., 1997.

Schneider, A. Gregory. *The Way the Cross Leads Home: The Domestication of American Methodism.* Bloomington, Ind., 1993.

Scholes, Percy A. *The Oxford Companion to Music.* 9th ed. London, 1955.

Schroeder, David P. *Haydn and the Enlightenment: The Late Symphonies and Their Audience.* Oxford, 1997.

Schwarz, John I., Jr., ed. "Two Symphonic Works by S. Wesley: Symphony in B-flat Major, 1802" and "One Symphony by S. S. Wesley: Symphony in C Minor, 1834." In *The Symphony, 1720–1840,* series E, vol. 3. New York, 1983.

Seed, Thomas. *Norfolk Street Wesleyan Chapel, Sheffield.* London, 1907.

A Selection of Hymns, to Be Performed on Christmas Day, at the Methodist Chapel, Leeds. Leeds, [c. 1798].

Sharpe, E. "Bristol Baptist College and the Church's Hymnody." *Baptist Quarterly* n.s. 28 (1979–80): 7–16.

Shaw, Giles, ed. *Annals of Oldham and District,* vol. 2. Oldham, 1904.

Shaw, H. Watkins. "Church Music in England from the Reformation to the Present Day." In Friedrich Blume, ed., *Protestant Church Music: A History,* 691–732. London, 1975.

Shay, Robert, and Robert Thompson. *Purcell Manuscripts: The Principal Musical Sources.* Cambridge, 2000.

Sherman, James. "Prefatory Letter." In *Novello's Congregational Music.* London, 1847.

Sixty Years of Cathedral Music, [ed. W. K. Stanton]. Church Music Society Occasional Paper 24. London, [1958].

Sketchley, James. *Sketchley's Bristol Directory.* Bristol, 1775.

Sloman, Susan. *Gainsborough in Bath.* New Haven, Conn., 2002.

Smith, Isaac, ed. *A Collection of Psalm Tunes.* London, [c. 1779.] (SmitICPT a)

Smith, John Stafford. *Anthems.* London, [1793].

Smither, Howard E. *The Oratorio in the Classical Era.* A History of the Oratorio, vol. 3. Oxford, 1987.

Snowman, Janet. "The Left and Right Hands of the Eighteenth-Century British Musical Prodigies, William Crotch and Samuel Wesley." *Laterality: Asymmetries of Body, Brain and Cognition* 15 (2010): 209–52.

Solomon: A Serenata [words only]. Bristol, 1759.

Souvenir History of the New England Conference. Volume 2: South District, ed. William Albert Thurston. Boston, 1897.

[Spence, Robert.] *A Pocket Hymn Book Designed as a Constant Companion for the Pious.* York, 1781.

———. *A Pocket Hymn Book Designed as a Constant Companion for the Pious.* New York, 1786.

Spencer, Jon M. *Black Hymnody: A Hymnological History of the African American Church.* Knoxville, Tenn., 1992.

Spitzer, John, and Neal Zaslaw. *The Birth of the Orchestra: History of an Institution, 1650–1805.* Oxford, 2004.

Stanford, Charles Villiers. *Pages from an Unwritten Diary.* London, 1914.

———. "The Post-Beethoven Period." In Stanford and Cecil Forsyth, *A History of Music,* chap. 15. London, 1916.

Stokes, Winifred. "The Place of Methodism in Georgian Psalmody." In Christopher Turner, ed., *Georgian Psalmody II,* 59–64. Corby Glen, 1999.

Summers, Thomas O. *Commentary on the Ritual of the Methodist Episcopal Church, South.* Nashville, 1874.

Sweet, Rosemary. *Antiquaries: The Discovery of the Past in Eighteenth-Century Britain.* Hambledon, 2004.

Tate, Nahum, and Nicholas Brady. *A New Version of the Psalms of David, Fitted to the Tunes Used in Churches.* London, 1696.

Telford, John. *Sayings and Portraits of Charles Wesley.* London, 1927.

———. *The Letters of John Wesley.* 8 vols. London, 1931.

Temperley, Nicholas. "Mozart's Influence on English Church Music." *Music and Letters* 42 (1961): 307–18.

———. "The Anglican Communion Hymn." *The Hymn* 30 (1979): 7–15, 93–101, 178–85, 243–51. Repr. in Temperley, *Studies in English Church Music,* 103–39. Aldershot, 2009. (1979a)

———. *The Music of the English Parish Church.* 2 vols. Cambridge, 1979. (1979b)

———. "Cathedral Music." In Temperley, ed., *The Romantic Age 1800–1914,* 171–213. Athlone History of Music in Britain, vol. 5. London, 1981.

———. *Works for Pianoforte Solo by Late Georgian Composers.* The London Pianoforte School, 7. New York, 1985.

———. "The Lock Hospital Chapel and Its Music." *Journal of the Royal Musical Association* 118 (1993): 44–72. Repr. in Temperley, *Studies in English Church Music,* 258–86. Aldershot, 2009. (199)

———. *The Hymn Tune Index.* 4 vols. Oxford, 1998. (*HTI*)

———. "Xenophilia in British Musical History." In Bennet Zon, ed., *Nineteenth-Century British Music Studies,* 1:1–19. Aldershot, 1999.

———. "Methodist Church Music." In Stanley Sadie and John Tyrrell, eds., *The New Grove Dictionary of Music and Musicians.* London, 2001.

———, ed. *William Sterndale Bennett: Lectures on Musical Life.* Woodbridge, 2006.

Temperley, Nicholas, and Sally Drage, eds. *Eighteenth-Century Psalmody.* Musica Britannica, 85. London, 2007.

Thistlethwaite, Nicholas. *The Making of the Victorian Organ.* Cambridge, 1990.

Thomas, John. *Three Welsh Hymns.* Bristol, 1762.

Thomson, John M. *The Oxford History of New Zealand Music.* Auckland, 1991.

Threinen, Norman J. "Friedrich Michael Ziegenhagen (1694–1776): German Lutheran Pietist in the English Court." *Lutheran Theological Review* 12 (1999–2000): 56–94.

Tiebout, John. *A Collection of Original and Select Hymns and Spiritual Songs.* New York, 1805.

Tomita, Yo. "Bach's Credo in England, an Early History." In Anne Leahy and Yo Tomita, eds., *Bach Studies from Dublin,* 205–27. Irish Musical Studies, 8. Dublin, 2004. (2004a)

———. "Pursuit of Perfection: Stages of Perfection of the Wesley/Horn 48." In Michael Kassler, ed., *The English Bach Awakening,* 341–77. Aldershot, 2004. (2004b)

Tourjée, Eben. *The Tribute of Praise. A Collection of Hymns and Tunes for Public and Social Worship.* New York, 1874.

Tyerman, Luke. *The Life and Times of the Rev: John Wesley.* 3 vols. 3rd ed. London, 1876.

Tyson, J. *Charles Wesley: A Reader.* New York, 2000 [paperback ed.].

Vaughan, William. *British Painting: The Golden Age.* London, 1999.

Vernon, Walter Newton. *The History of the United Methodist Publishing House.* 2 vols. Nashville, 1988.

Vincent, William. *Considerations on Parochial Music.* London, 1787.

Wainwright, Arthur W., ed. with Don E. Saliers. *Wesley-Langshaw Correspondence: Charles Wesley, His Sons, and the Lancaster Organists.* Atlanta, 1993.

Walker, Ernest. *A History of Music in England.* London, 1907.

Walker, R. J. B. *Regency Portraits.* 2 vols. London, 1985.

Walker, Ralph S., ed. *A Selection of Thomas Twining's Letters, 1734–1804: The Record of a Tranquil Life.* Lewiston, N.Y., 1991.

Walker, William. *Southern Harmony.* Spartanburg, S.C., 1835. Facsimile edition (based on 1854 revision), ed. Glenn C. Wilcox, Los Angeles, 1966.

Walmisley, Thomas Attwood. *Sacred Music.* London, 1857.

Ward, W. Reginald, and Richard P. Heitzenrater, eds. *Journal and Diaries V (1765–75).* The Works of John Wesley (33 vols., ed. Frank Baker), 22. Nashville, 1993.

Weber, William. *The Rise of the Musical Classics in Eighteenth-Century England: A Study in Canon, Ritual and Ideology.* Oxford, 1992.

Welch, Edwin. *Spiritual Pilgrim: A Reassessment of the Life of the Countess of Huntingdon.* Cardiff, 1995.

Wesley, Charles [the Elder]. *Hymns on God's Everlasting Love.* London, [1742].

———. *Hymns for Those That Seek, and Those That Have, Redemption in the Blood of Jesus Christ.* London, 1747.

———. *Hymns and Sacred Poems.* 2 vols. Bristol, 1749. (1749a)

———. *Hymns for New Years Day M.DCC.L.* Bristol, 1749. (1749b)

———. *Hymns for Those to Whom Christ Is All in All.* London, 1761.

———. *Short Hymns on Select Passages of the Holy Scriptures.* 2 vols. Bristol, 1762.

———. *Journal,* ed. Thomas Jackson. 2 vols. London, 1849.

———. *The Manuscript Journal of the Rev. Charles Wesley, M.A.,* ed. S T Kimbrough Jr. and Kenneth G. C. Newport. 2 vols. Nashville, 2007–8.

Wesley, Charles [the Younger]. *Sacred Harmony: A Set of Tunes Collected by the Late Revd. John Wesley. . . . Revised by His Nephew.* London, 1822.

Wesley, John. *A Collection of Forms of Prayer for Every Day of the Week.* London, 1733.

———. *A Collection of Psalms and Hymns.* Charlestown, S.C., 1737. Facsimile edition, ed. Frank Baker and George Walton Williams: *John Wesley's First Hymn-Book,* Charleston, S.C., 1964.

———. *A Collection of Psalms and Hymns.* London, 1738.

———. *A Collection of Psalms and Hymns.* [2nd ed.] London, 1741.

———. *A Collection of Tunes, Set to Music, as They Are Commonly Sung at the Foundery.* London, 1742. (#CTSF)

———. *An Earnest Appeal to Men of Reason and Religion.* London, 1743.

———. *Hymns and Spiritual Songs, Intended for the Use of Real Christians of All Denominations.* London, 1752.

———. *Select Hymns with Tunes Annext: Designed Chiefly for the Use of the People Called Methodists.* London, 1761. (Tune supplement: *TS Wes a)

———. *Select Hymns with Tunes Annext: Designed Chiefly for the Use of the People Called Methodists.* 2nd ed. London, 1765. (Tune supplement, "Sacred Melody," *TS Wes b)

———. *A Collection of Hymns for the Use of the People Called Methodists.* London, 1780.

———. "[Thoughts] on the Power of Music." *Arminian Magazine* 4 (1781): 104–7. (1781a)

———. *Sacred Harmony, or a Choice Collection of Psalms and Hymns.* [London?, 1781] (#SHCCPH) (1781b)

———. *The Sunday Service of the Methodists in North America.* London, 1784.

———. *A Pocket Hymn Book for the Use of Christians of All Denominations.* London, 1787.

———. *Sacred Harmony,* corrected by his nephew, Charles Wesley. London, 1822.

———. *A Collection of Hymns for the Use of the People Called Methodists . . . With a Supplement.* London, 1831.

———. *The Works of John Wesley.* 14 vols. London, 1872.

———. *The Works of John Wesley, with a New Supplement. Edition with Tunes.* London, 1877.

———. *A Representative Collection of his Writings,* ed. Albert Cook Outler. New York, 1964.

———. *The Works of John Wesley,* ed. Frank Baker. 34 vols. (In progress.) Oxford, 1975–.

Wesley, John, and Charles [the Elder]. *Hymns and Sacred Poems.* [Vol. 1.] London, 1739.

———. *Hymns and Sacred Poems.* [Vol. 2.] London, 1740.

———. *Hymns and Sacred Poems.* [Vol. 3.] London, 1742.

———. *A Collection of Psalms and Hymns.* [3rd ed.] London, 1743.

———. *Hymns for the Nativity of Our Lord.* ([London, 1744]).

———. *Hymns on the Lord's Supper.* Bristol, 1745. (HLS)

———. *Gloria Patri, &c., or Hymns to the Trinity.* London, 1746. (1746a)

———. *Hymns for Ascension Day.* Bristol, 1746. (1746b)

———. *Hymns for Our Lord's Resurrection.* London, 1746. (1746c)

———. *Hymns of Petition and Thanksgiving.* Bristol, 1746. (1746d)

———. *A Collection of Psalms and Hymns for the Lord's Day.* London, 1784.

Wesley, Samuel [1691–1739]. *Poems on Several Occasions.* London, 1736.

Wesley, Samuel [1766–1837], ed. *The Fitzwilliam Music . . . Three Hymns, the Words by the Late Rev. Charles Wesley, . . . Set to Music by George Frideric Handel.* London, 1826.

———. *Original Hymn Tunes.* London, 1828.

———. "Sketch of the State of Music in England, from the Year 1778 up to the Present." *Musical World* 1 (1836): 1–3.

Wesley, Samuel Sebastian. *A Few Words on Cathedral Music and the Musical System of the Church, with a Plan of Reform.* London, 1849.

———. *Anthems,* vol. 1. London, [1853].

———. *Anthems,* ed. Peter Horton. Vol. 1. Musica Britannica, 57. London, 1990.

———. *Anthems,* ed. Peter Horton. Vol. 3. Musica Britannica, 89. London, 2010.

Westerfield-Tucker, Karen. *American Methodist Worship.* Oxford, 2001.

Whitefield, George. *Divine Melody: or, A Help to Devotion.* London, 1739.

———. *An Account of Money Received and Disbursed for the Orphan-House in Georgia.* London, 1741.

———. *A Continuation of the Account of the Orphan-House in Georgia.* London, 1743.

———. *A Collection of Hymns for Social Worship.* London, 1753.

The Whole Booke of Psalmes, Collected into English Metre by T. Starnhold I. Hopkins & Others. London, 1562. (✻P E4)

Wild, W. *The History of the Stockport Sunday School and Its Branch Schools.* London, 1891.

Wilde, J[ohn]. *Favorite Hymns, Odes and Anthems, as Sung at the Methodist Chapels, in the Sheffield, Rotherham, Doncaster and Nottingham Circuits.* 5th ed. [N.p.], 1797.

Williams, Thomas. *Psalmodia Evangelica.* London, 1789. (WillTPE)

Williams, William. *Welsh Hymns.* Bristol, 1768.

Williamson, Malcolm. *12 New Hymn Tunes.* London, 1962.

———. *Six Wesley Songs for the Young.* London, 1963.

Williamson, Robert. *A Collection of Hymns.* Bristol, 1756.

Winters, W. *An Account of the Remarkable Musical Talents of the Wesley Family.* London, 1874.

Woodbury, Isaac B. *The New Lute of Sion.* New York, [c. 1856].

Woodmason, C[harles] H[yde]. *A Selection of Psalms from the New Version.* 2nd ed. East Dereham, 1813. (WollCSP 2)

Woodward, Josiah. *An Account of the Religious Societies, in London and Westminster, and Other Parts of the Kingdom.* London, 1698.

Wren, Brian A. *Praying Twice: The Music and Words of Congregational Song.* Louisville, Ky., 2000.

Wylde, J. B. *Jubal's Lyre: A New and Choice Selection of Psalm and Hymn Tunes.* London, [c. 1808]. (WyldJJL)

[Wylde, John.] *A Selection of Hymns, to Be Performed on Christmas Day, at the Methodist Chapel, Leeds.* Leeds, [1798?].

Yardley, Anne B. "Choirs in the Methodist Episcopal Church, 1800–1860." *American Music* 17 (1999): 39–64. (1999a)

———. "What Besides Hymns? The Tune Books of Early American Methodism." *Methodist History* 37 (1999): 189–201. (1999b)

Young, Carlton R., ed. *Companion to the United Methodist Hymnal.* Nashville, 1993.

———. *Music of the Heart.* Carol Stream, Ill., 1995. (1995a)

———. *My Great Redeemer's Praise.* Akron, Ohio, 1995. (1995b)

———. "John F. Lampe and *Hymns on the Great Festivals, 1746.*" In Lampe, *Hymns on the Great Festivals, and Other Occasions: A Facsimile of the First Edition,* ed. S T Kimbrough, 7–20. Madison, N.J., 1996.

———. "Methodist Episcopal Worship Music." In Edward Foley, ed., *Worship Music: A Concise Dictionary,* 199–200. Collegeville, Minn., 2000.

———. *Sacred Harmony: The Musical Wesley Family.* Dallas, 2007.

Young, Percy M. *A History of British Music.* London, 1967.

[Zinzendorf, Nikolaus Ludwig, Graf von.] *Hymns Composed for the Use of the Brethren.* London, 1749.

Zöllner, Eva. *English Oratorio after Handel, 1760–1800.* Marburg, 2002.

CONTRIBUTORS

STEPHEN BANFIELD (professor of music, University of Bristol), founding director of CHOMBEC, Bristol's Centre for the History of Music in Britain, the Empire and the Commonwealth, is author of *Sensibility and English Song* (1985), *Sondheim's Broadway Musicals* (1993), *Gerald Finzi* (1997), and *Jerome Kern* (2006).

JONATHAN BARRY (associate professor of history, University of Exeter) researches provincial society and culture in England, with emphasis on Bristol and the southwest, and has co-edited *Reformation and Revival in 18th-Century Bristol* and *The Middling Sort of People* (both 1994); *Witchcraft in Early Modern Europe* (1998); and *Identity and Agency in England, 1500–1800* (2004).

MARTIN V. CLARKE (associate lecturer in music, Open University) was awarded a PhD from Durham University in 2008 for his thesis *John Wesley and Methodist Music in the Eighteenth Century: Principles and Practice* and was a visiting fellow at Bridwell Library, Southern Methodist University, in 2007.

SALLY DRAGE was awarded a PhD by the University of Leeds in 2009 for her thesis *The Performance of English Provincial Psalmody c. 1690–c. 1840*. She has published in *Early Music,* the *Oxford Dictionary of National Biography,* the revised *New Grove,* and in edited volumes. She co-edited *Eighteenth-Century Psalmody* (Musica Britannica, 2007) with Nicholas Temperley.

PETER S. FORSAITH (research fellow, Oxford Centre for Methodism and Church History, Oxford Brookes University) is a historian specializing in the religion, society, and culture of eighteenth-century Britain. In 2008 he published an edition of the letters of John Fletcher to John and Charles Wesley, George Whitefield, and the Countess of Huntingdon.

PETER HOLMAN (professor of historical musicology, University of Leeds) is the author of the prize-winning *Four and Twenty Fiddlers: The Violin at the English Court, 1540–1690* (1993) and of studies of Henry Purcell (1994) and Dowland's *Lachrimae* (1999). His latest book, *Life after Death: The Viola da Gamba in Britain from Purcell to Dolmetsch,* will soon be published by Boydell & Brewer.

PETER HORTON (reference and research librarian, Royal College of Music) is editor of Sebastian Wesley's complete anthems for Musica Britannica and author of *Samuel Sebastian Wesley* (2004), and he has recently been working on editions of Vaughan Williams and Sterndale Bennett.

ROBIN A. LEAVER (visiting professor, Yale University, the Juilliard School, and Queen's University, Belfast) has published extensively in the cross-disciplinary areas of liturgy, church music, theology, and hymnology. His latest book, *Luther's Liturgical Music: Principles and Implications,* was published in 2007.

ALYSON McLAMORE (music professor, California Polytechnic, San Luis Obispo) has published *Musical Theater: An Appreciation* (2004) and various scholarly articles on aspects of late-eighteenth-century music.

GEOFFREY C. MOORE (PhD program in Religious Studies, Southern Methodist University) trained as a choral conductor and currently serves as creative director for the Arts District Chorale in Dallas. His scholarly work focuses on Wesleyan eucharistic theology, practice, and hymnody. He has held positions at the Dallas Opera and Brookhaven College, Dallas.

JOHN NIGHTINGALE is a conductor, accompanist, editor, and researcher who worked for many years on BBC Radio 3's planning team. He assisted Lionel Sawkins with his Lalande catalogue (2005) and with editions of works by Lalande and others. He has a long-standing interest in the Wesley composers and has edited and directed performances of much of their music.

PHILIP OLLESON (emeritus professor of historical musicology, University of Nottingham) is the author of *Samuel Wesley* (2003) and *Samuel Wesley: A Source Book* (2001, with Michael Kassler), and he is editor of *The Letters of Samuel Wesley: Professional and Social Correspondence 1797–1837* (2001).

NICHOLAS TEMPERLEY (emeritus professor of music, University of Illinois) has published *The Music of the English Parish Church* (1979), *The Hymn Tune Index* (1998), *Eighteenth-Century Psalmody* (Musica Britannica, co-edited with Sally Drage, 2007), and articles in the revised *New Grove* (2001) on Anglican and Methodist music, hymns, psalmody, and the Wesley family.

J. R. WATSON (emeritus professor of English, University of Durham) is the author of *The English Hymn* (1997) and *An Annotated Anthology of Hymns* (2002). He is currently engaged in editing the forthcoming *Canterbury Dictionary of Hymnology,* intended to complement the work of John Julian (1892, 1907).

ANNE BAGNALL YARDLEY (associate professor of music, Drew Theological School) is the author of *Performing Piety: Musical Culture in Medieval English Nunneries* (2006) as well as numerous articles on medieval music and other topics, including nineteenth-century Methodist music and the pedagogy of music in the seminary.

CARLTON R. YOUNG (emeritus professor of church music, Candler School of Theology) edited two revised Methodist hymnals and is the author of two books on hymns as well as *Music of the Heart: John and Charles Wesley on Music and Musicians* (1995). In 2007 he curated *Sacred Harmony: The Musical Wesley Family* for the Bridwell Library, Southern Methodist University.

INDEX

Abel, Charles Frederick, 185
Addison, Joseph, 11, 43, 67, 124, 233
African American singing, 78–79, 83, 106–7
African Methodist Episcopal Church, 78, 243
African style, 115
Aldrich, Henry, 221
"ancient" music, 149–50, 165, 169–70, 183–90
Anglicanism. *See* Church of England
anthems, 18, 63, 200, 222; in Methodist use, 18, 63, 65, 71–72, 84, 113; Sebastian Wesley's, 136–38, 203–15, 218–25
antiphony, 47
antiquarianism in music, 187–89, 196. *See also* "ancient" music
Arminianism, 45, 54
Arne, Thomas Augustine, 56, 189–90
Arnold, George Benjamin, 225, 226
Arnold, Samuel, 196, 221, 222
Asbury, Francis, 94, 100, 106
Ashe, Andrew, 122
Attwood, Thomas, 122, 135, 200, 220
Australia, 217, 225, 226

Bach, Johann Christian, xvii, 184, 185, 191, 193
Bach, Johann Sebastian, 189, 224; influence on Samuel Wesley, 133, 186, 197–98
Baker, Frank, 32–33
Balfe, Michael William, 122
bands in chapels, 72–76
Baptists, 148
Barbandt, Charles, 189
Barnby, Joseph, 81, 105, 219, 220
baroque musical style, 189–93. *See also* "ancient" music
Barrington, Daines, 185
Battishill, Jonathan, 237

Beaumont, John, 70
Beethoven, Ludwig van, 132, 133, 186, 196, 217
Beggar's Opera, 14
Bennett, William Sterndale, xviii, 224
Berlioz, Hector, xviii, 225
Best, William Thomas, 217
Betjeman, John, xiii
"better music" movement, 78, 80–84, 93, 99
Blow, John, xvii, 187, 220
Bolton (Lancs.), 68, 75
Book of Common Prayer, 41, 43–44, 46; revised by John Wesley, 50, 53, 111
Boyce, William, xvii, 123–24, 150, 203, 221; anthems, 200, 212; *Cathedral Music,* 187, 188, 196; dedicatee, 232; hymn, 235, 240
Bradbury, William B., 85
Bradshaw, Richard, 115
Brahms, Johannes, 222, 224
Brevint, Daniel, 88
Bridge, Frederick, 105
Bristol, 123, 141–53, 158, 226; hymn publications, 44–45, 50, 148–49; New Room, 5, 49, 159; organists, 143–46
Broderip, Edmund, 143, 144–45
Brough, Paul, 225
Brown, William C., 108
Buck, Percy, 221
Buck, Zechariah, 136
Buckley, James, 100–101
Bunyan, John, *Pilgrim's Progress,* 20
Butts, Thomas, 9, 14, 60; *Harmonia-Sacra,* 7–11, 14–15, 64–67, 90, 107
Byrd, William, 186, 224

Caldwell, John, 220
Calvinistic Methodists, 11, 15, 45–47. *See also* evangelicalism; Whitefield, George
Campion, Thomas, 10, 222, 224

camp meetings, 20, 78, 83, 107

Canada, 217, 225

Carey, Henry, 15

cathedrals, 151; choirs, xvi, 123, 145–46; music, xv, 18, 47, 147, 183; musical repertory, 148, 187, 200, 211, 221–25; organists, 135, 136, 145–48, 178

Cennick, John, 47

Chapel Royal, 105, 135, 187, 200, 202; choir, 123, 202–3

Chatterton, Thomas, 141, 188, 196

child prodigies, xiv, 141; Wesley boys, 142–44

Chinese melodies, 115

choirs, 6, 66, 84

chorales, 10, 64, 105, 108

choral festivals, 71–73, 144, 151

Church of England, xv, 43, 52, 146–47; attitude to hymns, 42, 56, 211; cathedral music, 200, 221–25; psalm tunes, 10, 43, 64, 96, 105; singing, 5, 41. *See also* cathedrals

Coke, Thomas, 50, 172

Collection of Forms of Prayer, 49

Collection of Hymns for the Use of the People Called Methodists, 41, 45, 50–51, 53, 88–90, 104; in America, 48, 77, 89–91; contents, 54; tunes for, 7, 90–91

Collection of Psalms and Hymns, 42–44, 48–51

Colles, H. C., 219–20

communion: hymns, 44, 49–50, 54, 56, 88–100; theology, 88–89, 99–102

Congregationalists. *See* Independents

congregational singing, 6, 12, 56, 61, 113–18; of anthems and set pieces, 66, 68, 72–76

Cooke, Benjamin, 188

Corelli, Arcangelo, xvii, 149, 169, 183–84

Corfe, John Davis, 136

counterpoint, 187, 191, 193–94; avoidance of, 18, 64

Cowley, Mrs., 239

Cramer, John Baptist, xvii

Cramer, Wilhelm, 185

Croft, William, xvii, 10, 186, 200, 212, 221; St. anne's, 91

Crosby, Fanny J., 85, 86, 112

Dannreuther, Edward, 219

Davie, Donald, 34

deism, xiv, 61

dialogue hymns, 47

dissenters (nonconformists), 5, 10, 63–76, 141, 146–47; alienated by Wesleys, xvi; singing styles, 6, 9, 17, 75

Doane, Howard, 85, 86

Dow, Lorenzo, 20

Downing, Joseph, 43

Dryden, John, 14–15

Dussek, Jan Ladislav, 122, 186

Dyer, Richard, 239

Dyer, William, 47, 142, 151

Dying Christian, 67–68

Dykes, John Bacchus: hymn tunes, 18–20, 81, 87, 105, 109; criticized, 219

Edson, Lewis, 80

Elgar, Edward, 219

Eliot, T. S., 30, 33–35, 39

Elly, Robert, 240

English Hymnal, 104, 105, 110

Eucharist. *See* communion

evangelicalism, 60–62, 100, 103, 147–48, 158; in America, 85–86, 93, 95, 99

Evangelical party (Church of England), 47, 157

Evans, James, 75, 90–94, 107

Everett, L. C., 78–80

Exeter cathedral, 139, 211, 216–17

extemporization: by Charles Wesley the younger, 123; by Samuel, 127–28, 131, 165, 185; by Sebastian, 140, 227

Fawcett, John, 75

Fellowes, Edmund H., 220, 221

figured bass: in Methodist tunebooks, 7, 74–75, 104; omitted, 65, 68

Fletcher, John, 49, 154–57, 171

Floyd, A. E., 225–26

folk hymns, 20, 22–24, 110, 112

Foundling Hospital, London, 65, 151

Foundry chapel, London, 5, 9, 49; *Collection,* 7, 10, 45, 49

Franck, César, 219, 224

Freylinghausen, Johann Anastasius, 10, 42

fuging tunes, 68, 80–81, 107–8; prohibited, 18, 106

Gainsborough, Thomas, 160

galant style in music, 18, 65, 124, 184–85, 189

Garrett, George Mursell, 218, 225, 226
Gatch, Philip, 100
Gatens, William, 139, 220
Gauntlett, Henry J., 105
Gay, John, 14, 239
Geminiani, Francesco, xvii, 144, 149, 169, 183
George III, 129, 179
George IV, 129, 136, 179
German influence on Methodist music, 10, 42
Giardini, Felice, xvii, 184, 185
Gibbons, Orlando, 8, 10, 221–22, 224
Gladstone, Francis, 2, 226
Glenn, Robert, 236
Gloucester cathedral, 215, 226, 227
Goodall, David S., 114
Goodall, Howard, 226
gospel hymns, 78, 86, 91, 109–12
Goss, John, 135, 200, 224; *The wilderness*, 204–6
Gounod, Charles, 220
grace doctrine, 51, 92, 99–101, 103, 112, 139
graces. *See* ornaments
Green, Fred Pratt, 113
Greene, Maurice, 186, 188, 200
Gwynne family, xiv, 147; Marmaduke, 142. *See also* Wesley, Sarah

hallelujahs, 20, 92; disapproved, 17, 21
Handel, George Frideric, 14–15, 56–58, 129, 149–51; adaptations of, 13–15, 56, 108, 240; admiration for, xvii, 72, 149, 184–86; influence of, 11, 17, 73, 75, 108; influence on Wesley musicians, 127, 142, 149–51, 169–70, 191; operas, 14; oratorios, 72–73, 149–51, 183–86; parodies of, 13–15
—compositions: hymn tunes, 59, 104; *Judas Maccabaeus*, 15, 149–50; *Messiah*, 149–50, 183; *Ode for St. Cecilia's Day*, 191; *Riccardo primo*, 13–14; *Samson*, 149–50, 183
Handel Commemoration (1784), 72, 73, 179
harmony, 7–8, 169; meaning "unison," 45; Romantic, 18–19, 136, 139, 228; Samuel Wesley's, 187, 191, 197; static, 82, 91, 93
harpsichord, 142, 155, 176; accompanying hymn singing, 8, 57, 65; concertos, 149, 198, 232; lessons, 144–46; solos, 197, 232–33
Harris, Howell, 49, 142

Harwood, Basil, 222
Harwood, Edward, 67
Hawes, William, 135, 227
Haydn, Franz Joseph, 108, 132, 187, 193–94, 224
Herbert, George, 30, 38, 42, 43
Hereford cathedral, 136, 203
Hickes, George, 43
high churchmanship, 6, 24, 43. *See also* Oxford movement
Hobson, James, 227
Holman, Peter, 56
Holy, Thomas, 71
Holy Club (Oxford), 41–43
homophony, 18, 80–81, 136, 187
homosexuality, 130
Hopkins, Edward J., 105
Horn, Charles Frederick, 133, 186, 198
Horton, Peter, 135–36, 138–39, 218, 222
Howells, Herbert, 113
Hulan, Richard Huffman, 20, 78
Hull, 70–71
Huntingdon, Selina, Countess of, 46, 157, 158; her "Connexion," 21, 47, 149, 151
Hymns Ancient and Modern, 33, 80, 105, 108
Hymns and Sacred Poems, 27, 44–45, 49
Hymns and Spiritual Songs, 45
hymns discussed: "A charge to keep," 107; "Amazing grace," 17, 24; "Author of faith," 35; "Christ, whose glory," 113–14; "Come Holy Ghost, all-quickning fire," 36; "Come let us anew," 33; "Come, O thou traveller unknown," 112, 113, 209; "Father, in whom we live," 31; "Father of everlasting grace," 30; "Glory to God," 28; "Hail, Jesus, hail," 55; "Happy the souls," 90; "Jesu, dear, redeeming Lord," 91; "Jesu, lover of my soul," 18, 39–40, 81–82, 109–10; "Jesu, thou soul of all our joys," 29; "Lamb of God," 55–58; "Let earth and heaven agree," 40; "Listed into the cause of sin," 13, 28; "Lo, he comes with clouds descending," 9, 82–83; "Love divine," 14–15, 28, 113; "O for a thousand tongues," 28–29, 82, 109; "O thou eternal victim," 94; "O thou who camest from above," 37; "Rejoice, the Lord is king," 58–59, 113; "Victim divine," 96
Hymns on the Great Festivals, 11, 52–62

Hymns on the Lord's Supper, 88–102
hymn tunes discussed: ABERYSTWYTH,
19; AURELIA, 218, 225; BEVERLY, 97–98;
CAMP ALDERSGATE, 116; CANAAN,
70; CHESHUNT, 64–65; CRUCIFIXION
(Lampe), 57–58, (Leach), 75; DENMARK,
65–66; DEVIZES, 91; EASTER HYMN,
10, 17; EMILY, 116; FROM STRENGTH TO
STRENGTH, 33; GOPSAL, 59, 104; HARTS,
92–93; HELMSLEY, 9, 82–3; HEREFORD,
xiii, 37, 218, 225; HOLLINGSIDE, 18;
HOTHAM, 9, 18–19, 81; HUTTON RUDBY,
115; INVITATION, 12; KINGSFOLD, 23;
LENOX, 80; MARTYN, 82, 110; MORN-
ING SONG, 11; NEW SARABAND, 113–14;
PLYMOUTH DOCK, 95; RESURRECTION
(Lampe), 58–59; SALVATION, 22; SELENA,
95; SHOUTING HYMN, 22; ST. ETHEL-
WALD, 33; "Vital Spark," 67–68; WEST-
MINSTER, 15; WOODBURY, 113–14

improvisation. *See* extemporization
Independents, 6, 9
India, 217–18
Ingalls, Jeremiah, 22–24
Ingham, George, 42
interlining, 109–10

Jackson, Thomas, 123, 130, 159
Johnson, Julian, 127
Johnson, Samuel, 161

Keeble, John, 188
Kelway, Joseph, 124, 126, 143, 183
Kelway, Thomas, 144
Kimbrough, S T, 30–32, 103, 115
Klocko, David, 22
Knapp, Phoebe, 85–86

Lampe, John Frederick, 12, 50, 52, 56;
contribution to Methodism, 50, 60–62;
hymn tunes, 7, 11–13, 52–60; musical
style, 12, 17, 56–57, 64
Lancashire singers, 72–76
Langhorne, John, 237
Leach, James, 70, 73–75
Leaver, Robin, 11, 12, 59
Leeds, 73, 87, 104; parish church, xv, 209,
211, 221, 228

Lightwood, James, 71, 104, 142
Lim, Swee Hong, 115–18
lining out, 4, 5, 20, 70; in African American
practice, 79, 107
Linley, Thomas the younger, 191
Liszt, Franz, xviii, 216, 219
liturgical calendar, 50, 52–53
Lloyd, Charles Harford, 222
Lock Hospital, London, 65, 69; *Collection,*
18, 65–66
Loh, I-to, 115, 117
Lombardic rhythm, 12, 57
London: base for Methodism, 5, 49, 60;
for musical career, 136; musical life of,
167–68, 198–99; portrayal in music, 134;
theatrical community, 60–61. *See also*
Chapel Royal; Foundry chapel; Maryle-
bone; St. Paul's cathedral; Surrey chapel;
Westminster Abbey
Long, Kenneth R., 220
Luther, Martin, 25
Lutherans, 42, 44; chorales, 10, 64, 105, 108
Lyon, Emma, 239
Lyttleton, George, Lord, 170

Madan, Martin, 18–19, 47, 65, 158
Madras cathedral, 217–18
madrigals, 183, 186–88, 227
Main, Sylvester, 108
Manchester, 72, 202
Marsh, John, 185
Martin, Charlotte, 189
Martin, Dennis, 56–57
Marylebone, 154, 161–62, 164; parish
church, xv
Mason, Lowell, 80, 84, 91, 108
Mason, William, 130
Matsikenyiri, Patrick, 115–16
McCutchan, Robert G., 110
Mead, Stith, 20
Mendelssohn-Bartholdy, Felix, 15, 193–96,
224; *Elijah,* 109, 124, 138, 217; influence
on Sebastian Wesley, 138, 217
Merbecke, John, 111
meters (time signatures), 92, 94, 96, 97, 113;
changes in, 68
meters (verse), 4, 26, 38, 43, 84; new, 10,
32–33, 80, 104
Methodist Church (British, 1795-), 18,

104–6; Conference, 20, 72; (USA, 1939-), 110, 242

Methodist denominational hymnals (USA), 242–43

Methodist Episcopal Church, 18, 50, 78, 89–101, 107–10, 242; Conference, 89, 96, 105, 108

Methodist Episcopal Church, South, 78, 80, 89–100, 109, 242–43

Methodist Hymn-Book with Tunes, 105–6

Methodist movement, 41, 62, 88; Conference minutes, 9, 17, 21, 64, 65–67; hymnals, 78–79, 103–18, 242–43; singing, 5–9, 53, 88; societies, 41, 45

Methodist Protestant Church, 91, 94, 243

Milgrove, Benjamin, 92

Miller, Mark A., 115–16

Miller, William Edward, 21

Milton, John, 26, 29, 211–13, 235

modal scales, 22–24, 115, 133–34, 188

Monk, William Henry, 33

Moody, Dwight, 85–86

Moore, Edward, 239

Moravians (Unitas Fratrum), 4, 10, 42, 147

More, Hannah, 237

Mornington, Garrett Wesley, Earl of, 161, 173

Mozart, Leopold, 171

Mozart, Wolfgang Amadeus, xiv, 126, 186–87, 191, 193; two-piano music, 197–98

Mulrain, George, 117–18

musical profession in England, 121; Wesleys' ambivalence to, 122–24, 144, 174, 177–82

Nares, James, 221

Naylor, Edward Woodall, 33

Negro spirituals. *See* spirituals

Nettl, Bruno, 3

New Version of Psalms (Tate and Brady), 42, 44, 56, 211, 236

New Zealand, 226

Noble, Thomas Tertius, 222

Noble, Yvonne, 14

nonconformists. *See* dissenters

Novello, J. Alfred, 68, 217, 225

Novello, Vincent, 83, 132, 186–87

"old Methodist" tunes, 90, 105

"Old Version." See *Whole Booke of Psalmes*

"old way of singing," 5

Olleson, Philip, 12, 130, 188, 197

oratorios, 72, 149–51, 171; miniature, 63, 74–76

organ concertos, 152, 185–86, 197; by Charles Wesley the younger, 125–26, 129, 232

organ duets, 130–31, 165, 170, 186

organ recitals, 203, 217

organs: in America, 77, 109; in England, 127, 128, 143–52, 156; in Methodist chapels, 7, 18, 69–76

organ voluntaries, 124–26, 147, 186, 233

ornaments, 16, 69, 145; in hymn tunes, 12–13, 17, 57–60, 64

Ouseley, Frederick Arthur Gore, 220, 224

Oxford movement, 80, 84

Palestrina, Giovanni da, xvii, 224

parish-church music, 5, 41, 66, 211

parody hymns (set to secular tunes), 13–15, 64, 113. *See also* folk hymns

Parry, Charles Hubert Hastings, 109, 220, 227

Penrose, Thomas, 237

Pepusch, Johann Christoph, 188

Pietism, 4, 42

Pilsbury, Amos, 22

Pocket Hymn Book: (Spence), 21, 91–94; supplement, 94–96; (Wesley), 21

Pope, Alexander, 67–68, 237, 238

Presbyterians, 6, 148–49

Primitive Methodists, 20–21

psalms, as sources for anthem texts, 200; metrical, 3–4, 42–43, 48, 148, 211

Purcell, Henry, 14–15, 150, 183, 186, 188; anthems, 203, 207, 224; influence on Wesleys, 126–27, 187, 191–93; Service in B flat, 187

Puritanism, 6, 18, 24, 53

Pye, Miss, 240

Quakers, 141, 147

"quartet" choirs, 84

renaissance music, 183, 187–88; "English musical renaissance," 218, 219

repeating tunes, 16, 68, 80, 105

revival hymnody, 19–24, 85–86, 91–92, 99, 107. *See also* Moody, Dwight
Roberts, Thomas, 51
Rogers, Nelme, 143–44
Roman Catholicism, 43, 178–80; church music, 9, 187, 189, 224
Rooke, Edward, 145
Rossini, Gioacchino, 136
Rousseau, Jean-Jacques, xiv
Routley, Erik, 110, 209, 218; hymn tune, 113–14
Russell, John, 4, 27, 155–56, 157–61

sacramental hymns. *See* communion: hymns
Sacred Harmony: (1781), 7–9, 12, 16, 21, 84; (1790), 7, 67; (1822), 104, 240; (1848), 84; tunes, 15, 65, 104
Sacred Harp, 22, 106
Sacred Melody. See Select Hymns with Tunes Annext
Sammartini, Giuseppe, 240
Savannah, Georgia, 4, 42–44, 158
Scarlatti, Domenico, 113, 240
Schubert, Franz, 138, 224
Schumann, Robert, 34, 138
Select Hymns with Tunes Annext (*Sacred Melody*), 7, 10, 45, 64; preface, 6, 12, 45, 60, 64; tunes, 18, 64–65, 82
services (settings of Anglican canticles), 221–22; by Samuel Wesley, 186–87; by Sebastian Wesley, 221
set pieces, 63–76
Shakespeare, William, 34, 37, 240
shape-note music, 84, 106
Shaw, H. Watkins, 220
Sheffield, Norfolk Methodist Chapel, 69–71
Shenstone, William, 237, 239–40
"shouting" hymns, 20–22, 83, 107
singing schools, 84, 106–7
Smart, Henry, 87, 216, 221
Smith, John Stafford, 202–3
Sosa, Pablo, 115
Spence, Robert, 21
spirituals, 20–22, 107; Negro, 77, 110, 111
Spohr, Louis, 196, 219, 220
Stainer, John, 139, 217, 218–20, 224; text setting, 200, 207–9, 215
Stanford, Charles Villiers, 217, 220–22, 224; opinion of Sebastian Wesley, 219

Sternhold and Hopkins. See *Whole Booke of Psalmes*
St. Paul's cathedral, 18, 135, 204
street music, 143, 152
Sullivan, Arthur Seymour, 105, 217, 218
Summers, Thomas O., 101
Sunday schools, 68, 72–76, 84–85, 108
Sunday Service of the Methodists, 50, 53, 111
Surrey Chapel, London, 68
Suter, Sarah, 202
Sydney (Australia), 217

Tallis, Thomas, 10, 222, 224
Tate and Brady. See *New Version of Psalms*
tempo, 63, 92, 94–96, 139
theater music, 14, 56, 59, 135, 177
time signatures. *See* meters (time signatures)
Trebeck, James, 239
Tregarthen, William Coulson, 226
trills, 12, 57, 68, 128
Trimnell, Thomas Tallis, 226
Trimnell, W. F., 212–14, 226
Trollope, Arthur William, 236
tune meters. *See* meters (verse)
Turle, James, 221

Unitas Fratrum. *See* Moravians
United Methodist Church, 111, 113, 243

Vaughan Williams, Ralph, 9, 22–24, 217
Victorian church music, 216–20; hymn tunes, 80, 81, 87, 105
Vincent, William, 3, 25
violin, 153; in chapel bands, 73–74; music, 124, 126, 132, 186; teaching, 144, 146, 185

Wagner, Richard, xviii, 136, 219
Walker, Ernest, 218–19
Walmisley, Thomas Attwood, 135, 200, 222
Walton, William, 227–29
Watts, Isaac, 6, 25, 36, 42–43; hymns, 21, 31, 65, 67, 70
Weber, Carl Maria von, 136
Wesley, Charles the elder, 26–28, 49, 103; awakening, 44; education, xiii, 41; as father, 123–24, 143–44, 175–82; house at Bristol, 142, 147, 152; at Marylebone, 154, 161–63; Methodist opposition to, 26, 41, 52, 176–77; ode, 237; satirical verse, xvii;

social standing, 123, 157; tricentennial, vii, 118
—attitudes: to family concerts, 168, 170–72; to Handel, xvii, 149–50; to harmony, 7, 29–30; to modern music, xvii, 17–18; to secular music, 14–15, 28, 142; to sons' up-bringing, xiv, 159, 171, 175–78
—hymns: importance to Methodism, 52–53; poetic quality, 26–40, 44; purpose, 51, 56, 60–61, 101; settings of, 11–19, 56–60, 79–83, 89–100, 102–18, 236; theology, 33–34, 52–55, 88–89, 103. *See also* hymns discussed; parody hymns
Wesley, Charles the younger, 124–30, 155, 160–61, 178–79; *Caractacus,* 128–29; catalogue of works, 231–41; character, 130, 178–79; conservative taste, xvii, 126, 149; editions by, 240; education, 142–46, 175–78; *Elijah,* 124; hymn tunes, 104; *I will lift up mine eyes,* 126; *Ode on the Death of Dr. Boyce,* 124, 237; organ playing, 127, 149, 179; organ voluntaries, 125–26; as prodigy, 142, 143; sonata in F minor, 128–29. *See also* extemporization
Wesley, Charlotte (née Martin), 180
Wesley, Eliza, 174
Wesley, Garrett. *See* Mornington, Earl of
Wesley, John, 4–5; awakening, 44; education, xiii, 41; in Georgia, 4, 42–44; hymn collections, 41–51; ministry, 49; musical taste, 16–19, 21, 25, 60; rules for singing, 6, 12, 45, 64; theology, 45, 54, 61–62, 88–89, 103; "Thoughts on the Power of Music," 8, 60, 177; translations, 4, 42, 77, 113; tune collections, 7, 10–13, 45, 101, 104; *Works,* 111
—attitudes: to anthems, 18, 65–67, 71; to choirs, 6, 66; to counterpoint, 17–18; to family concerts, 172–73; to harmony, 8; to modern music, xviii, 8; to oratorios, 151; to organs, 7–8; to secular music, 13–15; to set pieces, 63–67; to singing, 5–9; to verbal repetition, 17, 64
Wesley, Matthias Erasmus, 161
Wesley, Sally. *See* Wesley, Sarah ("Sally," 1759–1828)
Wesley, Samuel (1665–1735), xiii, 41
Wesley, Samuel (1690–1739), 42, 52
Wesley, Samuel (1766–1837), 122–23, 179–82, 183–99; anticipation of German

Romantics, 193–96, 199; antiquarianism, xvii, 183–99; arrangements of old music, 186; attitude to musical profession, 179–81; character, xvi, 130, 152–53, 178–80; education, 142–46, 175–78; interest in J. S. Bach, 186, 197–98; mental illness, 178, 182, 185; organ playing, 185; as prodigy, 143–44, 156, 160, 179, 183; Roman Catholicism, 179–80, 189; stylistic diversity, 133, 189–98. *See also* extemporization
—compositions, 130–35; anthems, xv; Grand Duet, 130–32; hymn tunes, 31, 104; Latin sacred music, 189–91; *Ode to St. Cecilia,* 191–92; organ concerto in D, 197; organ voluntaries, 128; "O sing unto mie roundelaie," 187–88; piano music, 132–34, 197; *Ruth,* 154, 183; service in F, 186–87; songs, 187; symphony in B flat, 193–96; trio for 3 pianos, 198
Wesley, Samuel Sebastian, 135–36, 201–2; career, 136, 203; character, xiv; depression, 210; *The Dilosk Gatherer,* 136; education, 202; hymn tunes, xiii, 37, 87, 218; influence, 225–29; musical style, 135–40, 218–19; reception, 221–25; religious feeling, 210–11; sons of, 210; standing as composer, 216–17; "symphony," 138–39; text setting, 203–15; worldwide reputation, 218–21
—anthems, 136–38, 203–15, 222–25; *Ascribe unto the Lord,* 138, 140; *Blessed be the God and Father,* 207, 222; *By the word of the Lord,* 211–13; *Cast me not away,* 209, 222; *The face of the Lord,* 211; *Let us lift up our heart,* 139, 217, 219; *O Lord, thou art my God,* 139–40, 207–9, 217; *The wilderness,* 203–7, 219, 227; *Thou wilt keep him,* 209–10, 222; *To my request,* 139, 211, 217, 222; *Wash me throughly,* 139, 219, 222, 228–29
Wesley, Sarah (née Gwynne, 1726–1822), 123, 176; background, 142, 150; extravagance, 168, 169; as mother, 142–43, 150, 166–67, 176; musicality, 142; portrait, 158; role in the family concerts, 164–69
Wesley, Sarah ("Sally," 1759–1828), 157, 179; artistic gift, 159; dress, 159, 168; as head of family, 179; singing, 168; verse by, 237
Wesley, Sebastian. *See* Wesley, Samuel Sebastian

Wesley, Susanna (née Annesley), xiii, xiv

Wesleyan theology, 55, 61–62, 79, 88–101, 103

Wesley family characteristics, xv-xviii

Wesley family concerts, 161–63, 164–74, 177–78; musical content, 169–71, 183–84, 241

Westminster Abbey, 72–73, 105, 187

Westminster School, xiii, 157

Whitefield, George, 3, 6, 148, 158; break with Wesleys, 45–47; hymnals, 11, 46–47, 148

Whole Booke of Psalmes ("Old Version"), 42, 44, 56, 211

Wiant, Bliss, 115

Wilde, John, 69–71

Williams, Charles Lee, 215

Williams, David, 143, 145

Williamson, Malcolm, 113–14

Winchester cathedral, 211–12, 218, 225

Wither, George, 13

women: as hostesses, 168; in hymn singing, 5–6, 9, 16, 47, 65–69, 73, 149; separate seating, 69

Wood, Charles, 222, 223

Wren, Brian, 61

Young, Carlton R., 26, 57, 66, 130; hymn tune, 116

Young, Percy M., 220

Zinzendorf, Count Nicholas, 42

The University of Illinois Press
is a founding member of the
Association of American University Presses.

Composed in 10.5/13 Adobe Minion Pro
with Meta display
by Jim Proefrock
at the University of Illinois Press
Manufactured by Cushing-Malloy, Inc.

University of Illinois Press
1325 South Oak Street
Champaign, IL 61820-6903
www.press.uillinois.edu